Salesforce.com Lightning Process Builder and Visual Workflow

A Practical Guide to Model-Driven
Development on the Force.com Platform

Jonathan Keel

Apress®

Salesforce.com Lightning Process Builder and Visual Workflow: A Practical Guide to Model-Driven Development on the Force.com Platform

Jonathan Keel
San Antonio, Texas, USA

ISBN-13 (pbk): 978-1-4842-1690-3   ISBN-13 (electronic): 978-1-4842-1691-0
DOI 10.1007/978-1-4842-1691-0

Library of Congress Control Number: 2016960575

Managing Director: Welmoed Spahr
Acquisitions Editor: Susan McDermott
Developmental Editor: Laura Berendson
Technical Reviewers: Philip Weinmeister, James Loghry
Editorial Board: Steve Anglin, Pramila Balen, Laura Berendson, Aaron Black, Louise Corrigan, Jonathan Gennick, Robert Hutchinson, Celestin Suresh John, Nikhil Karkal, James Markham, Susan McDermott, Matthew Moodie, Natalie Pao, Gwenan Spearing
Coordinating Editor: Rita Fernando
Copy Editor: Lori Jacobs
Compositor: SPi Global
Indexer: SPi Global
Cover Image: Designed by Freepik.com

Distributed to the book trade worldwide by Springer Science+Business Media New York, 233 Spring Street, 6th Floor, New York, NY 10013. Phone 1-800-SPRINGER, fax (201) 348-4505, e-mail orders-ny@springer-sbm.com, or visit www.springer.com. Apress Media, LLC is a California LLC and the sole member (owner) is Springer Science + Business Media Finance Inc (SSBM Finance Inc). SSBM Finance Inc is a Delaware corporation.

For information on translations, please e-mail rights@apress.com, or visit www.apress.com.

Apress and friends of ED books may be purchased in bulk for academic, corporate, or promotional use. eBook versions and licenses are also available for most titles. For more information, reference our Special Bulk Sales–eBook Licensing web page at www.apress.com/bulk-sales.

Any source code or other supplementary materials referenced by the author in this text is available to readers at www.apress.com. For detailed information about how to locate your book's source code, go to www.apress.com/source-code/.

To my children, Ashton, Janae, Logan, and Abigail, who bring me great joy in life and are so thoughtful, supportive, and patient.

Contents at a Glance

Contents

About the Author

Jonathan Keel is President and Founder of 6 Street Technologies, LLC, a consulting company specializing in Salesforce.com Sales Cloud and Commerce development as well as AppExchange and Lightning development. Since founding the company, he has helped many clients realize the full potential of Salesforce.com and the Force.com platform.

Jonathan is a Salesforce.com Certified Force.com Developer and has more than 16 years of experience delivering web applications using many technologies including Visualforce, Apex, Lightning, HTML, JavaScript, CSS, and Java. He has worked in many industries such as retail, education, finance, music, and technology. He has a Bachelor of Science in Computer Science and a minor in English from The University of Texas Pan-American in the Rio Grande Valley.

Jonathan currently lives in San Antonio, Texas. When he isn't working he spends his free time with his kids either at the movies, playing video games, or enjoying outdoor activities. You can read more about him at http://jonathankeel.com, read his blogs at the 6 Street Technologies blog at http://6st.co/blog/ or follow him on Twitter(@socialkeel). Jonathan can be reached at jonathan.keel@6st.co.

About the Technical Reviewers

Phil Weinmeister, Salesforce MVP is the senior director of product management at 7Summits, where he is focused on bringing together collaboration, content, and community and delivering innovative lightning products on the Salesforce platform. Phil is 10x Salesforce certified and has delivered numerous solutions to a variety of organizations on the Force.com platform since 2010. A graduate of Carnegie Mellon University with a double major in Business Administration (with a focus on information technology) and Spanish, Phil now resides in Powder Springs, Georgia. He spends most of his free time with his lovely wife, Amy, and his children, Tariku, Sophie, Max, and Lyla. When he's not finding ways to make his kids laugh or cheering on the Arizona Cardinals, Phil involves himself in various church-related activities with friends and families in the Cobb County area.

Stay updated on Phil's most recent insights and blog posts by following him on Twitter (@PhilWeinmeister).

James Loghry is a CRM Architect with Demand Chain Systems. He has over 10 years of experience with CRM customizations and integrations. James has 11 Salesforce certifications and has been nominated as Salesforce MVP by peers throughout the Salesforce community.

Acknowledgments

Writing this book has been a dream and a long adventure. Many people contributed directly or indirectly and I'd like to acknowledge and thank them here. Thank you for all your help and support.

- Susan McDermott (Apress): Susan gave me the opportunity to begin this book and her encouragement and patience pushed me to complete this huge undertaking. Thank you!

- Phil Weinmeister (7Summits): Phil has been an amazing friend! He believed that I could write this book and stepped in as Technical Reviewer. Phil, thank you for making all this possible!

- James Loghry (Demand Chain Systems): James has an amazing technical knowledge of Salesforce. His feedback resulted in changes that made this book better. Thanks!

- Rita Fernando (Apress): Rita kept me on my toes and made sure I hit the deadlines. She offered encouragement and help to tackle so much content in this book. Thank you!

- Noe Tamez (6 Street Technologies): Noe has been my best friend forever it seems. He has been there during the best times and the worst times. Noe left his previous job to join my small one-man consulting company to build something great. This book is possible due to his stepping in so many times with the avalanche of work we take on. Noe, thank you so much for everything!

- Patricia Obst: My Mom worked so many years as a single mom. She worked hard and encouraged me to seek knowledge growing up. Love you Mom!

- Kylie Campbell: When I told Kylie I was going to work on this book she probably thought I was crazy with my business workload. She said she would stay by my side and encourage me all the way to the finish line. Thanks for all your love, help, and encouragement!

- Ashton, Janae, Logan, and Abigail: My kids have put up with not getting to see their father much for months. They stepped up as well to help each other and help me in so many ways. I'm sure they will be glad to get their Dad back. I thank you and love you all so much!

Introduction

If you are looking to learn what Visual Workflow and Lightning Process Builder are, then you have come to the right place. You may be expecting this to strictly be a how-to book. While that is partly true, its intent extends beyond just a simple step-by-step instruction manual. This book's intent is also to teach sound development practices that have been practiced way before Visual Workflow and Lightning Process Builder even existed. One of the main goals of this book is to take those software development practices and teach them with Visual Workflow and Lightning Process Builder as the implementation tools. You may be thinking, "This is not a programming book," but you would be wrong! You see, while Visual Workflow and Lightning Process Builder do not have code that you type in, it is indeed software you are building. In fact, I would say that once you learn how to develop with Visual Workflow and Lightning Process Builder you are a small fraction of the way from developing with a computer programming language. The art of software development comes not from knowing "how to code" as some people think. It comes from learning how to break down problems into bite-size pieces of logic. This book takes you on a journey of real scenarios of gathering requirements, understanding them, breaking them down, and designing a system to meet those requirements. Finally, that design is implemented using Visual Workflow and Lightning Process Builder.

When Salesforce first introduced Visual Workflow my mind went crazy with the possibilities. I was not even sure if Salesforce realized what it had on its hands. I'm sure Salesforce did though, since it acquired the technology. I immediately recognized this for its potential as a replacement for a text-based programming language (to an extent). Indeed, Visual Workflow looked to me like the start of other graphical development tools I've seen people create. Those tools never seemed to get the level of adoption that their textual counterparts received. Tools such as Google Blockly or Yahoo! Pipes are great tools for visual programming, but one of the complaints is that it took quite a while to build something substantial. Text-based programming languages allow development with more brevity. Visual Workflow and Lightning Process Builder do so well, though, because they are on Salesforce.com and do not need to do everything under the sun to be successful. Instead, they need to be able to apply logic to common Salesforce constructs such as Objects, records, Chatter, E-mail Alerts, etc. By giving an administrator the ability to tie all these together with logic, these tools give the administrator a lot of power.

Why Develop with Visual Workflow and Lightning Process Builder?

If you attend any local Salesforce user groups or maybe attend some Salesforce events in which you run into other administrators then you probably have run into those who talk about Visual Workflow or Lightning Process Builder as though it is the most amazing thing on the planet. People who have started to use them quickly become excited about how it will help make them better and more efficient administrators. Not only have I seen administrators jump on the bandwagon, but I have seen developers do so as well! I've been in many meetings where someone is talking about writing an Apex Trigger (which uses code) only to have another developer stop him and say just to do it in Lightning Process Builder. It is that powerful that coders are adopting it in place of code. Why is that? Well let's look at some reasons to develop with Visual Workflow and Lightning Process Builder:

- They are graphical and can be easily understood since the logic is presented in a straightforward manner via a diagram.

- Development requires no unit tests because it is still considered "declarative," unlike development with Apex code.

- Maintenance is improved due to the logic being clearly visible, making it easier to see what the system is doing, and thus making it easier and faster to fix if needed.

- Versioning is now a possibility with both Visual Workflow and Lightning Process Builder so that if there is ever an issue or a change in business processes, the implementation can be rolled back to a previous version or forward to a more current version.

- Knowledge transfer is more efficient because the implementation is almost self-documenting. Someone can easily look at a what was created and see each step that is being performed.

What Is Model-Driven Development?

As stated before, when using Visual Workflow or Lightning Process Builder, you are essentially programming but it is not with code. You are programming or developing visually with graphical tools. There are many terms out there to describe this process, and it seems that everyone has his or her own terms, such as "visual programming" or "flow-based programming" to name a couple. Even the term "model-driven" has other meanings as well. For the context of this book, "model-driven development" describes developing using individual blocks or "models" that can be tied together to build a diagram that in turn is read and understood by the Force.com platform. The platform then in turn converts these models into real-time running programs. As you see, what is developed with Visual Workflow and Lightning Process Builder is essentially a model that is then run in the cloud to become a real process. To learn more about different types of development read about Programming Paradigms at https://en.wikipedia.org/wiki/Programming_paradigm.

Target Audience

This book assumes that the reader has a beginning knowledge of Salesforce administration. While it is a beginning to Visual Workflow and Lightning Process Builder, it assumes that the reader can create custom objects, custom fields, e-mail alerts, approvals processes, etc. It does not assume the reader has any knowledge of coding with Apex, but Salesforce developers who are familiar with Apex can learn a great deal by leaning about Visual Workflow and Lightning Process Builder because these tools give the ability to create solutions faster with little to no coding involved.

Salesforce Editions

Please be aware of the different Salesforce editions that exist and each of the features they provide. According to Salesforce documentation, Visual Workflow is available in Salesforce Classic and Lightning Experience in the Enterprise, Performance, Unlimited, and Developer Editions. Lightning Process Builder is available in Salesforce Classic and Lightning Experience in the Professional, Enterprise, Performance,

Unlimited, and Developer Editions. In addition to these tools there are other features that are important to understand in relation to the edition they are available on. You can find an overview of the different editions of Salesforce.com at `https://www.salesforce.com/editions-pricing/sales-cloud/`.

Development Environment

To implement the examples in this book it is highly recommended that you create a fresh development environment in which you can practice and build. Existing environments could have other processes in place that could hinder or skew your results. Salesforce provides free developer orgs that can be provisioned quickly. Visit `https://developer.salesforce.com/signup` and sign up for your own org. It is not necessary to create a new developer org for every example in this book. In fact, the book has several examples that build on each other. I hope you enjoy the adventure of reading this book as I've enjoyed the adventure of creating it.

CHAPTER 1

■ ■ ■

A History of Workflow and Graphical Development

There are many features that Salesforce.com has that make it the leader in the customer relationship management (CRM) space. The one aspect of Salesforce.com that puts it over the top of the competition is the level of customization one can make to fit the tool into a company's business process. This is by far better than how a lot of software works in which a company has to learn how a tool works and change its process to fit the tool. On top of all that, Salesforce.com does it with a cloud solution, meaning that the instance a company runs exists on the Internet to be accessed with a web browser and run on the Salesforce.com servers. No software is required to be loaded on an employee's laptop, desktop, or mobile computing device. It's truly a remarkable feat Salesforce.com has achieved by giving everyone universal access but at the same time distinct customizable instances for each of their customers.

To make the Salesforce.com experience unique for every of its customer's needs, it offers such powerful features as custom objects, custom fields, reports, dashboards, approval processes, validation rules, and workflow rules. With these features a Salesforce.com administrator has the power to tailor his or her organization (org) to fit the desired processes that the company needs. A seasoned administrator also knows that although these tools can be used to meet most requirements, they come with restrictions on what can and cannot be changed. When these restrictions are hit during configuration, other alternatives can be used (e.g., coding with Visualforce, Apex classes, and Triggers).

When these three aspects of Salesforce.com development (Visualforce, Apex classes, Triggers) are reached, you are leaving the famous Salesforce.com credo of "clicks, not code." Salesforce.com administrators must then resort to reaching out to a developer (whether in-house or a contractor) to come in and make the necessary updates to give more functionality than what can be achieved in standard Salesforce.com configuration. Writing code will get you to the core underlying functionality of the Force.com platform and has proven to be a good fallback for when clicks just aren't enough. What is a Salesforce.com administrator to do? What about the idea of "clicks, not code"? The answer is that Salesforce.com isn't done innovating!

By the end of this chapter you will

- Get a basic understanding of how current Workflow Rules work in Salesforce.com.

- Learn about the history of developing processes graphically rather than by code.

- Understand at a high level what Visual Workflow is.

- See how Salesforce.com took Workflow to the next level with Lightning Process Builder.

© Jonathan Keel 2016
J. Keel, *Salesforce.com Lightning Process Builder and Visual Workflow*, DOI 10.1007/978-1-4842-1691-0_1

Getting Some Logic with Workflow

Let's start off with getting Salesforce.com to react and have conditions set to perform actions for those different conditions. When developing with code, programmers have conditional statements they can use in their programming language to direct the program to perform different actions depending on the current state of the program. These are usually seen as "if," "then," and "else" statements. There are other variations, but for the most part these three conditional statements get the job done. The way these statements work is as follows: "IF (some test of the current state of the system is true) THEN (perform a set of actions) ELSE (perform a set of other actions)."

Let's look at an example of how an if-then-else conditional statement might look. To keep the example simple, let's assume that this code is only run when the "StageName" field of an Opportunity in Salesforce.com is updated. A developer on the Force.com platform would write Apex code as shown in Listing 1-1.

Listing 1-1. Apex Code for Sending E-mails for Either Opportunties Won or Other StageName-Related Updates

```
if(myOpportunity.StageName == 'Closed Won') {
    emailManager.sendOppWonEmail(thisOwner);
}
else {
    emailManager.sendOppStageUpdatedEmail(thisOwner);
}
```

In this example, a developer uses the if-then-else statement to send different e-mails depending on the value of the StageName of the opportunity when the opportunity is updated. Again, we will assume that this code is executed when there is any update to the StageName field on an opportunity in Salesforce.com. With that assumption in place, the code tests the current state of the opportunity by looking at the StageName field. So if the StageName field value is equal to "Closed Won," then send an e-mail to the owner of the opportunity letting the owner know that the opportunity is won. Otherwise, just send the owner an e-mail letting him know the opportunity StageName has been updated to a new value.

While Salesforce.com has functions, such as the "IF( )" function, that can give the ability to allow logic to be placed in areas such as formula fields or validation rules, these functions alone do not have the ability to start a process if the logical test comes back as true or false. These are only used to return back another value in their "then" or "else" clauses. They can return Boolean values such as true or false. They can return text values such as "closed" or "won." They can also return numbers such as 10, 20, 5.1, or 6.50. They alone cannot start a process such as sending an e-mail or updating a field on a record. Besides code, these actionable condition statements are reserved for a small subset of Salesforce declarative functionality such as Workflow Rules and Formulas to name a couple.

With Workflow Rules, criteria can be set to test for logical conditions. They can then be configured to perform a set of actions if the criteria for those conditions are met. This would mean that all conditions were found to be true. Notice that the conditions have to be true only and not false. Workflow Rules actually don't work with the same branching paradigm as the if-then-else conditional statements described in the earlier Apex example. They are very simple in that way. The Workflow Rule simply tests if the conditions are true, and then it performs the actions. There is a way to configure the Workflow Rules to perform an "else" action, but first let's look at how we would configure a Workflow Rule to perform the first test and action in the Apex code example earlier.

Before we start, let's review what each Workflow Rule must consist of according to the Salesforce.com documentation:

- Criteria that cause the Workflow Rule to run

- Immediate actions that execute when a record matches the criteria

- Time-dependent actions that queue when a record matches the criteria, and execute according to time triggers

Since the purpose of this book is to focus on Visual Workflow and Lightning Process Builder, the next few steps are not a step-by-step guide. They are merely to illustrate how to achieve something that is available via Apex code in a declarative tool such as Workflow Rules. This will be the bridge to more advanced rules in Visual Workflow and Lightning Process Builder.

From Code to Workflow Rule

When configuring a Workflow Rule to meet the same requirements, the criteria would have to be defined as seen in the Figure 1-1. Here is a Workflow Rule named "Opportunity is Won." There are several fields set here, but the main aspect we are focusing on is the Rule Criteria section. The Workflow Rule can be set to run when either "criteria are met" or "formula evaluates to true." In this example, the rule is set to run when the "criteria are met." The criteria can be multiple conditions strung together, but for this example it is just the Opportunity Stage field being equal to "Closed One" from the list of possible picklist values.

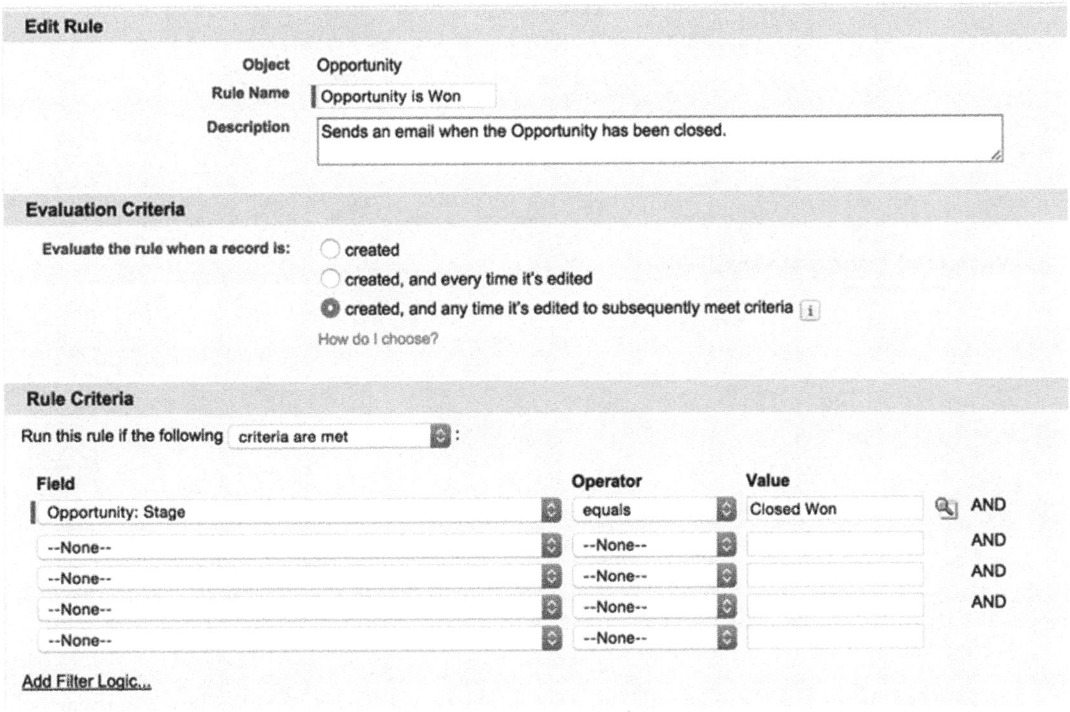

Figure 1-1. *Workflow Rule edit screen with Stage criteria*

■ **Note**   Previously, the Stage was referred to as StageName because in code, we must refer to the field by its "API" name. In configuration screens, we refer to fields by their labels, so it is simply just "Stage" in this example.

For this Workflow Rule there needs to be an action set up to run when all its criteria are met (i.e., when everything resolves to true). Figure 1-2 shows the configured Workflow Action.

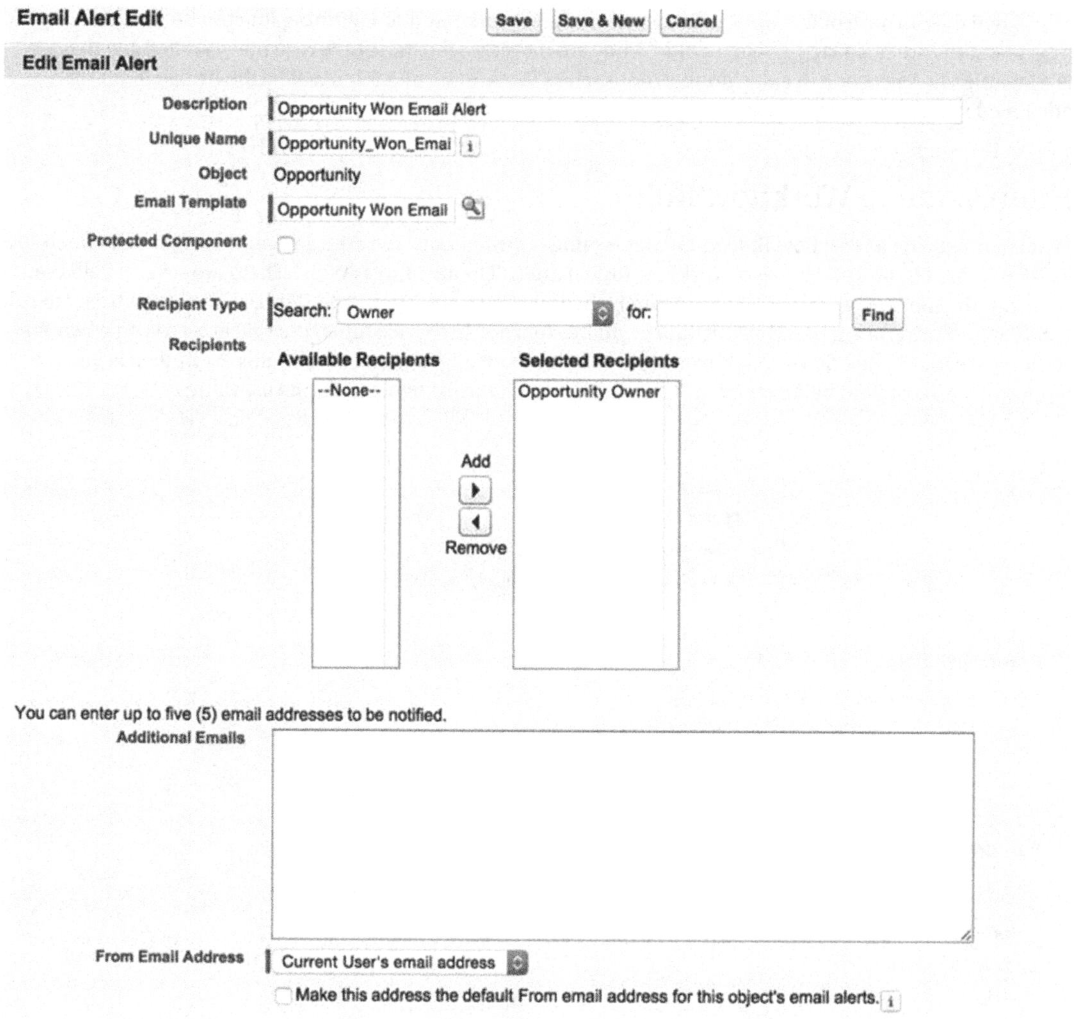

Email Alert Edit   Save   Save & New   Cancel

Edit Email Alert

Description	Opportunity Won Email Alert
Unique Name	Opportunity_Won_Emai [i]
Object	Opportunity
Email Template	Opportunity Won Email
Protected Component	☐

Recipient Type   Search: Owner   for: Find

Recipients

Available Recipients   **Selected Recipients**

--None--   Opportunity Owner

Add
▶
◀
Remove

You can enter up to five (5) email addresses to be notified.

Additional Emails

From Email Address   Current User's email address

☐ Make this address the default From email address for this object's email alerts. [i]

Figure 1-2. *E-mail Alert edit screen*

The Workflow Action is set to run on the Opportunity object, just like the Workflow Rule. There can be several types of Workflow Actions that can run, including the following:

- New Task: An activity that can be created and assigned to a user

- New E-mail Alert: An e-mail that can be sent out to one or more recipients

- Field Update: A action that will update a field on this same object

- New Outbound Message: A callout to a system outside Salesforce.com using a web service call

For this example, we have created an E-mail Alert. We will assume that the E-mail Template "Opportunity Won E-mail" was already created for use here. We are just focusing on what is needed to match the conditional requirements as well as the alerts needed, so we will assume that for both the Apex code example and this example an e-mail template was created and used by both. The Recipient Type is where you want to find the "who" to send the e-mail to. There are many different relationships a person can have to an opportunity, including:

- Account owner

- Case team

- Creator

- E-mail field

- Related contact

- Owner

- Public groups

- Related contact

- Related user

- Role

- Role and subordinates

- User

For our requirements the "Owner" option is selected. Selecting the "Owner" option then refreshes the list of Available Recipients and the option to choose "Opportunity Owner" becomes available. Add the "Opportunity Owner" by clicking the arrow pointing to the right. This will move "Opportunity Owner" to the right side of the option list. Everything else can be left as is and saved.

The final Workflow Rule should be set up and will look like the screenshot in Figure 1-3. If you look back at the original logic described as Apex code, you will see where the two perform the same functions for the IF-THEN statement. To get this Workflow Rule to work, do not forget to click the Activate button at the top. After doing so, when an opportunity is updated and the Stage is set to "Closed Won" an e-mail will be sent to the owner of the opportunity. Figure 1-3 shows the final Workflow Rule setup.

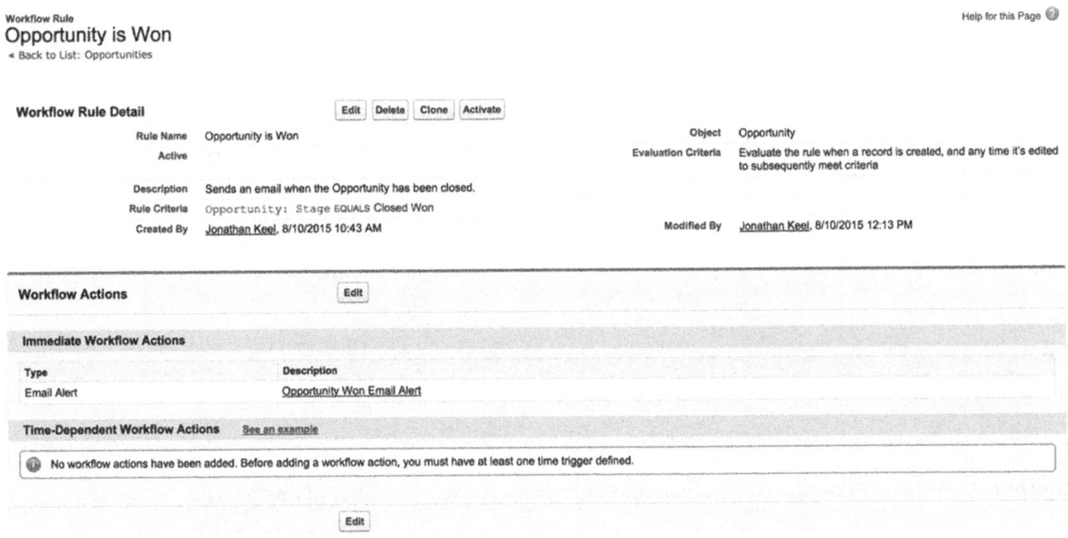

Figure 1-3. *Final Workflow Rule screen*

All right, that is all fine, but it only satisfies half of what was done with the Apex code we went over. What about the ELSE statement? As mentioned before, Workflow Rules do not function to have an action run if the criteria are not met. The actions only run when the criteria are met or a formula evaluates to true. In both cases all the conditions must be true. Actions do not run when the conditions are false. In the Apex code example it looks so simple. There is the single ELSE statement and the action to send an e-mail following it. How do we get this to work with a Workflow Rule?

The answer is to create a second Workflow Rule that would basically have the inverse of the criteria we just set up. So if the Evaluation Criteria option is set to "Evaluate the rule when a record is created, and any time it's edited to subsequently meet criteria" and the Rule Criteria is "Opportunity: Stage EQUALS Closed Won," then to achieve the same result as the else-clause in the Apex code, we would need it to fire any time the Stage field is updated but not to "Closed Won." So let's see what that Workflow Rule looks like.

To get the inverse, this Workflow Rule is a bit more complicated to make sure we account for not sending the e-mail when there is an update to the Stage but not when the update is for the Stage changing to "Closed Won." Figure 1-4 shows how to configure such a Workflow Rule.

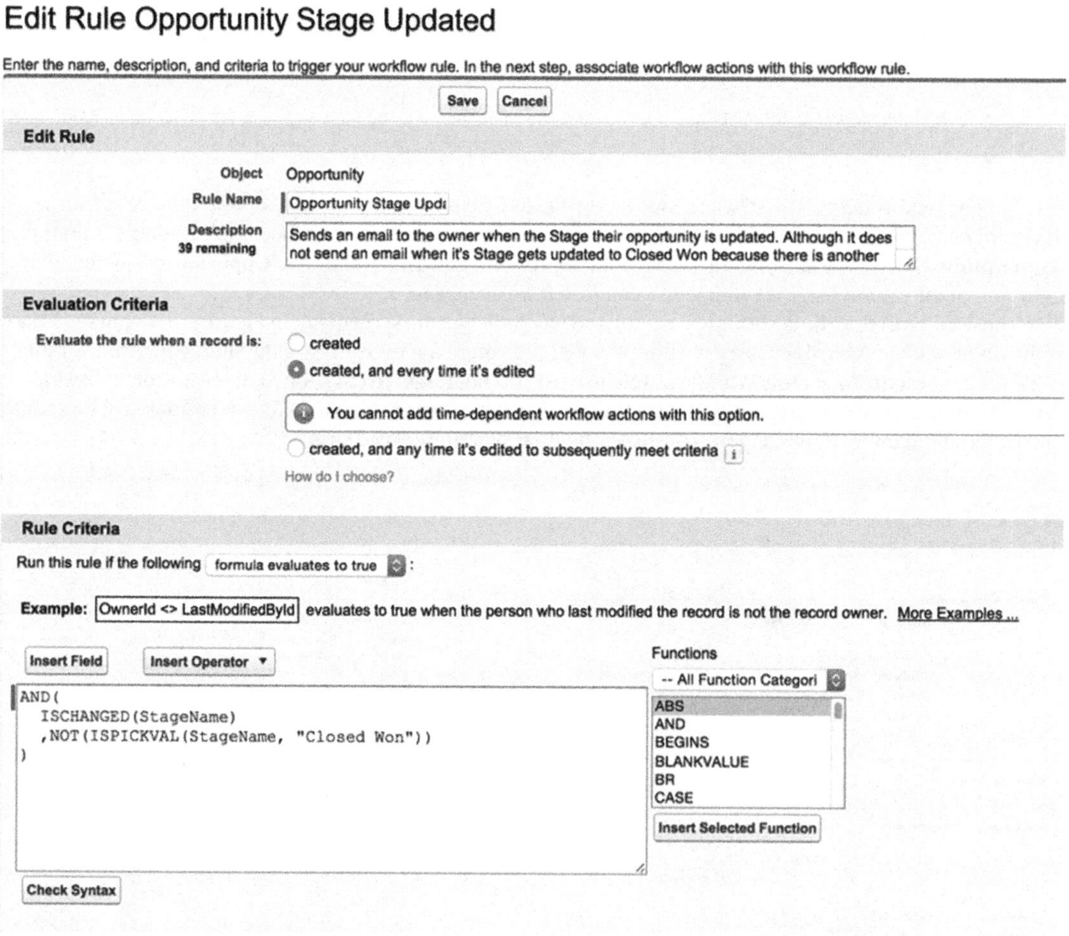

Edit Rule Opportunity Stage Updated

Enter the name, description, and criteria to trigger your workflow rule. In the next step, associate workflow actions with this workflow rule.

Save | Cancel

Edit Rule

Object	Opportunity
Rule Name	Opportunity Stage Upda
Description 39 remaining	Sends an email to the owner when the Stage their opportunity is updated. Although it does not send an email when it's Stage gets updated to Closed Won because there is another

Evaluation Criteria

Evaluate the rule when a record is:
- ○ created
- ● created, and every time it's edited

  ⓘ You cannot add time-dependent workflow actions with this option.

- ○ created, and any time it's edited to subsequently meet criteria ⓘ

How do I choose?

Rule Criteria

Run this rule if the following formula evaluates to true ⬍ :

Example: OwnerId <> LastModifiedById evaluates to true when the person who last modified the record is not the record owner. More Examples ...

Insert Field | Insert Operator ▼

Functions
-- All Function Categori ⬍

```
AND (
    ISCHANGED (StageName)
    ,NOT (ISPICKVAL (StageName, "Closed Won"))
)
```

ABS
AND
BEGINS
BLANKVALUE
BR
CASE

Insert Selected Function

Check Syntax

Figure 1-4. Workflow Rule screen for when opportunity is updated but not updated to Won

First, we need to set the Evaluation Criteria to "created, and every time it's edited" so that it's always checked when the opportunity is updated, no matter what. Next, the "formula evaluates to true" option is used so that we can test the prior value of the Stage.

■ **Note** The "formula evaluates to true" option gives more control over the Rule Criteria but is almost more complicated because a small amount of code must be used to build the formula.

Notice we check that two conditions are met using the AND function. First, we use the ISCHANGED function to check that the StageName field has been updated. Second, we check if the StageName field is not updated to "Closed Won" by using the ISPICKVAL function to check of the picklist value of StageName. Then we wrap that all in the NOT function to test for it being not equal to "Closed Won."

After putting all this together with a Workflow Rule it can get a little complicated. The small amount of code can be strange to look at for a non-developer. Code, when it gets lengthy, can be especially difficult to read. On the other hand, these screens we have walked through to set up these two Workflow Rules could appear complicated too. Someone else who may come along to make changes months or years later may not understand what the ultimate goal was when these Workflow Rules were configured.

Documenting Processes

To make processes more understandable, people will often document them as flow charts. Flow charts can have different shapes to represent the flow from one decision or action to another decision or action. They have a logical start and end. Typically, they are simply boxes with text describing an action the box represents and arrows pointing from one box to another. Decisions are typically represented as a diamond shape with text describing what the decision is asking. Decisions usually have multiple arrows branching out of them while boxes usually have a single arrow connecting it with the next shape.

■ **Note** A flow chart is a type of diagram that is used to represent a process, an algorithm, or logic.

Figure 1-5 is a flow chart representing the process we just reviewed in both the code and the Workflow Rules we configured.

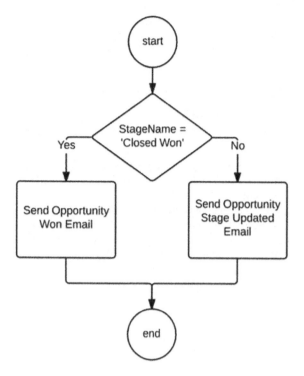

Figure 1-5. *The process we are developing shown as a flow chart*

To understand how to read this flow chart, let's review the shapes. The "start" circle is where the process flow begins. It is just designating where in the flow chart to start and where to continue following the connector arrows to. So it is read from "start" to the decision shape (the diamond). Decisions represent a part of the process where a test is made or a question is asked. It could be a test to see if the amount was over $1 million. It should be if a Contact's last name starts with the letter "K." Decisions also should ask only one question or be one test. It shouldn't test if the stage name is "Closed Won" and revenue is over $1 million. Instead, there would be one decision to test if the stage name is "Closed Won" and then if true or yes, have a connector arrow pointing to another decision asking or testing if the amount is over $1 million.

In this example, we only have one decision, so if StageName is equal to "Closed Won" then branch down to an action to send an e-mail stating that an opportunity was won. Otherwise send an e-mail stating that the opportunity Stage field was updated. After either one of those actions is performed, this flow is ended.

Flow charts are great because so much information can be easily communicated to other individuals. They are easily understood without much education on what the shapes mean and how to read them. Often when code must be written or Workflow Rules configured, the process or logic will be documented in a flow chart so that it can be understood and then translated into something software can understand and execute. A developer has to look at the diagram and physically type up the code for the system to run. Likewise, an administrator would look at the diagram and go through several screens to set up Workflow Rules. If only there was a way to have the system do all this work of taking a flow chart and turning it into code or Workflow Rules for us!

Graphical Development

There is a concept known as Dataflow Programming (DFP) that does this type of flow chart-to-code function. It is a way of performing graphical development. The general idea is that a program is built as a flow chart like the one discussed previously. The actions and decisions are represented in boxes called nodes. The connector lines branch out from one node to another. DFP has the goal of being easy to change and extremely flexible. Each node in the flow takes inputs and produces outputs. An individual employing software that supports development using DFP can use the series of inputs and outputs and move the nodes around to rearrange the logic and the sequence of events that occur in the application.

Using this series of inputs and outputs an individual can move nodes around in an application that can then be translated into usable software for an end user. DFP is not seen too often for a multitude of reasons. The main reason is that large programs can get extremely complicated and developing them as a large diagram can cause some issues with maintenance. The diagrams can get out of hand when what started off as an attempt to make system specifications more human readable will turn into a nightmare. Individuals will have a hard time trying to update or fix problems in the system with so many boxes and lines all over the place.

There are plenty of good applications though for DFP. It allows for rapid prototyping and implementation of certain systems. Salesforce.com would be such a system where DFP would fit nicely into since Salesforce.com is already set up to allow for quick and flexible changes with its configuration features such as custom objects and fields. DFP is also known for easing the process of providing end-user programming. That is, if a system is already designed, then that same system can allows users to modify its behavior using DFP. At the same time, expert developers can use DFP as part of their toolset when they feel it is appropriate, and it brings the most value and least risk to a project.

The Birth of Dataflow Programming

The concept of DFP has been around for about 50 years! In 1966, Bert Sutherland wrote his doctoral thesis ("The on-line graphical specification of computer procedures") while he was at MIT. Sutherland later was a manager at three well-known research labs, including Sun Microsystems Laboratories, the Systems Science Laboratory at Xerox PARC, and the Computer Science Division of Bolt, Beranek and Newman, Inc. In his thesis he describes a "graphical form of procedure specification and a working experimental system" based on the technique of graphically defining a process.

During the time of his writing, he stated that while there were some systems that dealt with graphical representation of data, the idea of dealing with an "on-line graphical procedure specification" was a neglected field. Sutherland saw the power of putting the instructions of procedures into a graphical form with flow charts rather than the text-based code that was being used at the time. A human without much training could easily understand it! Conversely, at the time it took a lot of training before someone could take a procedure and translate it into code that a computer could understand and execute.

Sutherland described how there could be bidirectional communication between a human and a computer. He explained that computers need a control language for them to understand. Normally this would be a written, text-based language. In his paper he said that instead of text, a computer could easily understand commands and show them as a flow chart to the person. The human would give the command via some input device and the computer would process and display the flow chart on the screen. At the time he threw out some ideas as light pen (a device to draw shapes similar to a stylus these days) to draw and manipulate shapes that appear on the screen.

Of course, technology at that time wasn't where it is today. There weren't any flat displays with touch screen interfaces like the cell phones, tablets, laptops, and monitors of today. There were large, heavy monochrome CRT (cathode ray tube) displays. These displays were not very mobile. Developers had to sit down in front of a screen and type away with a keyboard. The displays were heavy, were large, and offered limited ways of communicating with them. Even with a light pen individuals would have to hold their arms up for long amounts of time, causing fatigue. Although this paper was published in 1966, the computer mouse wasn't publicly unveiled until 1968.

Sutherland was ahead of his time in thinking of a new way of communicating with a computer to offer instructions to it describing procedures to follow. It might seem obvious to us now since we interact daily with our smart phones by touching and dragging objects about on their screens. When we are doing that, we are giving the computer processor in our phones instructions to follow and it follows and obeys our commands. In 1966, though, Sutherland stated that there was much to be done. He went on to say that better languages needed to be developed that could be used for such an interactive system. He says that new hardware devices for graphics needed to be developed. A foundation for a graphical/picture syntax needed to be developed so there could be a way to use pictures to describe and adequately represent processes.

So that brings us to today. It has been 50 years since his paper was published and our technology has advanced to a point that we can communicate very effectively now with computers. The bidirectional human-to-computer communication is pretty universal with the advent of touch screens and the explosion of mobile devices. It seems like almost everyone has a smart phone or a tablet these days. Young kids who can barely talk are able to communicate with a computer through the touch screen on a mobile device. Even animals such as monkeys and elephants can be seen accurately using touch screen devices in viral videos on the web. Yet it seems that for all that bidirectional communication with a computer, we still resort to text-based programming languages to define processes and procedures. As a Salesforce developer, one would use Apex and Visualforce. As an administrator, one can use Workflow Rules, but it just doesn't offer the power and flexibility to create as one could in a graphical development environment. Salesforce.com already is a powerful platform because it's designed to be flexible to fit the needs of its users. The creation of some sort of graphical development environment similar to what Sutherland envisioned would fit nicely on the platform.

Enter Visual Workflow

On December 31, 2009, Salesforce acquired Informavores, a company that developed what was described as business orchestration software. It was used by several call centers due to the power it had to create and change business process screens for call center associates. Informavores had designed a desktop application called "Firefly," which allowed the creation of complex business rules graphically as a decision tree. These business rules were saved as "Sparks" and could be used to create web-based forms that could interact with different data sources and deployed online. Someone using Informavores' software could now develop a web-based application that could take input from users and push or pull data all without writing code. Now someone who was familiar using diagramming software could easily use Firefly and create a complex web application without code. Sound familiar?

After the acquisition Salesforce rebranded Firefly as "Visual Process Manager" (very briefly) and then again to "Flow Designer." Several iterations through and the tool has moved from a desktop application to a cloud solution and is now known as "Visual Workflow." The tool used to build the "Flows" is called "Cloud Flow Designer." Now with Visual Workflow a Salesforce.com administrator can build pages that allow a user to interact by inputting data and saving and/or retrieving data from Salesforce. This used to be a task that a Force.com developer would have to be called to do by building Visualforce Pages and Apex Controllers.

Figures 1-6 and 1-7 show the progression of the tool used to build Flows. The first versions were FireFly and Flow Designer. Both were desktop tools that ran on Windows platforms. Flows developed in these tools had to be uploaded to the cloud. Figure 1-8 is the current Cloud Flow Designer. It is web-based and thus cross platform. The flows are editing directly in the cloud on Salesforce.com and there is no need to upload the flows like its predecessors.

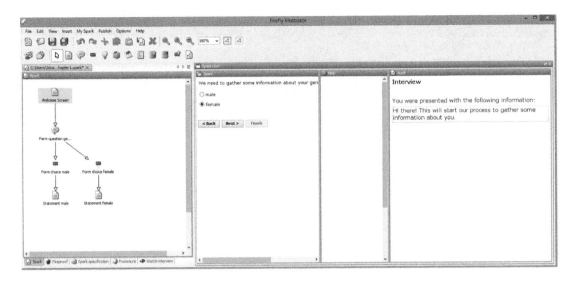

Figure 1-6. *The Informavores FireFly main screen with a basic Spark file opened for editing*

■ **Note**   FireFly did not function with Salesforce.com. The Spark files created were uploaded to Informavores servers online.

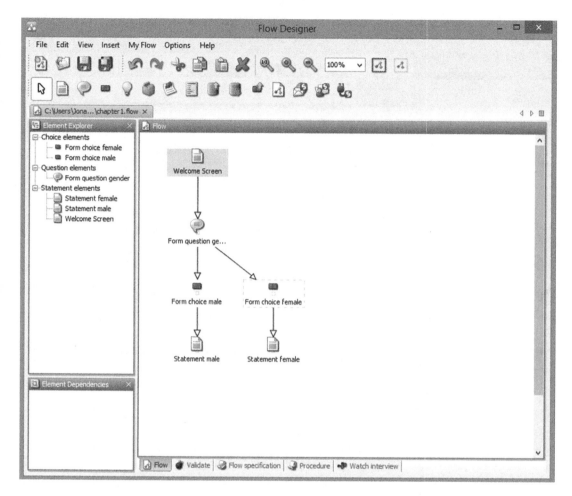

Figure 1-7. *The old desktop version of Salesforce.com Flow Designer with a basic Flow file opened for editing*

▪ **Note**   The first version of the Salesforce.com Flow Designer could open up Spark files and convert them to the new Salesforce.com Flow format.

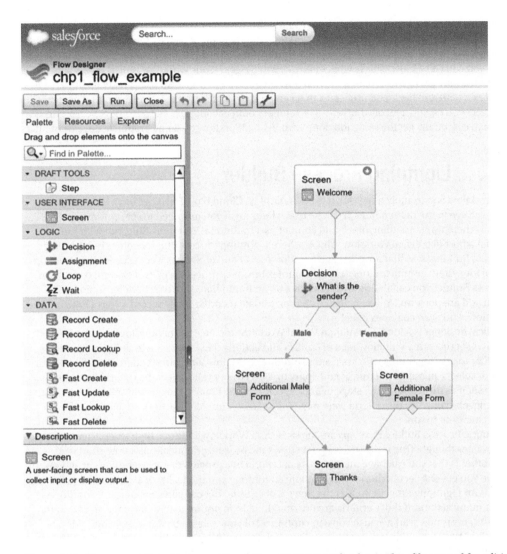

Figure 1-8. *The current Salesforce.com Cloud Flow Designer with a basic Flow file opened for editing*

Initially, all flows had to have these visual aspects to them (web-based screens). So if an administrator wanted to kick off a business process that didn't require human intervention, he or she would use Workflow Rules. In the case where the administrator wanted human intervention in a business process, then that's when he or she would use Visual Workflow to create web-based screens that flowed from screen to screen with business logic between them.

For several releases, Visual Workflow stayed in this paradigm of only creating pages for users to interact with. Administrators began to fall in love with the ability to graphically build a business process as a flow. Suddenly, having to build standard Workflow Rules by clicking a series of options in a web-based wizard seemed less appealing. Salesforce.com heard the ideas from its user base and finally the idea to allow Visual Workflow to create "headless" flows took root. Finally, Salesforce made the pilot release in 2014 and called these "headless" flows Flow Triggers.

With Flow Triggers you can create a Flow from Cloud Flow Designer with no screens for a user to interact with. It is 100% business logic similar to a Workflow Rule except, of course, these are more powerful as you can do more with Flows. You can then create a normal Workflow Rule, but as part of your action in the Workflow Rule you can call a Flow. This is what makes a Flow Trigger. Your Workflow Rule is essentially the trigger that calls the Flow. Now this is where the real power comes in. With Flows you can create both pages for users to interact with and back-end processes that can be kicked off based on some event that occurs. With Flow Triggers you can do a lot of what only a developer could accomplish in Apex Triggers. Now an administrator can essentially get the same job done with Visual Workflow by doing graphical development.

Next Up . . . Lightning Process Builder

While Visual Workflow is extremely powerful, it is also complex. Cloud Flow Designer has a lot of elements to it, which we will see in the next chapter. It can be overwhelming if you just need to set up some simpler processes. If only there was something that could simpler as a traditional Workflow Rule, but with the power of a visual editor like Visual Workflow. This is where Lightning Process Builder comes into play! Lightning Process Building was first unveiled at Dreamforce 2014 and attendees were excited. It opened up a huge platform for system administrators to build complex business processes with clicks, not code. With Lightning Process Builder you can define criteria to kick off an immediate and/or scheduled actions. The actions you can add are powerful. You can post to chatter, update records, create records, start Flows created in Visual Workflow, and even call Apex code!

The graphical designer is a lot different than Visual Workflow too. Instead of building processes out of decision trees it is set up with a Workflow idea of criteria and actions. This approach to building processes should be familiar to administrators who are used to building Workflow Rules. In standard Workflow Rules an administrator selects an object the rule would apply to. Then they would select the criteria that would trigger the rule, such as the Opportunity stage being a specific value. Finally, they would select the actions that would be triggered once all the criteria were met. They can be immediate actions or actions to be scheduled at a later time to run.

With Lightning Process Builder the steps are the same as a Workflow Rule at a high level. There are two main differences though. One is that its designer shows the process graphically as a flow chart (see Figure 1-9). Another is that you can have multiple sets of criteria in a process that trigger different actions. In a Workflow Rule you get one set of criteria with multiple conditions and then a list of actions to run after the criteria is met. With Lightning Process Builder the first set of criteria that contains one or more conditions can start one or many actions. If those criteria are not met there is an option to have another set of criteria to match against. This is powerful because you can contain all of your related business logic into this one process, whereas in Workflow Rules you would need several different Workflow Rules to catch the different scenarios in your requirements. The last major difference is that there are more options available to choose from in regard to the actions that can be taken.

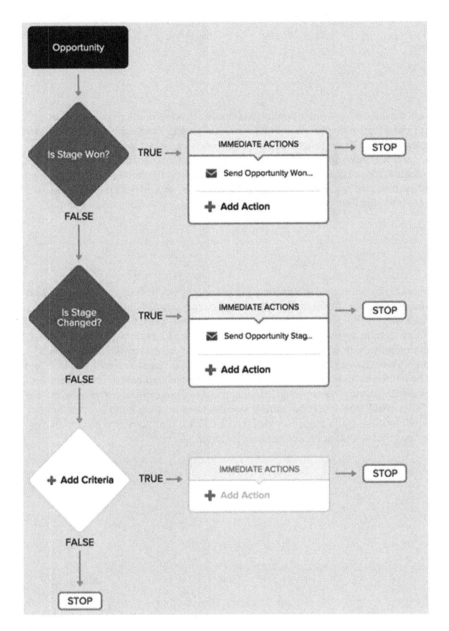

Figure 1-9. *The process we developed previously in Lightning Process Builder*

In Lightning Process Builder, an action can

- Run Apex code
- Create a record
- Send an e-mail
- Start a Flow created in Visual Workflow

- Post to chatter

- Run quick actions

- Submit for approval

- Update records

What's most interesting is that all this new functionality of Lightning Process Builder is actually just flows under the covers! That's right! Lightning Process Builder is basically a nice front end to the more complex Flows that we develop in Cloud Flow Designer. So when a Process is created it is actually a Flow. In later chapters this will be discussed more and how this fact affects the development and deployment of processes in Lightning Process Builder. For now, just realize they are one and the same and that is one reason why this book discusses these two Salesforce tools together. With that, let's dive into some details of Visual Workflow and start to build the foundation of our knowledge leading up to the newer Lightning Process Builder.

Recap

To understand where we are going, it's always a good idea to see where we've been. That way we can look at the progression of history and the decisions made to appreciate the current state of things. Salesforce.com is no different. We may wonder why current tools like Workflow Rules work the way they do in Salesforce. com. Why has advanced process development in Salesforce.com been a space for coders with text-based programming languages but not individuals who follow the "clicks, not code" mantra on which Salesforce. com is based? In this chapter, we have covered how Workflow Rules function in Salesforce.com and how they equate to a code that could be written in Apex. We also went over the history of graphical development of processes with an idea known as Dataflow Programming. Bringing these two concepts together in Salesforce. com we came to the feature known as Visual Workflow! Finally, we discussed how Lightning Process Builder give us more power than Workflow Rules by building on top of the Visual Workflow toolset to give us an easy way to kick off a variety of actions that are either immediate or scheduled.

CHAPTER 2

■ ■ ■

Visual Workflow Basics

Historically, Salesforce.com administration screens allow configuration through a series of web forms. That is, there would be a screen that you interact with by inputting data through a series of fields. Some fields would be required and some would be optional. Once the web form had at least the required fields entered, an administrator could move on to the next screen by clicking a button such as Next or Save. An administrator could also go back a screen by clicking the Previous button. Even a novice administrator will quickly find that most tasks in Salesforce.com follow this pattern of moving from screen to screen while performing data entry to configure apps, tabs, objects, workflow rules, and so on. Having the configuration of Salesforce.com set up as a wizard so that an administrator is guided through each step in the process helps to keep the amount of data entry from appearing too daunting. It also helps to break down each part of the setup process into manageable chunks.

Visual Workflow deviates from this pattern of being guided through a wizard of web forms. The Cloud Flow Designer is more open-ended and allows the Flow Administrator to quickly manipulate a Flow by adding, removing, and moving each piece of the configured Flow around. It is far different than any tool seen in the Salesforce.com toolset previously. Instead of forcing an administrator to follow specific steps, it allows complete flexibility and freedom to start at any point in the Flow design process. As we will see in this chapter, it essentially starts off with a blank Canvas with which to "draw" on. Although an administrator does not actually draw on the Canvas, he or she does have an enormous toolset represented as icons to drag onto the Canvas to build or "draw" out the Flow.

To provide a proper understanding of this complex tool, this chapter will first dive into the general concept of what a Flow is and what it represents. Also, in this chapter we will discuss the differences between standard Workflow Rule and Visual Workflow in more detail. Doing so will provide a better understanding of what a Visual Workflow can do and when it is appropriate to use a Flow from Visual Workflow vs. a standard Workflow Rule. Finally, before starting any development of Flows this chapter will go over the Cloud Flow Designer, its elements, and their purpose.

High-Level Concepts of Visual Workflow

Visual Workflow is a graphical development environment that allows you to build an application to automate business processes. Just like a developer can use Visualforce and Apex to build applications, you too can build custom applications using Visual Workflow. The features that it provides really go above and beyond how Salesforce.com already allows you to build applications with "clicks, not code." Most features of Salesforce.com have a series of data entry screens to configure your applications. You must follow these are restricted in what each feature does for you. For example, with Validation Rules you are only

© Jonathan Keel 2016

J. Keel, *Salesforce.com Lightning Process Builder and Visual Workflow*, DOI 10.1007/978-1-4842-1691-0_2

configuring the criteria for what is allowed to be entered in your application and the built-in functions you can use are restricted to those allowed for Validation Rules. If you want to have some sort of process kick off if you enter a specific type of data, then you have to leave Validation Rules and go over to Workflow Rules. There you can configure this type of logic. Still, if you want to do something simple like change the labels on a screen, you will have to leave Workflow Rules and go over to configure object labels or custom labels. As a Saleseforce.com administrator you need to know each of the tools and what they are used for and how to design your application to use each feature effectively. With Visual Workflow, you can bundle a lot of this together. That's not to say you will never configure a Validation Rule or a custom label. It just means that there are a lot of features that you can get out of this tool and if used right it can reduce the amount of configuration you have spread throughout your application. All of this gets bundled into what Salesforce.com calls a "Flow."

There are essentially three main aspects of Visual Workflow: designing, managing, and implementing business processes. The first is design. Salesforce.com provides the Cloud Flow Designer for creating flows. This is the graphical development aspect of Visual Workflow. With it, you can build your flow by dragging and dropping pre-defined elements onto a work area and connecting them together. The second aspect is management of the flows. Visual Workflow has configuration screens to allow the creation of flows, edit their properties, activate/deactivate them, delete them, and run them on demand. Part of the management of flows is versioning. Salesforce.com allows for creating versions (version 1, version 2, etc.) of the flows so that you can activate and deactivate the ones you want. The final aspect is the running of flows. Once a flow is activated it can be run from a custom button, a tab, a link, an Apex class, or a Process.

■ **Note**   When managing Flows in Visual Workflow, only one version at a time can be active.

What Is a Flow?

We keep talking about flows but what are they? They sound so nice! Almost like a relaxing Zen of configuration magic. A name like "Flow" might conjure up feelings of slowly writing calligraphy after your yoga workout. I don't want to paint too pretty of a picture. The graphical nature does make them easy to work with, but one should be aware of what flows are and when it's appropriate to use them. The Salesforce.com documentation states that "A flow is an application that can execute logic, interact with the Salesforce database, call Apex classes, and collect data from users." If you could take several of your configuration steps or chunks of Visualforce and Apex code and turn them into a flow chart that Salesforce.com understands and runs, that would be your flow. As discussed previously you can chart out the business logic of your IF-THEN-ELSEs onto the screen as in Figure 2-1. After drawing it out, you can run it to bring it to life. So cool!

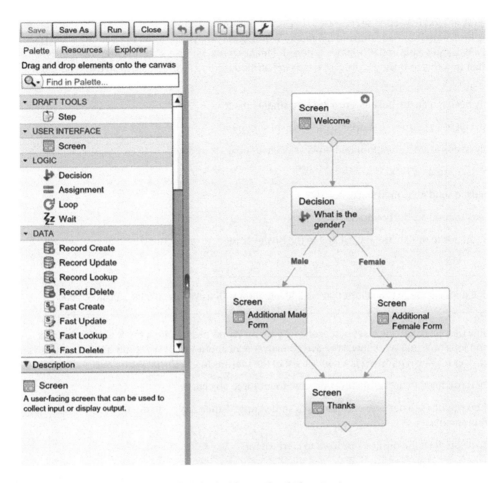

Figure 2-1. *Example of what a flow looks like in Cloud Flow Designer*

When to Use Visual Workflow vs. Workflow

Hearing the two names, Workflow and Visual Workflow, one would think they were related, but they really aren't. When you hear someone referring to "workflow" in Salesforce.com they are referring to the feature set of setting up Workflow Rules and Workflow Actions. This is the system that's been in place for many years using standard Salesforce.com data entry screens to set up the automated processes. While very simple to use, it has many limitations of what can be automated—such as being tied to a single object. When you hear someone referring to "flow" in Salesforce.com they are referring to the output of Cloud Flow Designer, the tool used to build Flows for Visual Workflow. Flows do not have the limitations that Workflow has. For example, a flow is not tied to a single object and can actually create, retrieve, edit, and delete records for multiple objects all without writing any code. Impossible you say? Nope, trust me! You are going to enjoy the ride we are about to embark on.

First, let's look at Workflow and the reasons to use it. While administrators can do a lot more with flows, Salesforce still allows Workflow to be utilized if needed. Workflow is pretty easy to set up. Its simple interface for configuring a Workflow Rule and Workflow Action still makes it the "go to" for a lot of administrators to fulfill most of their automated business process needs in Salesforce.com. Several reasons to use Workflow are that it

- only needs to tie the business process to a single object

- only needs to perform a simple if/then logical statement

- only needs to start an automated process when a record is updated

- needs to create a Task

- needs to send an E-mail alert

- needs to send an Outbound Message

- only needs to update the record tied to the business process or its parent

---

■ **Note**　An Outbound Message is a web service call to integrate with a system outside Salesforce.com.

All right, now that we have a clear set of reasons why to use Workflow, let's look more about what this book is about and look at Visual Workflow. We have gone over a lot about Visual Workflow already so we don't need to go over it again. Following is a concise list of the reasons to use Visual Workflow:

- When you need to tie the business process to multiple objects.

- When you need to perform complex logic and simple if/then logic will not meet requirements.

- When you need the business process to start when

- a user clicks a button or link

- a user accesses a custom tab

- a process starts (from Process from Process Builder starts)

- Apex code is called

- When you need to support user interaction.

- When you need to call Apex code.

- When you need to create records (besides Tasks).

- When you need to delete records.

- When you need to launch another flow.

- When you need to post to Chatter.

- When you need to send an E-mail alert.

- When you need to submit for approval.

- When you need to update ANY object record.

Visual Workflow Strengths and Limitations

Like any good tool, there is a time and a place to use it. Also, knowing your tools well will help to determine when it is best to use one tool vs. another for the job. As they say, "the right tool for the job"! We've listed some reasons to use Visual Workflow, but now let's dive deeper and discuss how the reasons equate to Visual Workflow's strengths and limitations.

Strengths

While we could go into a huge list of strengths of Visual Workflow, let's focus on three main aspects. First is the ability to tie business processes to multiple objects. The second is being able to implement complex logic that can incorporate multiple if-then-elses. The third is the ability to have multiple ways to start an automated process (a flow). Let's look a little closer at these three strengths.

Tie Business Processes to Multiple Objects

One of the most important strengths of Visual Workflow is its ability to tie a business process to multiple objects. While a standard Workflow must deal with one object at a time, this restriction does not exist when creating flows. In a flow you can have completely separate objects updated that are not even related by a lookup or master-detail record. A flow could look up a Contact record, and then use that Contact record to look for Opportunities that the Contact is related to. It could then update those Opportunities, or maybe just some of them depending on the criteria. The flow could then create a new record in a custom object to log the changes that were made and use some of the data from the User fields and Opportunity fields. There really isn't a limitation on how many objects can be used in a flow besides some governor limits, which we will discuss later. The main takeaway here is that these lookups and updates can happen to objects that really are not related in the data model. If you had a record for object A that had an external ID as a text field and wanted to use that text to look up another record but for a completely different object, object B, then you could develop that in a flow (see Figure 2-2).

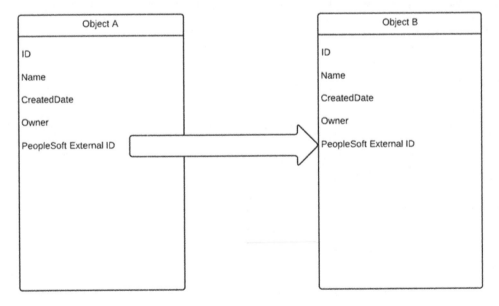

Figure 2-2. *Diagram showing the relation of two separate objects in Salesforce*

Complex Business Logic

When you need to perform complex logic and simple if/then logic will not meet requirements, the idea of building a Flow shines brighter than a newly purchased diamond ring.

Multiple Ways to Start a Flow

Visual Workflow allows you to start a Flow:

- when a user clicks a button or link

- when a user accesses a custom tab

- when a process starts from Lightning Process Builder

- from the Force.com REST API (application programming interface) to start an autolaunched flow

- from Apex to start an autolaunched flow or user provisioning flow

Limitations

There are some limitations, of course, to Visual Workflow. These range from Governor Limits to technical details about setting and accessing values in a flow to runtime considerations when the flow is executed.

Some runtime considerations are to be aware of what version of a flow is being run. Only one version of flow can be active at a time, but it is actually possible to have a newer version of a flow that is not active. Running an older version of a flow could cause issues because newer functionality or fixes could have been introduced to the most current version. Another consideration is that while testing a flow, even one that is inactive, delete operations still get run. This can cause some serious issues with data integrity, so it's best to be aware of what a flow does while testing and to be sure to run the flow in a sandbox for test purposes.

When a flow runs, it uses the permissions of the user. If a user is not set up properly to have the correct create, read, edit, and delete permissions and runs a flow, the user could receive an insufficient privileges error. Again, proper testing in a sandbox can help with this.

Finally there are several Governor Limits to be aware of, as described in Table 2-1.

Table 2-1. *General Flow Limits*

Description	Limit
Maximum number of versions per flow	50
Maximum number of executed elements at runtime	2000
Maximum number of active flows and processes per organization	500
Maximum number of flows and processes per organization	1000
Maximum number of flow interviews or groups of scheduled actions (from processes) that are waiting at one time	30,000
Maximum number of flow interviews that are resumed or groups of scheduled actions that are executed per hour	1000
Maximum number of relative time alarms defined in flow versions or schedules based on a field value in processes	20,000

For a more complete and up-to-date set, view the Visual Workflow documentation online at

https://developer.salesforce.com/docs/atlas.en-us.salesforce_vpm_guide.meta/salesforce_vpm_
guide/vpm_intro.htm

Intro to Cloud Flow Designer

By this point you are probably wondering when you are going actually see this thing and get your hands dirty. Let's take a look at the Cloud Flow Designer. First, you need to know how to get there. So after logging into the Salesforce.com Admin console, go to Setup ➤ Build ➤ Create ➤ Workflow & Approvals ➤ Flows. Figure 2-3 will show where this is at in the Salesforce.com console.

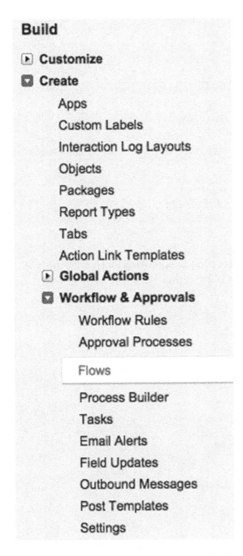

Figure 2-3. Setup navigation to get to the Flows screen within Salesforce

Once at the "Flows" screen there will be a list of active Flows, but if this is your first time then the list is probably empty. The view picklist also has other options to view inactive flows and all flows. On that screen is the New Flow button (see Figure 2-4). Any time you edit a flow or click this New Flow button you will be taken to the Cloud Flow Designer. Go ahead and click the New Flow button now so we can begin walking through all the pieces of it.

Figure 2-4. *The main Flows screen that shows all the flows in the Salesforce org*

Anatomy of Cloud Flow Designer

Once you have the Cloud Flow Designer open you will see three main components of the tool (see Figure 2-5). At the top is the Button Bar. To the left is the Toolbar and to the right is the Canvas.

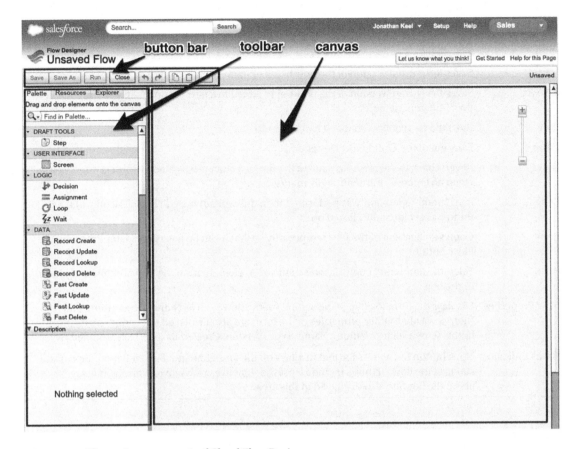

Figure 2-5. *The main components of Cloud Flow Designer*

Button Bar

The Button Bar contains all the buttons that perform functionality similar to what you would expect with a desktop application such as Save, Save As, Close, Copy, Paste, and so on. Table 2-2 provides a full list of each button and what it is used for.

Table 2-2. *Button Bar Features*

Button/Feature	Description
Save	Saves the current version of the flow being edited.
Save As	Saves the current version of the flow being edited to a new version (same name) or a new flow (different name).
Run	Runs the current flow so that it can be tested.
Close	Exits out of the Cloud Flow Designer.
Undo	Reverts back to the previous state of the flow if a change was made while editing. Useful when an edit was unintentionally made.
Redo	If an "undo" operation was performed then this will put the edit back. Useful when an undo was accidentally clicked on.
Copy	Copies an element of the flow temporarily so that it can be pasted at a later time with the Paste button.
Paste	Takes the temporary copy that was made of an element from the Copy button and puts in in the flow.
Flow Properties	Displays the form to change the settings of the flow such as Name, Description, and Interview Label. Other properties of the form are also displayed but cannot be changed in this screen such as Unique Name, Type, Version, Created By, and Last Modified By.
Status Indicator	Not a button but a message that displays on the far right of the Button Bar on the current status of the flow. Statuses include Unsaved, Inactive, and Active. Warning messages about the flow are also displayed in this area.

Toolbar

Below the Button Bar in the left panel is the Toolbar. The Toolbar has three tabs, each with different purposes to help in the building of flows: the Palette tab, the Resources tab, and the Explorer tab.

Palette Tab

The Palette tab has many different types of elements that can be used to create a flow (see Figure 2-6). It is supposed to help you "draw" out your flow just like an artist uses her palette of colors to paint a picture. To use an element, you just need to click and drag it over to the Canvas n the right side of the Cloud Flow Designer. Since there are so many elements that can be used, they are grouped into the following sections:

- **Draft Tools**: Currently, only the Step element is included here. It is used to quickly sketch out a flow and can be converted into a Screen element later. Before a flow can be activated, though, the Step element needs to be replaced.

- **User Interface**: Only the Screen element is in this section. The Screen element is used to create a user-interface screen for either showing information or collecting it in a form.

- **Logic**: This section has four elements used for building the business logic of the flow: Decision, Assignment, Loop, and Wait. These elements are used a lot to give your flow "intelligence" to behave differently depending on the inputs and data.

- **Data**: Contains elements to create, update, look up, and delete records. There are also "fast" versions of each of these elements that can act upon an sObject variable (a placeholder that represents a Salesforce object such as Account).

- **Flows**: A list of flows already in your Salesforce org. Flows can be reused so that a master flow can call a subflow. This is a very useful feature to keep flows concise and more maintainable.

- **Quick Actions**: This section has all the elements that have object-specific or global quick actions. These map to the Publisher actions that you can set up in your org.

- **Apex**: This section will show up only if there are any Invocable Methods or Apex classes which implement Process.Plugin in your organization.

- **E-mail Alerts**: This section has elements that allow you to send out preset E-mail alerts from the flow.

- **Static Actions**: The elements in this section have configuration actions such as Post to Chatter, Send E-mail, and Submit for Approval.

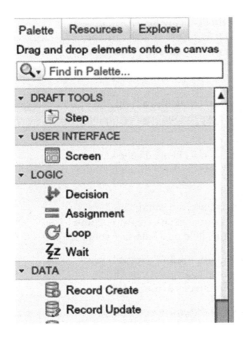

Figure 2-6. *The Palette tab*

Resources Tab

The second tab is Resources (see Figure 2-7). The items in it are focused on storing different types of values that can be saved and manipulated during the course of the flow being processed. Unlike the elements from the Palette tab, these values cannot be dragged onto the Canvas to "draw" the flow logic and behavior. Instead, these values can be created to be used by the elements in the Palette tab. To see them, you can access them in the Explorer tab, which we will discuss soon. You can access them in the elements that use them as well.

- **Variable**: An updatable value that can be referenced all throughout the flow. Each variable has a data type such as Text, Number, Currency, Date, Datetime, Boolean, Picklist, and Picklist (Muli-Select). Not only can these variables be referenced in the flow but they have scope too. They can have "Private," "Input Only," "Output Only," or "Input and Output" scope. The scopes are defined as:

  - Private: The variable cannot be passed into the flow and it cannot be accessed outside the flow.

  - Input Only: The variable values can be passed into the flow.

  - Output Only: The variable can be referenced outside the flow.

  - Input and Output: The variable can be passed into the flow and accessed outside the flow.

- **Collection Variable**: A collection or list of variables all with the same data types as a single Variable. This is essentially a way to group a logical set of variables of the same data type for use all throughout the flow. Collection Variables also have the same scope options as Variables.

- **SObject Variable**: An updatable variable that holds a single record for a specific object from Salesforce. Unlike a Collection variable, this SObject Variable can store many values of different types. Although, those values must be for valid fields on a standard or custom object in Salesforce. SObject Variables also have the same scope options as Variables.

- **SObject Collection Variable**: A collection or list of SObject Variables all with the same type of object. SObject Collection Variables also have the same scope options as Variables.

- **Constant**: A way to store a value that can be set once and not changed later. Very useful for defining default values or values that should never change throughout the course of the flow.

- **Formula**: Instead of storing a value, this type of value is a derived value. This means that you can use other flow resources to calculate this value that changes throughout the flow processing. It functions very much like a formula field on a Salesforce object.

- **Text Template**: Formatted text that can be used throughout the flow. Not only can this text be formatted with the rich text editor, but it can also display values from other resources within it. Usually used for displaying on screens to the end user.

- **Choice**: A single option to be used in a set of options that the end user can choose from on a screen. It contains both a label and a value associated with it that can be used throughout the flow. These are essentially fixed values that do not change at runtime.

- **Dynamic Choice**: The dynamic counterpart to the Choice resource. If you need to grab data from a Salesforce object and dynamically show it, then this is the resource for you!

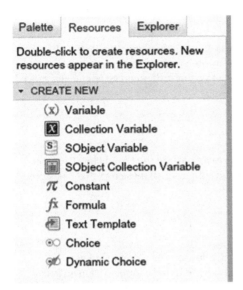

Figure 2-7. *The Resources tab*

Explorer Tab

The Explorer tab is simple a one-stop shop to find everything you created in your flow (see Figure 2-8). This is extremely useful when flows begin to get large and it is difficult to find items created from the Palette or Resources tab. The Explorer tab has a search field that will filter out items in the list as you type into it. It will save you loads of time when developing flows.

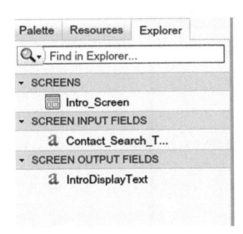

Figure 2-8. *The Explorer tab*

Canvas

The third and final section of the Cloud Flow Designer is the Canvas. It is like the paper in which to draw on. This is where your visual elements come together to form the step-by-step process that can then be run on Salesforce.com. You can click and drag items onto the Canvas, and once there, they can be edited and moved around rather easily.

Flow Elements

Now that we have gone over the highlights of what is in each of the main parts of the Cloud Flow Designer such as the Button Bar, Toolbar, and the Canvas, let's get into the fun subject of all these toys that Salesforce give us to play with!

Step

The Step element, as its name states, is used to represent a step in the flow during a drafting phase (see Figure 2-9). The Step element is very interesting as it is the only element that cannot exist in an active Flow. You can use it as long as your flow is being drafted and inactive so that it cannot be used. It is useful for brainstorming or when requirements are not set in stone and you do not want to spend a lot of time setting up the other elements only to have to delete them later. That said, you can put a Step element anywhere in the flow and put details into its settings as to the purpose of the Step so that you can replace it with the real step later. The Step element has the amazing ability to convert to a Screen element (another trait that no other element has) with the click of the bidirectional arrow icon on the element. It doesn't have to be replaced with a Screen element though. That is just the only element that it can convert to. If you happen to have the Step element on your Canvas to represent a place where you want to, at some point, do a Record Create, then you have to "rewire" your flow to take out the Step element and put in the Record Create element (which we will go over in this chapter).

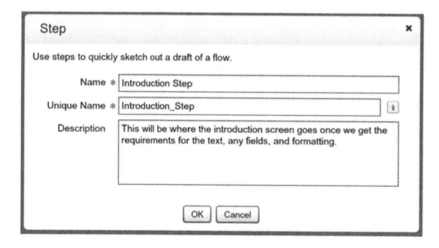

Figure 2-9. *The Set element configuration screen*

The Step element setup screen has a number of fields to fill out once it is dragged on the Canvas (see Table 2-3).

Table 2-3. *Step Element Fields*

Field	Description
Name	The friendly display name that you see on the Canvas. Think of it like a Label on a field.
Unique Name	The API name used by Salesforce to internally keep track of the data. Just like the API name on a field, this field cannot have spaces.
Description	Like the name says, it's the description of this element. Since this is a Step element to be replaced later, be sure to provide details as to the purpose and intent of this Step so that it can be properly converted or switched out for the appropriate element once drafting is complete.

■ **Note** As with other fields in Salesforce, the unique name field is used by API and managed packages. The name must begin with a letter and use only alphanumeric characters and underscores. The name cannot end with an underscore or have two consecutive underscores.

Screen

The Screen element is the bread and butter of a typical flow (not including autolaunched or user provisioning flows). Flows tend to look like step-by-step wizards, with one screen after another, that collect data from users and present information back to the screen. Due to all this user interaction, the Screen element has a lot of possible configuration options (see Figure 2-10). Let's try to go through them all but know that this is a creative element that allows endless possibilities of how to format a display to the user.

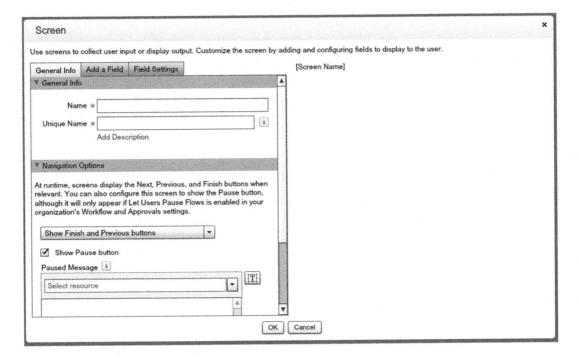

Figure 2-10. *The Screen element configuration screen with the General Info tab*

When you drag the Screen element to the Canvas, the setup screen that pops up has three tabs: General Info, Add a Field, and Field Settings. You will also notice something unique to this setup screen. On the far right side is an area where you design the screen by putting text, merge fields, and input fields. Just like the Canvas on the right side of the Cloud Flow Designer, you can design the screen on this right side of this setup window.

General Info tab

First let's look at what fields are on the General Info tab (see Table 2-4).

Table 2-4. *Screen Element Fields from General Info Tab*

Field	Description
Name	The friendly display name that you see on the Canvas. Think of it like a Label on a field.
Unique Name	The API name used by Salesforce to internally keep track of the data. Just like the API name on a field, this field cannot have spaces.
Add Description/Description	If you would like to add a description you first need to show the field by clicking the "Add Description" link. Doing that will display the Description field. Like the name says, it's the description of this element. Put whatever notes you want here to use as documentation as to why this element was created and its intention.
Next, Previous, and Finish buttons picklist	When they are running, screens in a flow will show navigation buttons such as Next, Previous, and Finish to help the user move forward and backward through the flow. This picklist gives you the option to configure which buttons you want to display so that the user can be limited in how they move about the flow. The available options are: • Show Finish and Previous buttons • Don't show Previous button • Don't show Finish button
Show Pause Button	Check this if you want to enable the Pause button in your flow navigation. This only works if you have the "Let Users Pause Flows" option enabled in the Workflows and Approvals settings for your organization.
Paused Message	The formatted text that will be displayed to users when they click the Pause button for the flow on this screen.
Help Text	The formatted text that will be displayed to help the user with this screen.

Add a Field Tab

The Add a Field tab is where the magic happens. If you look to the right side you will see the section to design the page as we discussed earlier. To design the page you just need to either double-click one of the field elements in the list or drag them over to the right. Notice that the elements are categorized by Inputs, Choices, Multi-Select Choices, and Outputs. When you move them over, you will see the fields appear on the screen mockup. The idea is to move over any fields you need to design the screen and then later modify each field with the Field Settings that we will discuss soon. Table 2-5 provides an explanation of each field.

Table 2-5. *Screen Element Fields from General Info Tab*

Field	Description
Text Box	Single line field to allow the input of general text.
Long Text Area	Multi-line field to allow the input of general text.
Number	Single line field to allow the input of a number.
Currency	Single line field to allow the input of a number as currency.
Date	Single line field to allow the input of a date formatted text. Also includes a date picker to allow the selection of a date form a calendar.
Password	Single line field to allow the input of text as a password. The text entered is masked so that it cannot be seen while typing.
Check Box	A standard check box field that can be checked or unchecked.
Radio Buttons	A field that allows a user to input one value from a list of several predetermined values displayed as radio buttons.
Drop-down List	A field that allows a user to input one value from a list of several predetermined values displayed as a picklist.
Multi-Select Check Boxes	A set of fields that allows a user to select multiple values from a list of several predetermined values as check boxes.
Multi-Select Picklist	A set of fields that allows a user to select multiple values from a list of several predetermined values as a multi-select picklist.
Display Text	An output field that is used to present a combination of text and merge fields to the user as formatted text.

■ **Note**   To remove a field from the screen, just move your mouse cursor over the field on the right side and an icon showing a trashcan will appear. Click the trashcan to remove a field.

Field Settings Tab

Once all the fields are added to the screen on the right side you will need to configure them. Each field has a different set of settings and the way to access them is to click the Field Settings tab and then click the field in the display on the right side. Every time you click a field that was added to the display screen, the configuration screens on the Field Settings tab will update with the fields that need to be configured (see Figure 2-11).

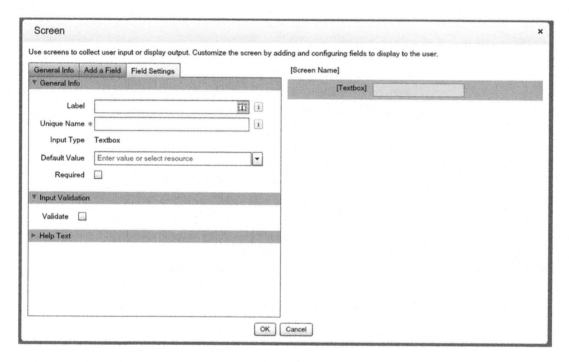

Figure 2-11. *The Screen element configuration screen with the Field Settings tab*

Decision

The Decision element provides the logic to give the flow intelligence. It is equivalent to IF-THEN-ELSE statements in programming languages. With the Decision element, the flows do not have to follow a straight line anymore. They can branch off in multiple directions called "Outcomes" based on a single condition or set of conditions (see Figure 2-12).

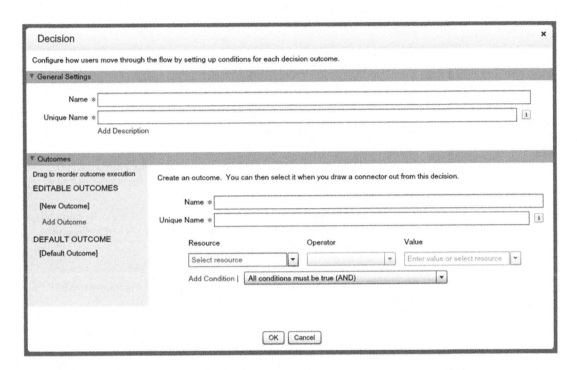

Figure 2-12. *The Decision element configuration screen*

Table 2-6 lists the Decision element setup screen fields to fill out once they are dragged on the Canvas.

Table 2-6. *Decision Element Fields Under General Settings Section*

Field	Description
Name	The display name that you see on the Canvas. Think of it like a Label on a field.
Unique Name	The API name used by Salesforce to internally keep track of the data. Just like the API name on a field, this field cannot have spaces.
Add Description/Description	If you would like to add a description you first need to show the field by clicking the "Add Description" link. Doing that will display the Description field. Like the name says, it's the description of this element. Put whatever notes you want here to use as documentation as to why this element was created and its intention.
Outcome Name	Asdf
Outcome Unique Name	Asdf

Under General Settings is another section for the Decision, called "Outcomes." Here one or many Outcomes can be created to branch the flow into different directions (see Table 2-7).

***Table 2-7.** Decision Element Fields Under Outcome Section*

Field	Description
Name	The display name that you see on the Canvas. Think of it like a Label on a field.
Unique Name	The API name used by Salesforce to internally keep track of the data. Just like the API name on a field, this field cannot have spaces.
Resource	The Resource (remember from the Resources tab) to pick from to compare it against a value.
Operator	A picklist with a list of types of ways to compare the Resource against the Value. Depending on the Resource the list of Operators in the picklist will change. For example, if the Resource is a Text box, then the Operators to pick from include equals, does not equal, contains, starts with, ends with, and is null. If the Resource is a Screen element, then the only operator available is "was visited."
Value	The value to compare against the Resource value. This value can be manually entered straight into this field or the down arrow can be clicked to show other Resources that can be compared against.
Add Condition	Clicking this link will add another Resource/Operator/Value
Conditional Logic Picklist	Select different ways of evaluating multiple conditions (if you have them). The options are: • **All conditions must be true (AND)**: every single condition created must evaluate to true. If even one value is false then the whole condition is not met. • One condition must be true (OR): at least one condition create must evaluate to true. The condition is only not met if all the conditions are false. • Advanced logic (combination of ANDs and ORs): choosing this option displays a new field to create a series of AND/OR statements with each condition noted by its place in the list. The first condition from the top is "1," then second condition from the top is "2," and so on. An example of an advanced logic statement would be (1 AND 2) OR 3

■ **Note**   It is recommended for ease of maintenance to not hard-code a value into the Value field, especially for complex flows. Rather, it is better to create a Constant (discussed later) and use the Constant in the Value field.

Assignment

The Assignment element gives the flow the ability to temporarily store values while the flow is running so that they can be used later. These values are not necessarily saved to the Salesforce database. Assignments are also useful when dealing with loops. With an Assignment element, values can be copied from one collection to another.

Figure 2-13 depicts an example of a more complex assignment. This assignment takes the value entered in a text field for the first name and assigns it to the First_Name variable. Then it takes the value entered in a text field for the last name and assigns it to the Last_Name variable. Finally, it combines the first name and last name (separated by a space) and saves it to a variable named Full_Name.

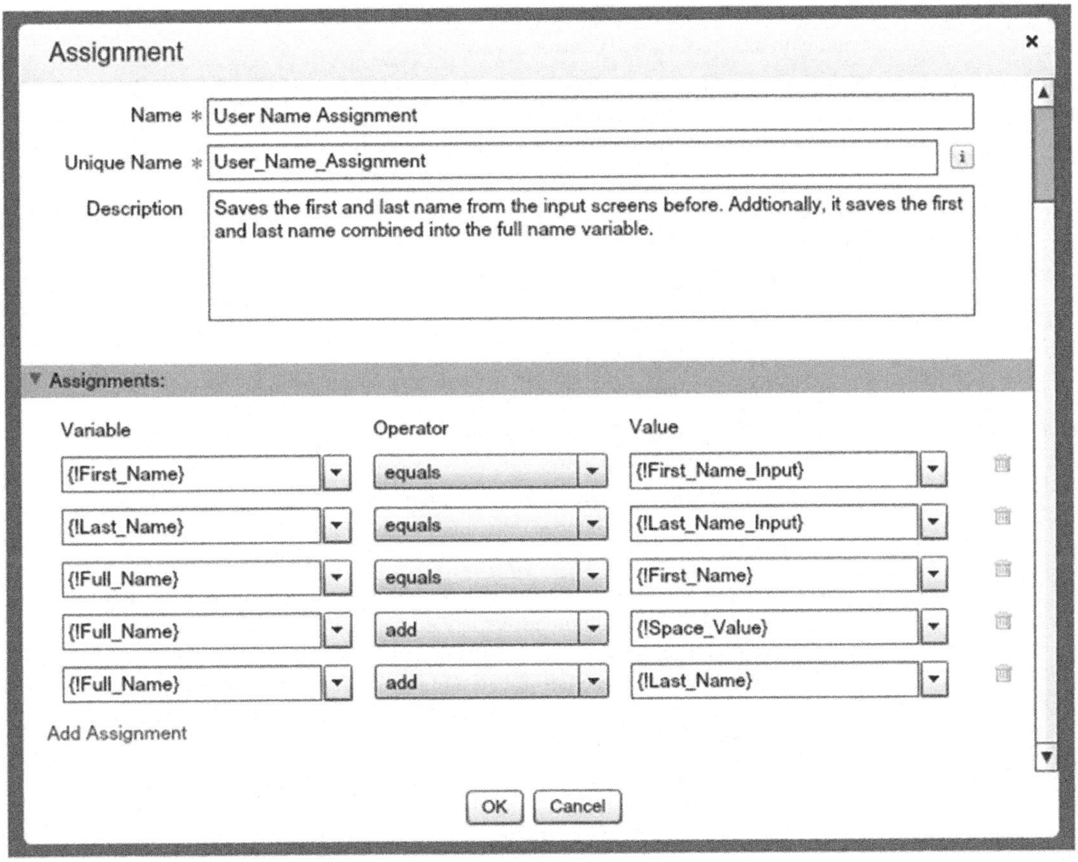

Figure 2-13. *The Assignment element configuration screen.*

■ **Note** To get the Space_Value to work you must create a Formula with a Text data type and a formula of " " & "".

Let's looks at what each of these fields does in Table 2-8.

Table 2-8. *Assignment Element Fields*

Field	Description
Name	The friendly display name that you see on the Canvas. Think of it like a Label on a field.
Unique Name	The API name used by Salesforce to internally keep track of the data. Just like the API name on a field, this field cannot have spaces.
Add Description / Description	If you would like to add a description you first need to show the field by clicking the "Add Description" link. Doing that will display the Description field. Like the name says, it's the description of this element. Put whatever notes you want here to use as documentation as to why this element was created and its intention.
Variable	The Resources to store the value into to save to use later. The only resources that can be set are: • Variable • Collection Variable • SObject Variable • SObject Collection Variable
Operator	The type of assignment that you want to occur to the Variable from the Value. The following types of Operators are: • **equals**: Takes the Value field and assigns it to the Variable field. Doing so replaces anything that was previously in the Variable previously. This is the most common Operator chosen. • **add**: Instead of replacing the Variable with the Value, it takes the original value in the Variable and adds the Value field to it. If the Variable is text, then concatenation occurs. This means that any text is just appended to the end of the original text. If the Variable is a number, then mathematical addition occurs. If the variable is a collection, then the element is added to the end of the collection. For example, if a Variable is "Work" and has an Operator of "add" and a Value of "flow," then the Variable will be changed to "Workflow." If the Variable is a number, then mathematical addition is performed. So, for example, if a Variable of "2" has an Operator of "add" and a Value of "1," then the Variable will be incremented to "3." If the Variable is a collection with one variable of "one" in the collection and then another variable of "two" is added, the collection will be "one," "two."
Value	The value to store into the Variable based on the type of Operator that was selected. A value can be a manually entered value straight in this field or it can be any Resource in the flow. To select a Resource, just click the drop-down arrow to the right to either create a new Resource or pick an existing one.
Add Assignment	Clicking this link adds another Variable/Operator/Value set. Multiple assignments can be added for one Assignment operator element on the Canvas. The assignments within one Assignment element are run in order from top to bottom. They can be removed by clicking the trashcan icon to the right of the assignment.

Loop

The Loop element allows the flow to go through a list of items in a Collection Variable or SObject Collection Variable (see Figure 2-14). Then, for each of the items it comes across in that collection, it will

- Assign the item to a loop-specific variable

- Execute a path in the flow that is specifically used for this loop

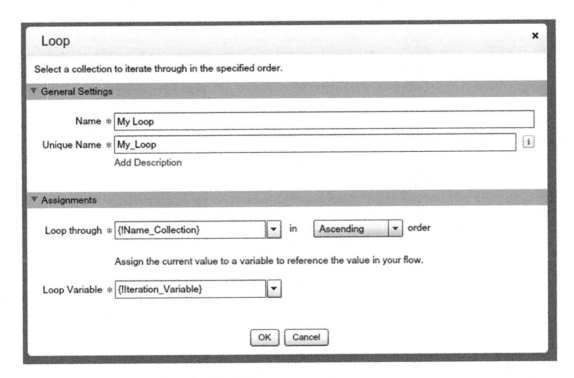

Figure 2-14. *The Loop element configuration screen*

Table 2-9 describes the fields that need to be configured for the Loop element.

Table 2-9. Loop Element Fields

Field	Description
Name	The friendly display name that you see on the Canvas. Think of it like a Label on a field.
Unique Name	The API name used by Salesforce to internally keep track of the data. Just like the API name on a field, this field cannot have spaces.
Add Description/ Description	If you would like to add a description you first need to show the field by clicking the "Add Description" link. Doing that will display the Description field. Like the name says, it's the description of this element. Put whatever notes you want here to use as documentation as to why this element was created and its intention.
Loop through	The Collection Variable or SObject Collection Variable that should be looped through for processing.
Order (picklist)	This picklist tells the flow whether to go from the first element to the last element (Ascending) or reverse order (Descending). Typically loops go in Ascending order.
Loop Variable	The variable that should hold the value of the current item that the loop is on during each iteration. This variable is necessary so that when the loop branches off into its subflow, this variable can be acted upon.

Additionally, there are some other aspects about the Loop element that need to be configured besides the fields mentioned. Once those are complete, you will need to attach the Loop element to the "Next element" you want to go to for each iteration of the loop. At the end of all processing you need to then attach an "End of loop" element, which is the element to go to next in the flow once out of the loop. Figure 2-15 shows an example of a Loop element configured with the "Next element" and "End of loop" connections.

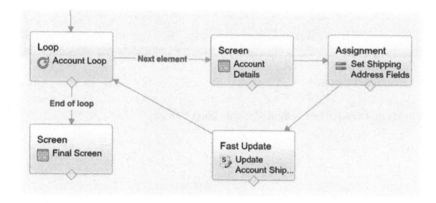

Figure 2-15. Example loop implemented to show "Next element" and "End of loop" connections

Wait

The Wait element is more of a reactive element in the sense that it is used to define events to wait for. Then, when those events occur, it can be configured to route to another part of the flow (see Figure 2-16). For example, you can have an update to an Opportunity Stage and you want to send an e-mail one day after it's updated. If that is the case, this is the element for you!

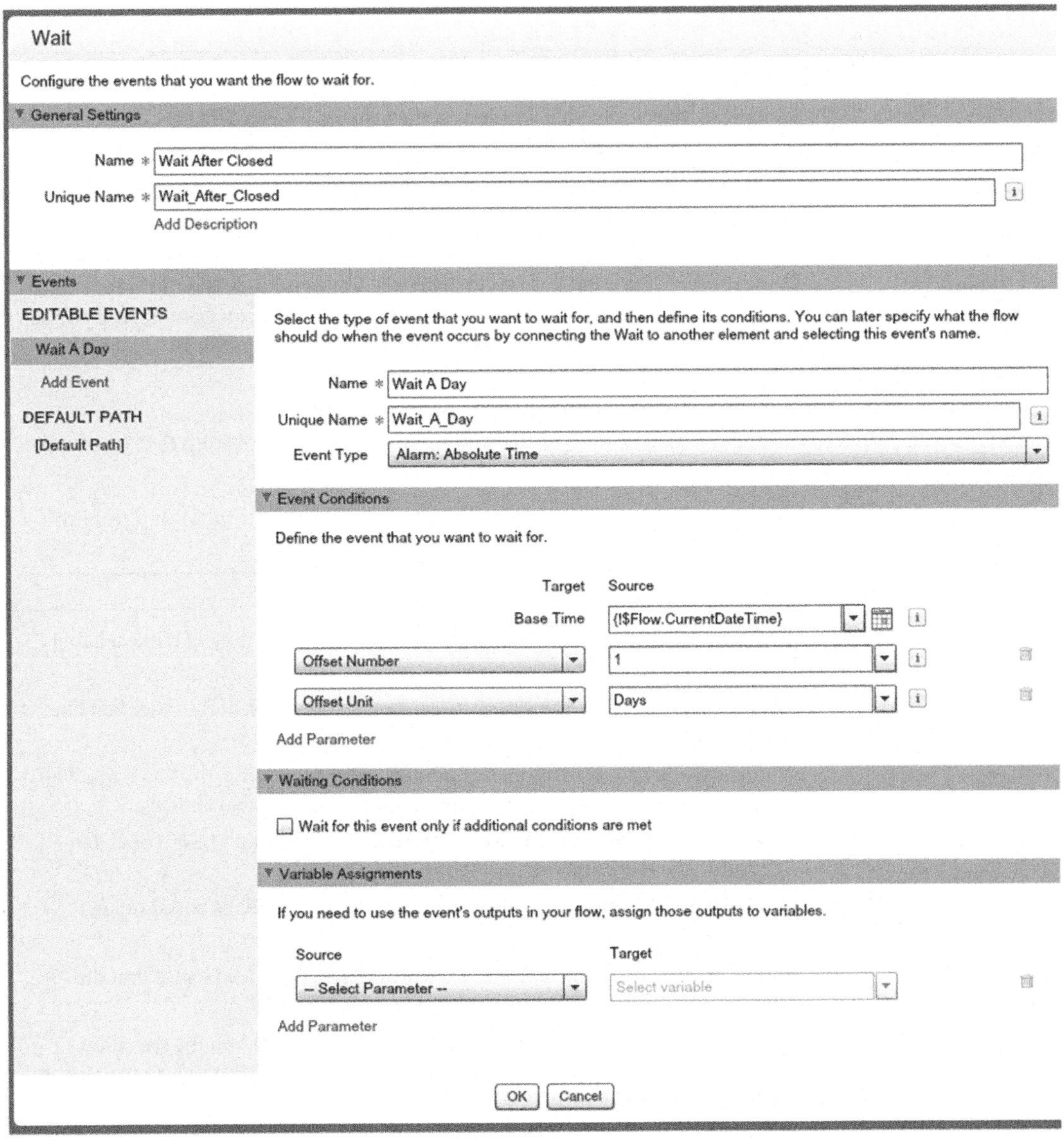

Wait

Configure the events that you want the flow to wait for.

▼ General Settings

Name * | Wait After Closed |

Unique Name * | Wait_After_Closed | [i]

Add Description

▼ Events

EDITABLE EVENTS

Wait A Day

Add Event

DEFAULT PATH

[Default Path]

Select the type of event that you want to wait for, and then define its conditions. You can later specify what the flow should do when the event occurs by connecting the Wait to another element and selecting this event's name.

Name * | Wait A Day |

Unique Name * | Wait_A_Day | [i]

Event Type | Alarm: Absolute Time | [▼]

▼ Event Conditions

Define the event that you want to wait for.

	Target	Source
Base Time		{!$Flow.CurrentDateTime} [▼] [🗓] [i]
	Offset Number [▼]	1 [▼] [i] 🗑
	Offset Unit [▼]	Days [▼] [i] 🗑

Add Parameter

▼ Waiting Conditions

☐ Wait for this event only if additional conditions are met

▼ Variable Assignments

If you need to use the event's outputs in your flow, assign those outputs to variables.

Source	Target
-- Select Parameter -- [▼]	Select variable [▼] 🗑

Add Parameter

[OK] [Cancel]

Figure 2-16. *The Wait element configuration screen*

Phew! The Wait element seems like a simple idea at first, but it's pretty powerful in what it can do. The power comes in that it can deal with timing of events and those events do not just have to kick off something after an event! Nope. You can also have it wait for a period of time BEFORE an event. We will have to dive further into the Wait element at another time, but an example of a "before" event is doing something a week before a contract expires. So in that case it is as though the flow is "watching" out for something to happen for you. Nice!

Table 2-10 shows a list of fields for the General Settings section of the Wait element setup screen.

Table 2-10. *Wait Element Fields for General Settings*

Field	Description
Name	The friendly display name that you see on the Canvas. Think of it like a Label on a field.
Unique Name	The API name used by Salesforce to internally keep track of the data. Just like the API name on a field, this field cannot have spaces.
Add Description/ Description	If you would like to add a description you first need to show the field by clicking the "Add Description" link. Doing that will display the Description field. Like the name says, it's the description of this element. Put whatever notes you want here to use as documentation as to why this element was created and its intention.

These fields are not really the important ones though. The entire configuration occurs within the Events section. You can add multiple events, but for each event there are a number of fields that you need to configure (see Table 2-11).

Table 2-11. *Wait Element Fields for Events*

Field	Description
Name	The friendly display name that you see on the Canvas. Think of it like a Label on a field.
Unique Name	The API name used by Salesforce to internally keep track of the data. Just like the API name on a field, this field cannot have spaces.
Event Type	The type of event that the flow element will base it's waiting on. Since the Wait element is a time-based piece of functionality you have two choices: • **Alarm: Relative Time**: waits for a defined time that's based on a date/ time field on a record • **Alarm: Absolute Time**: waits for a defined time that's based on an absolute date/time value
Record ID (Alarm: Relative Time only)	Enter the ID from the record that the alarm is based on. Make sure that the record is of the type put into the Object Type field.
Base Date/Time Field	Enter in the API name for a date or Date or Datetime field on the specified object. If you enter values for Offset Number and Offset Unit, this field value is the base for the offset.
Object Type	Enter the API name of the object whose field you want to base the alarm on (e.g., Account, Opportunity, or Product__c).
Base Time	The time field that this event should be fired off of. There are two system variables $Flow: CurrentDate and $Flow. CurrentDateTime can be used or a Resource in the flow can also be used.
Add Parameter (link)	Used to add a Parameter to the BaseTime field for calculation. If you want to have some offset (one week before, one day after, etc.) then a parameter will need to be added.

(continued)

Table 2-11. (*continued*)

Field	Description
Parameter	This picklist has two values to choose from: Offset Unit: The unit of measurement for time in the offset. The values allowed are "Days" or "Hours." Offset Number: The amount to offset from the Base Time. This can be a negative or a positive number. For example, -14 with a Days Offset Unit would be used for two weeks before the Base Time. Using 2 with an Hours Office Unit would be used for two hours after the Base Time.
Parameter Value	The value to use with the Parameter. As discussed in the Parameter picklist, this value would be different depending on what was picked in the picklist. For Offset Unit you can enter "Days" or "Hours." For Offset Number it can be a negative or positive number.
Waiting Conditions (check box)	Checking this box will give the ability to require additional conditions to be true. This way the Wait is on time and another set of conditions. Checking this box will then display a set of options similar to the Decision element where you can choose a Resource to be compared to a Value/Resource. One or many of these can be added and the way they are logically handled (AND, OR, Combination of ANDs and ORs) is available too.
Variable Assignments– Add Parameter	Clicking this link adds a Source/Target option to save the event's outputs to variables to be used later in the flow.
Parameter Source	There are two options available to save to a variable: • Base Time • Event Delivery Status
Parameter Target	The variable to store the Source to.

Record Create

The Record Create element is used to insert a new record for a standard or custom object into Salesforce. It takes individual variables to set each field on the record you want to create. This is different from the Fast Create element that takes an SObject Variable or SObject Collection Variable that already has all its values set to create a record. See Figure 2-17 and Table 2-12 for an explanation of the configuration of the Record Create element.

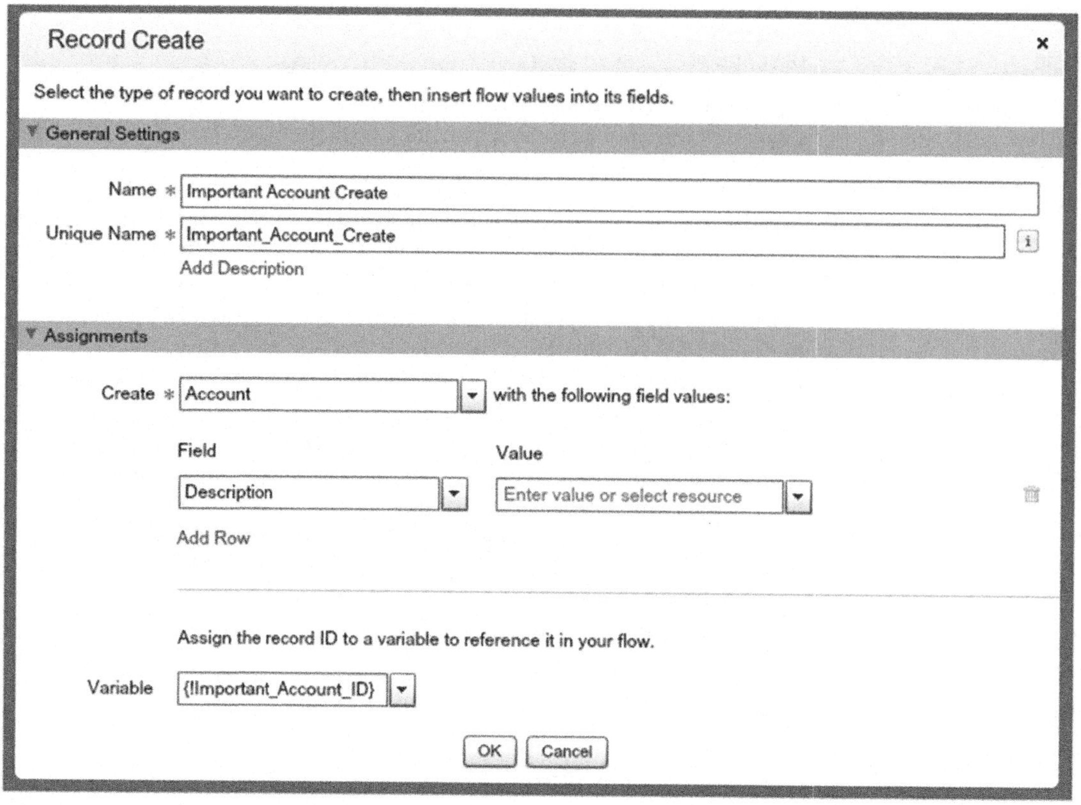

Figure 2-17. *The Record Create element configuration screen*

Table 2-12. *Record Create Element Fields*

Field	Description
Name	The display name that you see on the Canvas. Think of it like a Label on a field.
Unique Name	The API name used by Salesforce to internally keep track of the data. Just like the API name on a field, this field cannot have spaces.
Add Description/ Description	If you would like to add a description you first need to show the field by clicking the "Add Description" link. Doing that will display the Description field. Like the name says, it's the description of this element. Put whatever notes you want here to use as documentation as to why this element was created and its intention.
Create	The type of object to create.
Field	The field on the object created to set a value to.
Value	The value that to set in the object's field.
Variable	The variable to hold the Record ID from the newly created record.

Record Update

The Record Update element is used to update an existing record for a standard or custom object in Salesforce. It takes individual variables to set each field on the record you want to update. This is different from the Fast Update element that takes an SObject Variable or SObject Collection Variable that already has all its values set to update a record. See Figure 2-18 and Table 2-13 for an explanation of the configuration of the Record Update element.

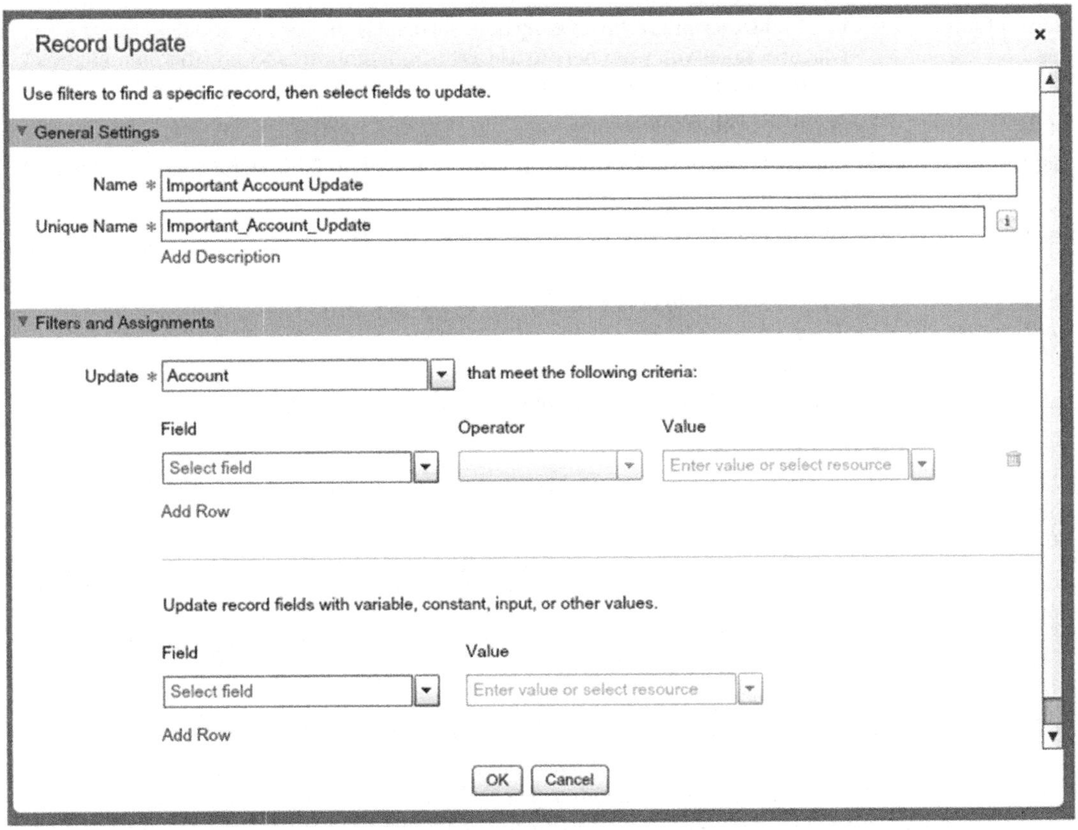

Figure 2-18. *The Record Update element configuration screen*

Table 2-13. *Record Update Element Fields*

Field	Description
Name	The display name that you see on the Canvas. Think of it like a Label on a field.
Unique Name	The API name used by Salesforce to internally keep track of the data. Just like the API name on a field, this field cannot have spaces.
Add Description/ Description	If you would like to add a description you first need to show the field by clicking the "Add Description" link. Doing that will display the Description field. Enter in whatever notes you want here to use as documentation as to why this element was created and its intention.
Update	The type of object to update.
Field (for Criteria)	The field from the object to use in defining a filter for finding the appropriate record to update.
Operator (for Criteria)	The operator to compare with against the Value field.
Value (for Criteria)	The value to use to define the criteria to find the appropriate record to update.
Add Row (link) (for Criteria)	Clicking this link adds another set of Field/Operator/Value fields to help further define the criteria for filtering out the appropriate record.
Field (for Assignment)	The field from the object to update.
Value (for Assignment)	The value to update the object's field to.
Add Row (link) (for Assignment)	Clicking this link adds another Field/Value assignment set to update more fields on the record.

Record Lookup

Similar to a SOQL (Salesforce Object Query Language) query in Apex, the Record Lookup element is used to retrieve an existing record for a standard or custom object from Salesforce. The Record Lookup element is used to find one record and set multiple variables in the flow from that record's fields. This is different from the Fast Lookup element that can find one record and assign its fields to a single SObject Variable or find multiple records and assign them to an SObject Collection Variable. See Figure 2-19 and Table 2-14 for an explanation of the configuration of the Record Lookup element.

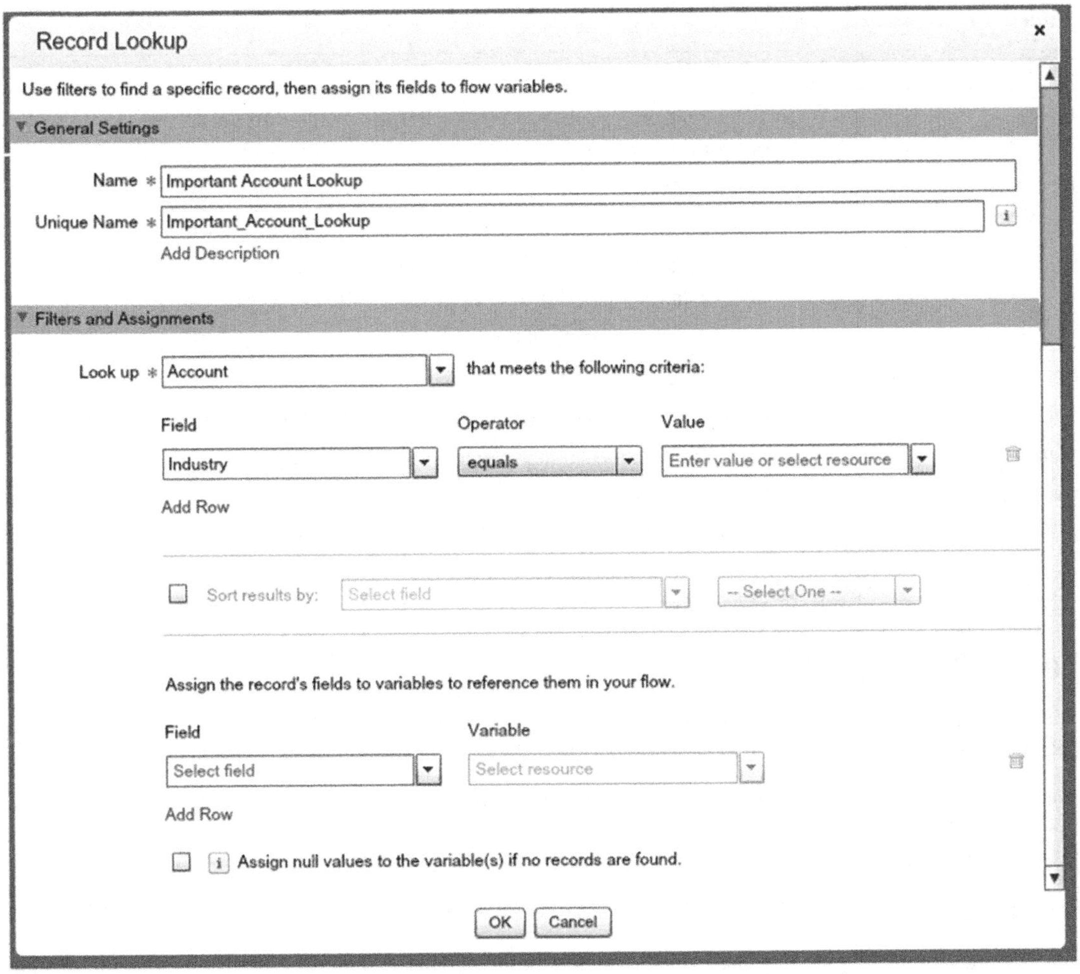

Figure 2-19. *The Record Lookup element configuration screen*

Table 2-14. *Record Lookup Element Fields*

Field	Description
Name	The display name that you see on the Canvas. Think of it like a Label on a field.
Unique Name	The API name used by Salesforce to internally keep track of the data. Just like the API name on a field, this field cannot have spaces.
Add Description/Description	If you would like to add a description you first need to show the field by clicking the "Add Description" link. Doing that will display the Description field. Like the name says, it's the description of this element. Put whatever notes you want here to use as documentation as to why this element was created and its intention.
Lookup	The type of object to lookup.

(*continued*)

Table 2-14. (*continued*)

Field	Description
Field	The field from the object to use in defining a filter for finding the appropriate record to lookup.
Operator	The operator to compare with against the Value field.
Value	The value to use to define the criteria to find the appropriate record to lookup.
Add Row (link)	Clicking this link adds another set of Field/Operator/Value fields to help further define the criteria for filtering out the appropriate record.
Sort Results by (check box)	Check to allow sorting of the results.
Sort Results by (field)	Select a field to sort by.
Sort Results by (order)	Choose between sorting Ascending or Descending.
Field	Field from the record to assign to use the value from.
Variable	Variable to assign the field value to.
Assign null (check box)	Assign a null to the variable if no records are found.
Fields	Select all the fields from the record to save in the variable.

Record Delete

The Record Delete element is used to remove an existing record for a standard or custom object from Salesforce. See Figure 2-20 and Table 2-15 for an explanation of the configuration of this element.

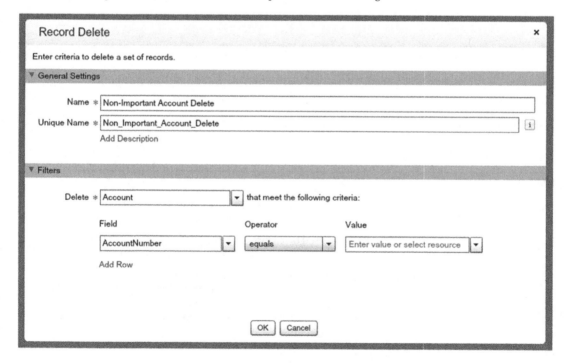

Figure 2-20. *The Record Delete element configuration screen*

Table 2-15. *Record Delete Element Fields*

Field	Description
Name	The display name that you see on the Canvas. Think of it like a Label on a field.
Unique Name	The API name used by Salesforce to internally keep track of the data. Just like the API name on a field, this field cannot have spaces.
Add Description/Description	If you would like to add a description you first need to show the field by clicking the "Add Description" link. Doing that will display the Description field. Like the name says, it's the description of this element. Put whatever notes you want here to use as documentation as to why this element was created and its intention.
Delete	The type of object to delete.
Field	The field from the object to use in defining a filter for finding the appropriate record to delete.
Operator	The operator to compare with against the Value field.
Value	The value to use to define the criteria to find the appropriate record to delete.
Add Row (link)	Clicking this link adds another set of Field/Operator/Value fields to help further define the criteria for filtering out the appropriate record.

Fast Create

The Fast Create element is used to insert a new record for a standard or custom object into Salesforce using the field values from an SObject Variable or SObject Collection Variable. This is different from the Create Record element that requires each of its fields to be set by separate variables. See Figure 2-21 and Table 2-16 for an explanation of the configuration of the Fast Create element.

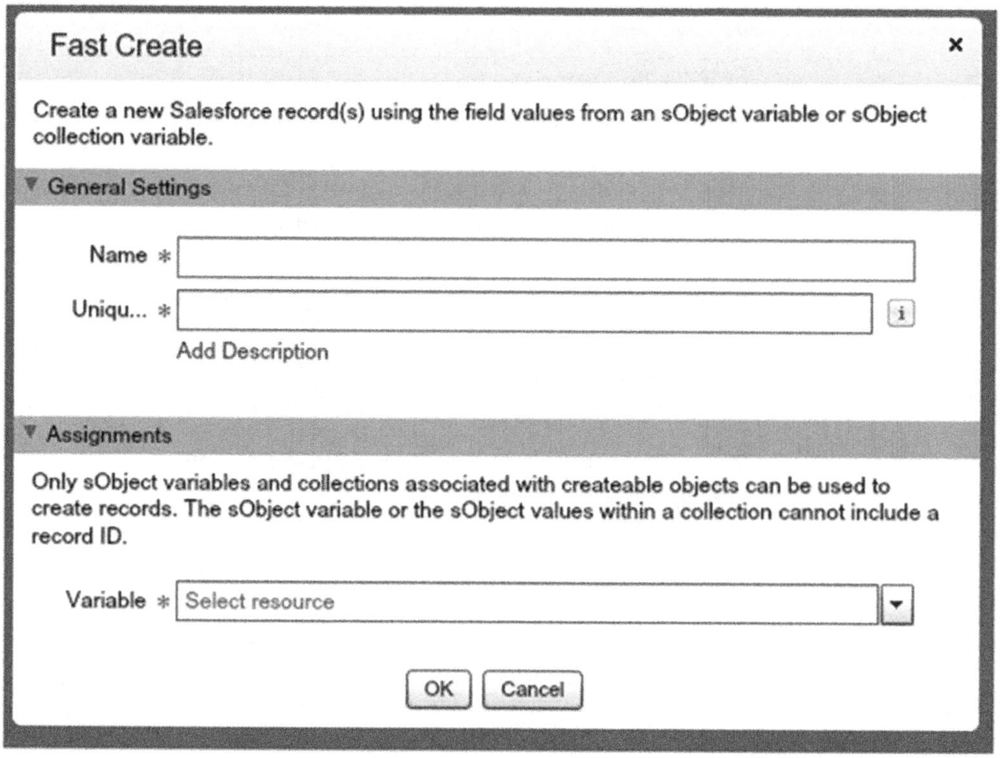

Figure 2-21. *The Fast Create element configuration screen*

Table 2-16. *Fast Create Element Fields*

Field	Description
Name	The display name that you see on the Canvas. Think of it like a Label on a field.
Unique Name	The API name used by Salesforce to internally keep track of the data. Just like the API name on a field, this field cannot have spaces.
Add Description/ Description	If you would like to add a description you first need to show the field by clicking the "Add Description" link. Doing that will display the Description field. Like the name says, it's the description of this element. Put whatever notes you want here to use as documentation as to why this element was created and its intention.
Variable	The SObject Variable or SObject Collection Variable associated with the Salesforce record to create. The variable cannot include a Record ID.

Fast Update

The Fast Update element is used to update an existing record or multiple records for a standard or custom object in Salesforce using the field values from an SObject Variable or SObject Collection Variable. This is different from the Update Record element that updates a single record by setting each of the fields for that record individually. See Figure 2-22 and Table 2-17 for an explanation of the configuration of the Fast Update element.

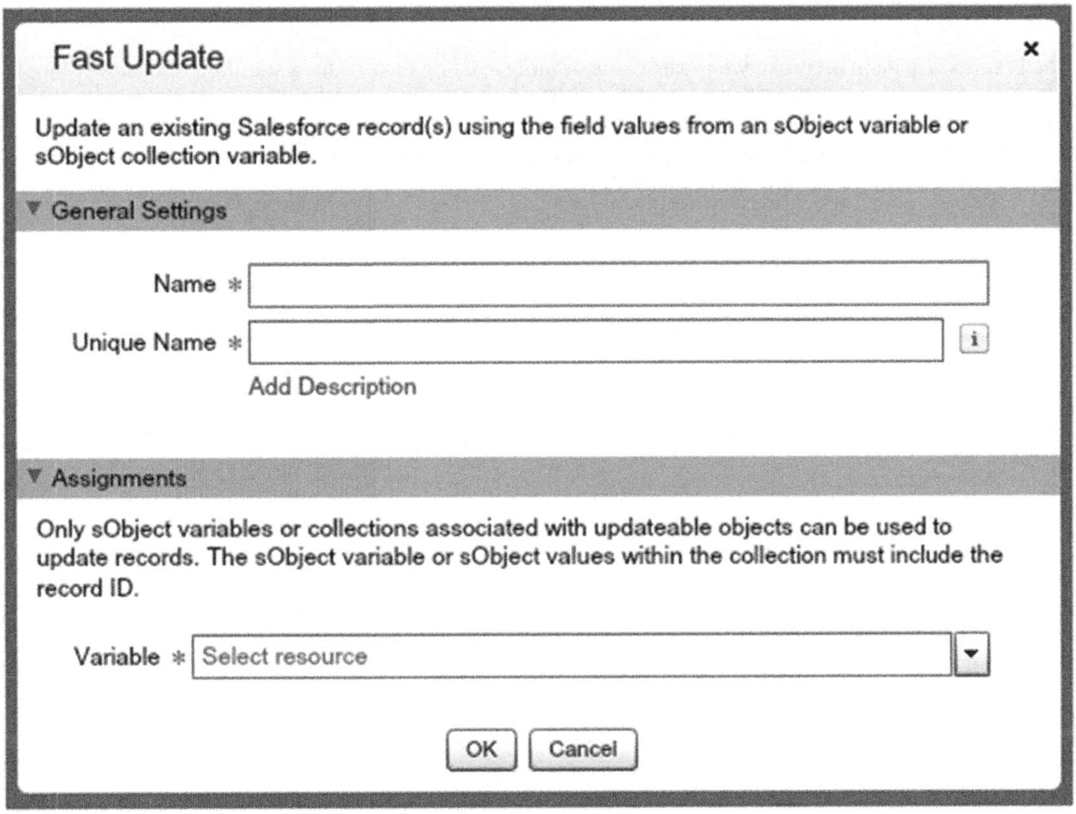

Fast Update ✕

Update an existing Salesforce record(s) using the field values from an sObject variable or sObject collection variable.

▼ General Settings

Name * [   ]

Unique Name * [   ] [i]

Add Description

▼ Assignments

Only sObject variables or collections associated with updateable objects can be used to update records. The sObject variable or sObject values within the collection must include the record ID.

Variable * [Select resource   ] [▼]

[OK] [Cancel]

Figure 2-22. *The Fast Update element configuration screen*

Table 2-17. *Fast Update Element Fields*

Field	Description
Name	The display name that you see on the Canvas. Think of it like a Label on a field.
Unique Name	The API name used by Salesforce to internally keep track of the data. Just like the API name on a field, this field cannot have spaces.
Add Description/ Description	If you would like to add a description you first need to show the field by clicking the "Add Description" link. Doing that will display the Description field. Like the name says, it's the description of this element. Put whatever notes you want here to use as documentation as to why this element was created and its intention.
Variable	The SObject Variable or SObject Collection Variable associated with the Salesforce record to update. The variable must contain a Record ID.

Fast Lookup

The Fast Lookup element is used to retrieve one or more existing records for a standard or custom object from Salesforce. If one record is found, it assigns fields from that record to an SObject Variable. If multiple records are retrieved, then it assigns them to an SObject Collection Variable. This is different from a Record Lookup element that finds one specific record and then assigns the record's fields to individual variables in the flow. See Figure 2-23 and Table 2-18 for an explanation of the configuration of the Fast Lookup element.

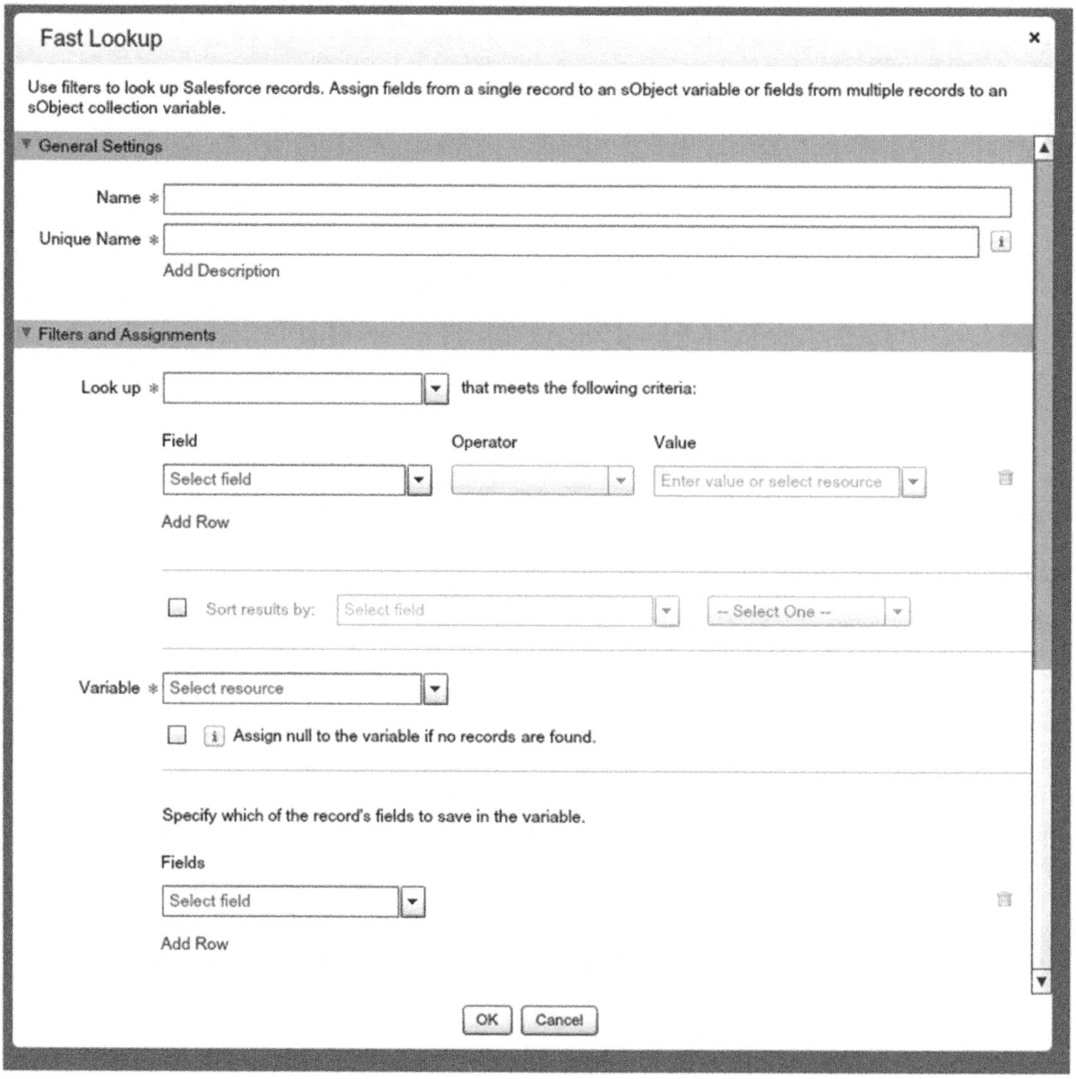

Figure 2-23. *The Fast Lookup element configuration screen*

Table 2-18. *Fast Lookup Element Fields*

Field	Description
Name	The display name that you see on the Canvas. Think of it like a Label on a field.
Unique Name	The API name used by Salesforce to internally keep track of the data. Just like the API name on a field, this field cannot have spaces.
Add Description/ Description	If you would like to add a description you first need to show the field by clicking the "Add Description" link. Doing that will display the Description field. Like the name says, it's the description of this element. Put whatever notes you want here to use as documentation as to why this element was created and its intention.
Lookup	The type of object to look up.
Field	The field from the object to use in defining a filter for finding the appropriate record to look up.
Operator	The operator to compare with against the Value field.
Value	The value to use to define the criteria to find the appropriate record to look up.
Add Row (link)	Clicking this link adds another set of Field/Operator/Value fields to help further define the criteria for filtering out the appropriate record.
Sort Results by (check box)	Check to allow sorting of the results.
Sort Results by (field)	Select a field to sort by.
Sort Results by (order)	Choose between sorting Ascending or Descending.
Variable	SObject Variable to assign record to.
Assign null (check box)	Assign a null to the variable if no records are found.
Fields	Select all the fields from the record to save in the variable.

Fast Delete

The Fast Delete element is used to remove one or more existing records for a standard or custom object from Salesforce associated with an SObject Variable or SObject Collection Variable. This is different from the Delete Record element that deletes a set of records by defining the set of matching fields individually. See Figure 2-24 and Table 2-19 for an explanation of the configuration of the Fast Delete element.

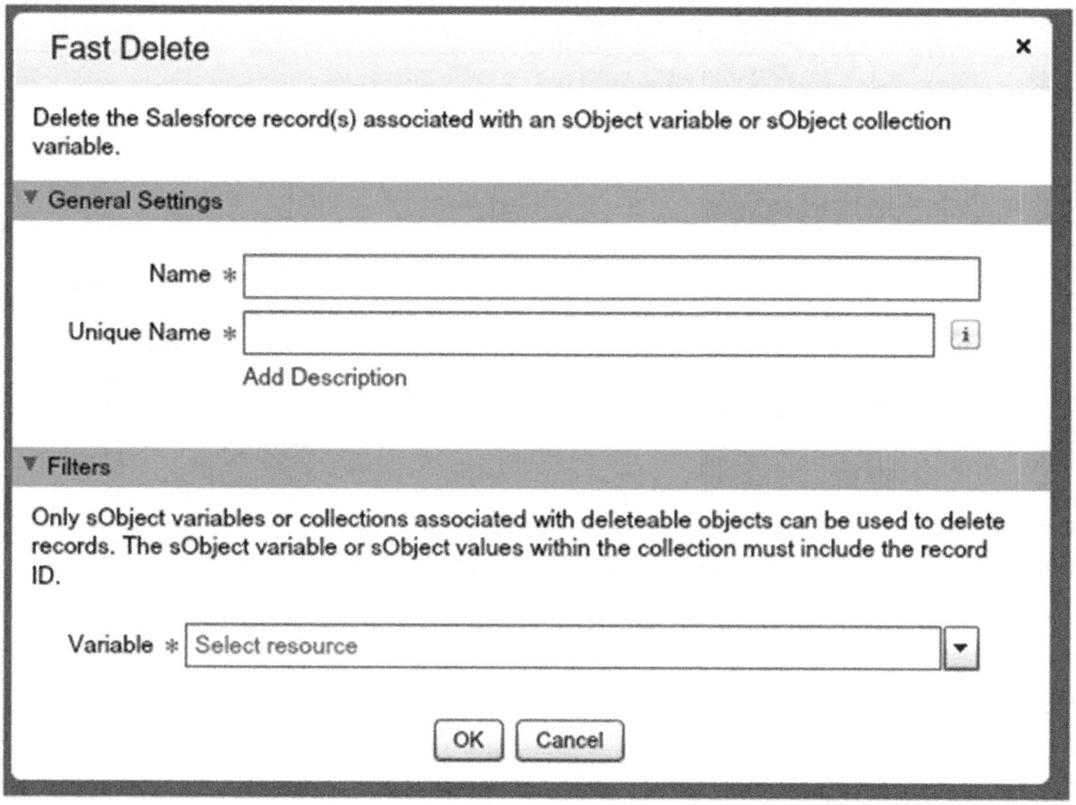

Fast Delete ✕

Delete the Salesforce record(s) associated with an sObject variable or sObject collection variable.

▼ General Settings

Name ∗ [   ]

Unique Name ∗ [   ] [i]

Add Description

▼ Filters

Only sObject variables or collections associated with deleteable objects can be used to delete records. The sObject variable or sObject values within the collection must include the record ID.

Variable ∗ [Select resource   ▼]

[OK] [Cancel]

Figure 2-24. The Fast Delete element configuration screen

Table 2-19. Fast Delete Element Fields

Field	Description
Name	The display name that you see on the Canvas. Think of it like a Label on a field.
Unique Name	The API name used by Salesforce to internally keep track of the data. Just like the API name on a field, this field cannot have spaces.
Add Description/ Description	If you would like to add a description you first need to show the field by clicking the "Add Description" link. Doing that will display the Description field. Like the name says, it's the description of this element. Put whatever notes you want here to use as documentation as to why this element was created and its intention.
Variable	The SObject Variable or SObject Collection Variable associated with the Salesforce record to delete.

Flows, Plug-ins, Quick Actions, Apex, E-mail Alerts, and Static Actions

You will notice there are a lot more elements in the Palette after these. They are included in the sections for Flows, Plug-ins, Quick Actions, Apex, E-mail Alerts, and Static Actions. These items have varied elements in their configuration screens and developers can add more elements into these sections. Following is a brief overview of each of these sections:

- **Flows**: Lists all the flows in the org that are either active or inactive so that they can be added to the current flow within the Canvas.

- **Plugins**: Lists any Apex classes that implement the Process.Plugin interface. These Apex classes are special in that they have their own custom configuration screens.

- **Quick Actions**: Lists any object-specific or global quick actions that are already been configured in the organization.

- **Apex**: Lists any Apex classes that have an invocable method defined so that it may be called from within a flow.

- **Email Alerts**: Lists workflow e-mail alerts so that they may be called from within a flow.

- **Static Actions**: List of actions provided by Salesforce for convenience which include Post to Chatter, Send E-mail, and Submit for Approval

Flow Resources

The second tab is Resources. It contains all the different types of ways of temporarily storing values to be used in the flow but not saved into the Salesforce database. Get acquainted with each of these because chances are you will use every single one of them at one point or another. While they all basically allow you to store and carry around data in the flow (or even out of the flow to another flow), they each have their specific purpose in life.

Variable

The Variable resource allows a value to be stored in the flow to be used later within the flow or even outside the flow. Figure 2-25 and Table 2-20 explain each of the fields.

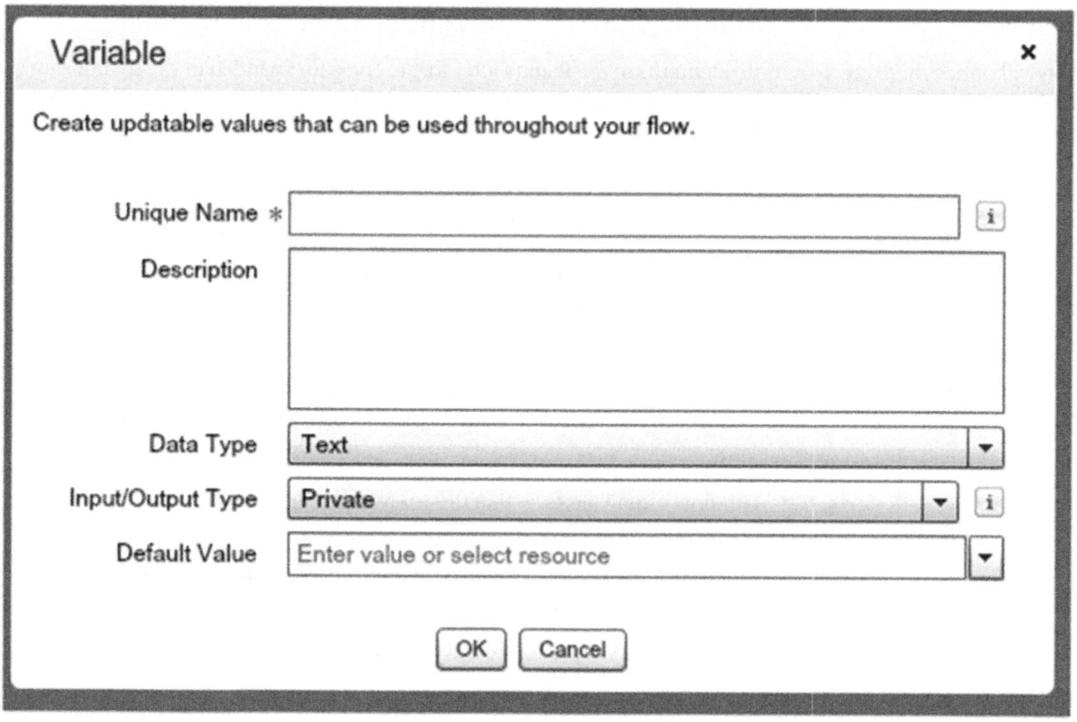

Figure 2-25. *The Variable resource configuration screen*

Table 2-20. *Variable Resource Fields*

Field	Description
Unique Name	The API name used by Salesforce to internally keep track of the data. Just like the API name on a field, this field cannot have spaces.
Description	Like the name says, it's the description of this element. Put whatever notes you want here to use as documentation as to why this resource was created and its intention.
Data Type	The type of value this resource should hold. Available options are: • Text • Number • Currency • Date • DateTime • Boolean • Picklist • Picklist (Multi-Select)

(continued)

Table 2-20. (*continued*)

Field	Description
Input/Output Type	Sets the permissions of how this resource is accessed in or out of the flow. Available options are:
	• Private: The variable cannot be passed into the flow and it cannot be accessed outside the flow.
	• Input Only: The variable values can be passed into the flow.
	• Output Only: The variable can be referenced outside the flow.
	• Input and Output: The variable can be passed into the flow and accessed outside the flow.
Default Value	The optional value that this resource should have when the flow first starts. A value can be manually entered or it can come from another resource. It can also be left blank so that the variable starts off with no value.

Collection Variable

The Collection Variable resource allows multiple values to be stored in the flow to be used later within the flow or possibly a calling flow. Figure 2-26 and Table 2-21 explain each of the fields.

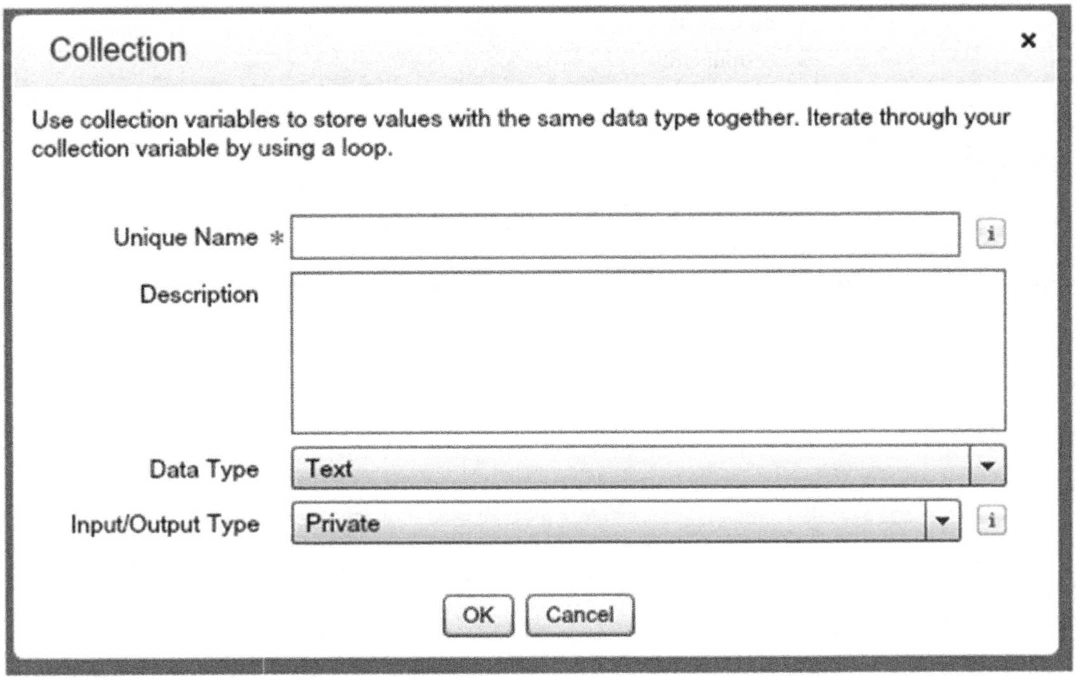

Figure 2-26. *The Collection resource configuration screen*

Table 2-21. *Collection Variable Resource Fields*

Field	Description
Unique Name	The API name used by Salesforce to internally keep track of the data. Just like the API name on a field, this field cannot have spaces.
Description	The description of this element. Put whatever notes you want here to use as documentation as to why this resource was created and its intention.
Data Type	The type of value this resource should hold. Available options are: • Text • Number • Currency • Date • DateTime • Boolean • Picklist • Picklist (Multi-Select)
Input/Output Type	Sets the permissions of how this resource is accessed in or out of the flow. Available options are: • Private • Input Only • Output Only • Input and Output

SObject Variable

The SObject Variable resource allows the storage of multiple field values that are a part of a type of object to be stored in the flow to be used later within the flow or possibly a calling flow. Figure 2-27 and Table 2-22 explain each of the fields.

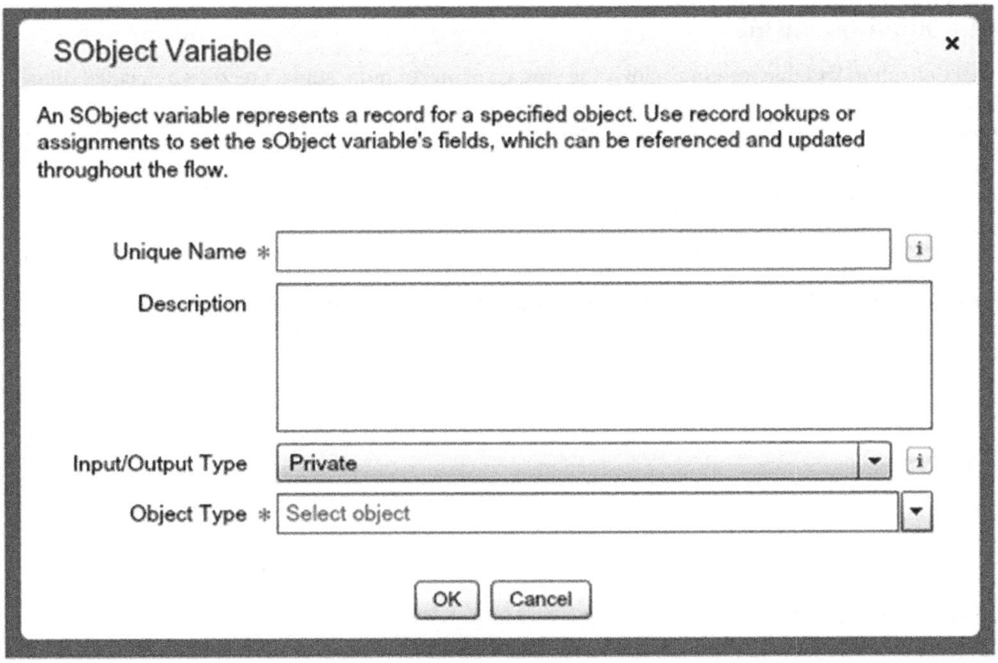

SObject Variable

An SObject variable represents a record for a specified object. Use record lookups or assignments to set the sObject variable's fields, which can be referenced and updated throughout the flow.

Unique Name *	
Description	
Input/Output Type	Private
Object Type *	Select object

OK   Cancel

Figure 2-27. *The SObject Variable resource configuration screen*

Table 2-22. *SObject Variable resource Fields*

Field	Description
Unique Name	The API name used by Salesforce to internally keep track of the data. Just like the API name on a field, this field cannot have spaces.
Description	Like the name says, it's the description of this element. Put whatever notes you want here to use as documentation as to why this resource was created and its intention.
Input/Output Type	Sets the permissions of how this resource is accessed in or out of the flow. Available options are: • Private: The variable cannot be passed into the flow and it cannot be accessed outside the flow. • Input Only: The variable values can be passed into the flow. • Output Only: The variable can be referenced outside the flow. • Input and Output: The variable can be passed into the flow and accessed outside the flow.
Object Type	The type of object that this SObject Variable will store.

SObject Collection Variable

The SObject Collection Variable resource allows the storage of one or more subject records as a collection. This collection of records is stored in the flow to be used later within the flow or even outside the flow. Figure 2-28 and Table 2-23 explain each of the fields.

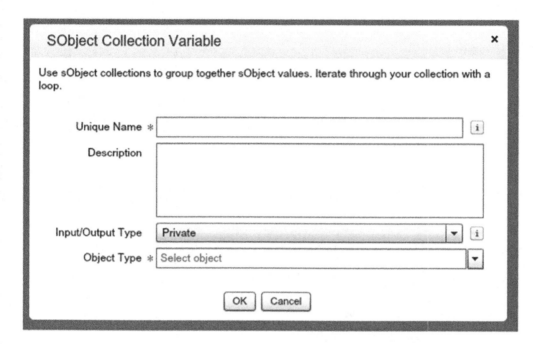

Figure 2-28. *The SObject Collection Variable resource configuration screen*

Table 2-23. *SObject Collection Variable Resource Fields*

Field	Description
Unique Name	The API name used by Salesforce to internally keep track of the data. Just like the API name on a field, this field cannot have spaces.
Description	The description of this element. Put whatever notes you want here to use as documentation as to why this resource was created and its intention.
Input/Output Type	Sets the permissions of how this resource is accessed in or out of the flow. Available options are: • Private: The variable cannot be passed into the flow and it cannot be accessed outside the flow. • Input Only: The variable values can be passed into the flow. • Output Only: The variable can be referenced outside the flow. • Input and Output: The variable can be passed into the flow and accessed outside the flow.
Object Type	The type of object that this SObject Collection Variable will store.

Constant

The Constant resource is used to store a value that cannot change but is read-only throughout the flow. Figure 2-29 and Table 2-24 explain each of the fields.

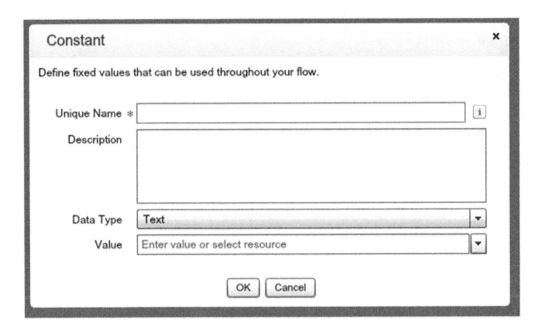

***Figure 2-29.** The Constant resource configuration screen*

***Table 2-24.** Constant Resource Fields*

Field	Description
Unique Name	The API name used by Salesforce to internally keep track of the data. Just like the API name on a field, this field cannot have spaces.
Description	The description of this element. Put whatever notes you want here to use as documentation as to why this resource was created and its intention.
Data Type	The type of value this resource should hold. Available options are: • Text • Number • Currency • Date • DateTime • Boolean • Picklist • Picklist (Multi-Select)
Value	The value that this resource should have when the flow first starts. A value can be manually entered or it can come from another resource. Once set, a constant's value cannot be changed.

Formula

The Formula resource is used to derive a calculated value at runtime during the flow execution using other values of resources and elements in the flow. Figure 2-30 and Table 2-25 explain each of the fields.

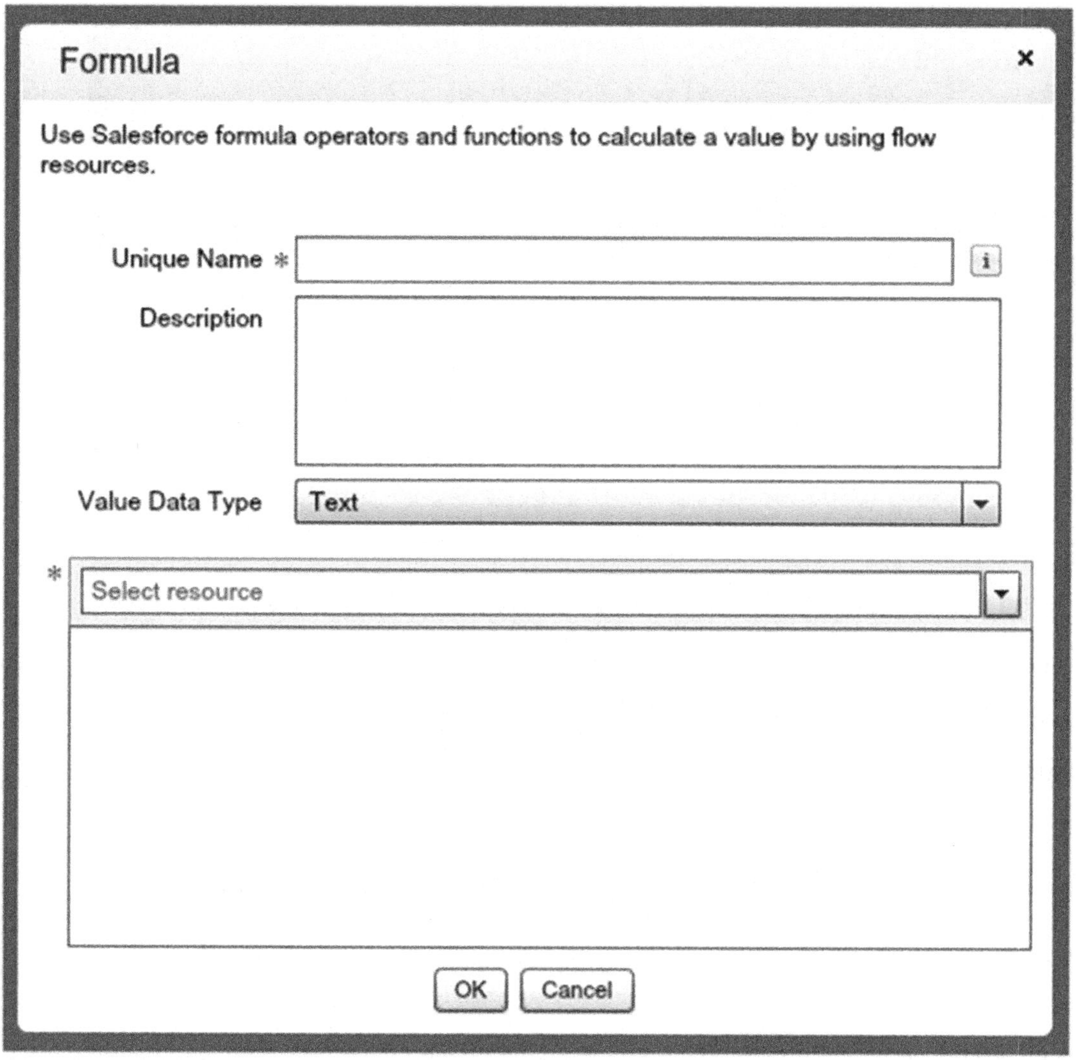

Figure 2-30. *The Formula resource configuration screen*

Table 2-25. *Formula Resource Fields*

Field	Description
Unique Name	The API name used by Salesforce to internally keep track of the data. Just like the API name on a field, this field cannot have spaces.
Description	The description of this element. Put whatever notes you want here to use as documentation as to why this resource was created and its intention.
Value Data Type	The type of value this resource should hold. Available options are: • Text • Number • Currency • Date • DateTime • Boolean
Formula (text box)	Just like a custom formula field on an Object in Salesforce, this text area is used to input the formula used to create the derived value for this field. You may use the drop-down to select a resource to find and insert a merge field into the formula text box below.

Text Template

The Text Template resource is used to store formatted text that can be used in the flow. Figure 2-31 and Table 2-26 explain each of the fields.

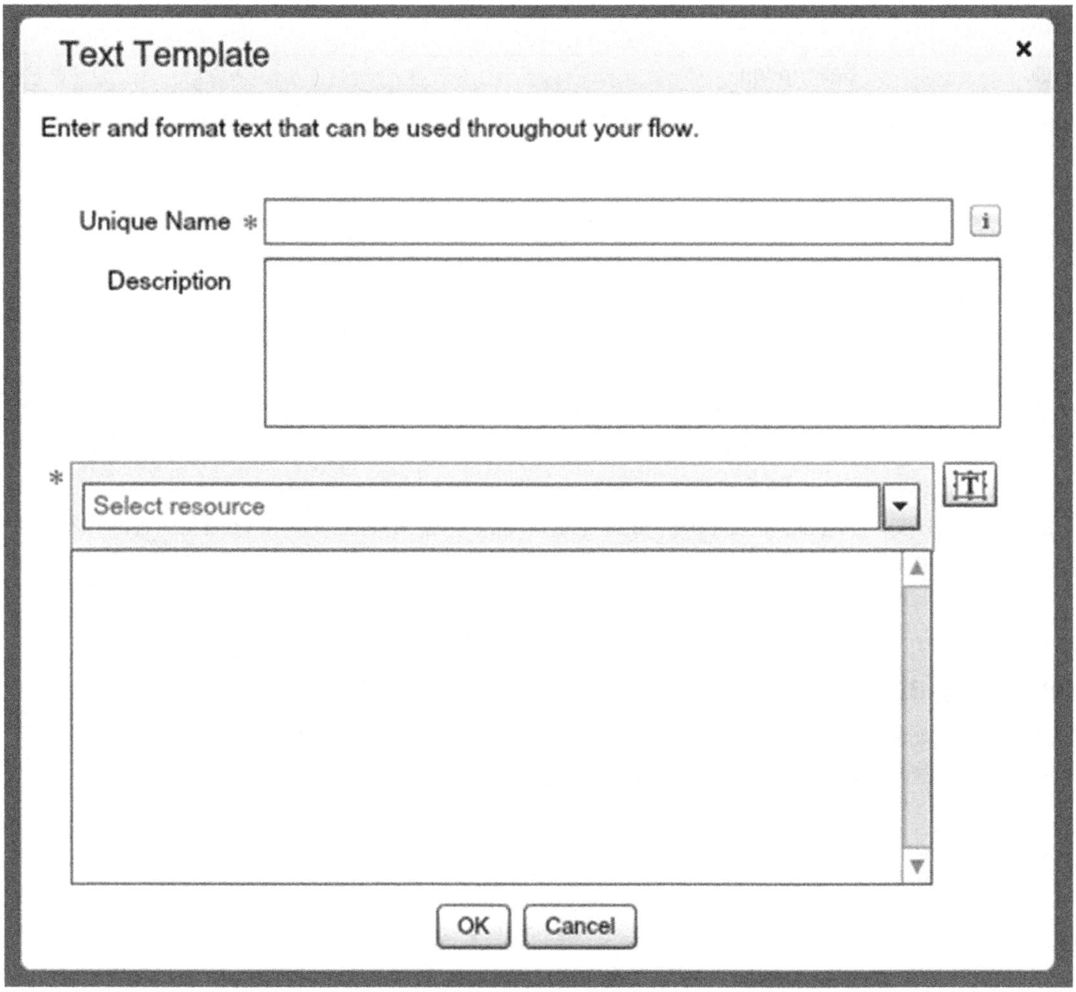

Figure 2-31. *The Text Template resource configuration screen*

Table 2-26. *Text Template Resource Fields*

Field	Description
Unique Name	The API name used by Salesforce to internally keep track of the data. Just like the API name on a field, this field cannot have spaces.
Description	The description of this element. Put whatever notes you want here to use as documentation as to why this resource was created and its intention.
Text (text box)	Enter in all the text (formatted or unformatted) into this area to be used elsewhere in the flow. Click the "T" icon to switch to formatted. Use the "Select resource" drop-down menu to select merge fields to use in the text.

Choice

The Choice resource is used to create a single choice option that can be used in the flow. This element is only reserved for flows with visual elements. This element cannot be used in autolaunched flows or user provisioning flows. Figure 2-32 and Table 2-27 explain each of the fields.

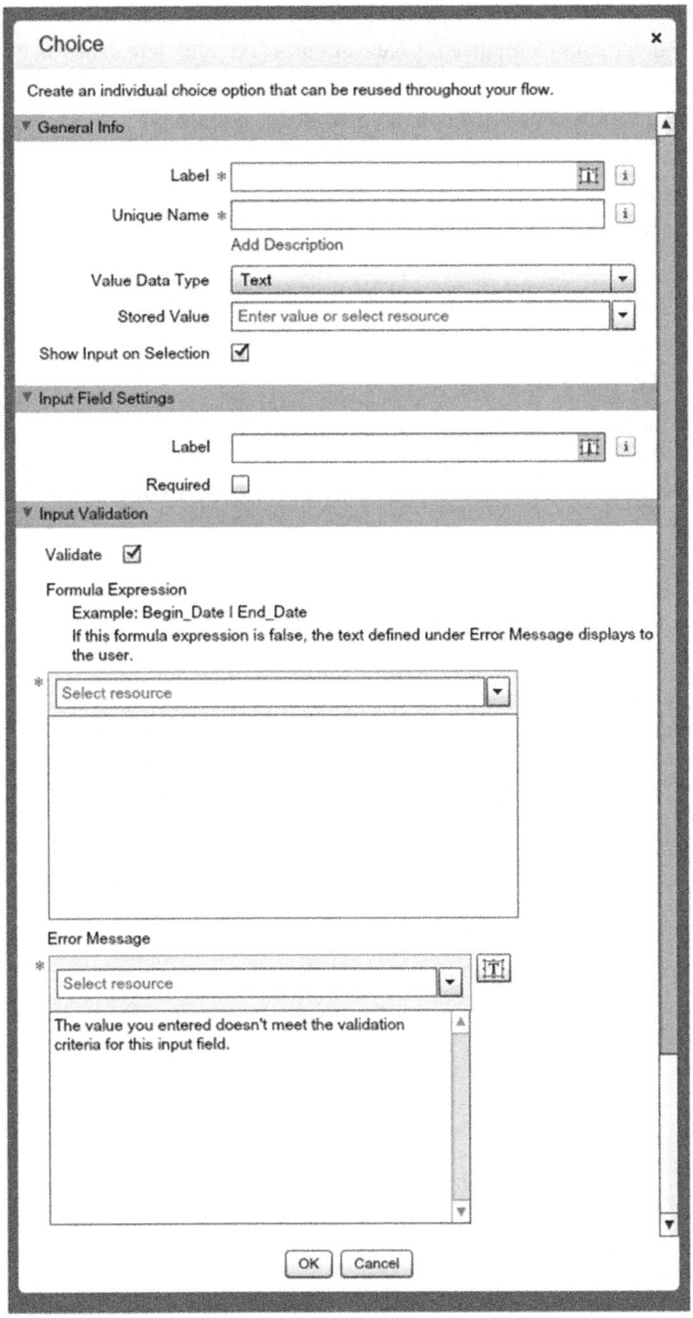

Figure 2-32. *The Choice resource configuration screen*

Table 2-27. *Choice Resource Fields*

Field	Description
Label	The display name for this Choice.
Unique Name	The API name used by Salesforce to internally keep track of the data. Just like the API name on a field, this field cannot have spaces.
Add Description / Description	The description of this element. Put whatever notes you want here to use as documentation as to why this resource was created and its intention.
Value Data Type	The type of value this resource should hold. Available options are: • Text • Number • Currency • Date • DateTime • Boolean
Stored Value	The value to be used for this single Choice.
Show Input on Selection	Check this box to display a user input field below the choice option. Not available if the choice's data type is Boolean.
Label (Input Field Settings)	The formatted value that the users see when this choice is used in a screen choice field.
Required (Input Field Settings)	Check this box if you would like this field to be required and a selection has to be made before moving to the next flow screen.
Validate (Input Validation)	Check this box if you would like to validate the input using a Formula Expression.
Formula Expression (Input Validation)	Just like a custom formula field on an Object in Salesforce, this text area is used to input the formula used to calculate if the value is not valid. If the formula returns false, then the Error Message field displays. You may use the drop-down to select a resource to find and insert a merge field into the formula text box.
Error Message (Input Validation)	A formatted text message to show if the Formula Expression is false. Merge fields may be used and the text can be formatted using the rich text box icon.

Dynamic Choice

The Dynamic Choice resource is used to create multiple choice options from a Salesforce object that can be used in the flow. This element is only reserved for flows with visual elements. This element cannot be used in autolaunched flows or user provisioning flows. Figure 2-33 and Table 2-28 explain each of the fields.

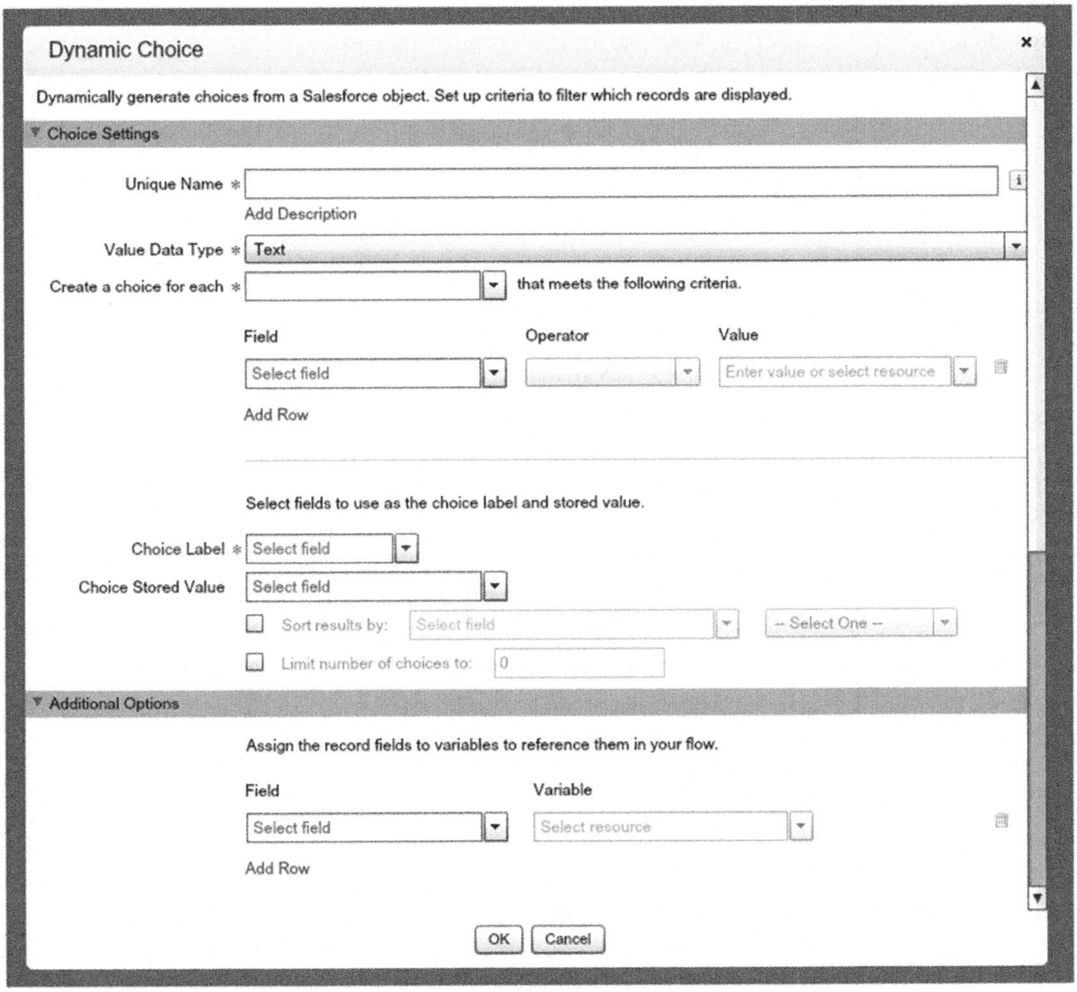

Figure 2-33. *The Dynamic Choice resource configuration screen*

Table 2-28. *Dynamic Choice Resource Fields*

Field	Description
Unique Name	The API name used by Salesforce to internally keep track of the data. Just like the API name on a field, this field cannot have spaces.
Add Description/ Description	The description of this element. Put whatever notes you want here to use as documentation as to why this resource was created and its intention.
Value Data Type	The type of value that these choices should hold. The possible types are: • Text • Number • Currency • Date • Boolean
Create a choice for each	Choose the type of object that should be used for the filter criteria.
Field (for Criteria)	The field from the object to use in defining a filter for finding the appropriate records to look up as part of the Choices.
Operator (for Criteria)	The operator to compare with against the Value field.
Value (for Criteria)	The value to use to define the criteria to find the appropriate record to look up as part of the Choices.
Add Row (link) (for Criteria)	Clicking this link adds another set of Field/Operator/Value fields to help further define the criteria for filtering out the appropriate records.
Choice Label	The field from the object record to be used as the display label for the choices.
Choice Stored Value	The field from the object record to be used as the value for the choices.
Sort results by (check box)	Check this box if you would like to choose how to order the records in the list of dynamic choices before displaying.
Sort results by (field)	The field to sort by.
Sort results by (order)	Select Ascending or Descending to choose how to order the records in the list of dynamic choices before displaying.
Limit number of choices to (check box)	Check this box if you would like to control the amount of choices that are populated from Salesforce.
Limit number of choices to (value)	Enter in a number to set a max amount of choices that should come back from Salesforce to populate the dynamic choices.
Field (for Assignment)	The field from the record use to update a variable.
Variable (for Assignment)	The variable to update the record's field to.
Add Row (link) (for Assignment)	Clicking this link adds another Field/Value assignment set to update variables from the fields on the record.

Recap

In this chapter we covered a lot of ground. First we learned what a flow is and what the difference is between Workflow and Visual Workflow. We also learned some strengths and weaknesses of Visual Workflow to help in meeting requirements when configuring Salesforce. A deep dive was also performed into the tool used to create flows called Cloud Flow Designer. All the pieces of the tool were discussed, such as the Button Bar, Palette tab, Resources tab, Explorer tab, and Canvas. Last but not least, every major element and resource was covered to discuss their purpose, show their setup screens, and provide a detailed explanation of every field in the setup screen.

CHAPTER 3

■ ■ ■

First Flow

We have covered a lot of information and have yet to actually create a single flow. You might have been wondering if you were ever going to get to the actual "how to" of this book, but alas here you are. Thank you for going through this journey of learning about graphical programming and the history of workflow in Salesforce. A major goal of this book—and something that I think makes it unique compared to any other book you will come across like it—is the goal to not just be a "how to" book. It is not all about walking through step-by-step instructions of building flows but instead to impart years of knowledge of development experience and apply them to developing flows. You see, while Visual Workflow is rather new to the Salesforce.com line of features, the concept of programming—whether it is through text-based code or graphical flows—remains the same. There are tried-and-true best practices and ways of thinking that can be a part of Visual Workflow development. These best practices can make the flows you develop easy to maintain and stand the test of time to be less brittle. Instead of going through all these best practices in one big swoop, we will instead start simply.

We will get our feet wet with building flows without worrying too much about every single aspect of design, efficiency, and maintainability. Instead, as we travel on this journey of building more and more complicated flows, we will slowly use more and more best practices to ensure a great design. After all, greater sophistication demands greater attention to detail. Creating a simple flow with three steps doesn't require hours and hours of an overarchitected design. Rather, the more complicated the flow, the more upfront design should be performed to create great quality software regardless of its being created with text-based programming or graphical programming.

By the end of this chapter you will

- Learn how to create a flow

- Create a welcome screen in the flow

- Create an input form screen

- Output the inputted data to a screen

- Test run the flow

Create That Flow!

To create a flow, go to the Salesforce.com Setup screen and traverse to Build ➤ Create ➤ Workflow & Approvals ➤ Flows. Once there you should see the Flows start page that we have shown before. On that page is the beginning of the beautiful world of flows. Click the New Flow button to start your journey for this chapter.

Once you click the New Flow button, the Cloud Flow Designer will open up with an empty flow. As explained earlier, the left side is the Palette and the right side is the Canvas. Think of the right side as a painting you are creating. The word "Palette" makes more sense when you think about it in this way. I like to think of all items on the left representing a toolbox to use in building flows. Whether painting or building, the main thing to keep in mind is that we are developing here—much like developers do with code—but here we are building with configurable blocks that we can chain together in any order to meet our requirements.

■ **Note**   When you first create new flow you will probably be prompted with an introductory video, the Visual Workflow Cloud Flow Designer. It is a great video to watch. If you want to watch the video at a later time, then click the Close button. Otherwise, if you don't want to be prompted again, click "Don't Show Again Check Box" and then click the Close button.

Requirements

Now before we start throwing elements on the canvas let's start off with a good development practice of writing down our requirements. There are many different types of requirements that can be researched and documented before building a system. They can be business requirements, functional requirements, non-functional requirements, design requirements, performance requirements, and many others. The two we are going to touch on for now are business requirements and functional requirements. The reason we are only covering these two is because most of the time when developing flows you are working from these types of requirements. You will likely be meeting with key stakeholders from the business side, such as Sales, Marketing, or a Service organization, to understand what they need before building a single thing. From there you define the business requirements and work toward defining the functional requirements.

When you meet with these stakeholders, they could be very specific about what they want and explain to you the following types of steps:

1.   Click a new Quick Contact button

2.   Open up a new window

3.   Fill in a form with First Name, Last Name, and E-mail Address

4.   Click a button to finish the process

While these are simple steps explained here, they are functional requirements. Functional requirements are a detailed list of steps that essentially explain the functionality that the system should provide. They don't have to be an ordered list of steps like this. They could be just a list of unordered requirements, but because flows will have a sequence of events that occur, most likely functional requirements will be in a list of ordered steps. The goal of functional requirements, though, is to provide enough detail to start designing and developing the implementation of whatever it is you are going to create. There really shouldn't be too many gaps to fill in once you document the functional requirements. We will dive more into the process of documenting functional requirements as we get to more and more complicated flows. For now just be aware of what they are.

More likely, though, you will not start with the functional requirements. Usually, the business unit will have a general goal in mind and you must build the functional requirements out of that goal. When you speak to the director of sales, for example, he or she may give you the following business requirement:

Implement a fast way to create a Contact with the minimum amount of data usually required by our department so that we can reduce the complexity and time taken to add new contacts into our CRM.

Notice how there are no steps? It's just a goal to work toward. It's up to the development team to think about the best way to design and implement the functionality to get to that goal. Most of the time this is the type of direction you will start from. Even if you go to the director of sales and he tells you the exact steps we listed for the functional requirements of the "Quick Contact" button, we should have him take a step back. We should then ask him what the goal is and then derive the business requirements from that goal. Doing this and getting the stakeholder (in this example, the director of sales) to agree and sign off on the business requirements ensures that you are working toward delivering to him the very thing the organization needs. This ensures a successful project where everyone is happy in the end!

Now that we have covered the differences between business requirements and functional requirements we will start this first example off assuming we have the business requirements documented already and out of them we came up with the following functional requirements:

1. Show an Intro or a Greeting Screen

2. Allow the user to click a button to get to a screen to enter in her full name in one field

3. Allow the user to click a button to get to the next screen to verify the data he entered

Okay, so this looks like it's a pretty simple flow, right? I mean, what are we doing with this full name being entered? So far nothing, but at this point we just need to get our hands dirty with creating a flow. So let's just walk through these functional requirements and create a flow from them. In later examples we will start off with business requirements, but to start things off simply we will go with functional requirements to ease into the development process.

Dragging and Dropping

The first thing you notice in the first functional requirement is an Intro/Greeting screen. Over in the Palette there is a Screen element in the User Interface section. Click the icon or name ("Screen") and then drag it over to the Canvas. Release the mouse button to drop it onto the Canvas. In Figure 3-1 you can see how it looks to drag and drop this element onto the Canvas.

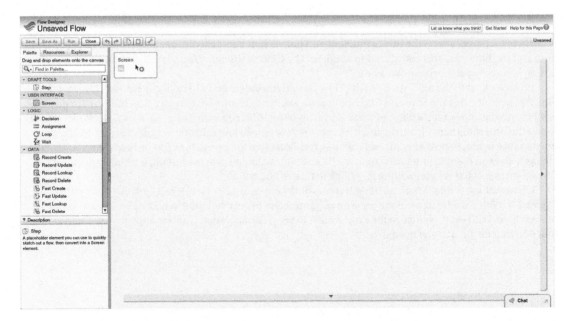

Figure 3-1. *Dragging and dropping the Screen element onto the Canvas*

Once the Screen element is dropped onto the Canvas the configuration window for the Screen element displays as seen in Figure 3-2. Remember that in Chapter 2 we went through each element and its settings. Use that chapter as a reference guide when configuring elements. For now, we will walk through setting this up.

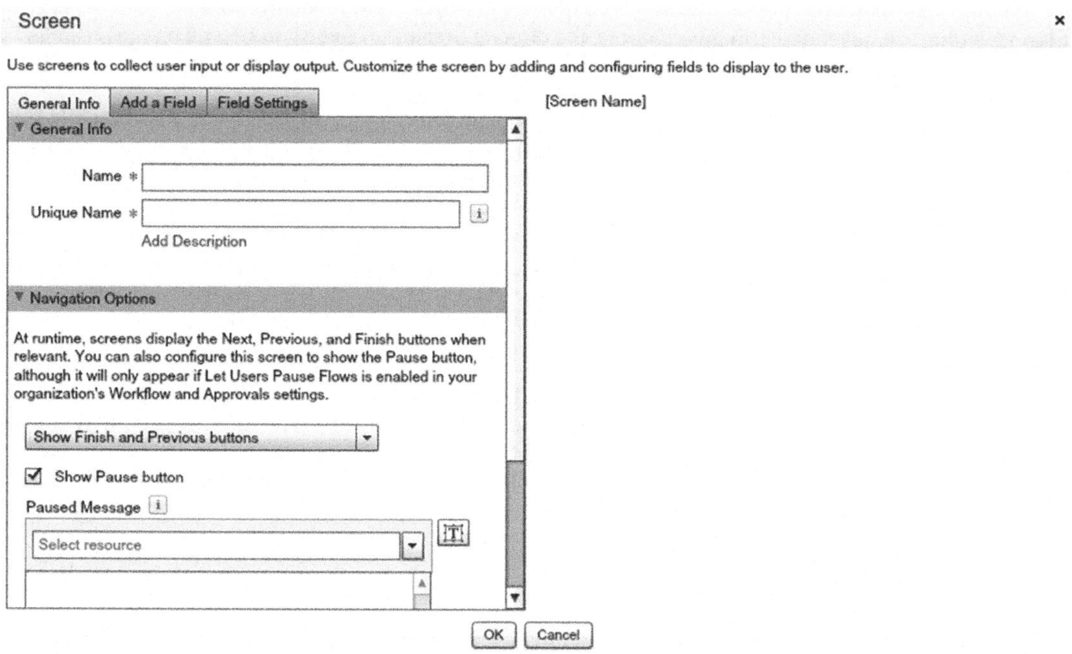

Figure 3-2. Screen element configuration window

In the Name field enter "Welcome" and then either hit the tab key to go to the next field, Unique Name, or click the Unique Name field with the mouse. Notice that the area off to the right shows "Welcome" as this is the name entered. This is the title of our Screen. There is much more to do, but at this point click the OK button at the bottom of this configuration window. The Canvas will now be updated to show the configured Screen element with the name "Welcome."

If you look up to the top left side of the Flow Designer window you will notice that it says "Unsaved Flow." Also notice that the Save and Close buttons are active while the Save As and Run buttons are not. We want to run this flow to see what a minimal flow with a single Screen with just a title looks like. We just want to test that this thing actually works and isn't some sort of smoke and mirrors. In order to run the flow we need to save it first. Repeat after me, we can only run flows that are saved. It would be nice if we could make changes and run them before saving to make sure they function the way we intend, but that is not the case. Always save! So what are you waiting for? Click that Save button!

Oh wow, look at that! Another configuration window appeared to save. It will look like the window in Figure 3-3. With Flow Designer there are a lot of parameters to get everything working, so you are seeing a pattern here. With every change to the flow, expect to see a configuration window appear so you can get it to function exactly the way you need it to.

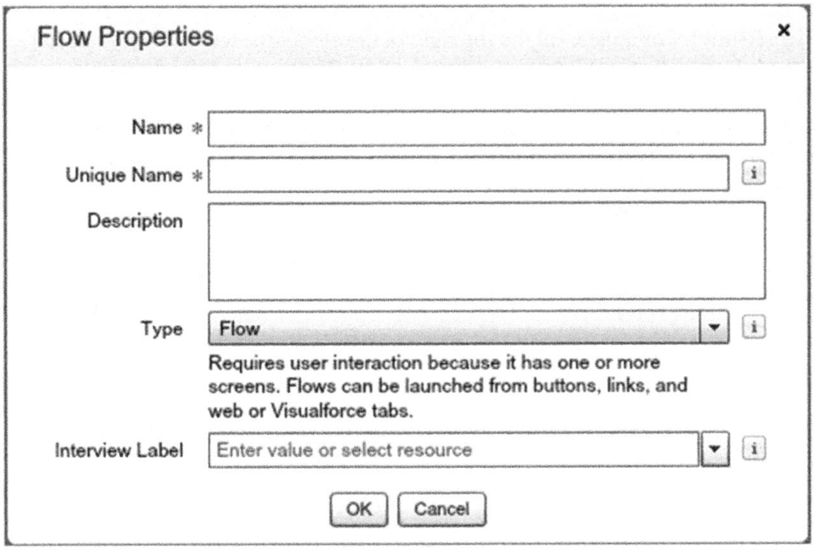

Figure 3-3. *The Flow Properties configuration window*

In the Flow Properties configuration screen enter in "My First Flow" in the Name field and either tab to or click on the Unique Name field. Again, you will see that Flow Designer automatically enters the Unique Name field just as it did for the Screen element we configured earlier. Flow Designer also updates the Interview Label. Accept all these default values and click the OK button to finally save—although, upon doing so you will notice a message box comes up telling you that while the save was successful, there were some warnings. Figure 3-4 shows the warning messages. The first message is that the flow must have a start item. Even though there is only one element on the Canvas, the flow does not know which element should be the first one to run. This is because there really should be more elements! That is why you see the second warning message stating that the Welcome Screen is not connected to anything.

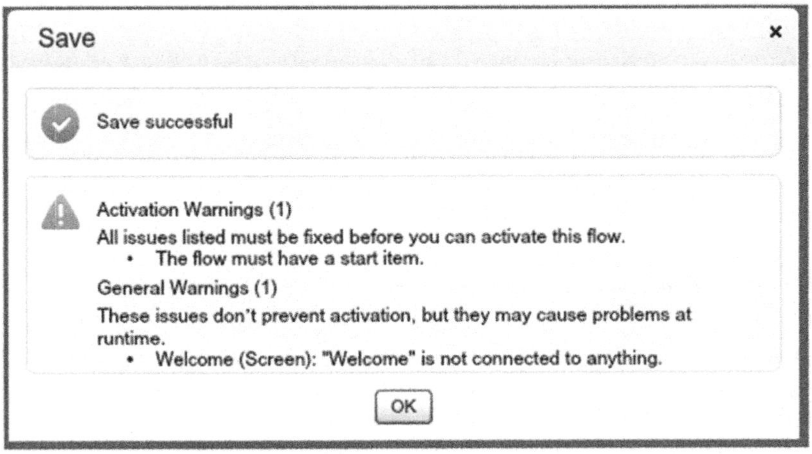

Figure 3-4. *The Save message box with warnings*

To fix the first warning, click OK to go back to Flow Designer. If you hover the mouse pointer over the Screen element you will see three tiny icons appear on the top right of the element. Figure 3-5 shows what these look like. You can see these icons when you hover over any element. The first icon that looks like a pencil is to edit the element. Clicking it will take you back to the element's configuration window so that you may make changes. The second icon is a trashcan and allows you to delete the element. The third icon, which looks like a green circle with an arrow pointing down, allows you to set this element as a start element. Since the first warning message was about the lack of a start element, go ahead and click this green icon to set the Welcome Screen as this flow's start element. You will notice that doing so will put a green border around the element and also cause the green icon to stay visible even when your mouse is not hovering over the element.

Figure 3-5. *The Welcome Screen element's edit, delete, and set start element icons*

Click Save to try to save the flow again. Now you will see the Save message box come up, but this time only with the warning about the Welcome Screen not being connected to anything. You can go ahead and click the OK button. Since the save was successful and these were just warnings, you can still run the flow. Go ahead and click the Run button. The flow should run and be rendered in a new window or tab (depending on how you have your browser configured). Your rendered flow should look like the flow in Figure 3-6.

My First Flow

Figure 3-6. *The rendered flow with only a single blank Screen element*

Notice that the name of the flow shows up at the top left and a Finish button shows up on the bottom right. This is how a flow is typically rendered without any changes to the look and feel. Since we only had a single Screen element there is not another Screen to go to. So we are left with this Finish button only. As we build onto this flow you will see that we will get more options to move forward and backward in the flow. For now, we can only "Finish" the flow. Go ahead and click the Finish button. Notice anything? It appears to just refresh! What's going on here? It might seem like it's broken, but actually it's not. When we are running this flow from the Flow Designer we are merely testing it out. Normally when you click Finish the flow window could close or redirect to another page depending on how it's set up and run after it's activated outside the Flow Designer. What is happening here is that after you click Finish on a flow run from Flow Designer, the runtime will start the flow over again from the start element that we configured so that you can test it over and over again without having to go back and forth between the rendered flow and Flow Designer. Since the flow's start element is also its last element, it just refreshes itself.

■ **Note** The window/tab that the rendered flow is in can be kept open. Every time the flow is saved in the Flow Designer, you can either refresh the window/tab with the rendered flow or click Finish on the flow and it will load up the saved changes and go to the start element again.

Screen Element Configuration

Let's return to Flow Designer and configure the Welcome Screen element so we can get some sort of content in the flow. While it is not needed for every flow, having a Welcome or Introduction screen helps to introduce users to the set of screens they are about to navigate through. Once implemented flows can be launched via buttons or links. Sometimes people click these buttons and links by accident, so it's good to let them know what they just entered into so that they can decide to continue or get out of Dodge!

To begin configuring the Welcome Screen mouse over the Welcome Screen element and the pencil icon will appear. Click the pencil icon and the configuration window for the Screen element will come up. Next click the Add a Field tab to get a list of all the fields that can be added to the screen. At the bottom of the list is a field named "Display Text." Double-click this field and the words "[Display Text]" appear on the right side of the configuration window. The right side is where all the fields you want on the screen are moved to in order to build it. Optionally, instead of double-clicking the field in the Add a Field tab to move it over, the field can also be dragged and dropped to the right side as well in order to add it.

Now the next step is to click on the text on the right side that says "[Display Text]." Doing so will change the left side to switch to the Field Settings tab. This tab will show all the possible settings you can configure for this field. Optionally, you could click the Field Settings tab first and then also click the [Display Text] field on the right to see the settings for this field. For the "Unique Name" setting, enter in "Welcome_Text." The Unique Name does not allow spaces, but we can use an underscore if we want, just as in custom field API names in Salesforce. Now in the text area below, enter in a welcome message for the user to see. Click or tab out of the text area to have the right side automatically update to the new text just entered. When complete, the final screen settings should look like Figure 3-7. Go ahead and click the OK button to save your changes. You will be returned back to the normal Flow Designer view.

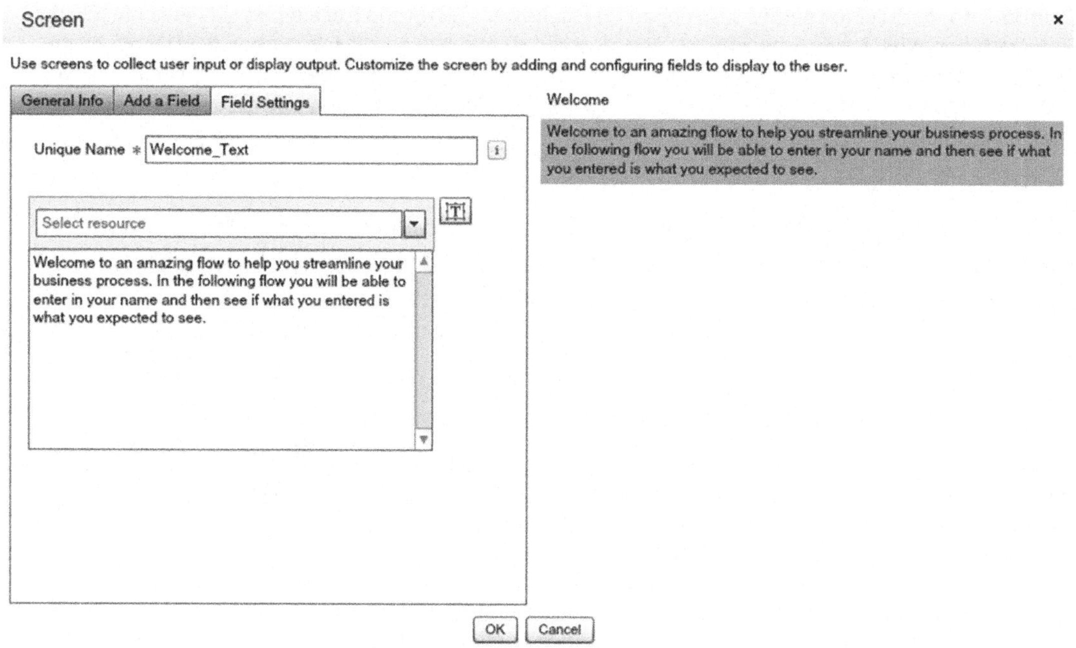

Figure 3-7. The field settings for a Display Text field

Now go ahead and move another Screen element to the Canvas. When the configuration window comes up, enter in the following values for the fields on the General Info tab:

- **Name**: End

- **Unique Name**: End

Next click Add a Field and move a Display Text field to the right panel. Click "[Display Text]" in the right panel to see its settings in the Field Settings tab. For the field settings, enter in the following values and click the OK button:

- **Unique Name**: End_Text

- **Text Area**: This concludes this process. Thank you for all that you do!

Once again you are returned to the main Flow Designer view. You will now see the Screen named "Welcome" and the other Screen named "End." At this point they are not connected and just floating on the Canvas. Flow Designer does not know that when we run this flow, not only do we want to start at the Welcome Screen, but we also want to go to the End Screen afterward. To get this to happen, we need to connect these elements. To connect the Welcome Screen to the End Screen is an easy process. Simply click and hold the diamond shape on the center bottom of the Welcome Screen element; then drag the mouse pointer over to the End Screen element and release when the mouse pointer is over the End Screen element. You will notice that while dragging, a line was drawn and when you released the line stayed connected to the End Screen element. Now these two elements are connected! Furthermore, you can tell the order in which they run by the direction in which the arrow that was drawn is pointing. It points from the Welcome Screen to the End Screen. So essentially we are telling Flow Designer, "Hey start at the Welcome Screen element, and go to the End Screen element next. Since the End Screen element is not connected to any other elements, this is where the flow will end." Your Canvas might look like Figure 3-8 now.

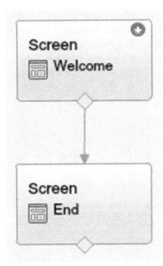

Figure 3-8. *The Welcome Screen element connected to the End Screen element*

The beauty of the Canvas in the Flow Designer is that you can lay out the elements any way you like as long as they are connected. Figure 3-9 illustrates some other ways these could possibly be laid out on the Canvas.

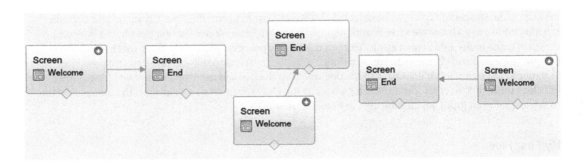

Figure 3-9. *Three of many possible ways to arrange elements*

Now that you know you can apply artistic license to flow layouts, go ahead and save this flow and run it to watch it in action. At this point you should see no errors and no warning messages when you save. You will see the majority of the Flow Designer dim, and depending on how long it takes to save, you may see a progress bar. You will then notice that the Save button is disabled now. That means you have Saved successfully, so there is no need to save again until you make some changes. When you click the Run button the flow will render as before, but this time you will see the changes we made when we saved.

■ **Note**   Always remember to save a flow before clicking run if you want to see any changes made.

The Welcome screen should appear like Figure 3-10, with the configured display text appearing for the user to see once the flow starts. Now I know it says that we are going to have the user enter his name, but we actually have not configured the flow to do that yet. Once this screen appears, there is a Next button on the bottom right. Think of this Next button representing the connection arrow we added between the Welcome Screen and the End Screen. Go ahead and click Next to go to the End Screen.

My First Flow

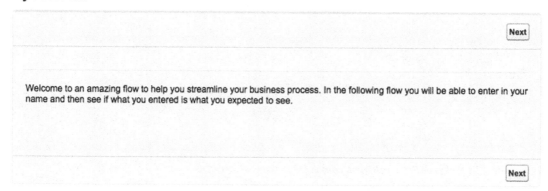

Figure 3-10. *The Welcome Screen rendered in the flow*

You should see the End Screen rendered as in Figure 3-11. Right now we have a simple message just letting the user know that she is done. At this point the user can actually click the Previous button to go back one step to the Welcome Screen, or he can click the Finish button to end the flow. Go ahead and click the Previous button to go back one screen, and then click the Next button once you get back to the Welcome Screen to come to the End Screen again. You can repeat this process indefinitely. Well, that's enough fun for now! Go ahead and click Finish. You will notice once again that since we ran this flow from the Flow Designer to test it out, it just goes back to the beginning so that we can run it again if we want. Go ahead and close this window/tab if you want and go back to the Flow Designer so we can start the next part of this exercise, adding an input field for the user to enter her name!

My First Flow

		Previous	Finish
This concludes this process. Thank you for all that you do!			
		Previous	Finish

Figure 3-11. *The End Screen rendered in the flow*

Adding an Input Field

While displaying text to the user is a fun exercise, it does not allow any real interaction between the user and the flow besides traversing back and forth through screens. In this next series of steps, we are going to allow a user to enter some data and then have it displayed back to her. We are going to have the user enter her name, save it within the flow, and then include it as part of the final message on the End Screen. This will make the message more personal and will show how data can be kept within a flow but not necessarily saved into any Salesforce objects or fields.

To allow a user to enter in his name we need to add an input field to one of the screens. We could add it to the Welcome screen, but to make this flow a little more interesting let's add an additional screen that will be inserted between the Welcome Screen and the End Screen. In the main view of the Flow Designer click the Palette tab to make sure we see all the elements we can add. Now add a Screen element to the Canvas. Remember, to do so, just click the element icon or name and drag it over to the Canvas and drop it there by releasing the mouse button. In the Screen configuration window that appears, enter the following values for the settings (leave all other options at their default):

- **Name**: Personal Info Form

- **Unique Name**: Personal_Info_Form

Next click the Add a Field tab and place a Display Text field on the Personal Info Form Screen by double-clicking or drag and dropping it to the right panel of the Screen configuration window. Now while the Add a Field tab is still active, place a Text box field to the right panel as well right below the Display Text field that was just added.

■ **Note**   Double-clicking fields to add them to a screen will automatically put them in sequential order from top to bottom of the screen. This is an efficient way to add fields.

After adding the Display Text and Text box fields to the Personal Info Form Screen the configuration window should look like Figure 3-12.

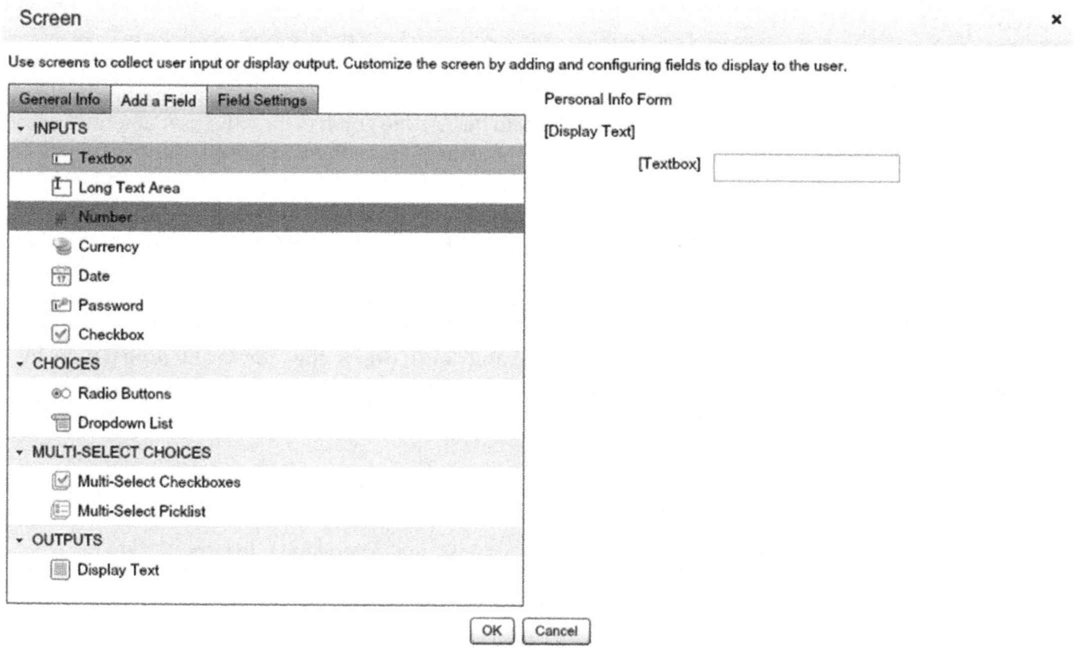

Figure 3-12. *Two newly added fields on the Personal Info Form Screen that are not yet configured*

Next click the Field Settings tab and then click the [Display Text] field on the Personal Info Form Screen. Enter the following values in the fields for the Display Text field:

- **Unique Name**: Form_Text

- **Text Area**: Please enter your name below. You can either enter your first name or your full name.

Next click the Text box field on the Personal Info Form Screen and the settings for it will show under the Field Settings tab. Enter the following values in the fields for the Text box field and leave other fields with their default values:

- **Label**: Name

- **Unique Name**: Name_Textbox

- **Required**: checked

Once complete, click OK and you will be taken back to the main Flow Designer view to see the newly configured Personal Info Form Screen on the Canvas, as in Figure 3-13.

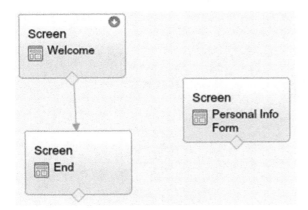

Figure 3-13. The Canvas with the Personal Info Form Screen element added but not connected yet

Now that we have this new element on the Canvas we want it connected so that the flow goes from the Welcome Screen to the Personal Info Form Screen to the End Screen. If you try clicking the diamond shape at the bottom of the Welcome Screen to drag a connecting arrow to the Personal Info Form Screen you will notice nothing happens. That is because it is already connected to the End Screen. We will need to disconnect these two elements now. In order to disconnect them just click the arrow and it will turn green. This means that it is selected. Now on your keyboard push the delete key. The arrow will disappear. Now you can connect the Welcome Screen to the Personal Info Form Screen. After that, connect the Personal Info Form Screen to the End Screen. Once they are connected let's organize the elements on the Canvas a bit to make the flow easier to read by stacking them in a straight line from top to bottom. Figure 3-14 shows the final layout on the Canvas. Click Save and then click Run to see the new changes in the flow.

Screen
Welcome
Screen
Personal Info Form
Screen
End

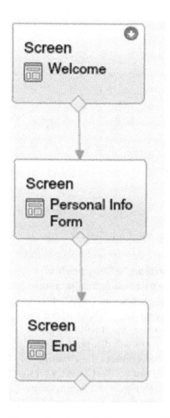

Figure 3-14. A nicely organized flow on the Canvas makes it more readable

After running the flow, navigate to the second screen we added with the text box labeled "Name." Notice that the field for the name has a red marker next to it, just like required fields on Salesforce edit pages for standard and custom objects. That is because we set it as required when we configured it. To see this required field in action, try clicking the Next button without entering any value in the field. You will be prompted to enter in some valid input as seen in Figure 3-15.

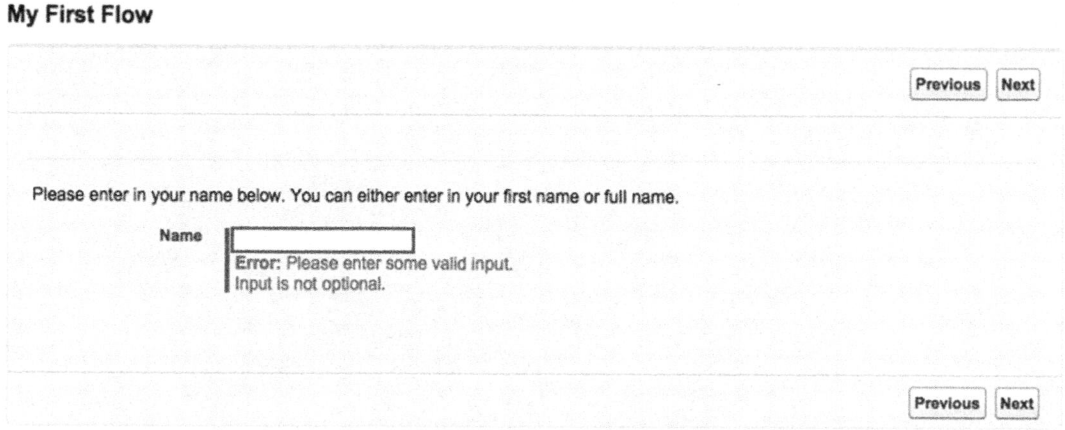

My First Flow
Previous
Next
Please enter in your name below. You can either enter in your first name or full name.
Name
Error: Please enter some valid input.
Input is not optional.
Previous
Next

Figure 3-15. The error message when no input is given for a required field

The nice thing about this is that now users cannot skip ahead through the flow without providing some input. We do not need to put in any sort of logic in the flow to check and then go back to the screen. The flow can be configured to prevent users from moving ahead in the flow if they don't satisfy the requirement to enter in valid input. Go ahead and enter your name and click "Next" to get to the End Screen.

The End Screen appears as before but without any sort of confirmation that the input was captured. This is the final piece to our example. Let's get this wrapped up with a nice bow on it! Go back to Flow Designer and edit the End Screen by hovering over the element to reveal the edit (pencil) icon. Click the pencil to edit this element. This will bring up the configuration window for the End Screen once more. Now click the display text that is on the right panel and the Field Settings tab will become enabled, showing the settings for this field.

On the End Screen we want to include whatever name was entered into the Name_Textbox field on the Personal Info Form Screen. Luckily, the current value from that field can be accessed anywhere in the flow. Of course this value would be blank before someone entered input, but by the time the flow gets to the End Screen we will have a value in this field. We can get the value of this field as a merge field similar to how merge fields are used in other aspects of Salesforce (e.g., formula fields). To add a merge field to the display text click the down arrow button for the Select resource field. A drop-down menu will appear with all the possible resources that can be used as merge fields. Figure 3-16 shows how this drop-down menu looks.

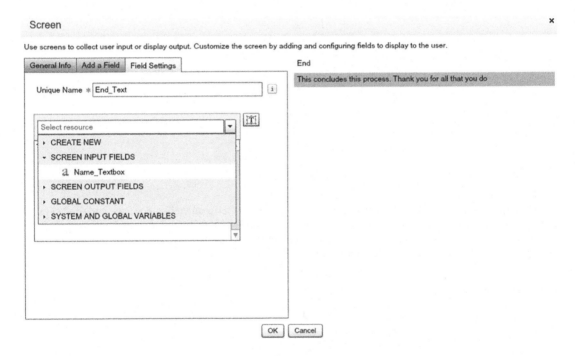

Figure 3-16. *Select resource picklist to select the Name_Textbox as a merge field*

Click "SCREEN INPUT FIELDS" to expand the list of input fields that are on any screens used in this flow. You will see only "Name_Textbox" since this is all was added for this flow. Now click "Name_Textbox" to have the merge field code "{!Name_Textbox}" added to end of the existing text in the text area field. This merge field code can also be manually typed in here as well, but if you do not remember the exact name of the field then using the drop-down menu makes things easier.

We still are not done yet. The text does not read right as the name will show up after the sentence. To make this proper, change the text to be the following:

"Thanks {!Name_Textbox} for all that you do! This concludes this process. You may click Finish now."

The final End Screen configuration window will look like Figure 3-17.

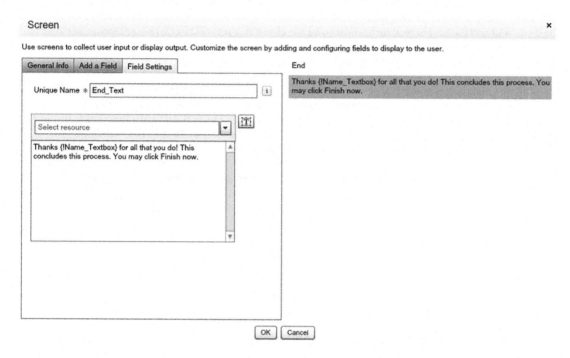

Figure 3-17. *Select resource picklist to select the Name_Textbox as a merge field*

Click OK to keep these settings and go back to the main Flow Designer view. Click Save and then click Run to watch this flow finally in all its glory! Traverse the second screen to enter your name and then click next to get to the last screen. Do you see your name? It should look like the screen in Figure 3-18 except that it is my name there. It's not yours, unless you are a Jonathan too!

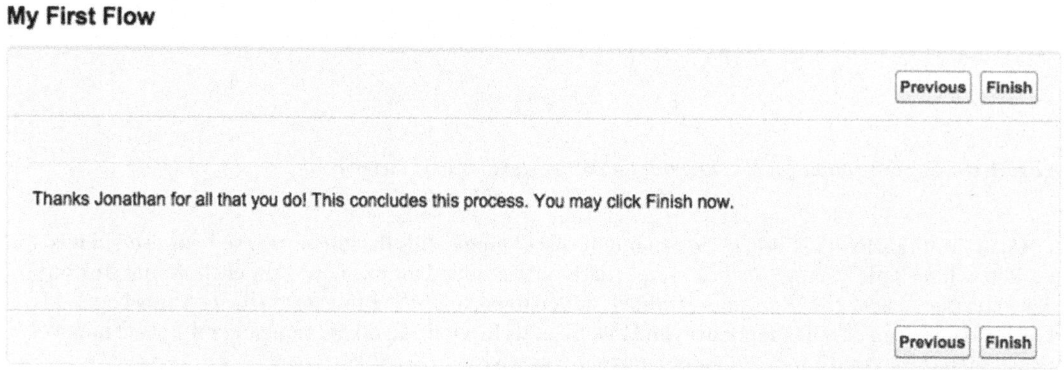

My First Flow

| | Previous | Finish |

Thanks Jonathan for all that you do! This concludes this process. You may click Finish now.

| | Previous | Finish |

Figure 3-18. *The End Screen in the flow with the name confirmed plus instructions on what to do next*

Recap

Until now, most of the information covered didn't give us any practical exercises to implement a flow and get our hands dirty. In this chapter we dived right in and created a simple flow to gain some hands-on experience in how to maneuver within Flow Designer. Instead of going straight through a series of steps to create a flow we started small and through an iterative process we built more and more on the flow to get a better understanding of how flows behave when run from the Flow Designer. We started off with a Welcome screen and then added an End Screen, letting the user know the flow is finished. We then added a screen between both of those to allow the user to enter input. Finally, we modified the end screen to have a message that displayed the input from the second screen. In doing so, this chapter showed the flexibility that Flow Designer gives to quickly change the process in the flows with ease.

■ ■ ■

CHAPTER 4

Creating a Wizard

Creating flows in Salesforce can be a pleasant experience. As seen in the previous chapter, you do not need to do a lot of upfront work to prepare for building a flow. Once an individual becomes acquainted with the Flow Designer and all of the elements, it becomes extremely easy to just create a new flow without a lot of planning. Since Flow development is in a graphical development environment, it lends itself to being very flexible. You can build a flow, then add in new elements, remove elements, and rewrite the whole thing in minutes. It could seem like a dream that so much power and flexibility are there in one tool, but as the saying goes, "With great power comes great responsibility."

In this chapter we are going to touch on that responsibility. While developing the next flow we will create a great design for the system by following best development practices. First we will understand the goals from a business objective and turn them into a series of requirements. Next we will take those requirements and before touching the Flow Designer we will sketch out a design. Once we have the design laid out, we will take that design and implement it in Visual Workflow. Try to resist the urge to go straight into development! Going through this process will make life much simpler when creating the final flow.

By the end of this chapter you will

- Translate business requirements into functional requirements

- Create a design to build a flow from

- Create a wizard flow to guide users

- Understand how to create Decisions and Outcomes in a flow

- Learn about the Assignment element

From Business Objective to Design

In this scenario we are working with a financial services organization named Original Recipe Bank and Trust. It is headquartered in Kentucky but you work out of the London office. It's a very nice office. It's the same office that the Jeff Rames, Director of Sales, works at. So you have the pleasure of being called into meetings with the Jeff a lot. One day you get a meeting invite with Jeff and several other people in the department. While the meeting details are vague, the title of the meeting, "Discuss climbing rate of incorrectly set up Accounts," clues you in on what the topic will be. Jeff kicks off the meeting with the main problem. He says, "I've been getting feedback that the number of problems with accounts being set up correctly has been going up steadily with the introduction of new financial products. Also, even small changes to existing products cause the amount of issues to increase as well." One of the other managers says that the department has been increasing the amount of training for new and modified products. He continues to say that training has helped but the overall percentage of accounts incorrectly set up continues to increase over time. Several team leads chime in with their perspective on the matter. They go into the details of how their sales teams have many different accounts to set up, including personal savings accounts, business checking accounts, CDs, money market accounts, and investments such as 529 College Savings plans. After each of these accounts is set up, information is transferred to other systems depending on the account. So, while the sales team may be filling out a ton of information for the new account set up in Salesforce, there could be vital information that is not getting to the integrated systems outside Salesforce. These systems, without all their required information, do not allow the accounts to be set up properly. Luckily, they have exception reports that are generated daily. With these reports, the sales team can go back and enter in the necessary information so that it can be pushed back out to the integrated systems again.

As the Salesforce administrator you are asked for some ideas. The first one that comes to mind is that you can set up more record types for accounts in Salesforce. Each type of account could have a different record type, so then the page layout could be different as well. Each page type could have different required fields and now the sales staff wouldn't be able to save an account unless they had all the information required.

People in the room liked this idea, but another team lead wondered if it just means that there will have to be increased training to let sales staff know which record type to pick. What if they choose the wrong record type? The team lead goes on further to say that he would like new hires to have less training to start doing their job and so far it seems that every year the amount of training needed for an individual to even begin to be productive just keeps going up. Soon everyone is chiming in with ideas again. After a while it seems like ideas are starting to run out and finally another sales lead in the meeting speaks up. It's Christine Thurman, VP of Sales from the UK business unit. She is new at the company but speaks up about how at her last company they were able to reduce the amount of training by have guided processes that stepped sales associates through a "wizard," a series of screens each with different questions. These wizards would guide sales associates through questions relating to the customer's needs and dealt with business questions instead of technical aspects of their sales system.

The Jeff Rames, Director of Sales, declares that he likes this idea and thinks this is the direction to go. To make sure everyone is clear on the business objectives he states them succinctly.

> *Our goal is to reduce the amount of errors in downstream systems during account setup and reduce required training through guided assistance.*

Next is the part every Salesforce administrator loves. Jeff looks over at you and asks, "Can you make this happen in Salesforce?" You look at Jeff and then around the room, noticing that it's quiet and still. All eyes are on you awaiting your answer. You aren't worried though. You've got this! You reassure everyone that you know what to do. Visual Workflow to the rescue!

So What Are the Requirements?

At this point you need to get the requirements of what's needed. You understand the business objective. You also know that a Flow can be used to create step-by-step forms with business logic embedded in them. You have the tools. What we need here is to understand what the business process is and what the requirements are for the system. What should it do? Who should be doing it? There are lots of details that you need to fill in as it is very important that you show that you can implement this new system flawlessly so that you can be the Salesforce admin superhero you know you were meant to be!

So you set off to do your due diligence by interviewing different individuals in the office who are responsible for each the business processes for each type of account. You also talk to individuals regarding the downstream systems into which those accounts get set up. From your experience working at Original Recipe Bank and Trust you have heard that the most straightforward new accounts to work with are personal savings accounts and money market accounts (surprisingly!).

First you set off to find out more about the requirements of setting up new accounts for personal savings. What you found are the following requirements:

- Req 01: All new personal savings accounts need a first name.

- Req 02: All new personal savings accounts can have an optional middle name.

- Req 03: All new personal savings accounts need a last name.

- Req 04: All new personal savings accounts need a mailing address (address line 1, address line 2, city, state, and zip code).

- Req 05: All new personal savings accounts need a primary/home phone number.

- Req 06: All new personal savings accounts can have an optional mobile phone number.

- Req 07: All new personal savings accounts can have an optional work phone number.

- Req 08: All new personal savings accounts need a social security number (SSN)/tax ID.

- Req 09: All new personal savings accounts receive a higher interest rate of 0.5% if the account owner has a checking account with the bank.

- Req 10: All new personal savings accounts receive a lower interest rate of 0.1% if the account owner does not have a checking account with the bank.

With this set of requirements, we can have a picture in our head about how this flow could be put together for setting up a new personal savings account. Next we will want to get a list of requirements for the money market account. Let's speed up through time and assume you have met with all the proper stakeholders regarding money market accounts and any systems that need to be integrated with Salesforce. Figuring out all the details you come up with a similar list of requirements for money market accounts.

- Req 11: All new money market accounts need a first name.

- Req 12: All new money market accounts can have an optional middle name.

- Req 13: All new money market accounts need a last name.

- Req 14: All new money market accounts need a mailing address (address line 1, address line 2, city, state, and zip code).

- Req 15: All new money market accounts need a primary/home phone number.

- Req 16: All new money market accounts can have an optional mobile phone number.

- Req 17: All new money market accounts can have an optional work phone number.

- Req 18: All new money market accounts need a social security number/tax ID

- Req 19: All new money market accounts can be either low-yield or high-yield.

- Req 20: Low-yield money market accounts have a 2% annual interest rate over a five-year period.

- Req 21: High-yield money market accounts have a 5% annual interest rate over a ten-year period.

From Requirements to Design

After getting these requirements you have a good idea of what type of data needs to be collected, but it does not describe exactly how it should be grouped onto a screen in the wizard. It also does not tell us what order each screen should be in. It is a good idea to not assume anything and instead get some feedback from the department leads who would be using this wizard as to how to make it most useful to them.

Again, you get them in a room and discuss the details. Everyone reviews the requirements together so they start on the same page of understanding. After much discussion, the following series of bullets were put together to represent the order of each of the screens.

- Introduction/Get Customer's Name

- Get Account Type

- Get Address

- Get Phone Numbers

- Get SSN/Tax ID

- Determine if customer wants Money Market Account OR Savings Account

    a. If Money Market Account then . . .

        i.   Get type of Money Market Account Terms

        ii. Show a review screen with all the selected options

    b. If Savings Account then . . .

        i.   Get the Checking Account Number (if customer has one)

        ii. If customer has a checking account number, give the customer a high-interest savings account

        iii. If the customer does not have a checking account number, give the customer a low-interest savings account

        iv. Show a review screen with all the selected options

The meeting is a success since everyone is in agreement with how the flow should go. While the bulleted list is helpful to quickly write up what's needed, we are going to do one more step before developing the Visual Workflow. We are going to take these bullets and translate them into a graphical design. We are going to create a flow chart. The purpose is that since the Flow Designer is a graphical development environment, it is easier to develop if you have a graphical design to work from like a blueprint. In a lot of industries the flow chart is the format for documenting business processes. We will do the same here. We want to get final approval of the design from management before the development of the flow begins. It is easier for management to approve something they can see and understand. While the bullet points are good, we decide to take them and build a flow chart.

There are many different tools to build a flow chart. There are desktop diagramming software packages that companies buy, and this has been the standard way people have created diagrams—besides good old pen and paper. These days, though, there are a lot of online diagramming tools also in the cloud. Most of these are free to use to develop a few diagrams. If you do not have access to any diagramming software within your company, then a simple web search should give you some options of free tools to use.

Going over how to use any of these tools is beyond the scope of this book. So please consult their documentation or perform another Internet search for tutorials or how-to videos to get a handle on how to use a diagramming tool to create a flow chart.

For now, I have taken the liberty of fast-forwarding the flow chart creation process and included a design based on the bullets that were documented. Please refer to Figure 4-1 as our final flow chart design. In a real-life scenario, the flow chart would be submitted for approval and once approved, you would be free to begin development.

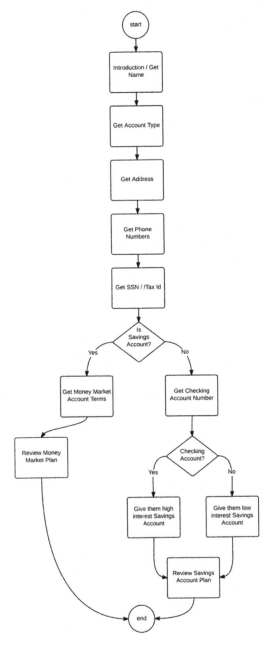

Figure 4-1. *Money Market/Savings Account design as a flow chart*

Building the Wizard

Now that we have taken the requirements and developed a flow chart, the rest should be merely implementing the diagram in Visual Workflow. So to start, create a new flow with the following name: "Account Creation Wizard."

According to the flow chart, the wizard should start with an introduction screen to welcome the customer and also capture his or her name. So after the flow is created and you are now in the Flow Designer, create a new Screen element with the following configuration settings under the General Info tab:

- **Name**: Introduction

- **Unique Name**: Introduction_Screen

Next add a Display Text field to the screen with the following configuration settings:

- **Unique Name**: Introduction_Text

- **Text Area**: Hello and thank you for calling Original Recipe Bank and Trust today. Before we begin can I please have your first and last name?

This Display Text will be the script that the customer support agent will read to ensure that each customer who calls in gets the same level of interaction across the department. Notice that the script is leading the customer to provide the details we want for this screen, which is his first and last name. Optionally, the customer can give her middle name too, so we will add all these three fields in here with the first and last name required and the middle name not required. Finally, we want to address the customer with the correct salutation of Mr., Ms., Dr., and so on, so we will have a required field for that as well.

Add the "Drop-down List" to the screen with the following configuration settings:

- **Label**: Salutation

- **Unique Name**: Salutation

- **Value Data Type**: Text

For this Drop-down List we could manually add all the salutations we need in here, but fortunately Salesforce already has a list of salutations in a picklist field on the Contact object. To promote reuse and to make this list dynamic, we are going to use the values from this picklist field as the values in this Drop-down List. To do so, follow these steps:

- Click the drop-down arrow for the Choice field under "Choice Settings"

- Click "CREATE NEW"

- Click "Picklist Choice"

A pop-up window will appear to configure the Picklist Choice. Enter these values:

- **Unique Name**: Salutation_Choice

- **Value Data Type**: Picklist

- **Object**: Contact

- **Field**: Salutation

The most important settings are regarding the Object and the Field. The settings here basically state to use the Salutation field that is found on the Contact object. So now if someone were to add a new value to the Salutation picklist it would show up as well for the user using this form.

Note Picklist Choices in flows will show every picklist value for that field even if record types are used to control which values show up.

After configuring the Picklist Choice and clicking "OK," the Field Settings should look like Figure 4-2:

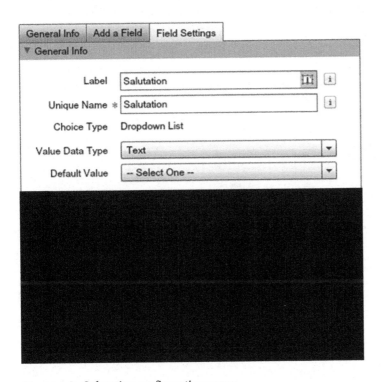

Figure 4-2. *Salutation configuration screen*

After adding and configuring the Salutation field, we need to add the other fields for First Name, Middle Name, and Last Name. Let's work on these fields next. You can quickly add three Text box fields to the screen right under Salutation. Then from top to bottom configure the three fields as described next.

First Name configuration settings:

- **Label**: First Name
- **Unique Name**: First_Name
- **Required**: <checked>

Middle Name configuration settings:

- **Label**: Middle Name
- **Unique Name**: Middle_Name
- **Required**: <not checked>

Last Name configuration settings:

- **Label**: Last Name
- **Unique Name**: Last_Name
- **Required**: <checked>

Once all these steps are complete, the Introduction Screen should look like Figure 4-3. Now you can click the OK button.

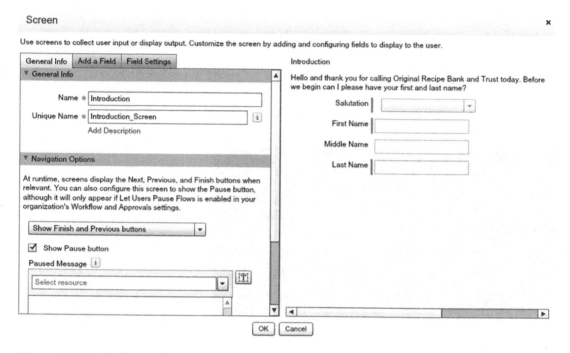

Figure 4-3. *Introduction configuration screen*

Before we forget, go ahead and hover the mouse pointer over the Introduction screen element on the Canvas to reveal the "Set as Start element" icon for this element. Click it to set the Introduction screen as the start element.

Account Type Screen

Now according to the flow chart we designed, the next step should be to find out what type of account the customer wants to set up. The requirements are, of course, to only worry about personal savings accounts and money market accounts. Other accounts will be handled in a later phase.

Again, add a new Screen element with the following configuration settings under the General Info tab:

- **Name**: Account Type
- **Unique Name**: Account_Type_Screen

Next add a Display Text field into the screen with the following configuration settings:

- **Unique Name**: Account_Type_Text

- **Text Area**: It's nice to meet you today, {!Salutation} {!Last_Name}. I understand you are calling today to open a new account. What type of account would you like to open?

Again, we will use the Display Text as the script that the customer support agent will read to ensure proper communication with the customer. Notice the merge fields, "{!Salutation}" and "{!Last_Name}" as a part of the text. With these fields pulling the values previously entered, we can now personalize the script the customer support agent uses in order to give the customer a more personal experience.

■ **Note** Merge fields can be manually typed into display text or they can be selected using the "Select resource" drop-down above the text area field for the display text.

The sole purpose of this screen according to the flow chart is to capture what type of account the customer wants to open. So let's add a Drop-down List field to the screen with the following configuration settings:

- **Label**: Account Type

- **Unique Name**: Account_Type

- **Value Data Type**: Text

For this Drop-down List we will manually add the two types of accounts we are required to deal with in this phase. To do so we need to create two new "Choices" and associate them with this Drop-down List.
To do so, follow these steps:

- Click the drop-down arrow for the Choice field under "Choice Settings"

- Click "CREATE NEW"

- Click "Choice"

A pop-up window will appear to configure the Choice. Enter the following values:

- **Label**: Personal Savings

- **Unique Name**: Personal_Savings

- **Value Data Type**: Text

- **Stored Value**: Personal Savings

Click "OK" to finalize these settings and return back to the configuration of the Drop-down List. Next we need to add a second Choice. To do so, click the "Add Choice" link right below the Choice you just added. Notice a new Select resource field appears. Go ahead and follow these steps to add another Choice:

- Click the drop-down arrow for the Choice field under "Choice Settings"

- Click "CREATE NEW"

- Click "Choice"

A pop-up window will appear to configure the Choice. Enter the following values:

- **Label**: Money Market

- **Unique Name**: Money_Market

- **Value Data Type**: Text

- **Stored Value**: Money Market

Click "OK" to finalize these settings and return to the configuration of the Drop-down List. Once all these steps are complete, the Account Type screen should look like Figure 4-4. Now you can click the OK button.

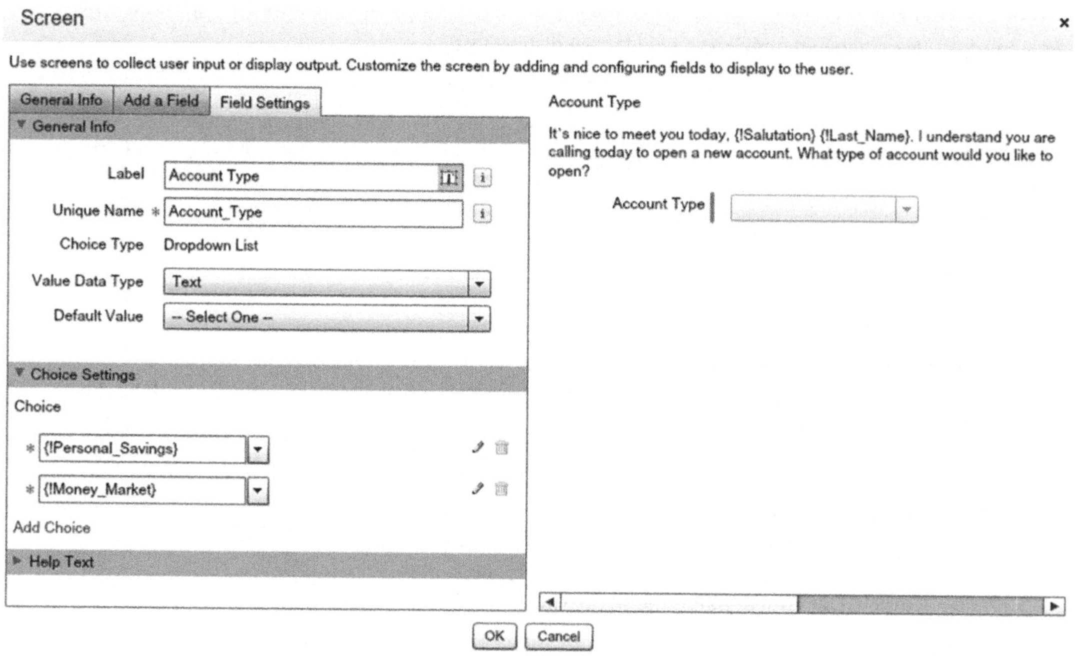

Figure 4-4. *Account Type configuration screen*

Presently, there should be two elements on the Canvas, the Introduction and the Account Type screens. While the Introduction screen is set as the start element, it is not connected to anything. Let's connect it to the Account Type screen and the elements on the Canvas to look like the flow chart that was designed. Remember, that in order to connect elements, you just click the diamond shape at the bottom of the element and drag over the arrow that appears over to the next element you want the flow to go to. The result should look like Figure 4-5.

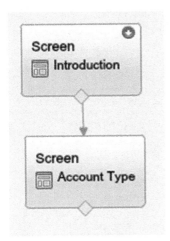

Figure 4-5. Introduction and Account Type screens connected on the Canvas

Address Screen

If we compare what the flow chart has to what the flow looks like currently, we can see that we are on the right track. Next up is the Address screen. While the flow chart shows this as the next screen that the user should come to it does not list the specific requirements for this screen. Looking back at the detailed requirements we see that we are capturing the mailing address, which consists of address line 1, address line 2, city, state, and zip code. OK, it seems simple enough. Let's get building!

Add a new Screen element with the following configuration settings under the "General Info" tab:

- **Name**: Address
- **Unique Name**: Address_Screen

Next add a Display Text field into the screen with the following configuration settings:

- **Unique Name**: Address_Text
- **Text Area**: OK {!Salutation} {!Last_Name}, I'm going to need some information from you to set up your new account. To begin can you provide me with your current mailing address?

This screen is a little more straightforward as there are no drop-down lists or choices to set up. The screen needs five text fields and all of them are required except for address line 2 since not all addresses need a second line. Add five Text box fields to the screen with the following configuration settings:

- Address Line 1 configuration settings:
  - **Label**: Address Line 1
  - **Unique Name**: Address_Line_1
  - **Required**: <checked>

- Address Line 2 configuration settings:
  - **Label**: Address Line 2
  - **Unique Name**: Address_Line_2
  - **Required**: <not checked>
- City/Province configuration settings:
  - **Label**: City/Province
  - **Unique Name**: City_Province
  - **Required**: <checked>
- State configuration settings:
  - **Label**: State
  - **Unique Name**: State
  - **Required**: <checked>
- Zip Code configuration settings:
  - **Label**: Zip Code
  - **Unique Name**: Zip_Code
  - **Required**: <checked>

You may be tempted to want to use a Number field for the Zip Code instead of the Text box but there are two things to consider here. One is that zip codes can have a dash with four extra numbers after them. The dash would not be allowed in a number field. There is also another reason that is very important to know when building flows. When using a Number field or a variable of a Number data type, Salesforce stores the values differently. Numbers will have a decimal form to them, so that 11331 will become 11,331.0. They can be configured to have a scale of zero, but even then 11331 will become 11,331 when trying to display the value. Either way, save yourself the trouble and keep the input as a Text box so that the value the user inputs is not changed.

■ **Note**   A good practice is to use number fields and number variables only when their values will be used for mathematical purposes. To ensure that input stays as intended by a user, a Text box or text variable will not modify the inputted value.

Once all these steps are complete the Address screen should look like Figure 4-6. Now you can click the OK button.

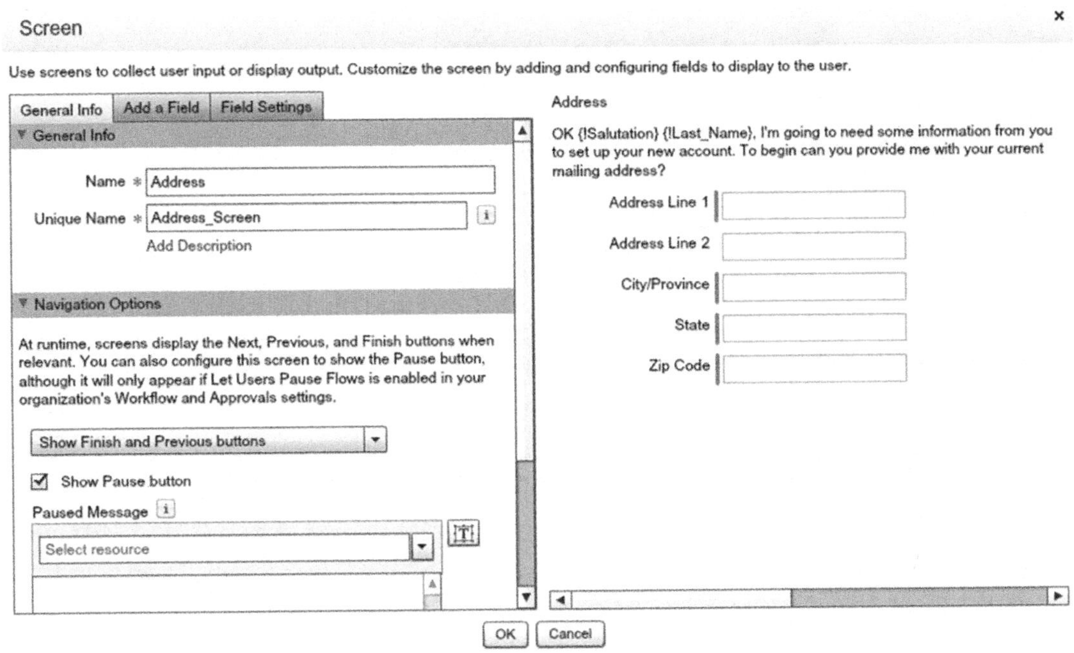

Figure 4-6. *Address configuration screen*

Now connect the Account Type Screen to the Address Screen in the flow. If we compare our flow chat with our current flow they should match so far. The flow should currently look like Figure 4-7.

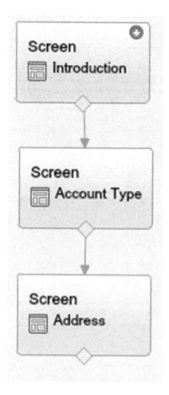

Figure 4-7. *Address screen connected on the Canvas*

Phone Numbers Screen

Next in our flow chart design is the Phone Numbers screen. It contains not one but three different possible numbers to capture. A primary or home phone, which is required, and then a mobile phone number and a work phone number. Both the mobile and work phone numbers are optional (not required). So while these are numbers, they do contain dashes, so we will make these text fields to keep the values unaltered. Let's make history!

Add a new Screen element with the following configuration settings under the "General Info" tab:

- **Name**: Phone Numbers
- **Unique Name**: Phone_Numbers_Screen

Next add a Display Text field into the screen with the following configuration settings:

- **Unique Name**: Phone_Text
- **Text Area**: Thank you {!Salutation} {!Last_Name}. Now can you give me your home or main contact phone number? Also, if you like, we can put additional contact numbers such as mobile or work into the application.

This screen is even more straightforward than the last. Three fields are needed, but only one is required: the Home Phone field. Add three Text box fields to the screen with the following configuration settings:

- Home Phone configuration settings:
    - **Label**: Home Phone
    - **Unique Name**: Home_Phone
    - **Required**: <checked>
- Mobile Phone configuration settings:
    - **Label**: Mobile Phone
    - **Unique Name**: Mobile_Phone
    - **Required**: <not checked>
- Work Phone configuration settings:
    - **Label**: Work Phone
    - **Unique Name**: Work_Phone
    - **Required**: <not checked>

Once all these steps are complete the Phone Numbers screen should look like Figure 4-8. Now you can click the OK button.

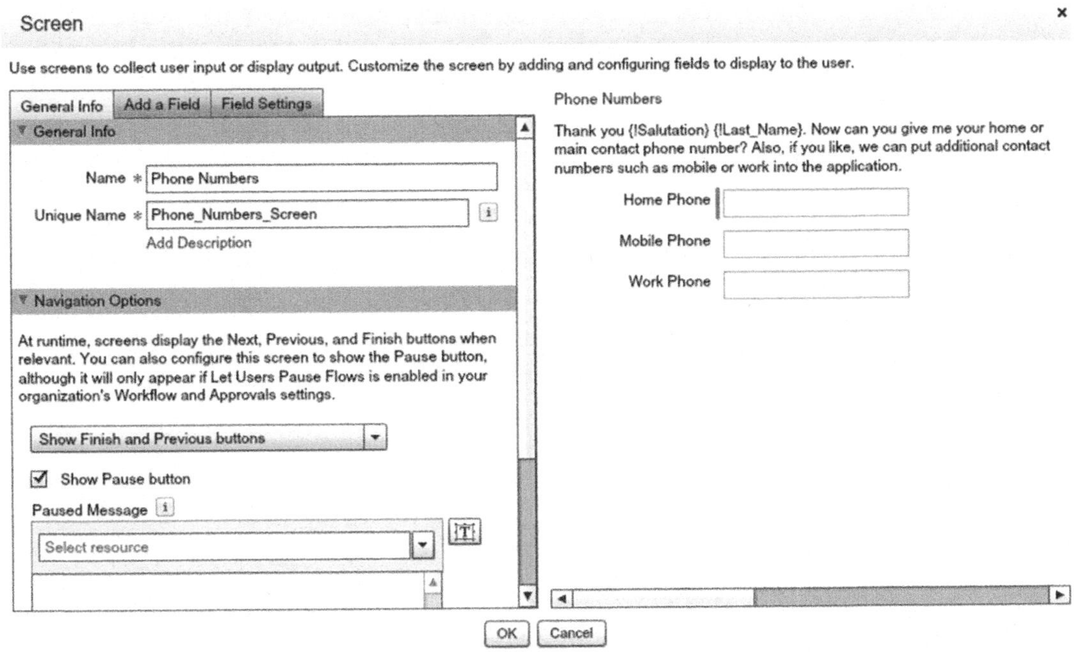

Figure 4-8. *Phone Numbers configuration screen*

Connect the Address screen to the Phone Numbers screen in the flow. The flow should currently look like Figure 4-9. Also, it might be a good time to click the Save button. We are working in the cloud and you never know when you might lose Internet connection or power. Losing all your work would be stressful! So click that Save button.

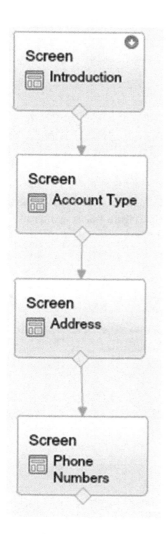

Figure 4-9. *Phone Numbers screen connected on the Canvas*

SSN/Tax ID Screen

Things are about to get interesting soon. I promise, but we have one more screen to go before we get to a fork in the road in this flow. We need to set up the SSN/Tax ID screen.

Add a new Screen element with the following configuration settings under the General Info tab:

- **Name**: SSN/Tax ID

- **Unique Name**: SSN_Tax_Id_Screen

Next add a Display Text field into the screen with the following configuration settings:

- **Unique Name**: SSN_Tax_Id_Text

- **Text Area**: Next, we need to associate your account to your federal tax ID. We need either your SSN or a federal tax identification number given to you by the IRS.

This screen is even easier! It's only one field, the SSN/Tax ID. Add one Text box field to the screen with the following configuration settings:

- **Label**: SSN / Tax Id

- **Unique Name**: SSN_Tax_Id

- **Required**: <checked>

When you are finished configuring everything the SSN/Tax ID screen should look like Figure 4-10. Now you can click the OK button.

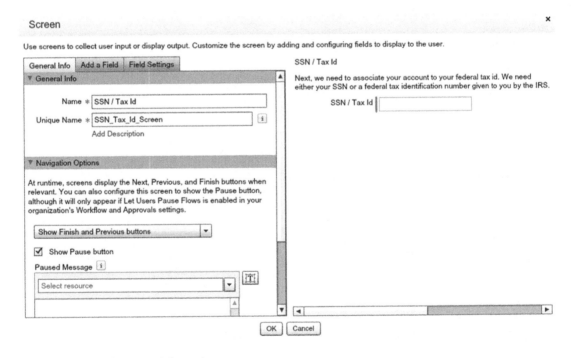

Figure 4-10. *SSN/Tax ID configuration screen*

At this point it all may seem a little too easy. Well, if you are feeling that it's because we did our due diligence in sorting out the requirements and the design. Once you have all that finished, it's just a matter of following your design like a blueprint. Before we forget, let's connect this last element and save because things are about to get a bit more complicated. Once you have connected and saved, your flow should look like Figure 4-11.

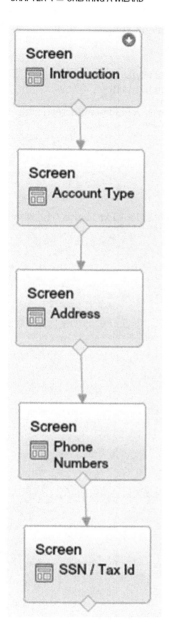

Figure 4-11. *SSN/Tax ID screen connected on the Canvas*

Money Market or Savings Account?

The design in the flow chart essentially was just a series of sequential screens allowing the user to input fields in a form and move on to the next step. It's important to note that depending on business requirements, we could have just had one large form on one screen where all the data was entered. These may seem like a way to simplify the design. I mean, after all, you would just build one screen instead of five. Sometimes this may be OK, but in this case we are separating them out into logical chunks. Why, you ask?

Well, mainly because that is what the business requested, but the core reason is since this is more of a call center application there is more going on here than just inputting data. If this were a wizard for internal use, then one form would probably be better. That's because after a while a power user would get tired of having to do so many extra clicks. Maybe in this case the call center representative might get tired too, but we are striving to achieve a conversation here. In call centers, it's important to engage the customer and appear as though you are not just filling in data in a form. That is why we break the process up into logical chunks with scripts for the representative to read in order to engage the customer in a back-and-forth conversation that seems more natural.

Now that we discussed the reasoning behind the multiple screens, let's get into some branching in this tree of logic. Looking at the design we are finally at the point where we have to check on what was entered previously to determine which screen to go to next. It is important to point out that if a developer had to create all this with code, it would be a bit complex to create the process that would check on what was entered previously and then route the user to the next screen. With Visual Workflow, it's just a matter of configuring the flow to go one way or the other by drawing it out. Let us begin!

Go to the Palette tab and drag over a Decision element to the Canvas. You'll be presented with the configuration screen for the element, but you will notice that it's a bit different than the other elements we have configured so far. In the settings that are available, configure them as follows:

- **Name**: Is Savings Acct?

- **Unique Name**: Is_Savings_Acct_Decision

■ **Note**   A good practice is to name Decisions as questions as a way to make it clear what the deciding factor is for branching off to one outcome vs. another.

Under the "Outcomes" section at the bottom of the Decision configuration window there is a special area to configure all the different outcomes (or branches) that will come from this Decision element. Each outcome will basically be a separate path in a "fork in the road," so to speak. When you initially add a Decision element the first outcome will just be named "[New Outcome]" (see the name on the left side of the window). Under this new outcome you have a few options to configure it. Use the following settings to configure the outcome:

- **Name**: Savings Account

- **Unique Name**: Savings_Account_Outcome

- **Resource**: {!Account_Type}

- **Operator**: equals

- **Value**: {!Personal_Savings}

- **Add Condition**: All conditions must be true (AND)

These last four settings need some explaining. While the Name and Unique Name have been seen before, the Resource, Operator, Value, and Add Condition settings are new to us. These last four settings are used to determine when this outcome should be used when the user is traversing through the flow. A way to read this logically is "go to the Savings Account outcome when the Account Type equals Personal Savings." The Resource is the item that it will be checking the value of. The Operator is how it is comparing and the Value is just the value it is comparing the Resource against. So far pretty straightforward right?

Well what about this "Add Condition" setting? That link, once clicked, will actually add another combo with a Resource, Operator, and Value. If we were to add several of these conditions then we would need to add some more instructions to the flow as to how to evaluate all of them together. Should all the conditions evaluate to true (AND) or should only one of them evaluate to true (OR)? What if it was complicated and you need some conditions to be true and some to be false? Well, then there is the "Advanced logic" option in the drop-down to help you configure those settings. At this point we do not need to get into all that. Our single condition is perfect for getting the job done here.

Now that we have set up the "Savings Account" outcome let's click the "Add Outcome" link on the left side. You'll notice a new set of Outcome configuration settings appears. This new set allows us to create another branch in this flow from this point. Essentially, every time you need a new path to follow in the flow chart we designed, you will need to be configure another outcome.

Use the following configuration settings for this new outcome:

- **Name**: Money Market Account

- **Unique Name**: Money_Market_Account_Outcome

- **Resource**: {!Account_Type}

- **Operator**: equals

- **Value**: {!Money_Market}

- **Add Condition**: All conditions must be true (AND)

Great! Now that you have these two outcomes configured click "OK" to return back to the flow. Go ahead and connect the SSN/Tax ID screen element to this new Decision element.

Even at this point the flow is a wizard in the sense that it is guiding the user screen by screen to help the user input a lot of information without overwhelming him. However, it is still linear and does not take the user on different paths during the processes based on input. Not yet anyway! In order to take a flow on an alternate path instead of just linear execution, we need a Decision element. We have one now and in it we configured two Outcomes. If the Account Type of "Savings Account" was chosen earlier in the flow then the Savings Account Outcome path will be taken. If the Account Type of "Money Market" was chosen earlier in the flow then the Money Market Account Outcome path will be taken instead. The name of the Outcome does not need to match any values as part of the logic such as Account Type. The names "Money Market Account" and "Savings Account" are used instead to display on the flow so that the flow is more readable when viewing it in the Flow Designer. Let's configure the next two screens so that we can see this concept in action! By the way, don't forget to save your progress thus far.

Money Market Account Terms Screen

The flow chart design created earlier shows that at this point the flow splits off in two directions. One direction goes to the Money Market Account Terms screen and the other direction goes to the Checking Account Number screen. It really does not matter which side you add and configure first in the flow. Everyone has a preference depending on how his or her mind thinks and comprehends. Since a lot of languages read left to right and top to bottom our flow goes top to bottom as well. Keeping with the left-to-right idea, let's start with the left side of the split from the linear flow so far. Obviously, not all languages and people share this idea of top to bottom and left to right. Some languages go right to left. If this is your preference then feel free to adjust the flow as you wish.

On the left side is the Money Market Account Terms screen. Go ahead and add a new Screen element with the following configuration settings under the General Info tab:

- **Name**: Money Market Account Terms

- **Unique Name**: Money_Market_Account_Terms_Screen

Next add a Display Text field into the screen with the following configuration settings:

- **Unique Name**: Money_Market_Account_Terms_Text

- **Text Area**: Now {!Salutation} {!Last_Name} we need to finally choose the terms for your money market account. We have two options to choose from. Each term option is beneficial based on your goals. Let me take this moment to explain them to you.

  High-Yield Term

  The high-yield Money Market term gives an interest rate of 5% annual interest over a ten-year period.

  Low-Yield Term

  The low-yield Money Market term gives an interest rate of 2% annual interest over a five-year period.

  Which term would you like to choose for this Money Market account?

Next we are going to add a choice field to allow the user to pick either a High-Yield or Low-Yield Money Market Term. Last time we added a choice field was with the Account Type, but it was a Drop-down List. Technically we could add a Drop-down List here as well, but since we are displaying the two different options in the Display Text field it probably makes sense to display both choices here as well. To do this we need to add a Radio Buttons field. Radio buttons are essentially a bullet list where the bullet can be clicked to select one of the items in the list. Unlike a Drop-down List where only one option is shown at a time unless you expand the list, a list of Radio Buttons will show all the options on the screen at once without having to click anything. This type of choice is good when there are not too many options to pick from or you do not mind taking up a lot of the screen space. A Drop-down list is good for longer lists or if you are trying to conserve screen space taken up by other fields on the page.

So let's add a Radio Buttons field to the screen with the following configuration settings:

- **Label**: Money Market Account Terms Radio Buttons

- **Unique Name**: Money_Market_Account_Terms_Radio_Buttons

- **Value Data Type**: Text

- **Required**: <checked>

■ **Note** While the Radio Buttons choice field has an option to be required or not required, the Drop-down List choice field does not have that option because that type of field is always required once added to the screen.

For these Radio Buttons we will manually add the two types of terms that can be chosen for a money market account. To do so we need to create two new "Choices" and associate them with this Radio Buttons field.

To do so, follow these steps:

- Click the drop-down arrow for the Choice field under "Choice Settings"

- Click "CREATE NEW"

- Click "Choice"

A pop-up window will appear to configure the Choice. Enter the following values:

- **Label**: High-Yield Money Market Term

- **Unique Name**: High_Yield_Money_Market_Term_Choice

- **Value Data Type**: Text

- **Stored Value**: high-yield

Click "OK" to finalize these settings and return to the configuration of the Radio Buttons. Next we need to add a second Choice. To do so, click the "Add Choice" link right below the Choice you just added.

Notice a new Select resource field appears. Go ahead and follow these steps to add another Choice:

- Click the drop-down arrow for the Choice field under "Choice Settings"

- Click "CREATE NEW"

- Click "Choice"

A pop-up window will appear to configure the Choice. Enter these values:

- **Label**: Low-Yield Money Market Term

- **Unique Name**: Low_Yield_Money_Market_Term_Choice

- **Value Data Type**: Text

- **Stored Value**: low-yield

Click "OK" to finalize these settings and return to the configuration of the Radio Buttons. Once all these steps are complete the Money Market Account Terms screen should look like Figure 4-12. Now you can click the OK button.

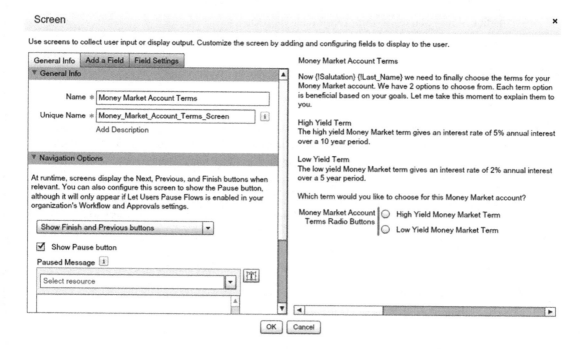

Figure 4-12. Money Market Account Terms configuration screen

Now that we have this new screen on the flow canvas, let's connect the "Is Savings Acct?" Decision element to this new "Money Market Account Terms screen" element like usual by clicking and dragging the connection point to the new screen element. Notice something different? You should see the Decision Routing pop-up just like in Figure 4-13.

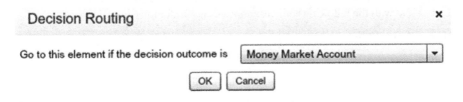

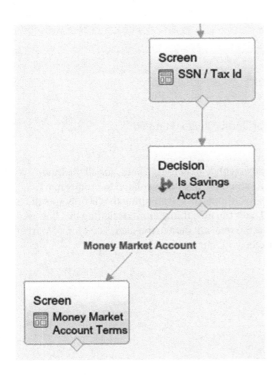

Figure 4-13. *Money Market Account Decision Routing pop-up window*

The Decision Routing pop-up allows you to choose which outcome will be connected to the next element on the Canvas. Normally when connecting two elements on the Canvas there is only one line (or path) available to connect them with. When connecting from a Decision element there are more paths to take. Each outcome is a path to split off from the Decision element to take the flow onto the next element when it is executing. Right now we want the "Money Market Account" outcome to then go to the "Money Market Account Terms" screen. Choose the "Money Market Account" option from the picklist if it is not already selected and then click "OK." The Canvas should look similar to Figure 4-14.

Figure 4-14. *Money Market Account Terms connected on the Canvas*

Money Market Review Screen

We have completed the difficult task of creating a Decision and its Outcomes to route the flow to the path for Money Market Accounts. So let's add the last screen in our decision for the Money Market side. It's the Money Market Review screen. The purpose of this screen is to have everything we have done so far in the flow represented on a single screen so that we can have the customer confirm before we finish.

Add a new Screen element with the following configuration settings under the General Info tab:

- **Name**: Money Market Review

- **Unique Name**: Money_Market_Review_Screen

Next add a Display Text field into the screen with the following configuration settings:

- **Unique Name**: Money_Market_Review_Text

- **Text Area**: OK {!Salutation} {!Last_Name}, I'm going to review everything before I submit this to open up your new account. Please listen carefully. What we have is . . .

  Account Type: {!Account_Type}

  First Name: {!First_Name}
  Middle Name: {!Middle_Name}
  Last Name: {!Last_Name}

  Address:
  {!Address_Line_1}
  {!Address_Line_2}
  {!City_Province}, {!State} {!Zip_Code}

  Main/Home Phone: {!Home_Phone}
  Mobile Phone: {!Mobile_Phone}
  Work Phone: {!Work_Phone}

  SSN/Tax Id: {!SSN_Tax_Id}

  Money Market Term: {!Money_Market_Account_Terms_Radio_Buttons}

  Does this sound correct?

This screen has no input fields of any type. It is simply text with a lot of merge fields for all the input fields we have added up to this point. All fields on this page should be fields only related to money market accounts or shared by money market and savings accounts. We shouldn't see anything that is only specific to savings Accounts on this page as that could be confusing. That's the nice thing about designing this flow as a wizard! We can tailor the pages to be specific and only show the relevant data to the user. The Money Market Review screen should look like Figure 4-15. Click "OK" to keep your changes.

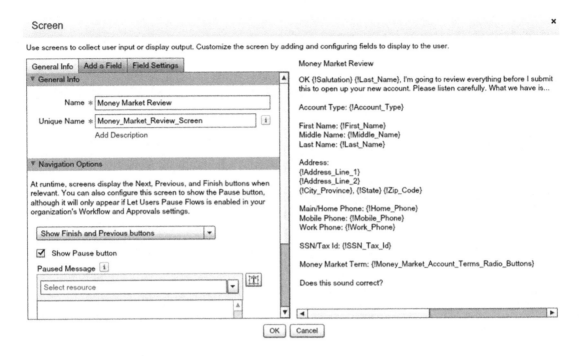

Figure 4-15. *Money Market Review configuration screen*

Now connect the Money Market Account Terms screen to the Money Market Review screen in the flow. The flow should currently look like Figure 4-16.

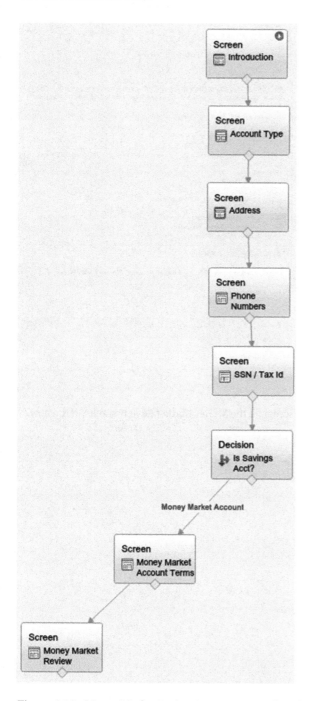

Figure 4-16. *Money Market Review Screen connected on the canvas*

Checking Account Number Screen

While the Money Market specific part of the flow is complete, the Savings Account portion still has more to it. We created two outcomes for the "Is Savings Acct?" Decision element. The outcome created for Money Market has been connected already but the "Savings Account" outcome has not. That outcome needs to connect to the Checking Account Number screen according to the flow chart design. Let's continue this journey by creating a new Screen element configured as follows:

- **Name**: Checking Account Number

- **Unique Name**: Checking_Account_Number_Screen

Next add a Display Text field into the screen with the following configuration settings:

- **Unique Name**: Checking_Account_Number_Text

- **Text Area**: We are almost finished with your account set up {!Salutation} {!Last_Name}. Did you know that if you have an existing checking account with us you could open this savings account with a higher interest account of 0.5% annual interest instead of the standard 0.1% interest?

  If you have an existing checking account can you give me the account number so we can add it to your file?

As you can tell by the text in this screen, the purpose is to allow customers to prove that they already have an account number. Doing so will give them better terms for their new savings account. This screen will need an input field to allow the service agent to type it in.

Add one Text box field to the screen with the following configuration settings:

- **Label**: Checking Account Number

- **Unique Name**: Checking_Account_Number

- **Required**: <not checked>

Notice that this Checking Account Number text box is not required since the customer may not have a checking account number.

■ **Note**   When none of the fields on a screen are required that screen can be skipped by users when they are running the flow.

When you are finished configuring everything, the Checking Account Number screen should look like Figure 4-17. Now you can click the OK button.

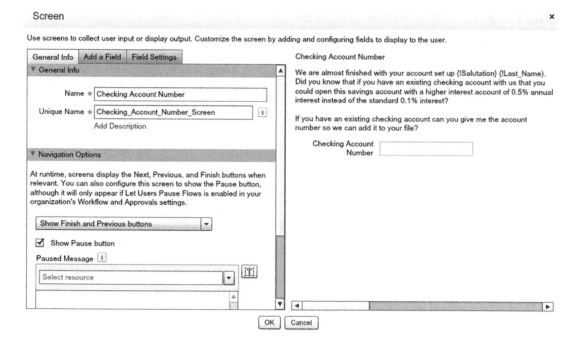

Figure 4-17. *Checking Account Number configuration screen*

Connect the "Is Savings Acct?" Decision element to the new "Checking Account Number" screen. A pop-up will appear as before, but this time choose the "Savings Account" outcome and click "OK." Figure 4-18 shows the Decision Routing pop-up window.

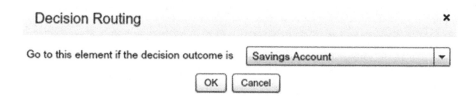

Figure 4-18. *Savings Account Decision Routing pop-up window*

To keep the flow clean and readable, position the new "Checking Account Number" screen element on the Canvas so that it's horizontally in line with the "Money Market Account Terms" screen element. Also move it so that it forms an upside down "Y" shape as in Figure 4-19. While it does not matter where elements are placed on the Canvas, it is a best practice keep the flow organized and readable. Some day in the future this flow will need to be maintained and changed in some way. Whether your or another individual does that work, it is best to keep the flow neat and tidy to not cause confusion when trying to figure out what the flow does. This will help to make future edits in the flow easy and also with less chance of an erroneous change. Different people have different ways of accomplishing this, but the main thing is to be consistent. In this book we will see other examples of laying out the flow for larger projects. For now, though, a simple flow going from top to bottom and fanning out as the logic splits works nicely because this flow is not large.

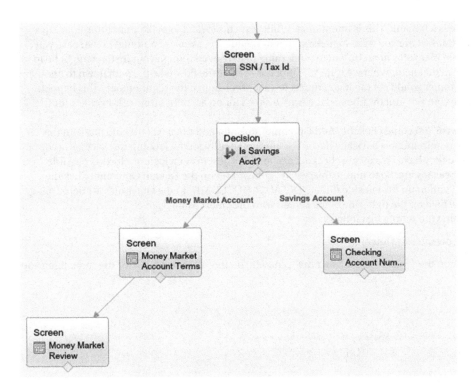

Figure 4-19. *Checking Account Number Screen connected on the Canvas*

Is Interest High? Decision

The next element to put on the Canvas is another Decision element. We have created one other Decision element in this flow already, so this should be a piece of cake. This Decision will be slightly different from the last though. Instead of having two Editable Outcomes and no Default Outcome, we will configure this one with a default and then one other outcome. Also, the comparison for determining which outcome will be a little different. Let's jump in!

Go to the Palette tab and drag over a Decision element to the Canvas. You'll be presented with the configuring screen for the element like before. In the settings that are available, configure them as follows:

- **Name**: Is Interest High?

- **Unique Name**: Is_Interest_High_Decision

Under the "Outcomes" section at the bottom of the Decision configuration window configure the "[New Outcome]" with the following settings:

- **Name**: High Interest Outcome

- **Unique Name**: High_Interest_Outcome

- **Resource**: {!Checking_Account_Number}

- **Operator**: does not equal

- **Value**:

- **Add Condition**: All conditions must be true (AND)

Notice the Value is left blank. This is intentional. While it seems logical to make something equal to a value, there will be times where you want to make sure that a value is . . . well . . . nothing! In that case you can just leave this field blank. It's not required to put a value in here even though your instinct might be to try to put something in that field. What we want to happen is to have the flow take the path down to another screen when the customer would get the high interest terms. According to the requirements, this happens when they do not have an account number. So the way to check for no account number is to check for the field to be blank.

Now here is a twist! You could click the "Add Outcome" link and add the next outcome there. In this scenario though the requirement is basically that all customers should get the low-interest savings account unless they can prove they have an existing checking account. It's best to keep logic as close as possible to how the business reasons are. So to mimic this, we are going to set up the Default Outcome. Click the "[Default Outcome]" option on the left side under "DEFAULT OUTCOME" in the Outcomes section. Doing so will show only one field on the right side of the screen with the label "Name."

Set the name using the setting that follows:

- **Name**: Low Interest Outcome

If you click back on the "High Interest Outcome" outcome on the left you should see the same thing you see in Figure 4-20.

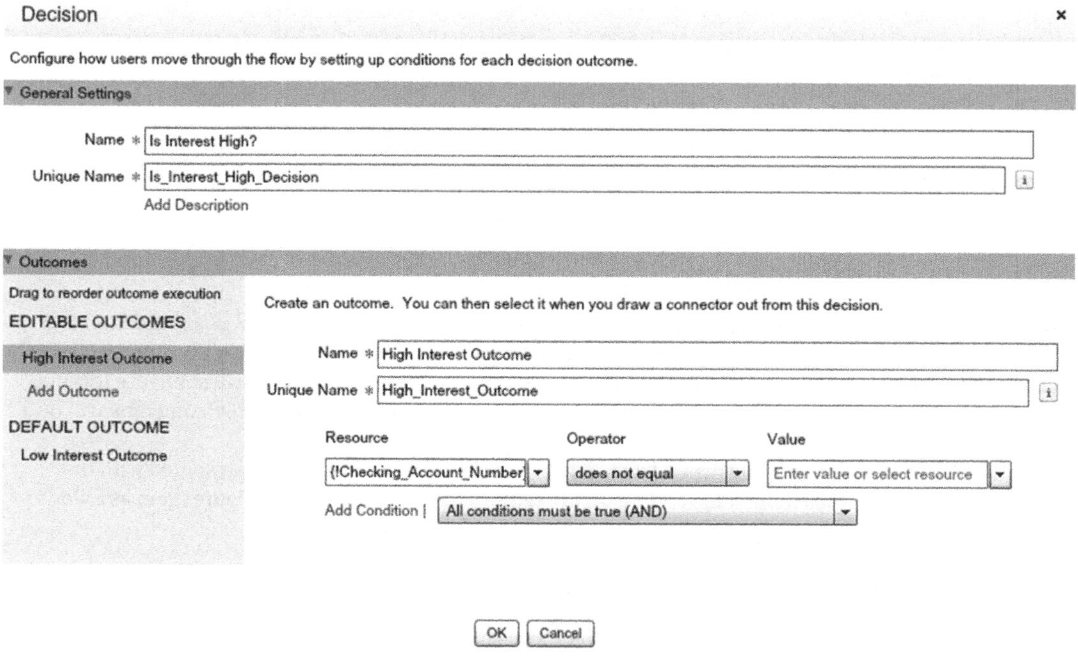

Figure 4-20. Is Interest High? configuration screen

Click "OK" to return to the Flow Designer Canvas. Make sure to connect the "Checking Account Number" screen to this new Decision element and then save the flow.

Assignments

We have been on a rampage creating screens, decisions, screens, more screens, and did I mention screens? Here we will get into a new element we have not used before, the Assignment element. In the Palette under the "LOGIC" section is the Assignment element. It has a green equals icon to signify making one value equal to another. Essentially, we use the Assignment element to store a value to be used later on in the flow. At this point we have been storing values in the Text box fields themselves. Sometimes though we need to set a value that may not necessarily come from a user-entered field. In this case, Assignments work nicely. As a part of the process we are about to embark on we will need to create some variables. These variables can be created beforehand, but we are going to create them just as we go along. So let's start assigning!

Drag a new Assignment over to the canvas and use the following settings to configure it when its configuration window appears:

- **Name**: Set Interest to High

- **Unique Name**: Set_Interest_to_High_Assignment

On the lower section of this window is the Assignments section. It's where the real work gets done. There are three fields: Variable, Operator, and Value. The Variable field holds the variable that we will use as storage to keep the value in. The Operator tells the Assignment how to store the value. Usually the option of "equals" is picked to simply store the value in the variable, although depending on the type of variable used the types of Operators change. Table 4-1 illustrates the different Operators and which types of Variables they apply to.

Table 4-1. *Operator to Variable Assignment Mapping*

Variable Type	Data Type/Object Type	Available Operators
Variable	Text	equals, add
Variable	Number	equals, add, subtract
Variable	Currency	equals, add, subtract
Variable	Date	equals, add, subtract
Variable	DateTime	equals
Variable	Boolean	equals
Variable	Picklist	equals, add
Variable	Picklist (Multi-Select)	equals, add, add item
Collection Variable	Text	equals, add
Collection Variable	Number	equals, add
Collection Variable	Currency	equals, add
Collection Variable	Date	equals, add
Collection Variable	DateTime	equals, add
Collection Variable	Boolean	equals, add
Collection Variable	Picklist	equals, add
Collection Variable	Picklist (Multi-Select)	equals, add
SObject Variable	standard, custom	equals
SObject Collection Variable	standard, custom	equals, add

As you can see, there are a lot of ways to store values and, depending on how those values are stored, different ways of using the Assignment element with them. What we need to store though is a number. We need the High-Interest value to be stored, so click the drop-down arrow to show the different types of variables we can add. Under "CREATE NEW" click "Variable."

The Variable configuration window will appear. Set the fields to the following values:

- **Unique Name**: Interest

- **Data Type**: Number

- **Scale**: 1

- **Input/Output Type**: Private

- **Default Value**: 0.1

The Variable configuration window should look like Figure 4-21 now. Click OK to go back to the Assignment configuration window.

Variable   ✕

Create updatable values that can be used throughout your flow.

Unique Name *	Interest
Description	
Data Type	Number
Scale	1
Input/Output Type	Private
Default Value	0.1

OK   Cancel

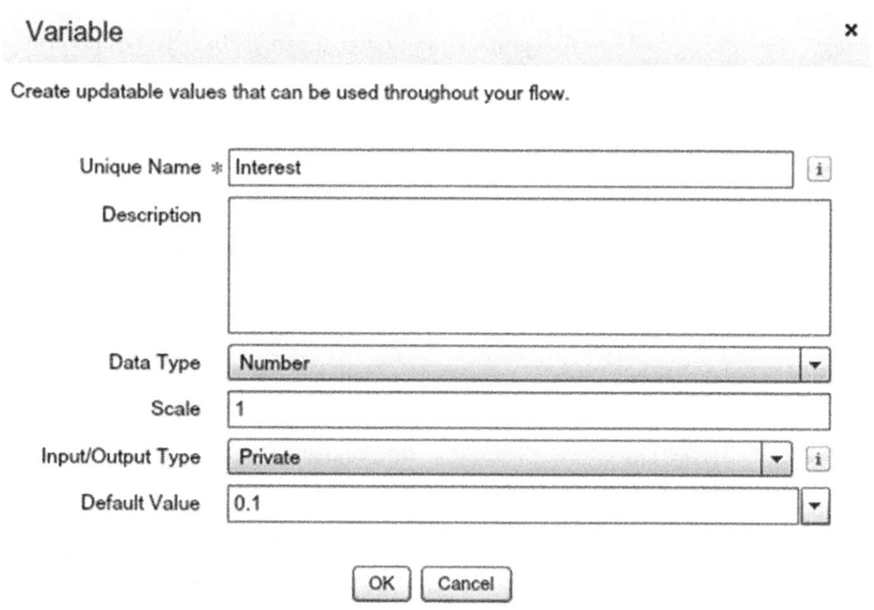

Figure 4-21. *Interest configuration screen*

Now that we are back to the Assignment configuration window, select the following values for the remaining fields:

- **Operator**: equals

- **Value**: 0.5

Notice that there is an "Add Assignment" link. Clicking this link will provide the ability to assign another Value to another Variable. Using this link, you can assign many values in one step! This is a nice feature because if it didn't exist you would have to drag and drop many Assignment elements on the Canvas, causing the flow to be extremely messy and unreadable. So, a word to the wise, if you are connecting Assignment elements together, then you are doing it wrong. Consolidate those into one element to keep your flow clean! Now that we have that tidbit out of the way, go ahead and click the OK button to finish up here.

Finally, on the Canvas, go ahead and connect the "Is Interest High?" Decision element to the "Set Interest to High" Assignment element. The Decision Routing pop-up will appear. Choose the "High Interest Outcome" option from the drop-down list and click "OK."

We still have another Assignment to go. The "Is Interest High?" Decision element has two outcomes. We connected one, but the default outcome named "Low Interest Outcome" has not been connected yet. Let's make it happen! Since we just finished up configuring an Assignment element, we will speed through this next one because it is almost identical except for the value assigned to the "Interest" variable. Place another Assignment element next to the element you just created and use the following settings to configure it:

- **Name**: Set Interest to Low
- **Unique Name**: Set_Interest_to_Low_Assignment
- **Variable**: {!Interest}
- **Operator**: equals
- **Value**: 0.1

Click "OK" to return to the Canvas and connect the "Is Interest High?" Decision element to the newly created "Set Interest to Low" Assignment element. This time it will just connect without presenting the pop-up window to select the appropriate outcome. The reason is that besides the default outcome, all the other outcomes have been used. So it will automatically use the default outcome to connect to this last element. Go ahead and move the elements around to give a clean look to the flow like in Figure 4-22.

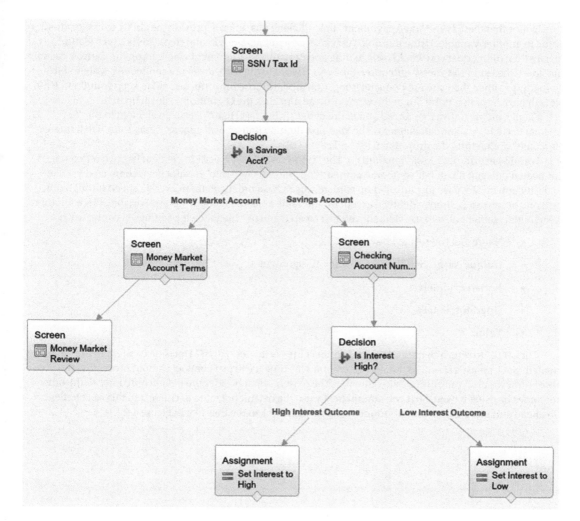

Figure 4-22. Is Interest High? Decision and Assignment elements connected on the Canvas

Personal Savings Review Screen

We are in the home stretch! Let's review the design in the flow chart. According to the design, we need to add a final screen. Just like the path in the flow to the Money Market Review screen, there is a similar path to a Personal Savings Review screen. By this point we are pros at creating Screen elements. So go ahead and create a new Screen element with the following configuration settings:

- **Name:** Personal Savings Review
- **Unique Name:** Personal_Savings_Review_Screen

Now add a Display Text field with the following configuration settings:

- **Unique Name**: Personal_Savings_Review_Text

- **Text Area**: OK {!Salutation} {!Last_Name}, I'm going to review everything before I submit this to open up your new account. Please listen carefully. What we have is . . .

  Account Type: {!Account_Type}
  First Name: {!First_Name}
  Middle Name: {!Middle_Name}
  Last Name: {!Last_Name}

  Address:
  {!Address_Line_1}
  {!Address_Line_2}
  {!City_Province}, {!State} {!Zip_Code}

  Main/Home Phone: {!Home_Phone}
  Mobile Phone: {!Mobile_Phone}
  Work Phone: {!Work_Phone}

  SSN/Tax ID: {!SSN_Tax_Id}
  Checking Account Number: {!Checking_Account_Number}

  Interest Rate: {!Interest}%

  Does this sound correct?

When you are finished configuring everything the Personal Savings Review screen should look like Figure 4-23. Now you can click the OK button.

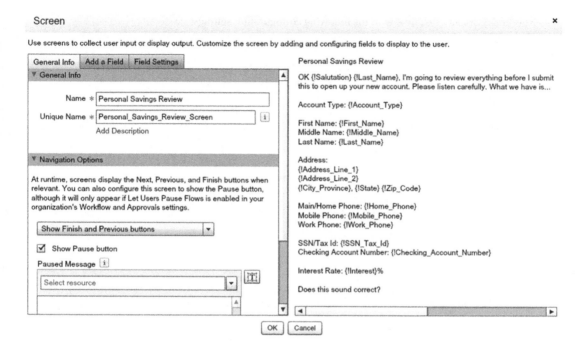

Figure 4-23. *Personal Savings Review configuration screen*

We are about to do something we have not seen before. Up to this point we have only ever had an element pointed to by one other element. We have never pointed two or more elements to the same element! Our flow has been fanning or expanding out as it went further and further through the steps, but we have not seen it get narrower. Instead it has always been getting wider. We could have created two review screens. One for the High-Interest path and one for the Low-Interest path, but we are keeping our design clean and concise. The fewer elements we have, the less chance of something going wrong and the more readable the flow will be. For this reason, we are going to connect the "Set Interest to High" Assignment element and the "Set Interest to Low" Assignment element to the "Personal Savings Review" element. Go ahead and try to connect them! You will notice that Flow Designer allows it. If arranged in a similar fashion to how we have been arranging the previous parts of the flow, the final flow should look like Figure 4-24.

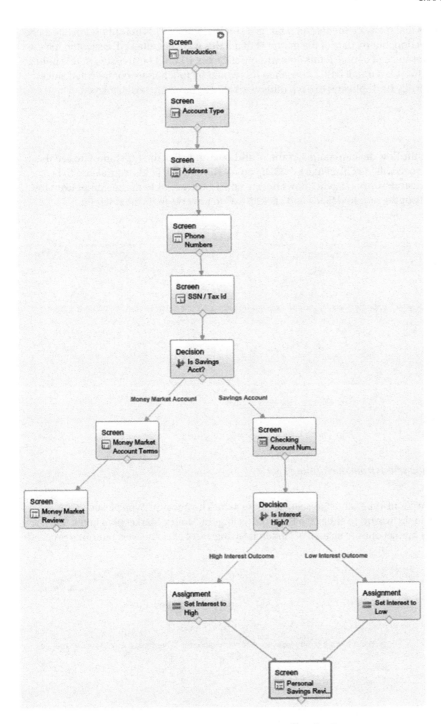

Figure 4-24. *Personal Savings Review screen connected on the Canvas*

The fact of the matter is that many elements can point to a single element. This may not seem like a big deal since we just saw it in action, but the fact of the matter is that if this were not allowed, we would have to create two screen elements instead of one. If this flow was much larger, it could be an issue. At this point, it is not as big a deal, but if this was a much larger flow, then this would be much more complicated since multiple screens would basically be duplicates of each other with almost the same text displayed.

Save It, Run It!

Everything is complete with the flow development. Go ahead and save and click the Run button to see this wizard in action. The first screen will look like Figure 4-25. If you recall, all these fields were set up to be used later in the flow so that the custom support agent knows how to consistently refer to the customer from the call script. Go ahead and fill out the required fields and click "Next" to traverse to the next screen.

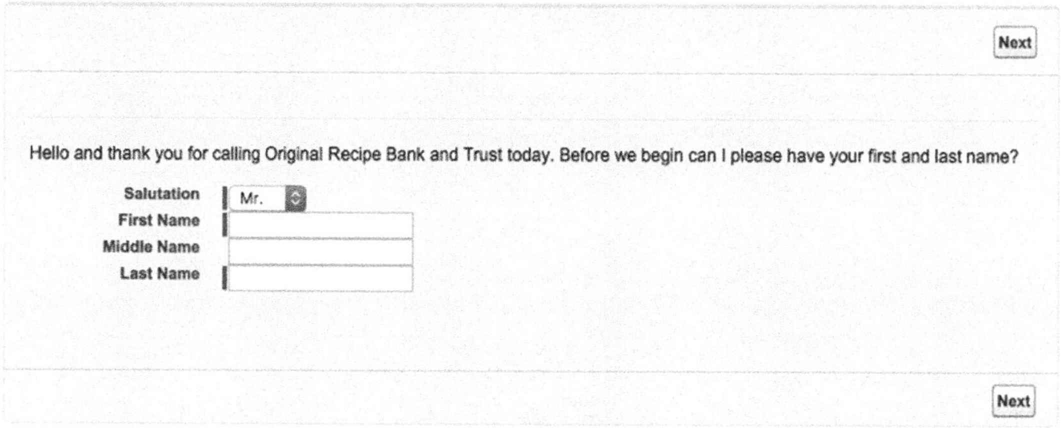

Next

Hello and thank you for calling Original Recipe Bank and Trust today. Before we begin can I please have your first and last name?

Salutation	Mr.
First Name	
Middle Name	
Last Name	

Next

Figure 4-25. *The Introduction screen from the running flow*

The next screen is the Account Type screen as seen in Figure 4-26. The Account Type picked at this screen will change the path in the wizard to either the Personal Savings or Money Market path in the flow. At this point choose the Money Market option, instead of Personal Savings, and click the Next button to proceed.

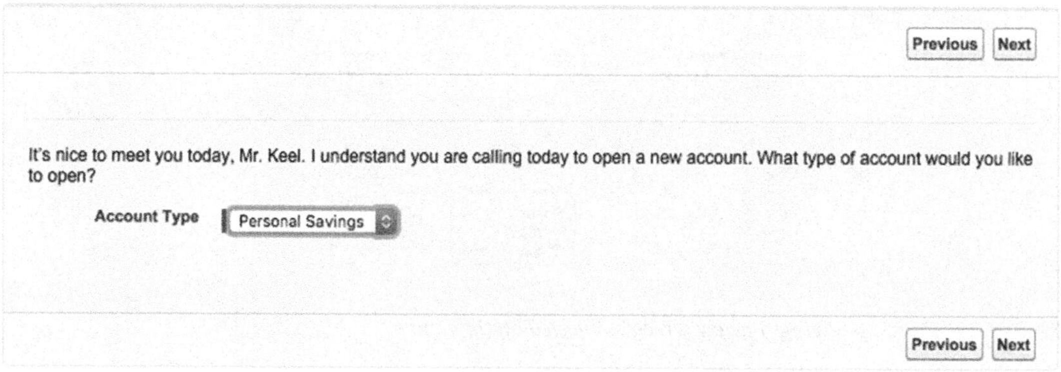

Previous   Next

It's nice to meet you today, Mr. Keel. I understand you are calling today to open a new account. What type of account would you like to open?

Account Type	Personal Savings

Previous   Next

Figure 4-26. *The Account Type screen from the running flow*

The following screens will be encountered now as you traverse through the flow in the Money Market path as seen in Figure 4-27, Figure 4-28, Figure 4-29, and Figure 4-30.

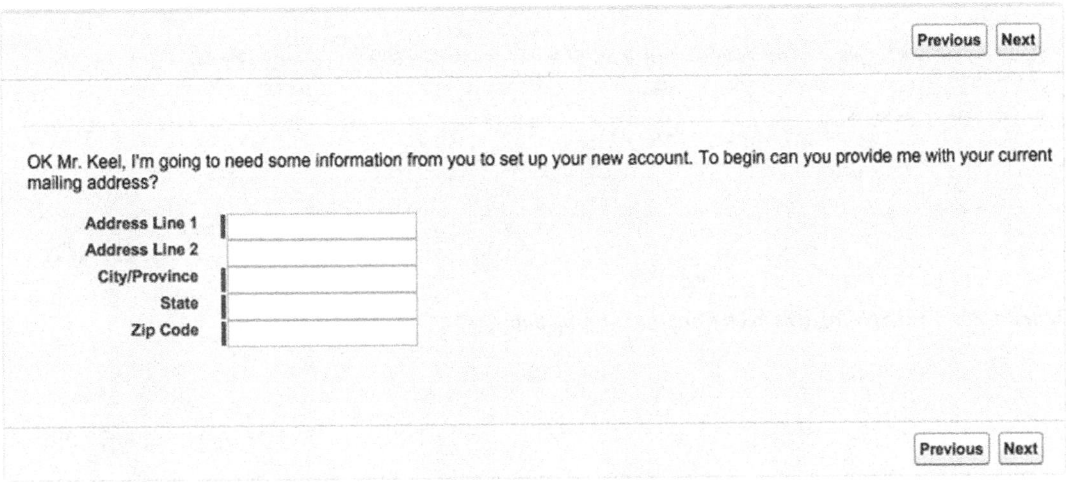

Figure 4-27. *The Address screen from the running flow*

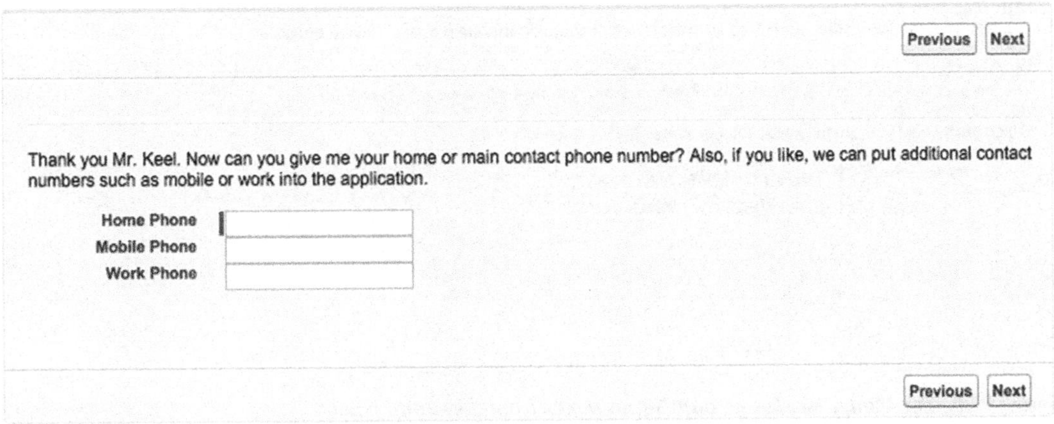

Figure 4-28. *The Phone Numbers screen from the running flow*

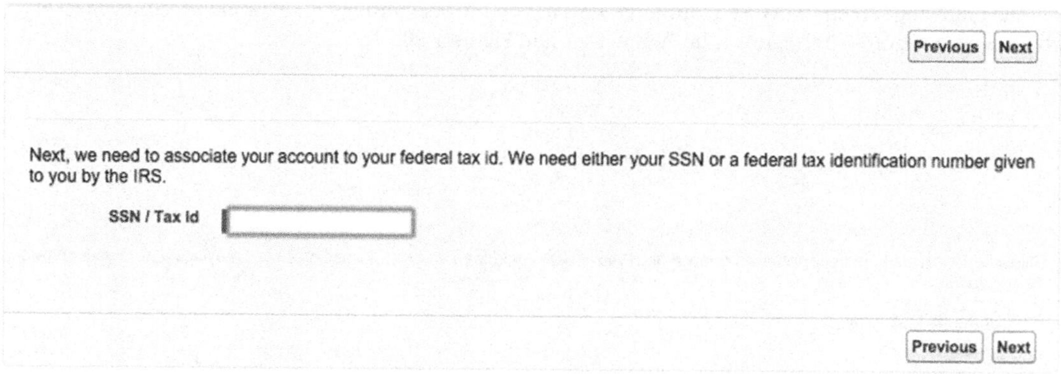

Figure 4-29. *The SSN/Tax ID screen from the running flow*

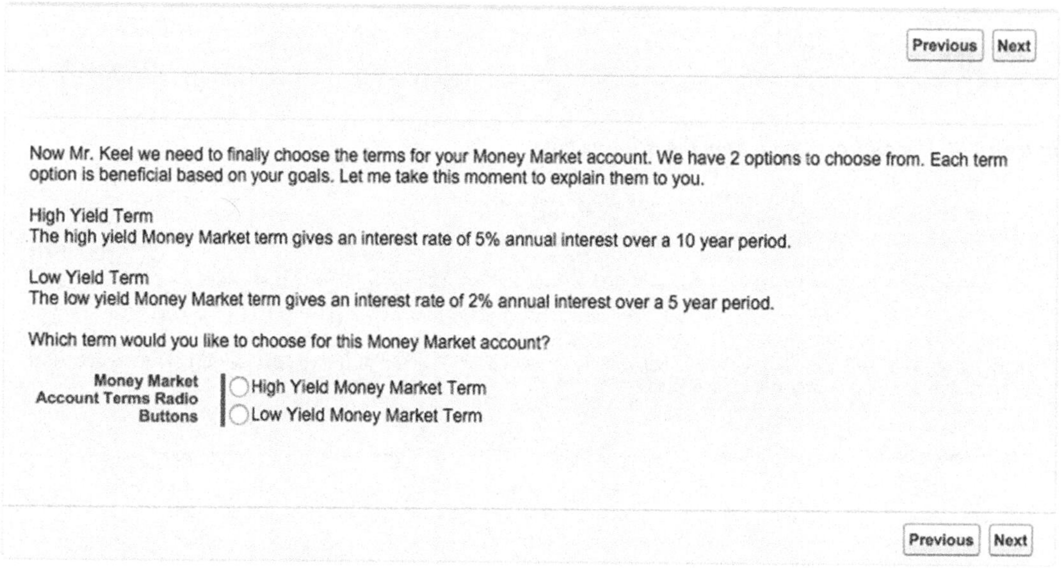

Figure 4-30. *The Money Market Account Terms screen from the running flow*

Finally, you should end up at the Money Market Review screen and, depending what values were entered in, those values should show up on this screen as seen in Figure 4-31. Look through carefully and make sure that all the values are showing up correctly. It is very common for merge fields to be mistyped if they are manually typed in. Also, formatting can be a concern so feel free to go back to the flow and make any adjustments with the spacing or which lines the information appears on. To end the flow, click the Finish button. Notice that the flow just starts from the beginning. This is normal. Go ahead and close the tab or window that the flow opened up in and return back to the flow in Flow Designer.

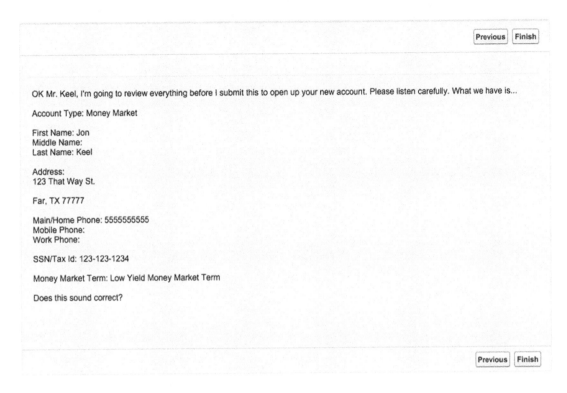

Figure 4-31. The Money Market Review screen from the running flow

Feel free to play around with the flow by running it again, but try all the different combinations of paths so that you are certain that the screens and data presented to the user are in alignment with the requirements, the design, and the implementation that we just went through. Once complete, make sure to save and take a nice break. Job well done!

It is worth noting that with this example we just went through, none of this data entered is saved anywhere permanently. We did not insert or update any records in Salesforce. If we were to do so, then we would have done it after the review screens. Don't worry though. Learning to save records into Salesforce is something we will cover later on.

Recap

The creation of wizards is a common practice with flows as they fit perfectly with the benefits of Visual Workflows since flows have a user interface and can guide the user down different paths depending on what is entered on each screen. There were a lot of steps involved in this flow, but most were very similar. At this point you should be getting comfortable with the creation of each of the elements in the flow generated in this chapter because a lot of the configuration was the same from element to element. It is amazing to think that just in this chapter we created a foundation for how to develop flows by covering how to translate business requirements into functional requirements and then to a design. Then we covered how to take that design and use it as a blueprint to implement the actual flow in Flow Designer. A new topic covered in this chapter was the creation and configuration of decisions and outcomes in a flow.

CHAPTER 5

■ ■ ■

Salesforce Data and Loops

The flows created so far have covered several techniques of dealing with business processes that one might run into in the real world. From a simple linear flow to a flow that branches out depending on user-selected choices, a lot can be achieved with what you have learned in the last chapters—although everything covered so far has not dealt with a scenario of having multiple records to work and iterate over while a flow is in the process of running.

This chapter will cover the concept of loops in Visual Workflow and how they can be used with data in Salesforce. Loops allow the flow to have a collection or a series of data to loop or iterate over. In doing so, the loop can apply a repeatable process for each item it iterates over in the flow. So while the knowledge gained in the last chapters can help build a flow that deals with a single Account or a single Contact, this chapter will cover building a flow when dealing with many records from Salesforce. Once you reach the end of this chapter you will be able to build flows that can deal with several Accounts or any other Salesforce object for that matter and repeat through them to perform a business process all in the same flow.

By the end of this chapter you will

- Learn the concept of Collections and Loops

- Learn about Salesforce lookups

- Learn about Salesforce updates

- Create a flow that handles multiple records from Salesforce

Collections and Loops

In standard Force.com development using the Apex language, there is a concept known as Collections. This is what is known as a data structure. A data structure is a way to hold information in software development. The concept of the Collection data structure has existed before Apex in other programming languages. A Collection is a group of the same type of object. For example, it could contain zero or more Accounts, or it could instead contain zero of more Opportunities. It would not, however, contain a mix of Account and Opportunity records. Actually, in Apex it is possible to do some mixing, but that discussion is outside the domain of this book. For now, think of Collections in Visual Workflow as being pure. No mixing of different types of objects is allowed.

To further illustrate the general idea of what a collection conceptually looks like imagine a series of boxes filled with the same type of items. We are not talking about Salesforce objects or variables right now. Just what a real-life collection would be. Let's say you are a stamp collector. You would like a way to organize your stamps so instead of just putting them in a pile you decide to have each one in a box so you can clearly see the individual stamp and what it looks like in detail. At this point you have five stamps and you want to display them in a row for all to see. Once you set them out in a row, you realize that maybe you want to order

© Jonathan Keel 2016
J. Keel, *Salesforce.com Lightning Process Builder and Visual Workflow*, DOI 10.1007/978-1-4842-1691-0_5

them in some way instead of in a random order like they currently are. How will you order them? Will it be by the year they were in circulation? Will it be by their value? This is something to be aware of and to decide on if you don't like the idea of them just being randomly ordered in their boxes. You decide to leave them in their boxes and just shift them around so that the oldest is the first (or the far left as seen in Figure 5-1) and the newest is the last (to the far right). Now you have an ordered collection.

Figure 5-1. *A collection is conceptually an ordered or unordered group of items such as this example of a collection of stamps*

This description of a collection of stamps, believe it or not, is a nice way to imagine the concept of a collection in a Flow. In a Flow there are two types of collections:

- Collection Variable: A type of collection that contains Variables all of the same type such as Text, Number, Currency, Date, DateTime, Boolean, Picklist, or Picklist (Multi-Select).

- SObject Collection Variable: A type of collection that contains SObject Variables that are all of the same type of Standard or Custom object.

No matter which type of collection you are dealing with, the concept is the same. The collection can have zero to many items in it. It may be strange thinking of a collection with zero items in it, but this is called an empty collection. With the collection of stamps, if you had not yet pulled that first stamp into your collection it does not mean that the intent to fill it is not there. You may have the stamps elsewhere and just have not pulled them together. The same occurs in a Flow. The values may exist in Salesforce already and they just have not yet been pulled together into the collection.

Another interesting concept to go over is that items can belong to multiple collections simultaneously in a Flow. Technically, there could be an SObject Collection of Accounts that contains all Accounts. Then there could be another SObject Collection of Accounts that only contains Accounts located in the United States. It is possible that the US collection could be a subset of what is contained in the All Accounts collection. It is also possible that these two collections are identical if there are no Accounts in other countries besides the United States.

Collections are just a way to group and order items. In a Flow, collections are used to group and order variables and SObject variables! They are a very flexible and an invaluable tool to use when dealing with data in a Flow.

Riding on the Loop

Usually the best way to understand a concept is to just get your hands dirty and put it into practice. Let's build a Flow that has a loop element in it so we can see how collections and loops work. That approach solidifies the visual concept in one's head and fills in the gaps from the interpretation we get from just words on a page. It takes things from theoretical to practical. With that, let's get to it!

The following example will now show the concept of doing a lookup and an update. Specifically, we will be implementing the flow with the Fast Lookup and Fast Update elements along with the Loop element to put together a simple example of iterating (or looping) over a collection. When we get to the point of introducing the Fast Lookup and Fast Update elements we will dive into more details about them, but at this point we will be using them basically to retrieve or look up records from Salesforce. After retrieving the records with the Fast Lookup they will be stored in a collection. A Loop element will be utilized to go over each item in the collection to make some updates to the items. Then, once all the items are iterated over and the loop is complete we are going to use the Fast Update to put all the changes back into Salesforce so that anyone else using Salesforce can see the changes made.

Looping Story and Requirements

To be consistent with our methodology let's start with the business case for why this Flow needs to be developed in the first place. As the Salesforce administrator you find yourself in yet another meeting about some issues noticed by the sales team. While looking through reports several sales reps have noticed that many accounts have billing address information but not shipping address fields filled out. In these cases the billing addresses have been used, but known issues have arisen where the shipping address needs to be different. Instead of correcting this retroactively, the team decides during the meeting that they want a process put together to proactively correct the issues. The idea decided on during the meeting is for Salesforce to present them with all the accounts for a specific city and state combination and one of the sales reps can go through each account and correct the shipping address.

As the Salesforce administrator you are tasked with following up with the leads from the sales team to gather detailed requirements. Several meetings are scheduled with the appropriate personnel and the following requirements are documented:

- Req 01: The system should allow a sales rep to search for his or her territory by searching on a city/state combination

- Req 02: The system should find accounts that match the criteria of the city/state

- Req 03: The system should present each account to the sales rep on one page that includes all the billing address information on file plus the phone number so that the sales rep can call and gather the shipping Address information.

- Req 04: The system should have fields on the same page as the Account Billing Address/Phone Number page to enter in the shipping address information, including the street, city, postal code/zip

- Req 05: The system should allow sales reps to update the shipping address information and go on to the next account that the system found from their city/state search

- Req 06: After each Account Shipping Address is updated, the account should be queued up to update all the accounts before the process ends

- Req 07: If during the research to find the shipping address it is discovered that the billing address information needs to be updated, then the system should allow the sales rep to update the billing address as well.

Notice the last requirement regarding the billing address. Sometimes unexpected requirements come up during discussions that end up being great ideas. This is one of them. During all the research and updating for the shipping address it would be a shame if the billing address was also incorrect but the system would not provide a way to update it as well. So this extra requirement was added during the discussions and might actually be a blessing during the implementation of the Flow.

Designing the Loop

Next up in our process is taking these requirements and creating a design to work from. Again, Flow Designer does make it so easy to sketch out a Flow quickly. While this is great, my recommendation is to only skip the design step if you need to prototype a concept quickly. In the case of needing to implement a production worthy Flow, it is best to create a design first because several drafts will be worked through probably before a final design is settled on in real life. Once that design is finalized, taking it as a blueprint and creating the Flow in Flow Designer is going to be a very easy task.

If we look at the requirements we can see the steps needed. According to Req 01 a sales rep starts the process and should have a screen to search for accounts by a city and state. The system should then search in Salesforce for accounts that are missing shipping address information in the city and state searched on. At this point the system should loop through each account and present one screen at a time to the sales rep so that he or she may update the address information. Before the system goes to the next account, though, it should update the account with the address information entered.

Putting these steps into a flow chart should look something like Figure 5-2. It is a lot easier to comprehend and see the process visually instead of looking just at a bulleted list of requirements. In the diagram all the steps are laid out from the starting point through the different screens and steps. Notice this diagram has the loop in it. The loop is the part that asks the question, "Next Account?" In other words, "Is there another account in the collection? This question starts the loop. If there is another account, then we have some steps to follow. Almost like a mini-flow. If there are no more accounts in the collection, then the diagram continues as though the loop never happened. In this diagram it goes to the final screen.

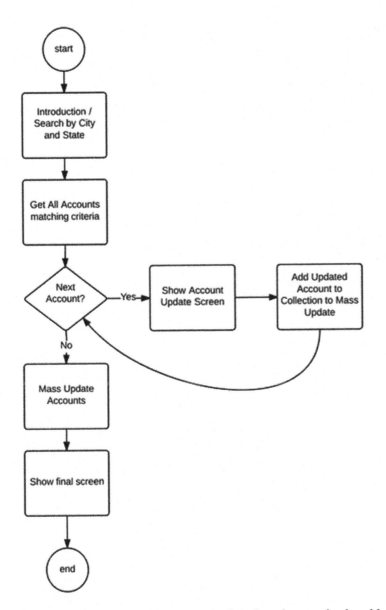

Figure 5-2. *The design of the system as a flow chart that was developed from the requirements.*

Most of the complexity for this flow is going to be in the loop. Every time that question of "Next Account?" is answered with a "Yes," then the next steps of showing an update screen for that account's address fields and then the step of updating the records in Salesforce will occur. Again, the reason for diagramming this out on paper or digitally is because it is far easier to move a bunch of boxes and lines around than it is to configure elements if the flow is half baked. We need our understanding of what's needed to be set in stone, so that following the blueprint for creating the flow in Flow Designer will be an easy task.

Implementing the Loop

At this point, we are all set. Start in the way we have so far by creating a new Flow in Flow Designer. Save it with a name such as "Shipping Address Updates" before continuing so that we can easily save periodically once we've started implementing this flow.

According to the design, the flow should start with an introduction screen that allows a search to be performed to allow users to search by city and state. Create a new Screen element with the following configuration settings under the General Info tab:

- **Name:** Introduction

- **Unique Name:** Introduction_Screen

Next add a Display Text field into the screen with the following configuration settings:

- **Unique Name:** Introduction_Text

- **Text Area:** Find accounts that lack all the necessary shipping address info by searching by city and state.

To have a field to search by city add a Text box field into the screen with the following configuration settings:

- **Label:** City

- **Unique Name:** City_Textbox

- **Required:** checked

To have a field to search by state add another Text box field into the screen with the following configuration settings:

- **Label:** State

- **Unique Name:** State_Textbox

- **Required:** checked

After configuring the Picklist Choice and clicking "OK," Field Settings should look like Figure 5-3:

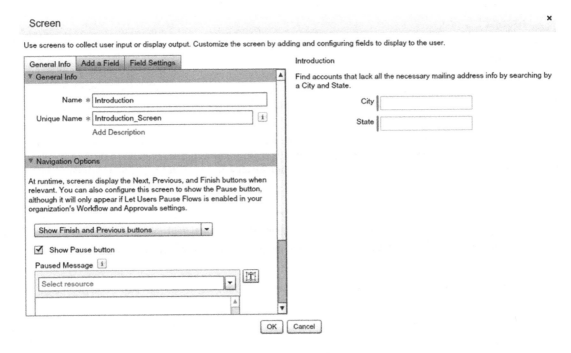

Figure 5-3. The configuration window for the Introduction screen

Click "OK" to be taken back to the Canvas. You should see your first element just created there. Go ahead and make it the start element and save the flow before continuing on to the rest of the implementation. A quick look at the design created previously shows that so far this flow is in line with it. The start element of the flow is the introduction screen where a user can search by city and state. Perfect!

Data Lookups

Looking at the next item in the design we see "Get All Accounts matching criteria." Up to this point when creating flows we have not pulled data from Salesforce. We've been working with user entry data and showing the information captured back to the user without retrieving previously saved data from Salesforce. So how does one pull data from Salesforce? In the Palette there is a Data section. Within that section there are two items. One is "Record Lookup" and the other is "Fast Lookup". Before deciding which lookup is the most appropriate let's dive into the details of each type of lookup to get a better understanding.

Record Lookup

First let's look at the standard "Record Lookup" element. If you click on the element in the Palette there is a description that shows at the bottom. We can see the description for the Record Lookup in Figure 5-4.

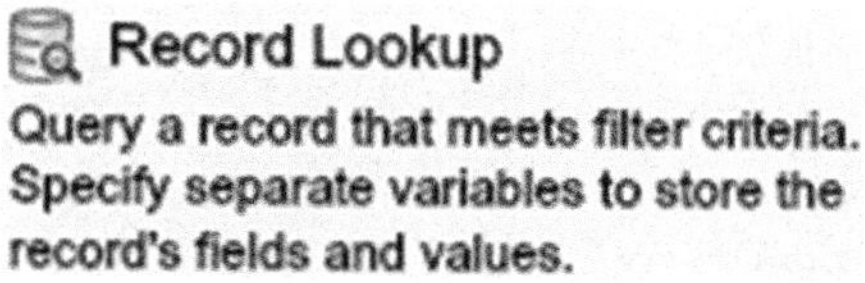

■ Record Lookup
Query a record that meets filter criteria.
Specify separate variables to store the
record's fields and values.

Figure 5-4. *The description of that Record Lookup element that shows in Flow Designer*

Please note the second sentence in that description. It says that separate variables are used to store the record's fields and values. What this means is that when using this type of lookup, you will need to have each field in the returned lookup to be stored individually to hold each value in the return from the lookup criteria against Salesforce.

■ **Note**   There is an option in a Record Lookup to hold each of the returned field values from the lookup into different fields in a single SObject variable rather than having multiple variables to hold the data.

To further illustrate how you must store the returned values from the Record Lookup element please refer to Figure 5-5.

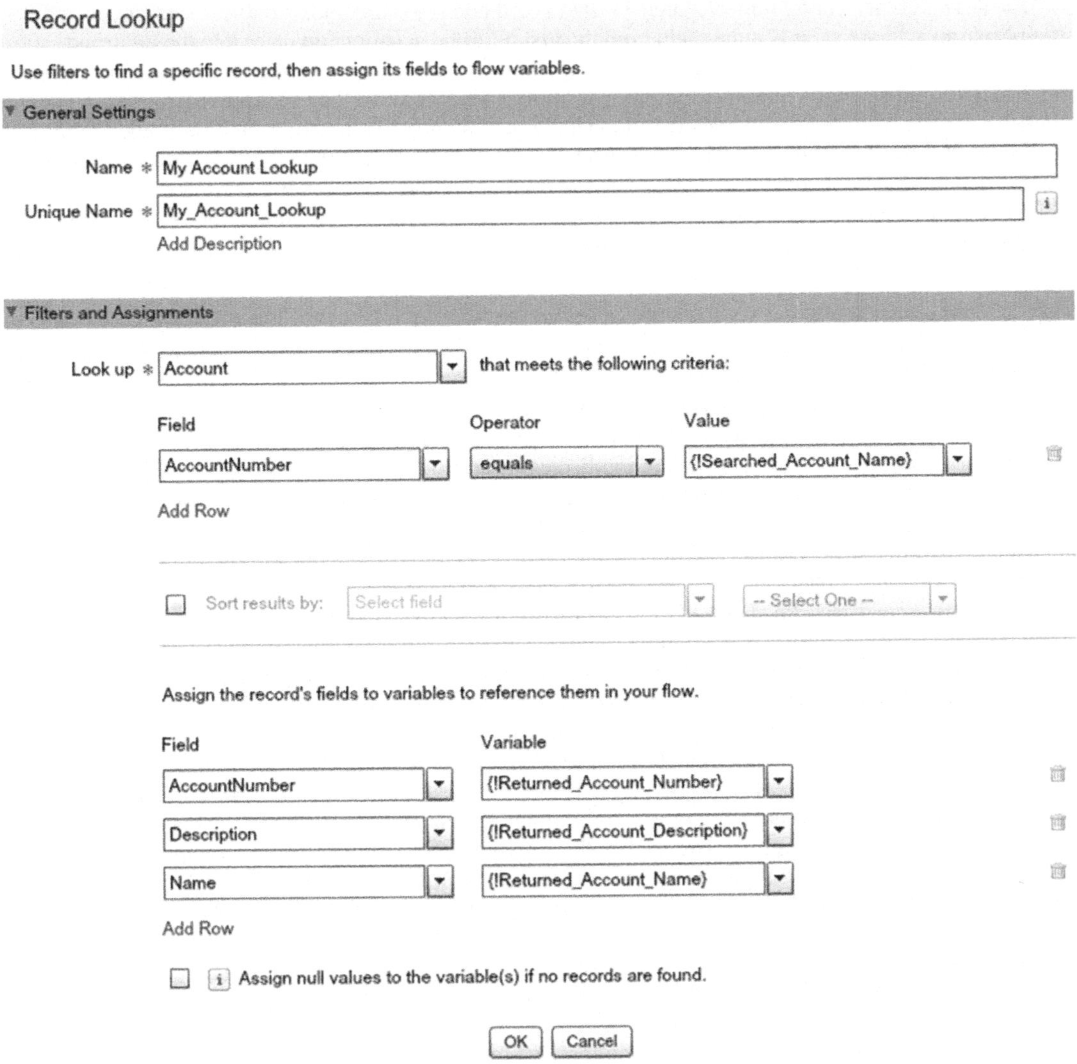

Record Lookup

Use filters to find a specific record, then assign its fields to flow variables.

▼ General Settings

Name ∗ | My Account Lookup

Unique Name ∗ | My_Account_Lookup | [i]

Add Description

▼ Filters and Assignments

Look up ∗ | Account ▼ | that meets the following criteria:

Field	Operator	Value	
AccountNumber ▼	equals ▼	{!Searched_Account_Name} ▼	🗑

Add Row

☐ Sort results by: | Select field ▼ | -- Select One -- ▼ |

Assign the record's fields to variables to reference them in your flow.

Field	Variable	
AccountNumber ▼	{!Returned_Account_Number} ▼	🗑
Description ▼	{!Returned_Account_Description} ▼	🗑
Name ▼	{!Returned_Account_Name} ▼	🗑

Add Row

☐ [i] Assign null values to the variable(s) if no records are found.

[OK] [Cancel]

Figure 5-5. *An example of the Record Lookup element configuration window*

In this example the Record Lookup is configured to find an Account with a matching account name that is stored in the "Searched_Account_Name" variable. Notice that I said "an Account." That's the big thing to note about the Record Lookup element. If multiple accounts are matched with the criteria you specify, then only the first account is returned. Then how do you know you have the right account? In this example, the criteria are matching by account name. Chances are you will find the correct account, but it isn't guaranteed, especially if you were matching on other criteria like city and state.

■ **Note**   It is very important to check the "Sort results by" check box and specify how to sort them so that the first result is the one you are interested in.

The last part of the configuration screen for the Record Lookup is for field/variable assignments. In the example we take the Account Number field from the first returned account and place it in the Returned_Account_Number variable. The Description value is placed into the Returned_Account_Description variable and the Name value is placed into the Returned_Account_Name variable. If these three variables had previous values in them they would be overridden if the account record returned had values pulled from Salesforce. If for some reason the values pulled from Salesforce were empty then there would be no values to override the variables with. Below the field/value assignment section is a check box that states "Assign null values to the variable(s) if no records are found." If checked, and no records are found, then any variables will be overridden with null.

Fast Lookup

While using the Record Lookup element makes it easy to pull out only one single record from Salesforce, our design requires that we pull multiple records from Salesforce. We need a collection! This is where the Fast Lookup element comes in. Unlike its counterpart, the Record Lookup, it does not just pull one record at a time. The Fast Lookup allows a flow to pull multiple records at a time, into a collection!

Under the "DATA" section in the Palette, you will find the Fast Lookup element. It is very similar to the Record Lookup. In the configuration screen you will see a way to filter criteria by the type of object (the "Lookup" field) and its field's values, although what is different is that there is the option to store multiple records into an SObject Collection. You still have to specify which fields are to be saved, but this time they are saved into the corresponding fields of each instance of the SObject in the collection.

In Figure 5-6 we can see the configuration screen for an example Fast Lookup element. This one has been configured similarly to the Record Lookup seen previously. This time though it is expected to pull back many records. Those many records need to be saved to an SObject Collection. The first section of the configuration window is General Settings. It is the standard element section where the Name and Unique Name are defined so that this element can be distinguished uniquely from other elements in the flow.

The second and most important section is the Filters and Assignments section. This section can further be broken up into three main parts: filtering, sorting, assigning. First is filtering where the Lookup field and the list of criteria can be defined. The Lookup field is where we define what type of standard or custom object we are performing the lookup on. The list of criteria is a combination of that lookup object's field name, an operator for comparing, and the value to compare against. Multiple rows of criteria can be added using the "Add Row" link below them. To the right of each row is a trashcan icon. Clicking the trashcan icon will remove the row from the list of criteria. The criteria list can be thought of as the list of criteria when developing a report. You can search with one field being equal to a value and also have a second field as being less than or greater than another value.

The second section is for sorting. This is optional though. The results returned from the lookup will be random if you do not check this option. Once it is checked, though, you must select a field from the drop-down to sort by. You must also choose what direction to sort the results. They can be ascending or descending—which means that they can be sorted so that the values at the beginning of the results start at the lowest value and increase as they continue or the other way around.

The last part is for assigning the objects and fields. The Variable field is for defining which SObject Variable or SObject Collection Variable should be used to store the results from the lookup. There is an optional check box to assign null to the variable in the event that no results are returned from the lookup. The last section is a list of rows for selecting which fields should be assigned to the variable returned. If a field from an SObject Variable or an SObject Collection Variable is going to be used in the flow elsewhere, then it is required to be in this list. Otherwise an error will occur if the flow tries to access that field.

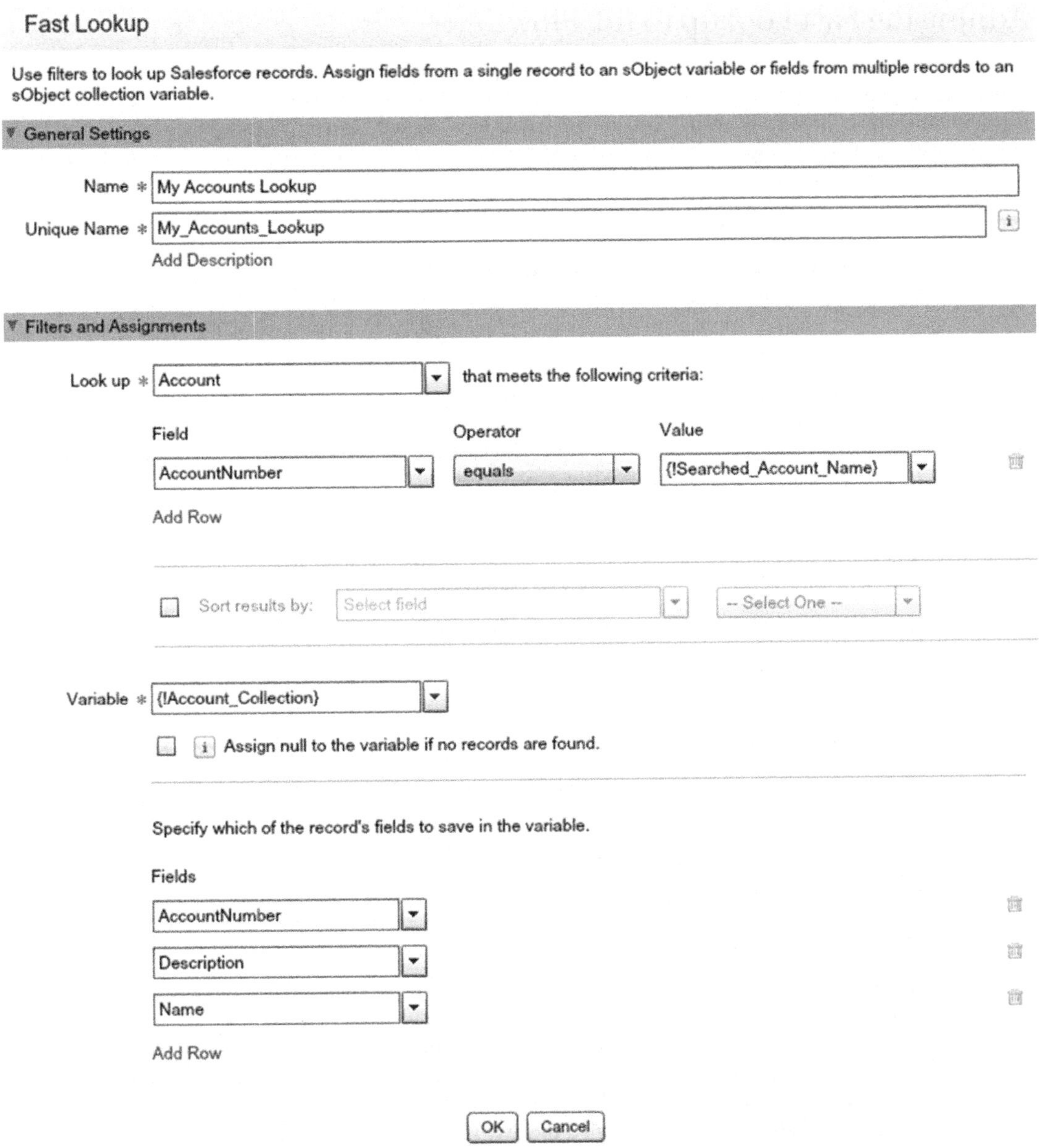

Fast Lookup

Use filters to look up Salesforce records. Assign fields from a single record to an sObject variable or fields from multiple records to an sObject collection variable.

▼ General Settings

Name ✴ | My Accounts Lookup |

Unique Name ✴ | My_Accounts_Lookup | [i]

Add Description

▼ Filters and Assignments

Look up ✴ | Account | ▼ | that meets the following criteria:

Field	Operator	Value
AccountNumber ▼	equals ▼	{!Searched_Account_Name} ▼	🗑

Add Row

☐ Sort results by: | Select field | ▼ | -- Select One -- | ▼ |

Variable ✴ | {!Account_Collection} | ▼

☐ [i] Assign null to the variable if no records are found.

Specify which of the record's fields to save in the variable.

Fields

AccountNumber ▼	🗑
Description ▼	🗑
Name ▼	🗑

Add Row

[OK] [Cancel]

Figure 5-6. *An example of the Fast Lookup configuration window*

Adding the Fast Lookup to the Flow

We have dived into a lot of details on the two different types of lookups, but it was necessary to know which element would be the best one to use for the design. So let's start where we left off. The flow has the Introduction screen already. Now the Fast Lookup needs to be added. So let's go about the same process and drag over the Fast Lookup element to the Canvas just under the Introduction screen. Use the following configuration settings for it:

- **Name:** Account Lookup By City and State

- **Unique Name:** Account_Lookup_By_City_and_State

- **Lookup:** Account

- **Lookup Criteria:**

    - **Field:** BillingCity equals {!City_Textbox}

    - **Field:** BillingState equals {!State_Textbox}

- **Sort results by:** Name (Descending)

Now the next configuration setting, "Variable," is the variable to store the record(s) that are returned from the Fast Lookup. Since we are expecting zero or more records, we need an SObject Collection Variable. We do not have an SObject Collection Variable yet so follow these steps to create one:

- Expand the Variable drop-down list by clicking the expand icon (upside down triangle)

- In the drop-down menu choose "CREATE NEW"

- Select "SObject Collection Variable"

The configuration screen for the SObject Collection Variable will appear. Use the following settings to configure it:

- **Unique Name:** Account_Collection

- **Input/Output Type:** Private

- **Object Type:** Account

The "Unique Name" is of course just the name to reference this in the flow. It's the same as other elements, variables, and so on, created in flows. The "Input/Output Type" is the scope of the life of this variable. The option "Private" was selected because this collection is only going to be used within the flow. If we needed to pass information into the flow so that it could be accessed immediately from the start element, we would have selected "Input Only" or "Input and Output." If we wanted the collection to be pass out of the flow to be used after the flow had ended then we would have chosen "Output Only" or "Input and Output." We are instead pulling data from Salesforce to put into this SObject collection variable just during the lifetime of this flow so that we can make updates and save the data back to Salesforce. Once the flow has ended, there will be no need to keep the actual SObject collection variable around since the data will be saved eventually into Salesforce.

Finally, there is the Object Type. Account was chosen because per the requirements and design, the flow needs to retrieve all the accounts that lack shipping address information. It is good to note, however, that even though Account is a standard object, we can also choose custom objects. SObject collection variables are very flexible tools to get the job done when you need to work with multiple records of information. Notice that you can choose only one object type at a time. An SObject collection variable cannot be comprised of, let's say, Accounts and Opportunities. That would break the concept of what a collection is in the first place.

After typing all the settings into the SObject Collection Variable configuration screen, it should look like Figure 5-7. Go ahead and click "OK" to go back to the Fast Lookup configuration screen.

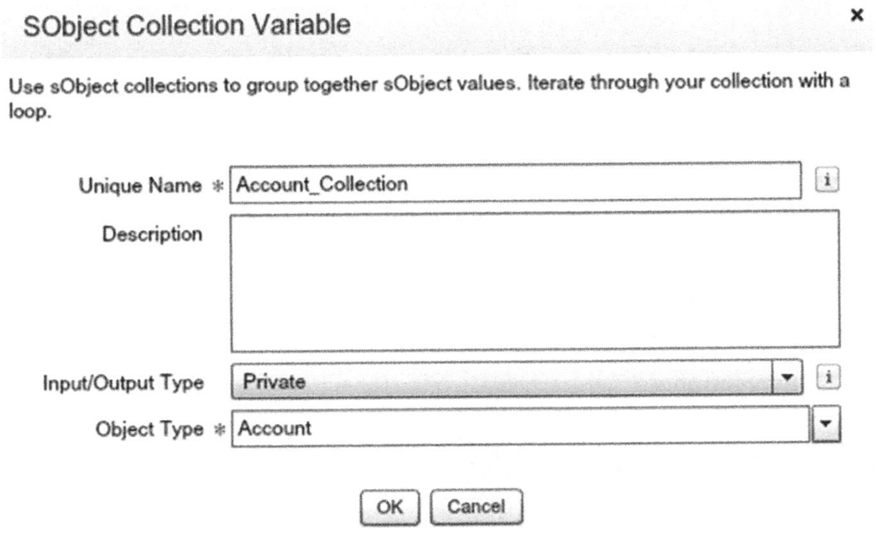

Figure 5-7. *The configuration window for the SObject Collection Variable*

Once we are back to the configuration screen for the Fast Lookup there is one last section to complete. This section is where we tell the Fast Lookup which fields are to have their values pulled for storage in the collection. It has a drop-down to add a field to the list. The drop-down allows you to pick from either a standard field or a custom field. Under the drop-down is a link titled "Add Row," which allows you to add a new field to be retrieved for accessing later. To the right is a trashcan icon. Clicking the icon allows the removal of the field on this configuration screen so that you do not retrieve it from Salesforce.

> ■ **Note** Just as in other aspects of Salesforce such as SOQL (Salesforce Object Query Language) or reports, you must be explicit about which fields need their values retrieved in a lookup. If you try accessing a field not retrieved later in a flow an error will occur.

It does not matter what order the fields are retrieved in because there is no way to reorder them in the list.

For our requirements, let's configure the Fast Lookup to pull the following fields as seen in Figure 5-8. Also, note the location of the link/icons to add or remove rows in this list:

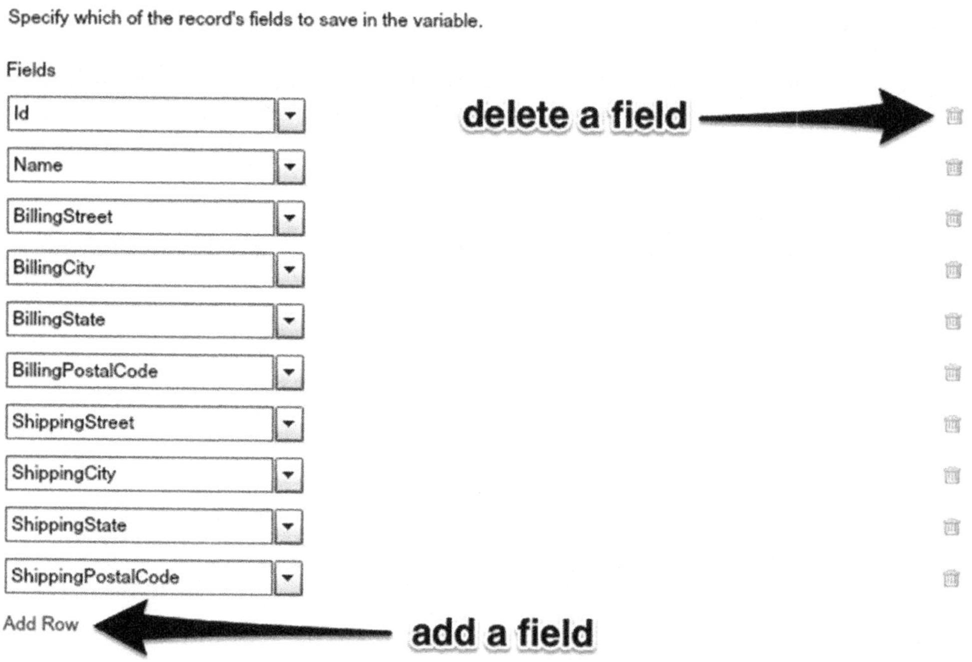

Figure 5-8. Field assignment section of the Fast Lookup configuration screen

Once you have all the fields set up, go ahead and click "OK." You will be taken back to the Canvas where you can connect the Introduction screen to the Fast Lookup just created. Please save the flow so you do not lose any time. At this point, the flow should look like Figure 5-9.

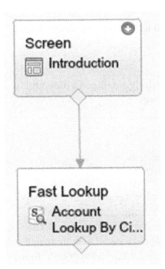

Figure 5-9. The flow with the Introduction screen and Fast Lookup element

Account Loop

The next big chunk of work will be getting the loop set up to iterate over the collection of account records. In the Logic section of the Palette there is the Loop element. Drag and drop the Loop element onto the Canvas to begin configuring the next part of the design. The design requires that each account record that is found needs to have a screen presented to the user for it in which the user can update the address information. Mainly the goal is to update the shipping address, but it was also a requirement to allow for the update of the billing address. If, during the course of research, you find that the billing address also needs to be updated, you can do so at the same time.

When the Loop element is added to the Canvas the configuration screen appears. Go ahead and set up the "General Settings" section as follows:

- **Name:** Account Loop

- **Unique Name:** Account Loop

Next comes the "Assignments" section. This section is the main configuration section of a loop. The first field, Loop through, is where we enter in the unique name of the collection to iterate over. You are only allowed to loop through one collection at a time. The next field that is a picklist is for the order in which to loop through. We'll call this the Order field and the options available are "Ascending" and "Descending." While this terminology sounds a bit vague for how to determine which way to loop through the collection, it basically determines if the loop is forward or backward. Ascending is forward or starting from the beginning of the collection and going through each item in the collection to perform some step we will configure later until it gets to the end. Descending is backward or starting from the end of the collection and going through each item in the collection to perform some step we will configure until it gets to the beginning. Usually loops are done start to end or Ascending! Rarely do you see loops going backward or Descending through a collection. It just depends on the requirements and how the collection was sorted prior to being used by the Loop element.

■ **Note**   It is important to have a collection sorted prior to being used in loop so that looping either ascending or descending will give the expected result.

Understanding how the Loop through and Order fields work now we can configure them to meet the design expectations. Set up the two fields with the following configuration settings:

- **Loop through:** {!Account_Collection}

- **Order:** Ascending

Of course, while looping through each item in the collection how does the flow know what the current item is that is being looked at in the loop? In this case the loop is iterating over an SObject Collection Variable made up of accounts. To know which account is the current Account being iterated over the Loop element allows you to put it in an SObject Variable so that you can access it by a unique name in the rest of the flow. Since the flow is going to execute and possibly loop through hundreds of accounts it would be difficult to try to keep track of which account we are working with at the time unless we had a name to call that current account. If we had to say, "Now use the first account," then "now use the second account," then "now use the third account," and so on, it would get really messy. Some actual programming languages work this way. They require developers to keep track of which number they are on when looping through a collection. The way that Salesforce has implemented Loops in Visual Workflow is way more efficient and readable. Loops simply step through each element. In a way, it's like a queue at a government office and the person at the counter is simply saying "next . . . next . . . next. . . . ." We don't need to track what number we are on in the collection. The loop simply says "next" and the next one that comes up is the new current Account. The previous account that used to be current is now just tossed to the side. It doesn't matter anymore. We only care about the current one. This current one is what is called the "Loop Variable."

The Loop Variable is the last configuration setting we need to set up for this loop. It requires an SObject Variable since our loop is working with SObject Collection Variables. If our loop were instead iterating over a normal Collection Variable, then this Loop Variable would need to be of the type Variable and not SObject Variable. Flow Designer will make sure you don't choose the wrong type though. Depending on what type of collection is in the Loop through field, you will only be presented with the compatible type for the Loop Variable.

At this point, though, we have not created an SObject Variable that we can use in this setting, but like all the other settings in Flow Designer, you can create them on demand. In the Loop Variable drop-down menu choose Create New and then SObject Variable. Use the following settings for it:

- **Unique Name:** Current_Account

- **Input/Output Type:** Private

- **Object Type:** Account

Click "OK" to be returned back to the Loop configuration screen. You should see the setting updated to "{!Current_Account}." Excellent! At this point the Loop configuration screen should look like Figure 5-10. If all looks good, then click "OK" to accept these settings and return to the Canvas.

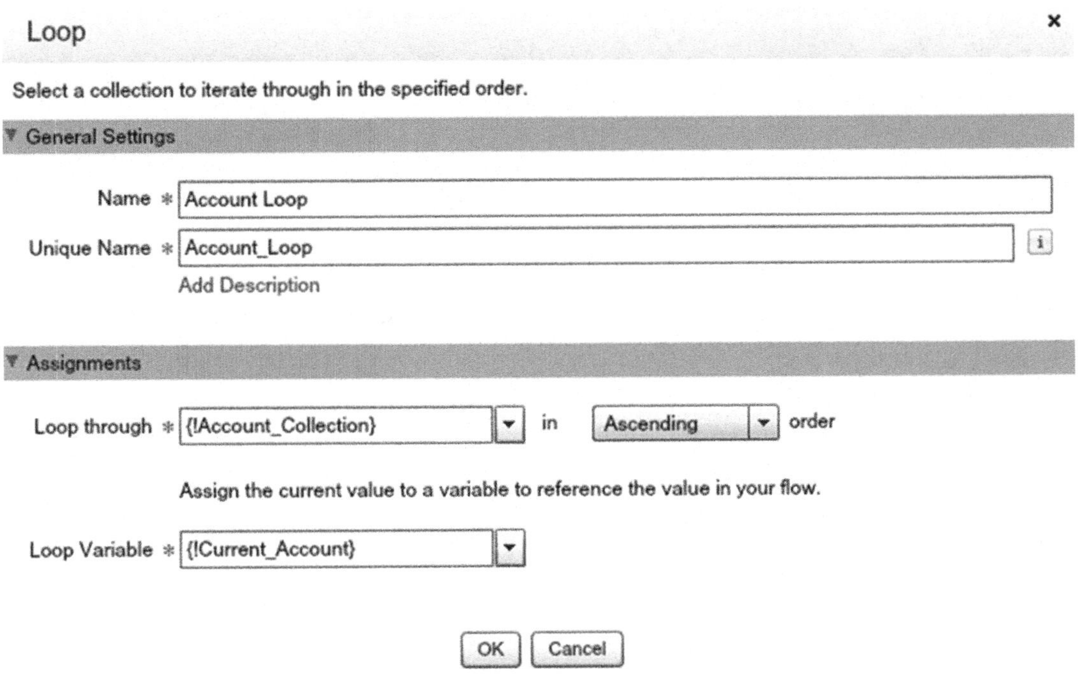

Loop

×

Select a collection to iterate through in the specified order.

▼ General Settings

Name ∗ | Account Loop |

Unique Name ∗ | Account_Loop | [i]

Add Description

▼ Assignments

Loop through ∗ | {!Account_Collection} | [▼] in | Ascending | [▼] order

Assign the current value to a variable to reference the value in your flow.

Loop Variable ∗ | {!Current_Account} | [▼]

[OK] [Cancel]

Figure 5-10. *The configuration window for the Loop element*

Connect the Fast Lookup element to the newly created Loop element and then click Save to make sure you don't lose ground on everything done so far. Depending on how you have the elements arranged on the Canvas, the flow should currently look something like Figure 5-11.

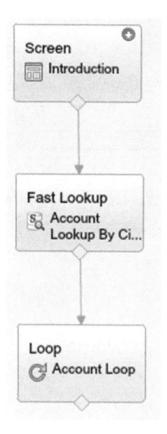

Figure 5-11. *The flow with the Loop element added*

Defining the Body

Using the Loop element we have defined what collection to iterate over, what direction to iterate, and the variable to access each item in the collection for the loop. So now that all that is set up we need to actually define what happens with the current item in an iteration of the loop. This part we will call the "Loop body." The Loop body can almost be thought of as a mini-flow within this flow. During an iteration of the loop, the flow will branch out and perform another set of steps. Once each item in the collection has gone through the Loop body, normal execution of the flow will continue.

Looking at Figure 5-12, the design for this process calls for an update screen to be presented each time there is a next account in the collection. Once data is updated on this screen and the user moves on, the account needs to be added to the collection to do a mass update at the end of the flow. To get this working in our flow we need to create the update screen. This screen is just a normal screen with input fields like we have created in the past.

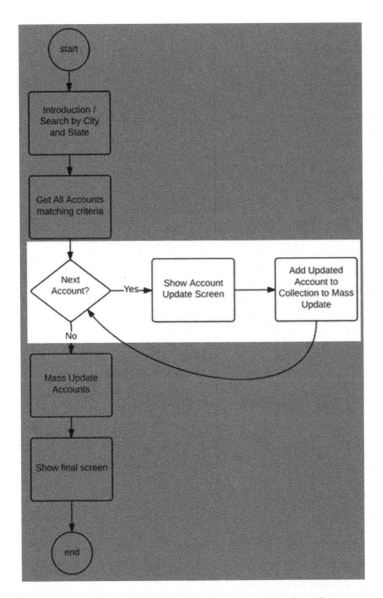

Figure 5-12. *The loop highlighted in the original flow chart design*

To create the Account update screen, place a Screen element on the Canvas to the right of the Loop element. Set up the screen configure screen with the following settings:

- **Name:** Account Details
- **Unique Name:** Account_Details

Next, add a Display field with the following settings:

- **Unique Name:** See_Next_Record_Text

- **Text:** Account Details for {!Current_Account.Name}

- **Account Name:** {!Current_Account.Name}

Now we need to add all the fields that can be updated to the screen to allow for the user to modify their values. Following is the list of Text boxes to add and their settings:

- **Billing Street**

  - **Label:** Billing Street

  - **Unique Name:** Billing_Street

  - **Default Value:** {!Current_Account.BillingStreet}

- **Billing City**

  - **Label:** Billing City

  - **Unique Name:** Billing_City

  - **Default Value:** {!Current_Account.BillingCity}

- **Billing State**

  - **Label:** Billing State

  - **Unique Name:** Billing_State

  - **Default Value:** {!Current_Account.BillingState}

- **Billing Zip**

  - **Label:** Billing Zip

  - **Unique Name:** Billing_Zip

  - **Default Value:** {!Current_Account.BillingPostalCode}

- **Shipping Street**

  - **Label:** Shipping Street

  - **Unique Name:** Shipping_Street

  - **Default Value:** {!Current_Account.ShippingStreet}

- **Shipping City**

  - **Label:** Shipping City

  - **Unique Name:** Shipping_City

  - **Default Value:** {!Current_Account.ShippingCity}

- **Shipping State**

    - **Label:** Shipping State

    - **Unique Name:** Shipping_State

    - **Default Value:** {!Current_Account.ShippingState}

- **Shipping Zip**

    - **Label:** Shipping Zip

    - **Unique Name:** Shipping_Zip

    - **Default Value:** {!Current_Account.ShippingPostalCode}

Phew! Now that all those input fields are added the configuration screen should look like Figure 5-13. Go ahead and click "OK" to accept all these changes.

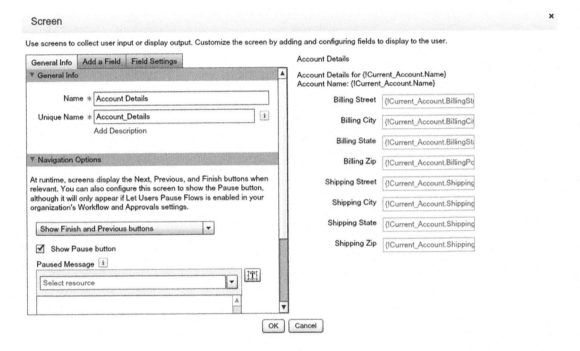

Figure 5-13. *The configuration window for the Account Details screen*

Once back on the Canvas, connect the Account Loop element to the Account Details screen element like normal, although this time when connecting an additional screen pops up with the following two options:

- for each value in the collection

- when there are no more values to process

The first option is used to connect the Loop to the Loop body. The second option is to connect the Loop to the next element when the loop is finished. You may be thinking, "What happens when the collection is empty? Does an error occur?" The answer is that you don't have to worry about that scenario unless there are some special requirements for when there are just no records to begin with. Luckily the Loop element in a flow is gracious and simple in how it handles iterating over a loop. It is simply seeing if there is another item in the collection and getting it to process. If there is not another element, whether because it reached the end or there just were never any elements in the collection to begin with, then the loop ends and follows the "when there are no more values to process" path.

Since we are just starting the loop at this point with the update screen, select "for each value in the collation" and click "OK". Figure 5-14 shows the selection to make for this connection.

Loop Routing ✕

Go to this element | for each value in the collection ▼

OK Cancel

Figure 5-14. *The Loop Routing pop-up window*

What you see on the Canvas now should resemble Figure 5-15. The arrow connecting the Account Loop element to the Account Details screen element will have a display name of "Next element" on it to distinguish the purpose of this special connection. We are not finished yet though. Having an input screen is fine for capturing user input, but it does not update Salesforce. The design says that we need to do the update before going on to the next Account in the collection.

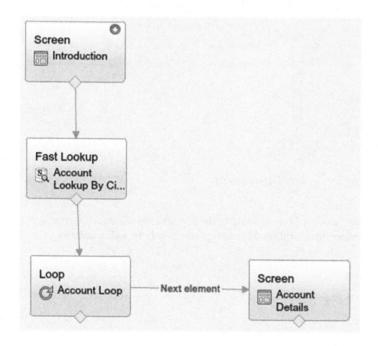

Figure 5-15. *The flow with the Account Details screen added as the next element during the loop*

Assignment

Let's fast-forward a bit to what we are going to need to do. We plan on updating the Account with the Fast Update element, but the way it works is by configuring it to update a single SObject, the current Account in the Loop. However, on the Account Details screen the fields do not update the Account's SObject directly. The Text boxes were initialized to the value of the fields we pulled from the Account. If the user updates those values they are not put right back into the SObject for that Account. They just update the values in the Text boxes. There is no binding or link from the Text box's values to the SObject's field values. To get the updated values from the Text boxes to the SObject we need to use the Assignment element.

We've used the Assignment element before. This time we will use it to copy the Text box values back into the SObject which holds the current iteration's Account data. That way the Fast Update can be used effectively. Add an Assignment element to the Canvas to the right of the Account Details screen. When the configuration window appears, set it up with the following values:

- **General Settings**
    - **Name:** Set Shipping Address Fields
    - **Unique Name:** Set_Shipping_Address_Fields
- **Assignments**
    - {!Current_Account.ShippingStreet} equals {!Shipping_Street}
    - {!Current_Account.ShippingCity} equals {!Shipping_City}
    - {!Current_Account.ShippingState} equals {!Shipping_State}
    - {!Current_Account.ShippingPostalCode} equals {!Shipping_Zip}

Once the configuration screen is set up it will look like Figure 5-16.

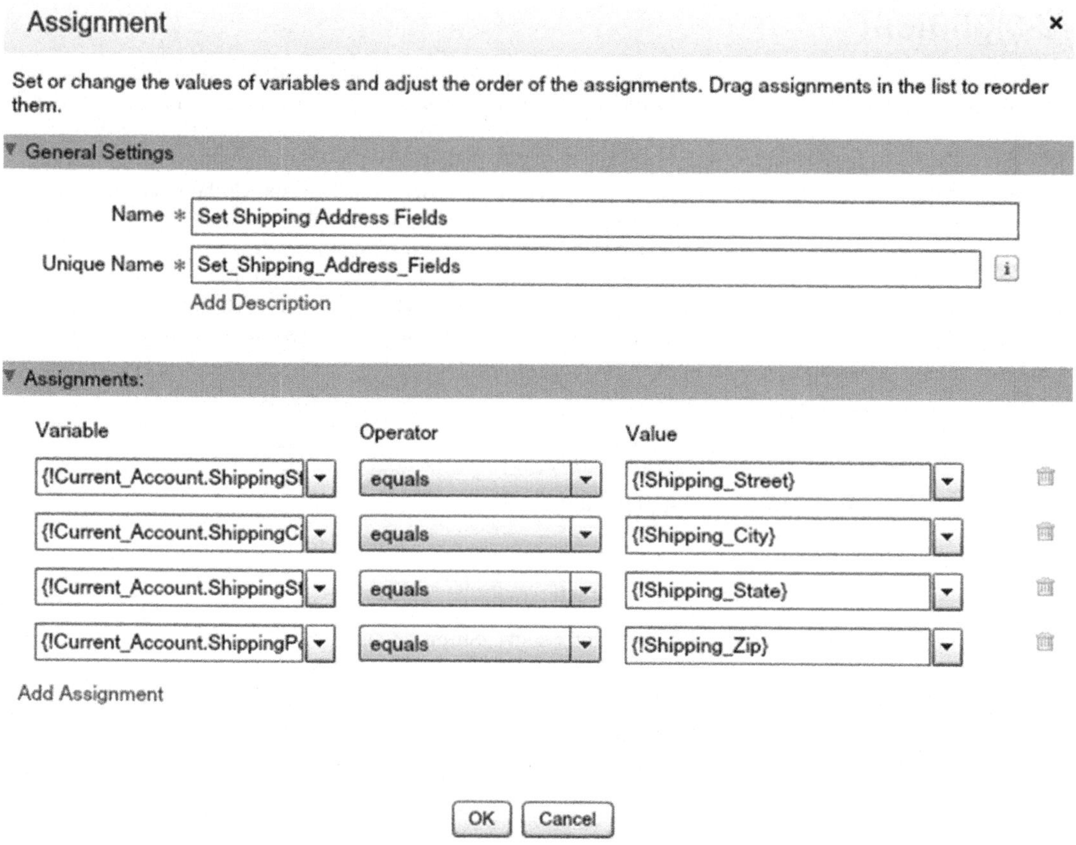

Assignment   ✕

Set or change the values of variables and adjust the order of the assignments. Drag assignments in the list to reorder them.

▼ General Settings

Name ✱ | Set Shipping Address Fields

Unique Name ✱ | Set_Shipping_Address_Fields   [i]

Add Description

▼ Assignments:

Variable	Operator	Value	
{!Current_Account.ShippingS⁞ ▼}	equals ▼	{!Shipping_Street} ▼	🗑
{!Current_Account.ShippingC⁞ ▼}	equals ▼	{!Shipping_City} ▼	🗑
{!Current_Account.ShippingS⁞ ▼}	equals ▼	{!Shipping_State} ▼	🗑
{!Current_Account.ShippingP⁞ ▼}	equals ▼	{!Shipping_Zip} ▼	🗑

Add Assignment

[OK] [Cancel]

Figure 5-16. *The configuration window for the Assignment element*

Click "OK" to accept these the changes and return to the Canvas. Now connect the Account Details screen to the newly created Set Shipping Address Fields Assignment element. Save the flow. It should look similar to Figure 5-17.

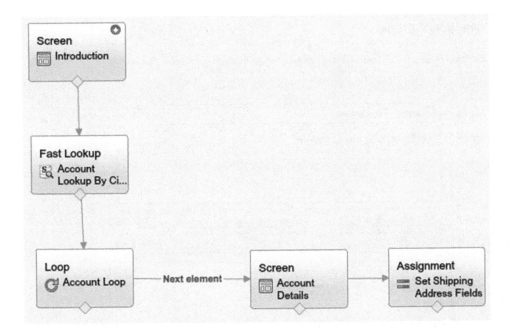

Figure 5-17. *The flow with the Assignment added to the loop after the Account Details screen*

To make this flow efficient we are now going to add the updated SObject variable to a new SObject collection variable. This way we can build a collection that will be updated all at once at the end of the flow. The first step is creating the SObject collection variable. In the Resources tab double-click "SObject Collection Variable" to add it to the flow. When the configuration window appears, set it up with the following values:

- **Unique Name**: Accounts_To_Update
- **Description**: The list of Accounts to update.
- **Input/Output**: Private
- **Object Type**: Account

It should look similar to Figure 5-18. After finishing, click "OK" to accept the changes.

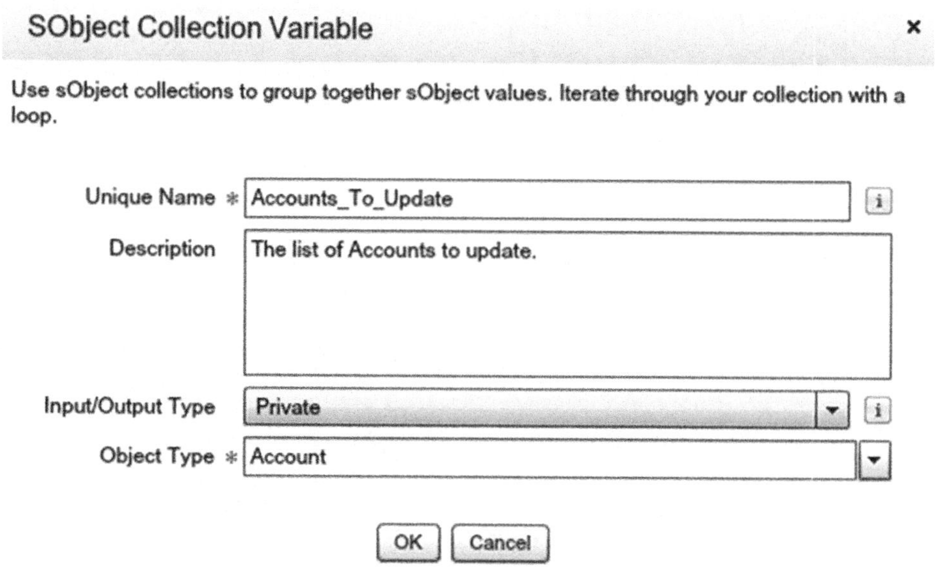

SObject Collection Variable ✕

Use sObject collections to group together sObject values. Iterate through your collection with a loop.

Unique Name *	Accounts_To_Update
Description	The list of Accounts to update.
Input/Output Type	Private
Object Type *	Account

[OK] [Cancel]

Figure 5-18. The configuration window for the SObject Collection Variable

Now drag another Assignment element to the canvas. This one will be for adding the updated "Current_Account" SObject variable to the new "Accounts_To_Update" SObject collection variable we just created. When the configuration window appears enter the following values:

- **General Settings**:
  - **Name**: Add Account To Update List
  - **Unique Name**: Add_Account_To_Update_List

- **Assignments**:
  - **Variable**: {!Accounts_To_Update}
  - **Operator**: add
  - **Value**: {!Current_Account}

It should look similar to Figure 5-19. After finishing, click "OK" to accept the changes.

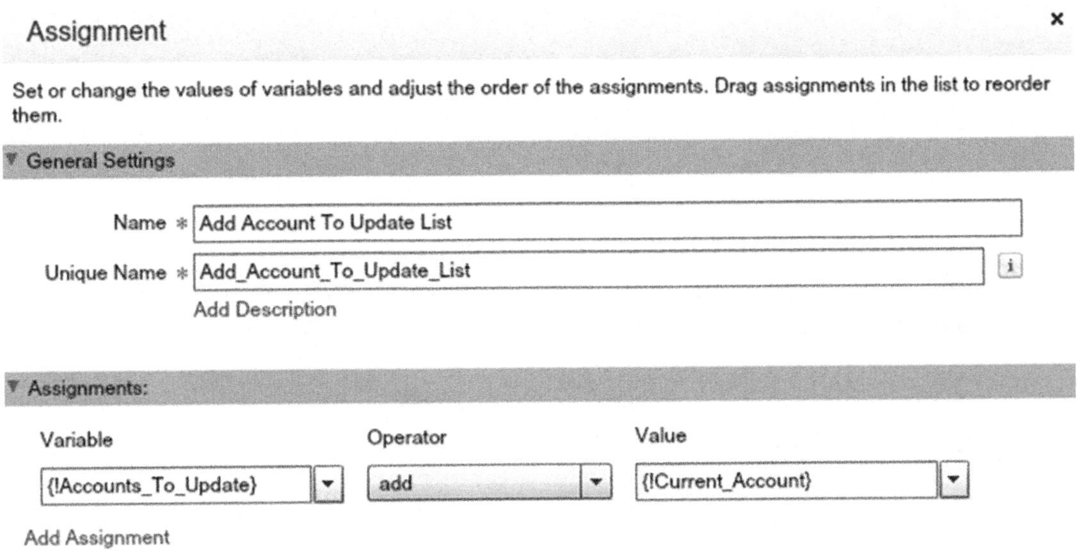

Assignment ✕

Set or change the values of variables and adjust the order of the assignments. Drag assignments in the list to reorder them.

▼ General Settings

Name ✳	Add Account To Update List
Unique Name ✳	Add_Account_To_Update_List	ⓘ

Add Description

▼ Assignments:

Variable	Operator	Value
{!Accounts_To_Update} ▾	add ▾	{!Current_Account} ▾

Add Assignment

Figure 5-19. *The configuration to do an "add" assignment to an SObject Collection Variable*

Once you return to the Canvas, connect the Add Account To Update List Assignment element to the Loop element. This closes our loop. Save the flow. It should look similar to Figure 5-20.

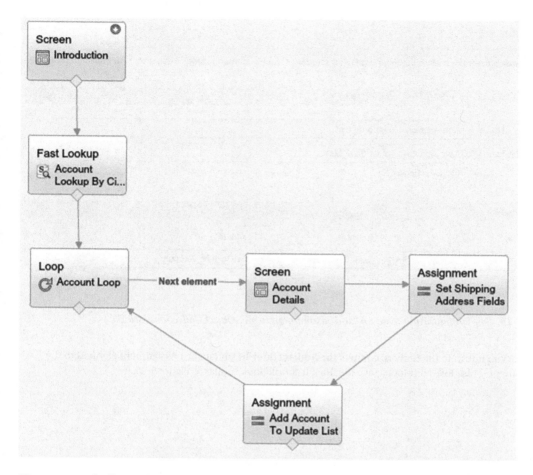

Figure 5-20. *The flow with the Assignment to add to the collection implemented*

When the loop finishes adding the SObject to the SObject collection variable it will check if there are more elements. If there are more, it will loop again. If not, it will need to end. There is an "End of loop" connector that can be attached to an element that comes after the loop is complete and there are no more elements. We want the collection that we were building to be used to update all its records it once. We can look at two options.

Updating Records

The SObject collection variable that is holding all of the accounts is being updated, but only within the flow. It still is not being updated in Salesforce. We need to get this data out of this flow and into Salesforce! The Fast Update was mentioned briefly, but let's go over it in more detail here. Also, we will compare it to its sibling, the "Record Update."

Fast Update

The Fast Update is fast because there is not much to setting it up. The Fast Update element assumes that you have an SObject that has been updated and that the SObject needs only to be saved to the Salesforce database. It's a pretty simple process that only does one thing only, the update! The only requirement is that the SObject or SObject Collection needs to have the ID field for each SObject so Salesforce knows which record to update.

Figure 5-21 shows the configuration screen for the Fast Update element. Notice that it is pretty simple. Besides the standard two fields that you usually see (Name and Unique Name), the only other required field is the Variable field. The Variable field takes either a single SObject Variable or an SObject Collection Variable. As long as that single SObject Variable has the ID field, or all the SObjects in an SObject Collection Variable have an ID field, it can successfully perform the update in Salesforce.

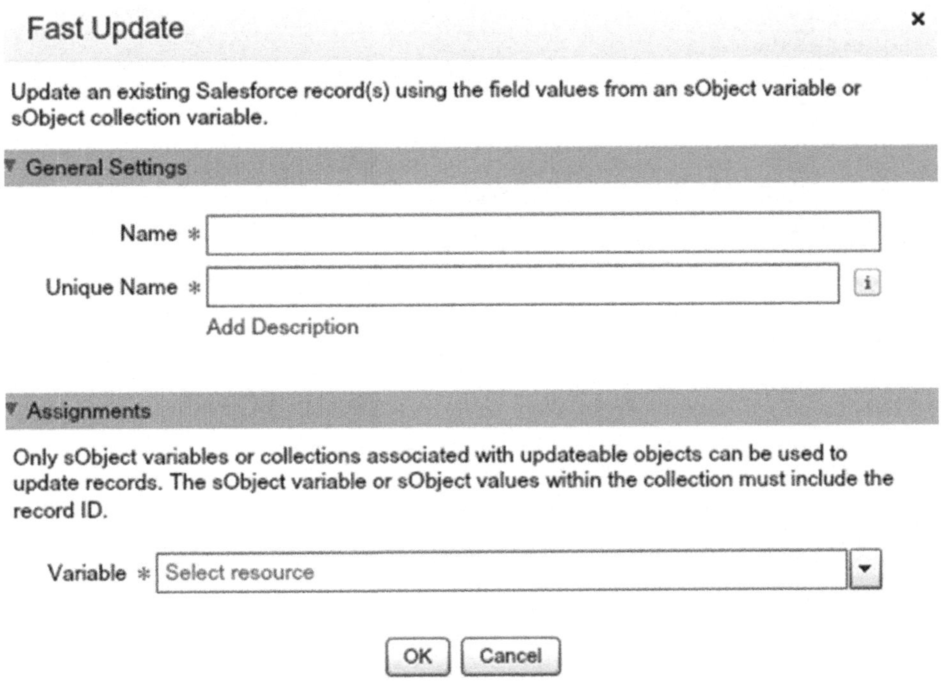

Figure 5-21. *The Fast Update configuration window*

Record Update

The Record Update element is a lot different from the Fast Update element. While the Fast Update element requires that you have the SObject Variable or SObject Collection Variable data all collected and ready, the Record Update element does not.

The Record Update works by finding and updating records in Salesforce all in the element itself. With the Fast Update element, the flow needs to find the records first, just as we did with the Fast Lookup. The Record Update element can find the records to update and then update immediately. The great thing about the Record Update element though is that instead of updating based on an SObject Variable or SObject Collection Variable, it can perform the update using normal flow resources such as variables, constants, formulas, and so on. It can even use an SObject Variable and be configured to pick out which field to use.

159

Let's look at Figure 5-22 to see what the configuration screen for the Record Update element looks like to get a better understanding. The main section is the "Filters and Assignments" section. The Update field is where you select what type of object this element will be retrieving and updating. Under that is a combination of fields. They are the field, operator, and value. These function just like the filter criteria fields in the Fast Lookup. One or many rows can be added here to fine-tune the lookup to find the record to update. Underneath that section is where the actual updates occur. It is a list of rows of which fields from the object to update matched with their values to update from. This section allows one or many rows of field/ values to have updated.

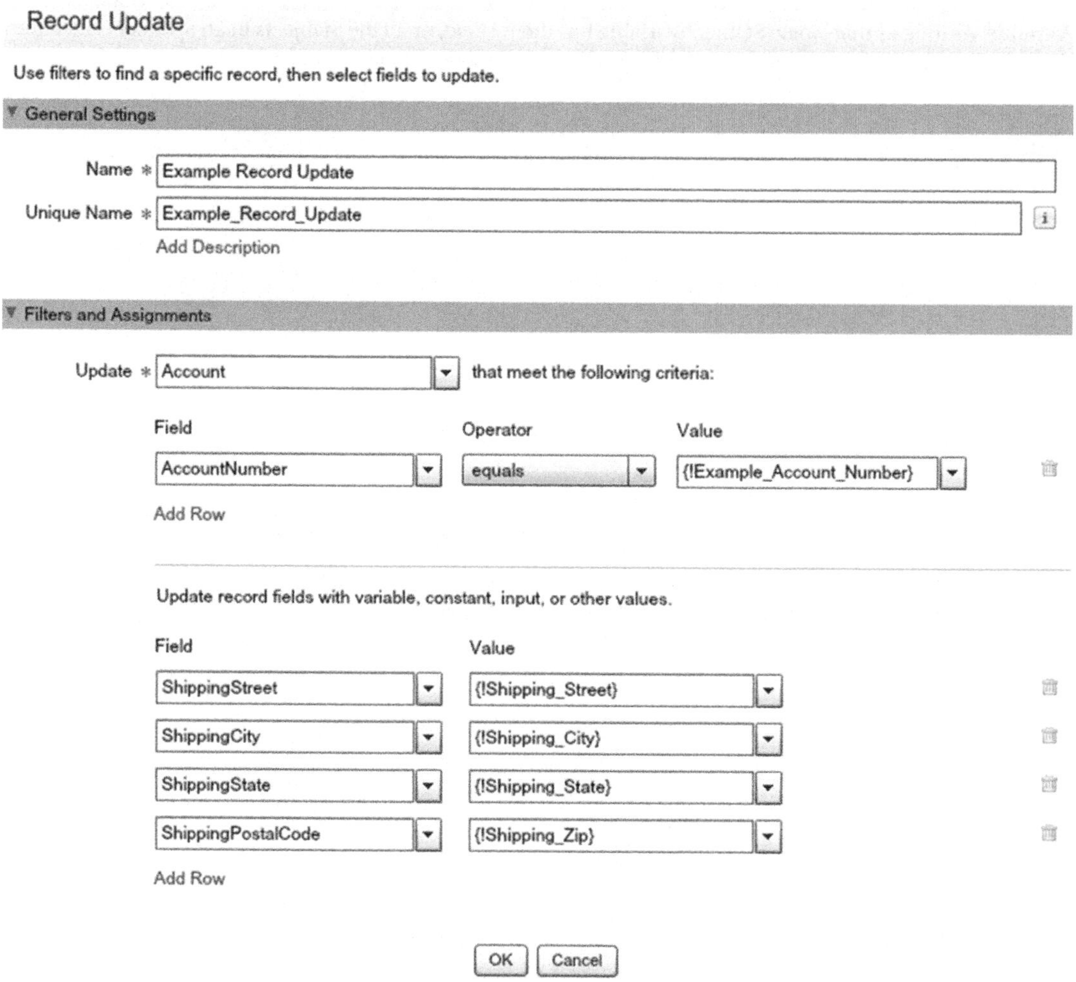

Record Update

Use filters to find a specific record, then select fields to update.

▼ **General Settings**

Name *	Example Record Update

Unique Name *	Example_Record_Update	ⓘ

Add Description

▼ **Filters and Assignments**

Update * | Account | ▼ | that meet the following criteria:

Field	Operator	Value
AccountNumber ▼	equals ▼	{!Example_Account_Number} ▼	🗑

Add Row

Update record fields with variable, constant, input, or other values.

Field	Value
ShippingStreet ▼	{!Shipping_Street} ▼	🗑
ShippingCity ▼	{!Shipping_City} ▼	🗑
ShippingState ▼	{!Shipping_State} ▼	🗑
ShippingPostalCode ▼	{!Shipping_Zip} ▼	🗑

Add Row

[OK] [Cancel]

Figure 5-22. *An example of the Record Update element configuration window*

Reviewing these two types of updates, the Fast Update will meet our requirements. The design required pulling a list of accounts, displaying them to the user for possible edits, and then updating them. The pattern of Fast Lookup, Screen, Assignment, and Fast Update works very well with the expected process. To finish this next step, place a Fast Update element on the Canvas and configure it with the following settings:

- **Name:** Update Account Shipping Address

- **Unique Name:** Update_Account_Shipping_Address

- **Variable:** {!Current_Account}

The final Fast Update configuration screen should look like Figure 5-23.

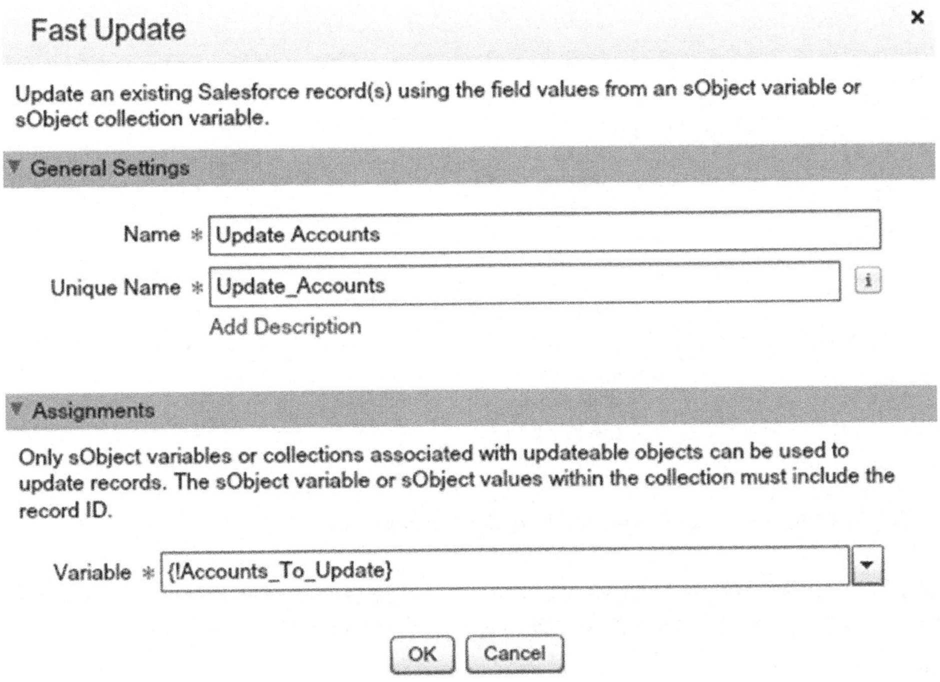

Figure 5-23. The Fast Update configuration window with the settings for the flow

If all looks good, then click "OK" to accept the changes and be taken back to the Canvas. Once at the Canvas connect the "Account Loop" element to the "Update Accounts" element. Notice that the connector has the "End of loop" label. The flow on the canvas should look like Figure 5-24.

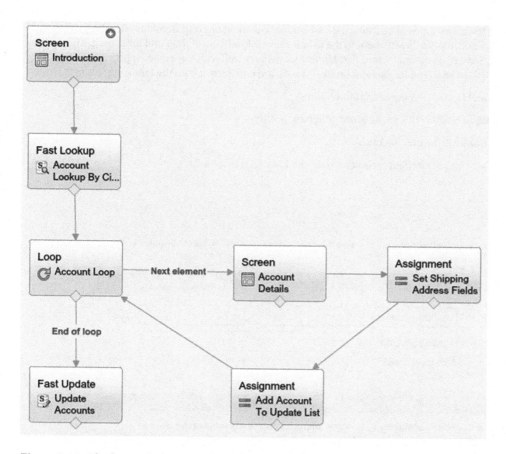

Figure 5-24. *The flow with the Fast Update element added after the loop ends*

We are almost complete with this flow. The last touch is the final screen that occurs after the fast update. Create the new Screen element with the following configuration settings under the General Info tab:

- **Name:** Final Screen
- **Unique Name:** Final_Screen

Next add a Display Text field into the screen with the following configuration settings:

- **Unique Name:** Final_Screen_Text
- **Text Area:** Process complete. No more records found.

Click "OK" to accept the changes. Now connect the "Update Accounts" element to the "Final Screen" element. Go ahead and save the flow. The flow now should look like Figure 5-25.

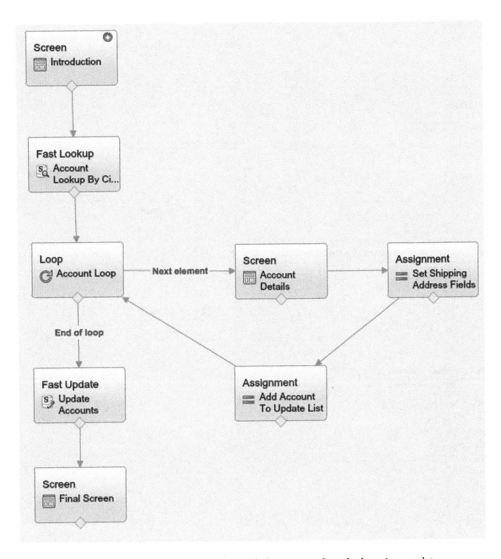

Figure 5-25. The flow with the Final Screen added to occur when the loop is complete

Run the Flow

Click the Run button to start the flow and make sure if it performs in the expected way. You should be presented with the Introduction screen, and then, depending on how many accounts are found for the search criteria, you will see the Account Details screen for each one. At the end you will see the final screen. You should be able to repeat the process again after completion and it would take you straight to the final screen after the introduction because all the account information would be updated (if you made it all the way through the list of accounts). With no accounts found by the lookup criteria, there would be an empty collection and nothing to loop through. You can see an example of a run in Figure 5-26, Figure 5-27, Figure 5-28, and Figure 5-29.

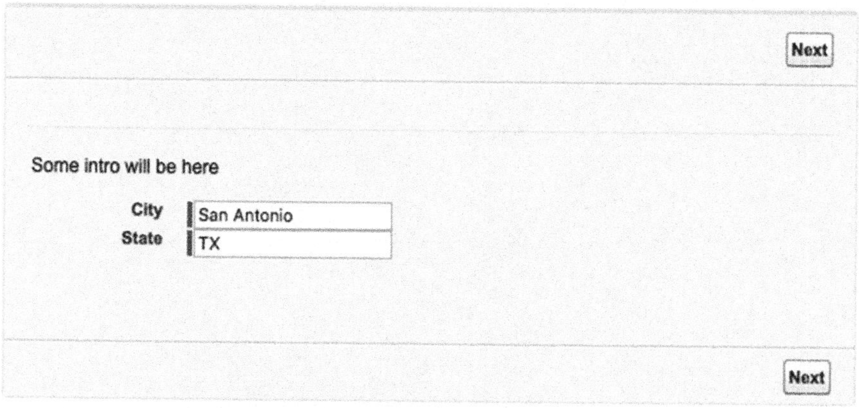

Figure 5-26. *The Introduction screen of the running flow*

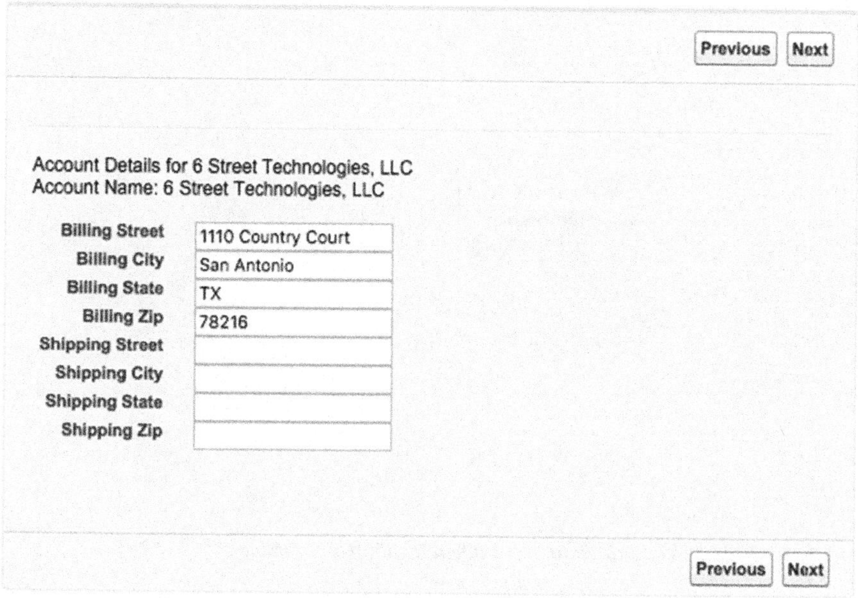

Figure 5-27. *The Account Details screen of the running flow in the first iteration of the loop*

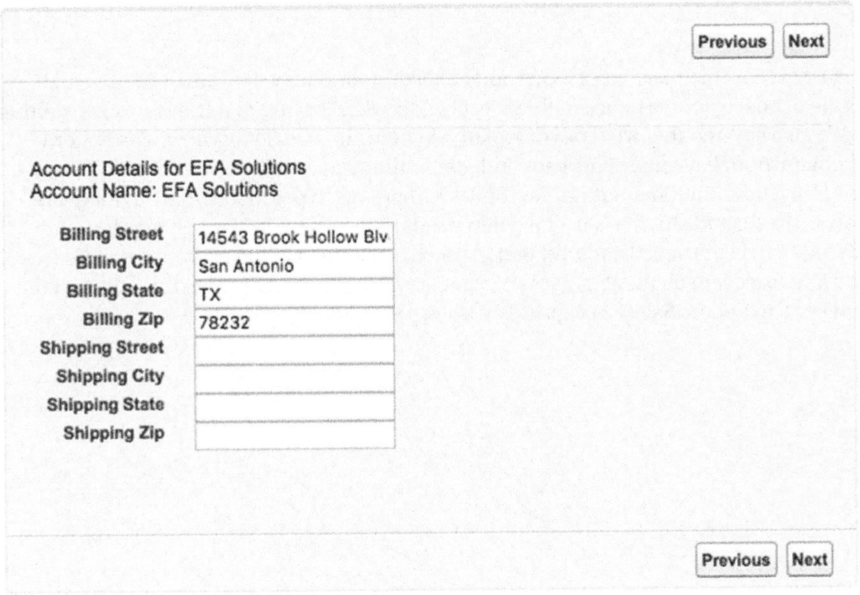

Figure 5-28. The Account Details screen of the running flow in the second iteration of the loop

Figure 5-29. The Final Screen of the running flow

Recap

In this chapter we focused on the core concept of loops and collections and how they are used in Visual Workflow. Collections are a great resource to use in flows, especially when having to retrieve or save multiple records in Salesforce. We also covered the two types of lookup elements in Visual Workflow. The Record Lookup and the Fast Lookup. Both have their purposes and, depending on the requirements and design, each one will work better in a flow implementation. Not only are there two types of lookups but there are also two types of updates. The Record Update is useful when the design calls for updating records with specific criteria so that they can be retrieved and updated in one flow element using existing resources in a flow. The Fast Update is an excellent element to use when you have one or many SObjects ready with the data they need and you need to update Salesforce quickly with the SObject's current state.

CHAPTER 6

■ ■ ■

Call Center Application

We have covered a lot of ground as we dived into Visual Workflow and the many examples of how to use Cloud Flow Designer and the many elements necessary to build a flow. All these elements are at your fingertips and give you some real power to develop applications that normally would require Apex code. Now they can be developed graphically. They can be easily understood because the flows created are edited and viewed as diagrams. This helps in making these flows easily maintainable. So far we have been dealing with specific examples to highlight some important features of Visual Workflow. What about creating an app in Visual Workflow? Is it meant just to complement other aspects of Salesforce and fill in a hole where configuration can get you only so far?

Let us just think about the power of Visual Workflow for a minute. Here we have a system that allows a lot of the same constructs that a programming language offers. It offers data access, variables, collections, and looping to just name a few. Apex development is usually the go-to when you need to implement a solution on the Salesforce platform and configuration just does not cut it anymore—although that's not the case now! As just stated, Visual Workflow offers a lot of the same constructs. Yes, it's not everything that Apex offers, but it offers enough to meet a lot of requirements. In this chapter we will cover just how powerful Visual Workflow can be by creating a call center application.

What Is a Call Center App?

This application will be a basic 1.0 version of what representatives at a call center can use to script the calls they receive. Call center representatives receive a call script for use when a call first comes through and they are talking to a real customer on the other end of the phone line. Without proper training, it can be very difficult to respond to all possible questions accurately. On top of the initial training they need to keep up with constantly changing rules, policies, and laws. To reduce risk, companies develop call scripts to guide phone representatives through daily communication with customers. Not only does it reduce risk by making sure information is passed on correctly, but it keeps communication uniform and consistent across the company. No matter which representative gets the call his or her communication with a customer should be roughly the same as that of another representative who might have received the call.

There are other aspects to a call center application such as computer-telephony integration (CTI), which is a term to describe the practice of tying your phone and computer systems together. For now we will assume this aspect is in place and separate for the app we are about to build. Implementing CTI is a whole other animal and there are several CTI apps on the Salesforce AppExchange such as Talkdesk, which can give this functionality for a call center. In case you are unfamiliar with Salesforce AppExchange it is an app store where free and paid apps are available to extend the functionality of Salesforce. It is very similar to the Apple App Store or the Google Play Store. In this case it is for Salesforce instead of for a mobile device.

With that, let's begin with the requirements as usual. In this scenario we are building a call center for a university known as Logan Alexander University. It's a prestigious university and only a select few are able to get in. Since only a select few can get into the university the campus has not had to worry too much about

© Jonathan Keel 2016

J. Keel, *Salesforce.com Lightning Process Builder and Visual Workflow*, DOI 10.1007/978-1-4842-1691-0_6

having a call center to handle incoming calls. This coming year though there is planned growth. Several buildings, staff, and faculty have been added to accommodate a larger incoming freshman class. With all the new students the university expects that there will be an increased demand for information as the new students get used to the university. Naturally student retention is important, and one major way of keeping retention high is by serving the students' needs as best as possible. The university leaders have discussed and come up with the following high-level requirements for a call center application that will guide the phone representatives when students dial their main university help line:

- Create a basic call center scripting application that is initiated via a button click on an Account record. The button will be titled "Student Call Center."

- Upon clicking the "Student Call Center" button the call representative will go through a series of questions and answers in what is called the decision tree.

- The first screen the call center representative should see is a screen with a standard greeting script that he or she should read to thank and welcome the caller.

- The decision tree will be simple with this 1.0 version, with a set of just a few questions and their corresponding answers.

- The first question would be to determine whether the student is an undergraduate or graduate student, but it should be pulled from the student's Account record and not verbally asked over the phone.

- If the answer is "graduate," then present the phone representative with the phone number of the specific college's graduate help number so the representative may transfer the caller.

- If the answer is "undergraduate," then have the call representative ask how he or she can help the student.

- Based on the information from the student, the call representative should then choose an option on the screen that best fits the appropriate category including:

  - Curriculum

  - Housing

  - Student Life

  - Financial Aid

- If the category is "Curriculum," present the phone representative with the phone number of the specific college's undergraduate help number so the representative may transfer the caller.

- If the category is "Housing," have the representative ask if it is related to "On-Campus" or "Off-Campus" housing. Based on the type of housing, present the call representative with the help number so the representative may transfer the caller to either the On-Campus Department of Housing or the Off-Campus Department of Housing

- If the category is "Student Life," then present the call representative with the help number so the representative may transfer the caller to the Student Life department.

- If the category is "Financial Aid" ask if it is related to "Scholarships," "Grants," or "Loans." Based on the type of financial aid, present the call representative with the help number so the representative may transfer the caller to either of the three financial aid departments.

- The department phone numbers should be stored in Salesforce as a Main Number field on custom object named "Department."

- The application should be flexible to add more questions and answers later.

As you can see, this is just a beginning. Call center representatives are really just routing the calls to the appropriate office. Using these requirements we will then move to the next step of creating a design.

Designing the App

The more advanced and complicated a flow is, the more important it is to design how it should function before implementing it. In the other chapters we covered the design phase before jumping straight to implementing the flows, and this time it is even more important than ever that we complete this phase of the development process. Let's start off with what we know from the requirements.

The whole process begins when that call comes in from the student. Since the requirements assume we have an account first, the design needs to show that step of the call representative to look up the student's account. With this basic system we will just use the standard Salesforce Account object. On that account record for a student, there will be just one Contact with the student's information. Now in Salesforce you can also use the concept of Person Accounts to do just this. Salesforce's data model supports the concept of contacts associated with specific companies/organizations, as well as contacts that are not associated with a "parent" organization and serve as their own account ("Person Accounts"). Some people like the concept of Person Accounts, but others find it confusing because the Account and Contact records become almost the same thing. For our needs, just having one Contact under an Account works and keeps it simple.

■ **Note** If Person Accounts are enabled in a Salesforce organization, they cannot be disabled, so be sure about the decision to turn them on.

Let's look at the interaction of the student and the call center representative in Figure 6-1. This is the design not of the flow implementation but of how the interaction will work before the flow gets kicked off. We are looking at this because we will need to do some work that is outside Cloud Flow Designer. Here we have the student calling into the main number for help. By calling this one single number the student can get access to what he or she needs. While there are a lot of different departments at the university, the call center representative's job at this point is to redirect the call to the appropriate department in order to better serve the needs of the student. Then, after the student calls in, the representative would take his or her information and look the student up in Salesforce. The goal is to look for the student's account record. His account would have the necessary information to help direct the call. Information that would be available includes whether the student is a graduate or undergraduate student, the student's classification (freshman, sophomore, junior, senior), and what college the student is enrolled in. On the student's account page, the representative would click the "Student Call Center" button to begin finding out what the student needs.

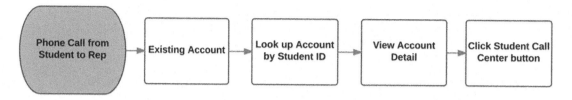

Figure 6-1. *Design showing the student to call center representative interaction*

Looking at the design we can see that the account will need these new fields, plus the Student Call Center button on the page layout that the representative will be using.

Onto the Flow Design

Once you click the Student Call Center button, the flow will be started. Taking the requirements, we come up with the design in Figure 6-2. We see first that the flow needs to take in some input parameters to know some information about the student's account. We can pass in anything that is on the Account record since the button is on the account detail page. Also, we can pass in any related information that can come from a cross-object formula field or a lookup field. Essentially, if there is a relationship that you can get to in a formula field you should be able to pass it to the flow as an input parameter.

After getting the necessary information, the flow would then determine automatically whether the student was a graduate or an undergraduate. If an undergrad, the flow would prompt the representative to transfer the call to the undergraduate department number. The undergraduate number would be located as a field in the custom Department object. If it was an undergraduate student, then present the representative with a screen that has a script to ask the student if his call is related to his curriculum, housing, student life, or financial aid. If the student's question is related to his curriculum, then the representative will choose that option from the screen and know what college the student is enrolled in. The flow would prompt the representative to transfer the call to that college's main number.

If the student has a question regarding her housing situation then the flow should have the script for the representative to ask the student if she wants on-campus or off-campus housing. Depending on the selection, the representative would click that particular option on the flow screen. At that point the next flow screen should prompt the representative to transfer the call to either the on-campus department or the off-campus department number.

If the student has a question about student life at the university then the flow screen should prompt the representative to transfer the call to the main number for the department of student life. Finally, if the student has a question about financial aid, the representative should be prompted to ask him what type of aid he has (scholarships, grants, loans, etc.) and then should be prompted to transfer the call to the main number of any of those departments. Again there would need to be a custom Department object created with a main number field so that we can get it dynamically. Although the number could be put into the flow, it is not advisable because a change to any one phone number would require a new version of a flow to be built, deployed, and activated in production. That is a lot of work just to change a phone number. It is instead better to externalize data to the flow so that the flow can be as dynamic as possible.

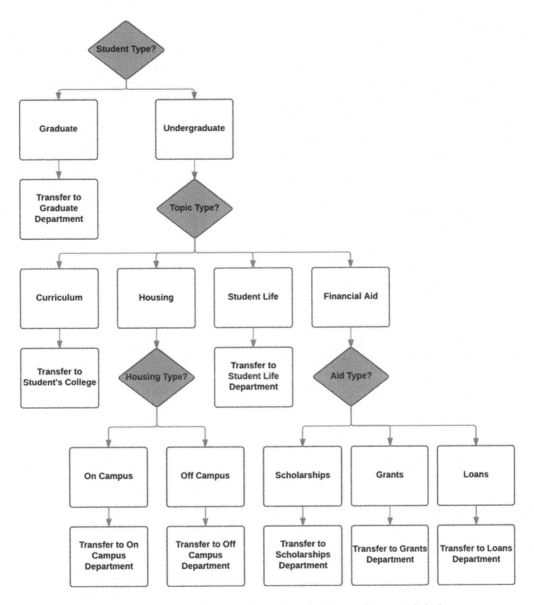

Figure 6-2. *Design showing the call flow after the Student Call Center button is clicked*

With these two designs we have the entire flow for version 1.0 of the Call Center application. These designs show us the basic functionality that the application will have and how it will behave. There is a lot of work ahead of us now. We need to implement this design and it's going to call for the custom Department object along with its fields. It is also going to require some custom fields on the Account object, including a picklist with "Graduate" and "Undergraduate" values. Another custom field will be a lookup to the College in which the student is enrolled. That means we will need a custom College object with some fields such as "Name" and "Main Number" to start off with. We will need to add a custom Student Call Center button and then have that placed on the appropriate page layout. Then, finally, we need to get to all the work associated with building the flow that is going to drive the representative's interaction on these calls. We have a lot of work ahead of us. Let's not delay!

Implementation

First let's start off by getting all of our objects in Salesforce ready. Looking back at our design we talked about two new custom objects. One is the College object. It will have a Name field (which comes by default) and a Main Number field (which is a custom field). The other object we need is Department. It is also a custom object with a Name field and a Main Number field. As time goes on these two objects will probably become more distinct (meaning they will have different fields), but in the meantime, we just need a Name and a Main Number to transfer to. Let's go ahead and add those two objects and their fields now.

First let's tackle the College object. Go to Setup > Build > Create > Objects and click the New Custom Object button. Once there, use the following configuration to create the College object and click the Save button when complete:

- **Label**: College
- **Plural Label**: Colleges
- **Object Name**: College
- **Description**: Represents a College at the University
- **Record Name**: College Name
- **Data Type**: Text

When creating an object, the Name field (labeled "College Name" here) is automatically added so now you only need to create the Main Number field. On the Object detail page under the "Custom Fields & Relationships" section, click the New button to create this field. Use the following configuration settings to set up the Main Number field:

- **Data Type**: Phone
- **Field Label**: Main Number
- **Field Name**: Main_Number
- **Description**: The main phone number of the college.
- **Required**: Checked

After entering all the values, selecting the appropriate field-level security, and adding to your page layouts, go ahead and click the Save button. The detail page should look like Figure 6-3.

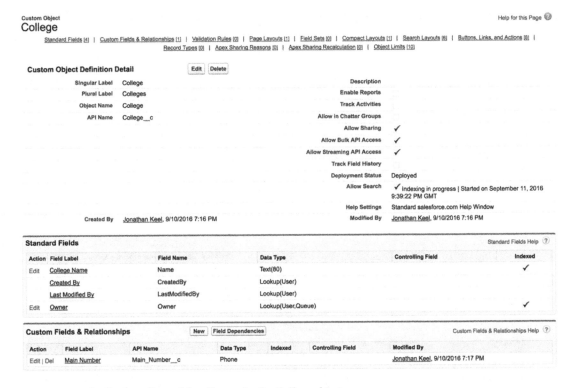

Figure 6-3. *The final configured detail page for the College object*

Now we have our College object set up with the fields to get our call center app working. Next we need to set up the Department object. It is going to be very similar. Go to Setup > Build > Create > Objects and click the New Custom Object button. Once there, use the following configuration to create the Department object:

- **Label**: Department
- **Plural Label**: Departments
- **Object Name**: Department
- **Description**: Represents a Department at the University
- **Record Name**: Department Name
- **Data Type**: Text

Again, the Name field (labeled "Department Name" here) is automatically added so now you only need to create the Main Number field. On the Object detail page under the "Custom Fields & Relationships" section, click the New button. Use the following configuration settings to set up the Main Number field:

- **Data Type**: Phone
- **Field Label**: Main Number
- **Field Name**: Main_Number
- **Description**: The main phone number of the college.
- **Required**: Checked

173

After entering all the values, selecting the appropriate field-level security, and adding to your page layouts, go ahead and click the Save button. The detail page should look like Figure 6-4.

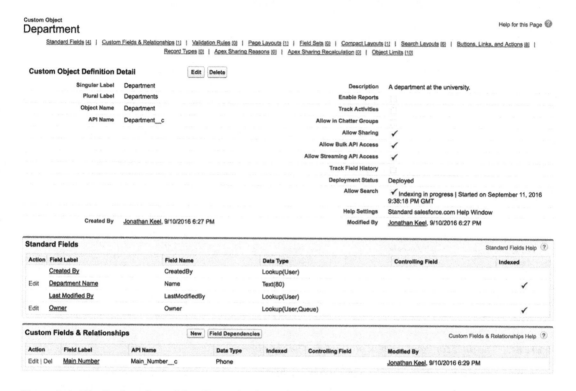

Figure 6-4. *The final configured detail page for the Department object*

There we go! We have our two new custom objects to get us through setting up our call center app. We still have some custom fields on the Account object to set up though. They should be simple. One is a picklist field that has the options of "Graduate" and "Undergraduate." We will call it the Student Type field. Then the second field is also on the Account object, but it is a lookup to the College object we just created. That way every student who has an account will have a relationship with the college in which they are enrolled for their major. We will simply call this the College field. To add these fields go to Setup ➤ Build ➤ Customize ➤ Accounts ➤ Fields and click on the New button under the Account Custom Fields & Relationships section.

Once there we need to configure our Student Type field. Select the picklist data type and then use the following values in Figure 6-5 to configure the Student Type field:

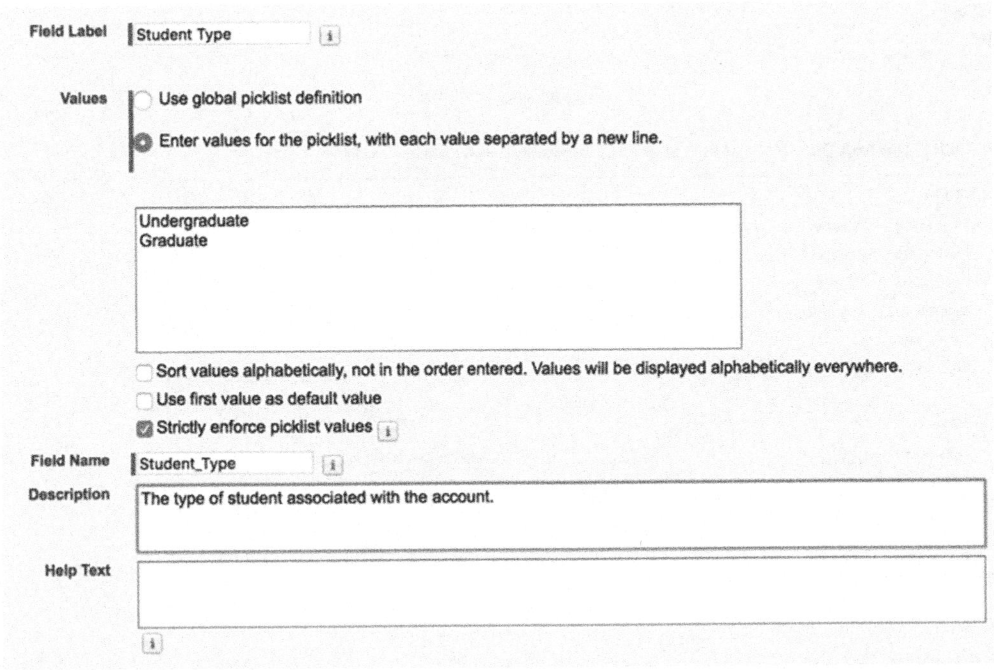

Figure 6-5. *The configuration settings for the Student Type field on the Account object*

After entering all the values, selecting the appropriate field-level security, and adding to your page layouts, go ahead and click the Save button.

Let's wrap up configuring the Account object by adding the College field. This will be a lookup to the College object we created earlier. On the Account detail page click the New button again under the Account Custom Fields & Relationships section. Once there we need to configure our College field. Use the following values to configure the College field:

- **Data Type:** Lookup Relationship

- **Related To:** College

- **Field Label:** College

- **Field Name:** College

- **Description:** The College associated to the student's account.

- **Child Relationship Name:** Accounts

Leave everything else as the default settings. Then go ahead and select the appropriate field-level security and add the field to the page layouts. After clicking the Save button the detail page should look like Figure 6-6.

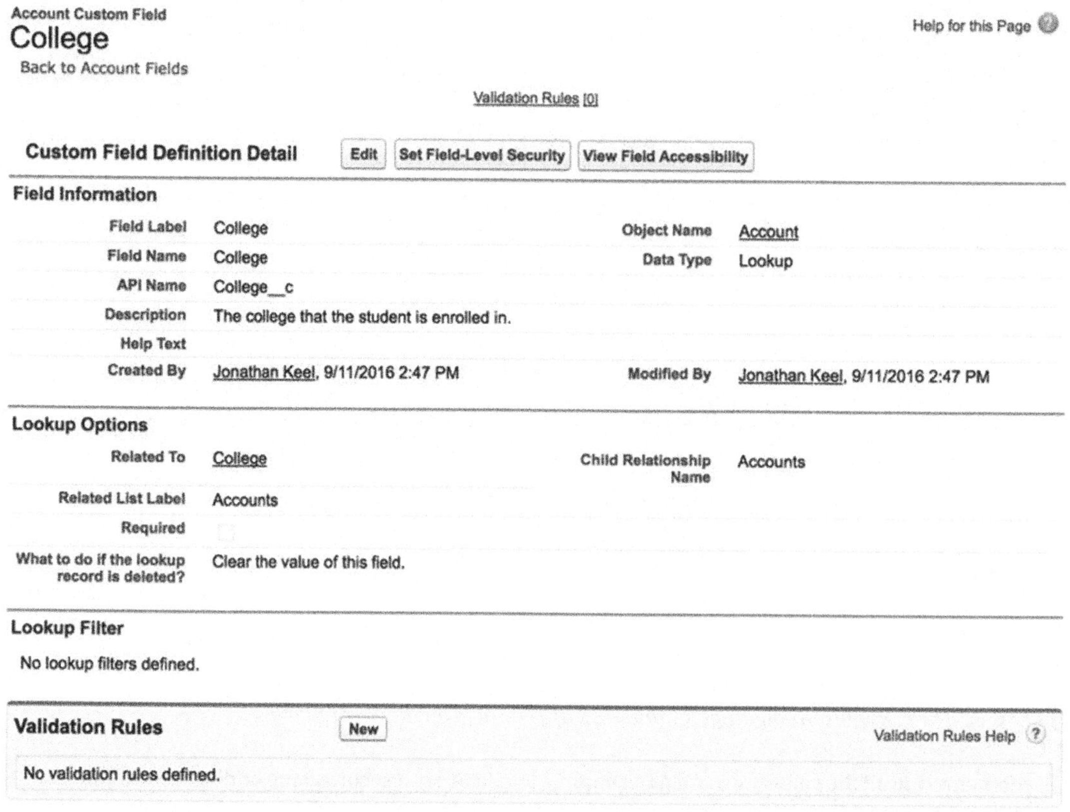

Account Custom Field

College

Back to Account Fields

Validation Rules [0]

Custom Field Definition Detail | Edit | Set Field-Level Security | View Field Accessibility |

Field Information

Field Label	College	Object Name	Account
Field Name	College	Data Type	Lookup
API Name	College__c		
Description	The college that the student is enrolled in.		
Help Text			
Created By	Jonathan Keel, 9/11/2016 2:47 PM	Modified By	Jonathan Keel, 9/11/2016 2:47 PM

Lookup Options

Related To	College	Child Relationship Name	Accounts
Related List Label	Accounts		
Required	☐		
What to do if the lookup record is deleted?	Clear the value of this field.		

Lookup Filter

No lookup filters defined.

Validation Rules | New | Validation Rules Help ⍰

No validation rules defined.

Figure 6-6. *The final configured detail page for the College field*

Call Center Transfer Subflow

Now we are cookin'! We have our prep work finished. Just like a chef has to do prep work before making a meal, we too need to prep our configurations before getting down to the implementation of our creation. Trust me when I say it's going to taste good at the end. We need to get the flow put together using Cloud Flow Designer. There are a lot of elements in the design and by now we are familiar with creating flows and adding elements on the Canvas. So to speed things up following is a series of configuration setting screenshots for each element to be added to the Canvas along with which element it should be connected to.

First there is going to be some common logic for getting data and presenting it to the call center representative for a transfer screen in a flow. Instead of duplicating this logic over and over again within one massive flow we will instead create a flow that will be called by the main flow. We will refer to this flow as a subflow since it will not be useful without the main flow calling it. Go to Setup ➤ Build ➤ Create ➤ Workflow & Approvals ➤ Flows and click the New Flow button to create the subflow.

Start off by creating a few variables we will need in this flow. First the flow needs to know whether this is a transfer to a Department or a College. We will create a Transfer_Type variable to hold this information. Since it is coming from the main flow (which we have not created yet) it will be an Input Only variable. See Figure 6-7 for the full configuration settings.

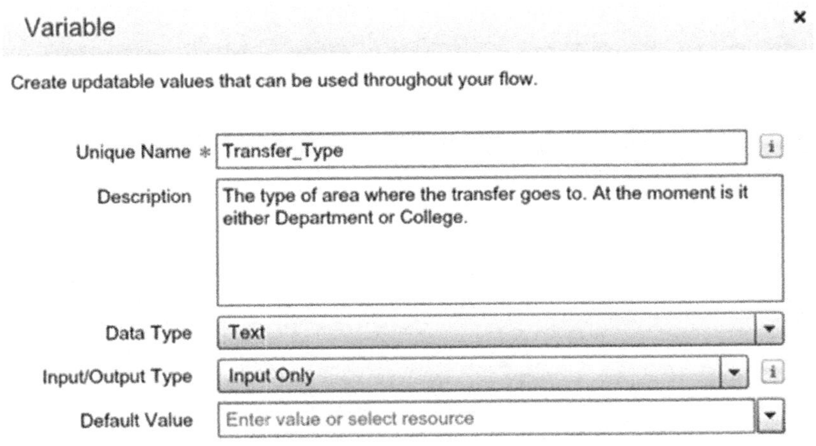

Variable ✕

Create updatable values that can be used throughout your flow.

Unique Name *	Transfer_Type ⓘ
Description	The type of area where the transfer goes to. At the moment is it either Department or College.
Data Type	Text ▾
Input/Output Type	Input Only ▾ ⓘ
Default Value	Enter value or select resource ▾

Figure 6-7. *The configuration screen for the Transfer_Type variable*

The next variable we need is the Department_Name variable. Also an input variable, it needs to pass the name of the department to which the transfer is occurring. See Figure 6-8 for the configuration settings for this variable.

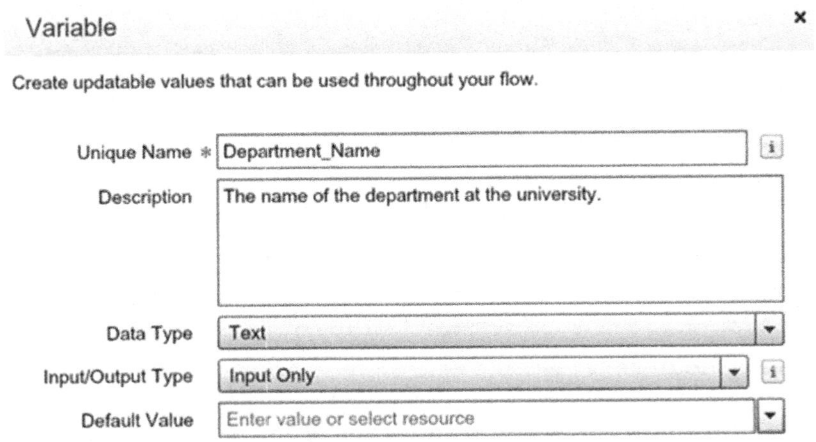

Variable ✕

Create updatable values that can be used throughout your flow.

Unique Name *	Department_Name ⓘ
Description	The name of the department at the university.
Data Type	Text ▾
Input/Output Type	Input Only ▾ ⓘ
Default Value	Enter value or select resource ▾

Figure 6-8. *The configuration screen for the Department_Name variable*

Like the Department_Name variable there needs to be another variable to hold the College name when it is passed to this flow as an input variable. Refer to Figure 6-9 for the configuration settings for the College_ Name variable.

177

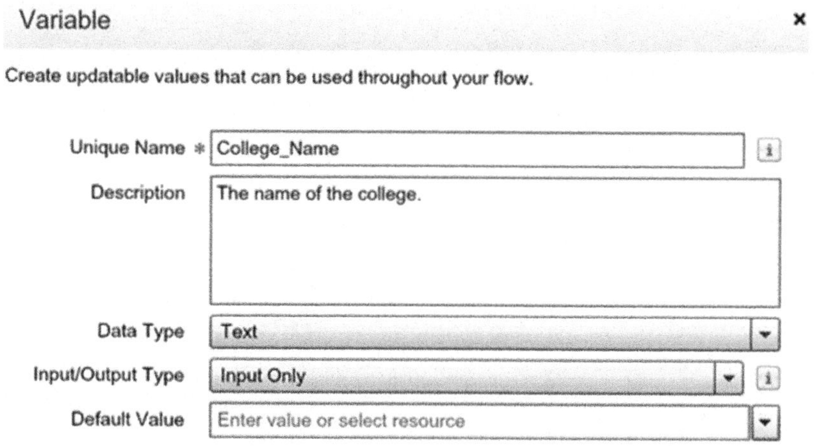

Variable ✕

Create updatable values that can be used throughout your flow.

Unique Name ✱	College_Name ⓘ
Description	The name of the college.
Data Type	Text ▼
Input/Output Type	Input Only ▼ ⓘ
Default Value	Enter value or select resource ▼

Figure 6-9. *The configuration screen for the College_Name variable*

We plan on also doing a lookup get the main number for the department or college. We will need a variable to hold that value. Use the settings in Figure 6-10 to create the Main_Number variable in the flow. It is a private variable because the value will not be shared outside this flow.

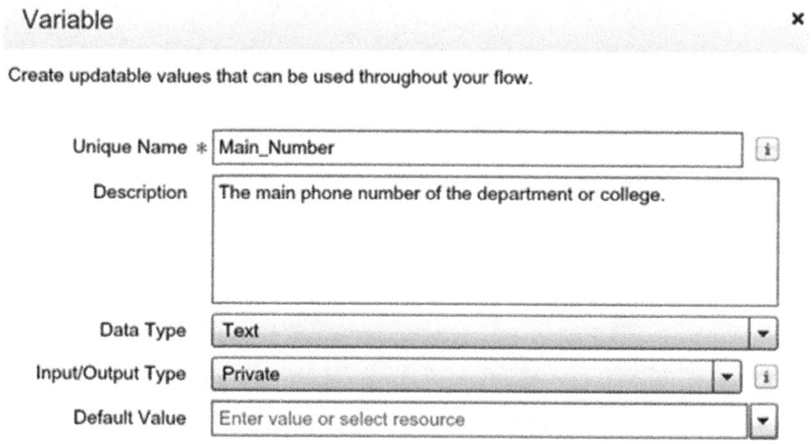

Variable ✕

Create updatable values that can be used throughout your flow.

Unique Name ✱	Main_Number ⓘ
Description	The main phone number of the department or college.
Data Type	Text ▼
Input/Output Type	Private ▼ ⓘ
Default Value	Enter value or select resource ▼

Figure 6-10. *The configuration screen for the Main_Number variable*

With the variables created, let's continue by creating a new Decision element with the settings in Figure 6-11. Notice that there are two outcomes. One is the Department Outcome that occurs when the `Transfer_Type` variable equals the "Department" value. The other outcome is the default outcome. The default outcome does not need to be renamed, but in order to make the flow more readable on the Canvas, let's rename it "College Outcome." After this element is completely configured, set it as the start element for the flow.

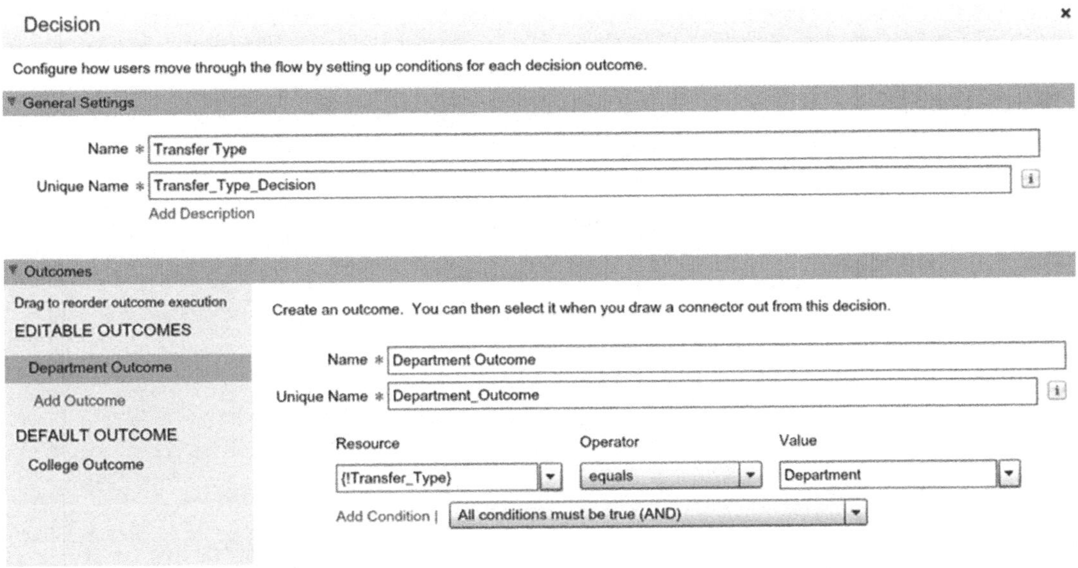

Decision   ✕

Configure how users move through the flow by setting up conditions for each decision outcome.

▼ General Settings

Name ∗	Transfer Type
Unique Name ∗	Transfer_Type_Decision ⓘ
	Add Description

▼ Outcomes

Drag to reorder outcome execution

Create an outcome. You can then select it when you draw a connector out from this decision.

EDITABLE OUTCOMES

Department Outcome

Add Outcome

DEFAULT OUTCOME

College Outcome

Name ∗	Department Outcome
Unique Name ∗	Department_Outcome ⓘ

Resource	Operator	Value
{!Transfer_Type} ▼	equals ▼	Department ▼

Add Condition | All conditions must be true (AND) ▼

Figure 6-11. The configuration screen for the Transfer_Type_Decision element

Once the transfer type is determined the flow must move on in that direction. If it is a Department transfer type then there needs to be a screen to show department-specific information. If it is a College transfer type then there needs to be a screen to show college-specific information. First let's configure the path of the Department transfer. The first thing to do before showing the Department transfer screen is to do a lookup to get any additional department information we need. At the moment we just need the Main_Number field from the Department object. Drag over a Record Lookup element to the Canvas to begin configuring it. In Figure 6-12 we see the configuration settings for getting the Department record's information.

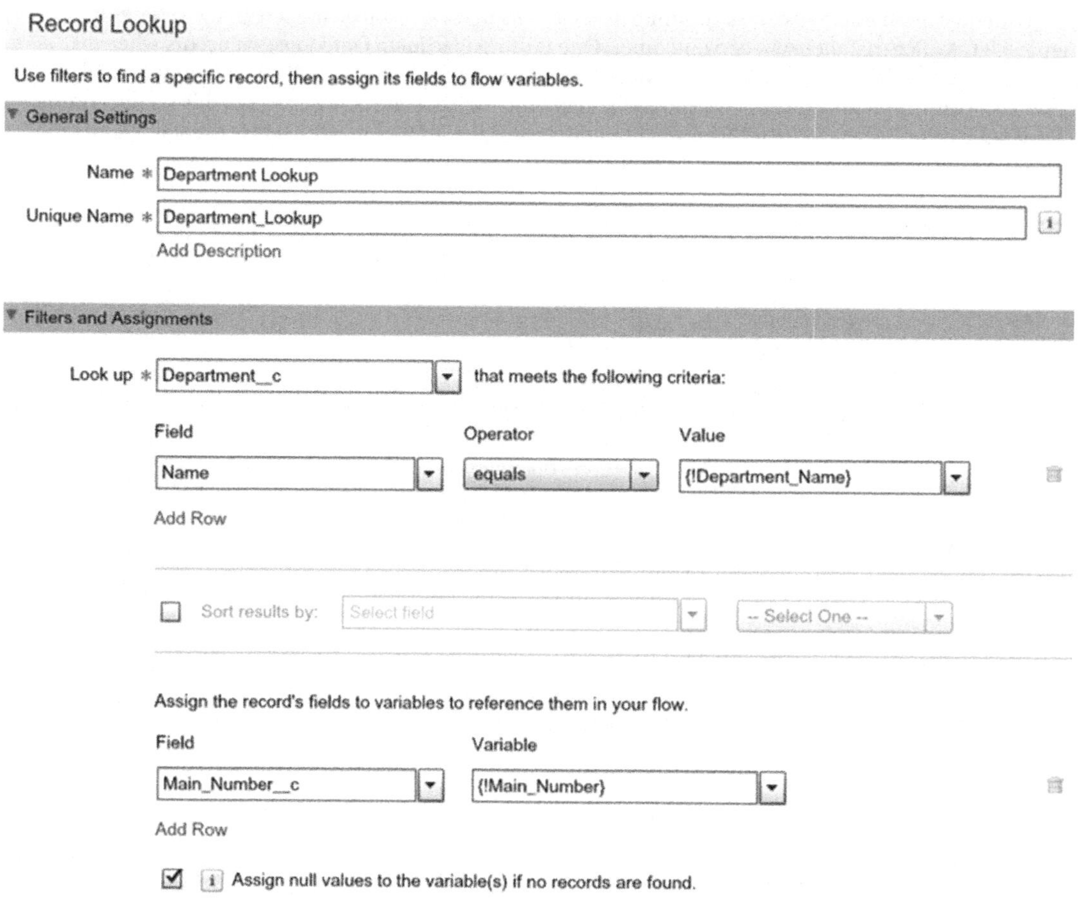

Record Lookup

Use filters to find a specific record, then assign its fields to flow variables.

▼ General Settings

Name ✱ | Department Lookup

Unique Name ✱ | Department_Lookup | ⓘ

Add Description

▼ Filters and Assignments

Look up ✱ | Department__c ▾ | that meets the following criteria:

Field	Operator	Value
Name ▾	equals ▾	{!Department_Name} ▾	🗑

Add Row

☐ Sort results by: | Select field ▾ | -- Select One -- ▾

Assign the record's fields to variables to reference them in your flow.

Field	Variable
Main_Number__c ▾	{!Main_Number} ▾	🗑

Add Row

☑ ⓘ Assign null values to the variable(s) if no records are found.

Figure 6-12. *The configuration screen for the Department_Lookup Record Lookup element*

Once complete and back to the Canvas, connect the Transfer_Type_Decision element to the Department_Lookup element. A pop-up should appear to let you pick which outcome goes to this Department_Lookup element. Choose the "Department Outcome" option.

When you successfully perform record lookup, the next step is to have a screen displayed to the call center representative that gives him not only the script he should read from but also the directions he should take to successfully transfer the phone call. Drag a Screen element to the Canvas and configure it with a Display Text field as seen in Figure 6-13.

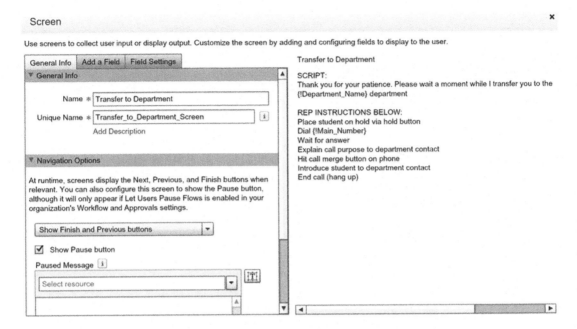

Figure 6-13. The configuration screen for the Transfer_to_Department_Screen element

Once complete with the configuration of that element, connect the Department_Lookup element to the Transfer_to_Department_Screen element. When you perform a record lookup there is always a possibility that an error could occur. The Screen element we just connected is the "happy path" of this record lookup. The first time you connect an element to a Record Lookup element, it travels the path where it successfully retrieves data without an error. Even if it does not find the data in the lookup, the flow will still continue down this success path. If there is some unforeseen error, though, the flow offers the "Fault" path to handle errors gracefully. To handle this fault scenario, drag a Screen element to the Canvas and configure it as in Figure 6-14. Notice that it has a Display Text field and in it is a reference to $Flow.FaultMessage. That is a variable found when selecting a resource to add to the Display Text. It is found under SYSTEM AND GLOBAL VARIABLES ➤ $Flow ➤ FaultMessage.

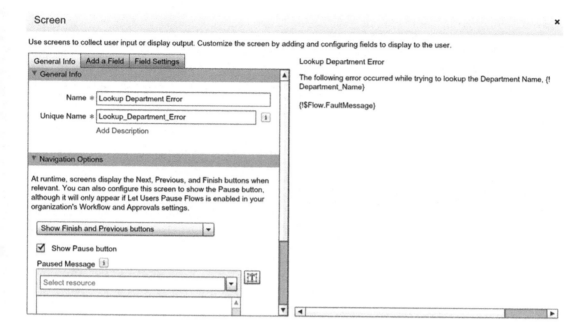

Figure 6-14. The configuration screen for the Lookup_Department_Error element

After finishing configuring the element, connect the Department_Lookup element to the Lookup_
Department_Error element. Notice that when doing so the arrow on the Canvas has the "FAULT" label on it.
This is the non-success path that occurs during the Record Lookup.

■ **Note** While adding a FAULT path is not required, it is highly recommended. Otherwise, when an error
occurs there will be no meaningful message to the user.

After the call has been transferred we can give the call center representative one final instruction to
close the call script window. Go ahead and drag a Screen element to the Canvas and configure it with the
settings in Figure 6-15.

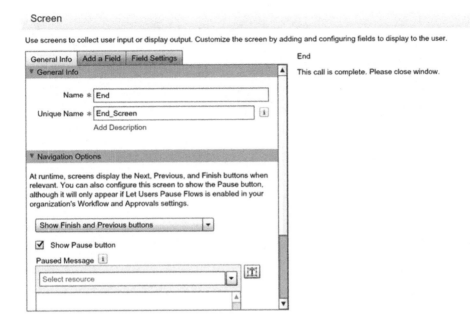

Figure 6-15. *The configuration screen for the End_Screen element*

After that is done, connect the Transfer_to_Department_Screen element to this End_Screen element. That concludes the transfer to a department side of this flow. Now we need to set up the transfer to a college. Drag over another Record Lookup element to the Canvas as we did for the department lookup. This time, though, we will configure this Record Lookup element to look up a college by name. Use Figure 6-16 as a reference to set up this element.

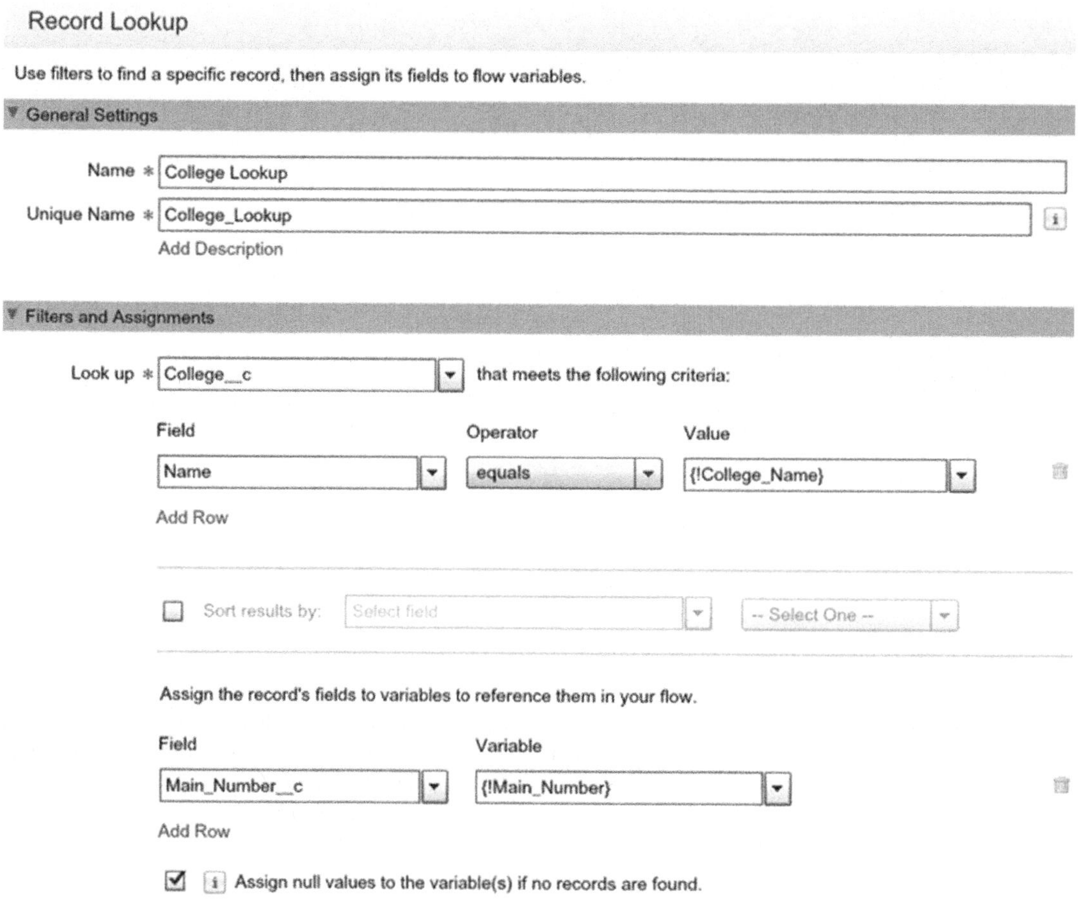

Record Lookup

Use filters to find a specific record, then assign its fields to flow variables.

▼ General Settings

Name * | College Lookup

Unique Name * | College_Lookup [i]

Add Description

▼ Filters and Assignments

Look up * | College__c [▼] | that meets the following criteria:

Field	Operator	Value
Name [▼]	equals [▼]	{!College_Name} [▼] 🗑

Add Row

☐ Sort results by: | Select field [▼] | -- Select One -- [▼]

Assign the record's fields to variables to reference them in your flow.

Field	Variable
Main_Number__c [▼]	{!Main_Number} [▼] 🗑

Add Row

☑ [i] Assign null values to the variable(s) if no records are found.

Figure 6-16. *The configuration screen for the College_Lookup element*

Once complete, connect the Transfer_Type_Decision element to this newly created College_Lookup element. The default outcome will automatically be chosen for you. If you remember, we renamed the default outcome to "College Outcome," so that will be visible on the Canvas. The College_Lookup element will get the data required for the next transfer screen we are about to create for the transfer to a specific college. Drag a Screen element to the Canvas and use Figure 6-17 as a reference to configure it.

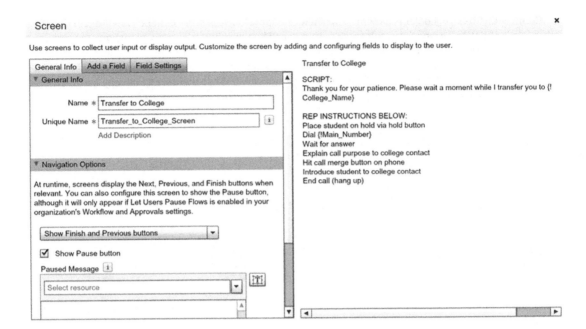

Figure 6-17. *The configuration screen for the Transfer_to_College_Screen element*

Once complete, connect the College_Lookup element to the Transfer_to_College_Screen element. This is the success path from the Record Lookup again. We will need a fault path. So add another Screen element to the Canvas and set it up as in Figure 6-18.

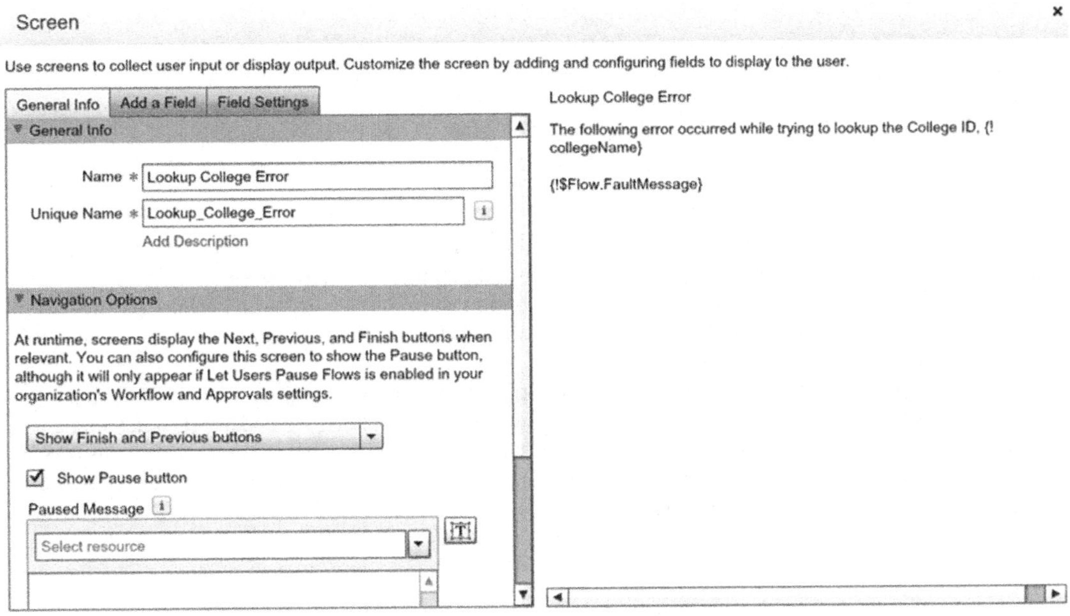

Figure 6-18. *The configuration screen for the Lookup_College_Error element*

Connect the College_Lookup element to this new Lookup_College_Error element. Notice again that the path is labeled "FAULT" to show that this is the path that will be taken in the event of an unexpected error.

We no longer need to add any more new elements. Simply connect the Transfer_to_College_Screen element to the End_Screen element. Once we do that we have just about completed this flow. Go ahead and save it with the name "Call Center Transfer Subflow" and activate it. While there are many ways to organize the elements of this flow on the Canvas, one way would be to organize it as in Figure 6-19.

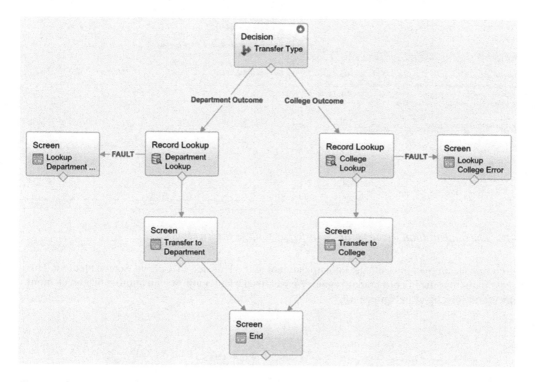

Figure 6-19. *The completed "Call Center Transfer Subflow" flow*

Call Center Flow

While it was a bit of an undertaking to set up the "Call Center Transfer Subflow," it almost feels bittersweet because we can't really use it yet. The subflow was created so that it can be called by our main "Call Center" flow which we have yet to create. As you see, we have to build this from the bottom up because if the main flow is to call into the subflow, then of course the subflow needs to exist first. Looking back at the design, this is going to be the long part of the process.

First, we are planning to have this flow be called from a button on the Account page. While we have not yet dived into the technicalities of how this is going to work, the one thing we do know is that some data needs to be passed into this main flow from the student's account. It may not be obvious yet how this is even possible, but trust that we will get to that part. Let's first set up the variables that will store the data that will be passed to this flow from the account detail page.

Create a new flow and once in Cloud Flow Designer create four variables using the configuration settings as seen in Figure 6-20, Figure 6-21, Figure 6-22, and Figure 6-23. Pay special attention to the Input/Output Type of each variable as some are inputs into this main flow only while others are not only inputs to this main flow but also outputs to be used as inputs into our just created subflow.

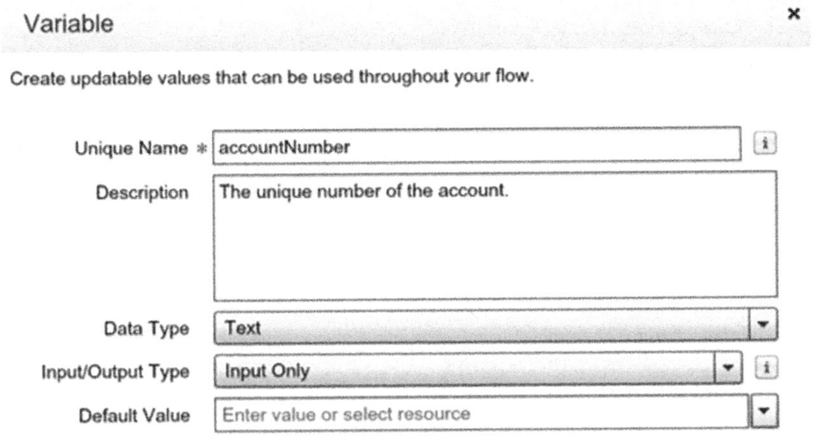

Figure 6-20. *The accountNumber variable configuration*

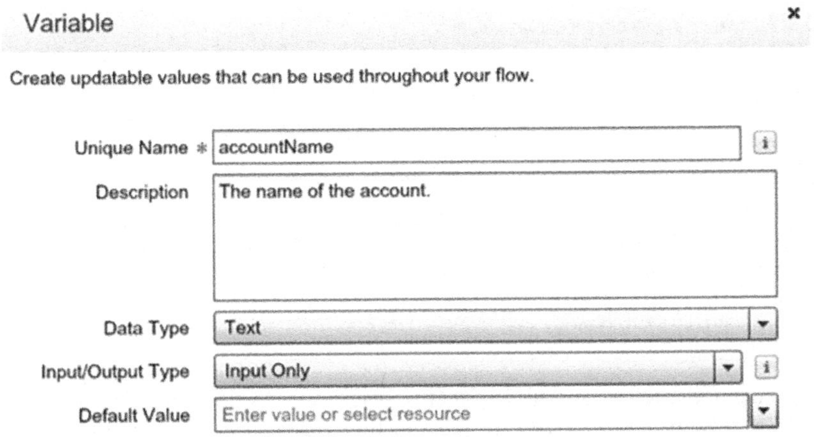

Figure 6-21. *The accountName variable configuration*

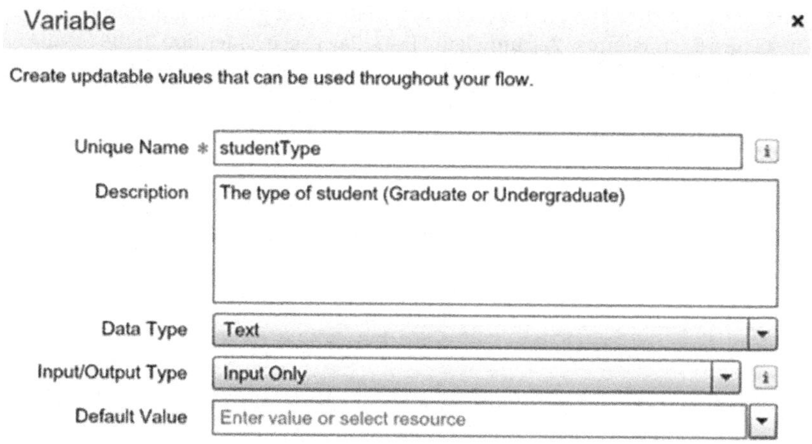

Variable   ✕

Create updatable values that can be used throughout your flow.

Unique Name *	studentType	ⓘ
Description	The type of student (Graduate or Undergraduate)	
Data Type	Text	▼
Input/Output Type	Input Only	▼ ⓘ
Default Value	Enter value or select resource	▼

Figure 6-22. *The studentType variable configuration*

Variable   ✕

Create updatable values that can be used throughout your flow.

Unique Name *	collegeName	ⓘ
Description	The ID of the college the student is enrolled in.	
Data Type	Text	▼
Input/Output Type	Input and Output	▼ ⓘ
Default Value	Enter value or select resource	▼

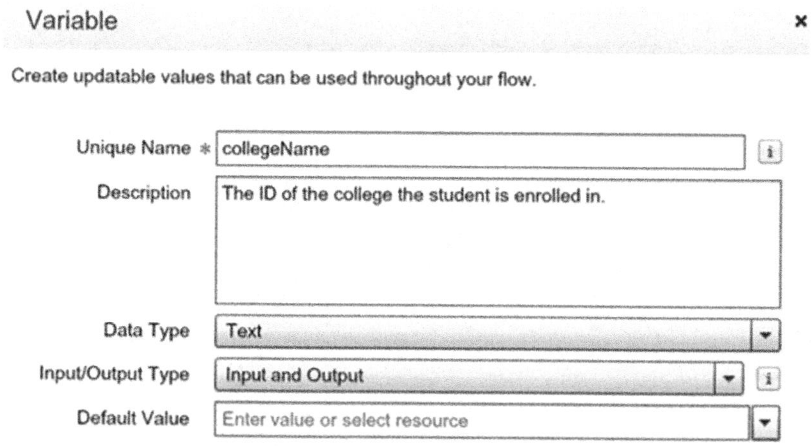

Figure 6-23. *The collegeName variable configuration*

Now that the variables are set up we need a constant too. On the Resources tab add a new constant using the configuration settings as seen in Figure 6-24. We are creating this constant so that it can store the name of the university to be used on any screens in the flow. Instead of adding this as a variable that can be modified, we are instead setting it as a constant that cannot be changed once a flow has started. Constants are very handy for setting up data that should be protected from being altered.

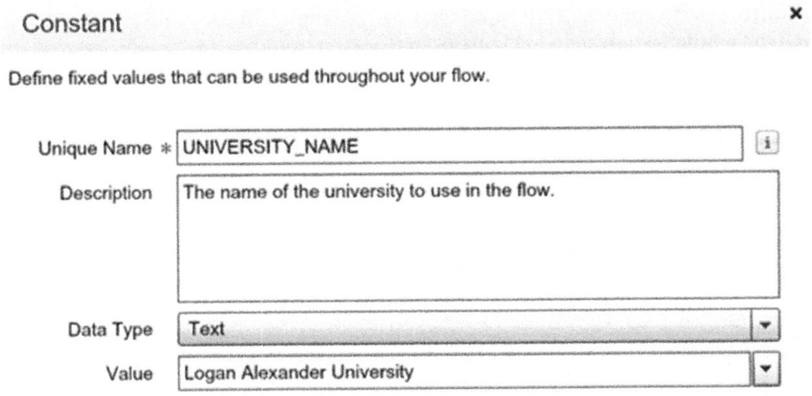

Constant ✗

Define fixed values that can be used throughout your flow.

Unique Name ✱	UNIVERSITY_NAME [i]
Description	The name of the university to use in the flow.
Data Type	Text ▼
Value	Logan Alexander University ▼

Figure 6-24. *The UNIVERSITY_NAME constant*

Now let's begin adding elements onto the Canvas! This time let's add and configure all the elements on the Canvas and then connect them all at the end to speed things along. First, add a Screen element to the Canvas and configure it to match Figure 6-25.

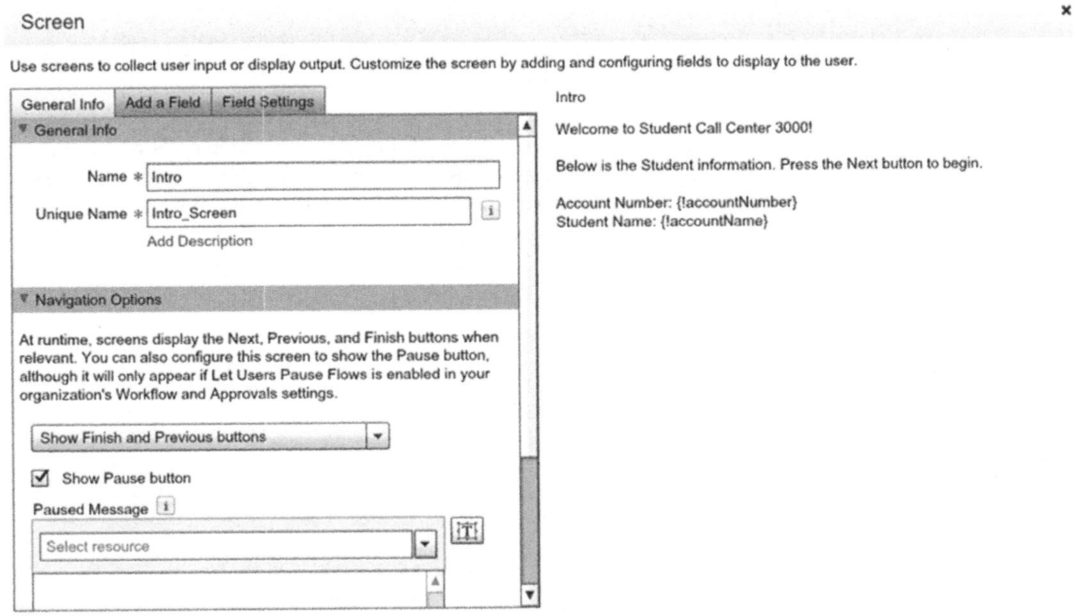

Screen ✗

Use screens to collect user input or display output. Customize the screen by adding and configuring fields to display to the user.

General Info	Add a Field	Field Settings

▼ General Info

Name ✱ Intro

Unique Name ✱ Intro_Screen [i]

Add Description

▼ Navigation Options

At runtime, screens display the Next, Previous, and Finish buttons when relevant. You can also configure this screen to show the Pause button, although it will only appear if Let Users Pause Flows is enabled in your organization's Workflow and Approvals settings.

Show Finish and Previous buttons ▼

☑ Show Pause button

Paused Message [i]

Select resource ▼

Intro

Welcome to Student Call Center 3000!

Below is the Student information. Press the Next button to begin.

Account Number: {!accountNumber}
Student Name: {!accountName}

Figure 6-25. *The configuration for the Intro_Screen element*

Once complete, set this Intro_Screen element as the start element. Second, add a Decision element to the Canvas. Set it up to match the configuration seen in Figure 6-26.

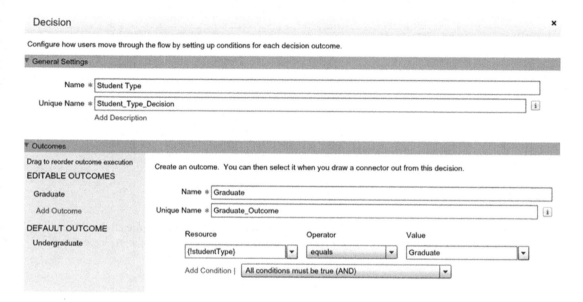

Figure 6-26. *The configuration for the Student_Type_Decision element*

This next step requires us to use the "Call Center Transfer Subflow" flow we created earlier. You can find it in the Palette under FLOWS. Simply drag it over to the Canvas and use the configuration settings seen in Figure 6-27 to configure an instance of the "Call Center Transfer Subflow" for use in this flow.

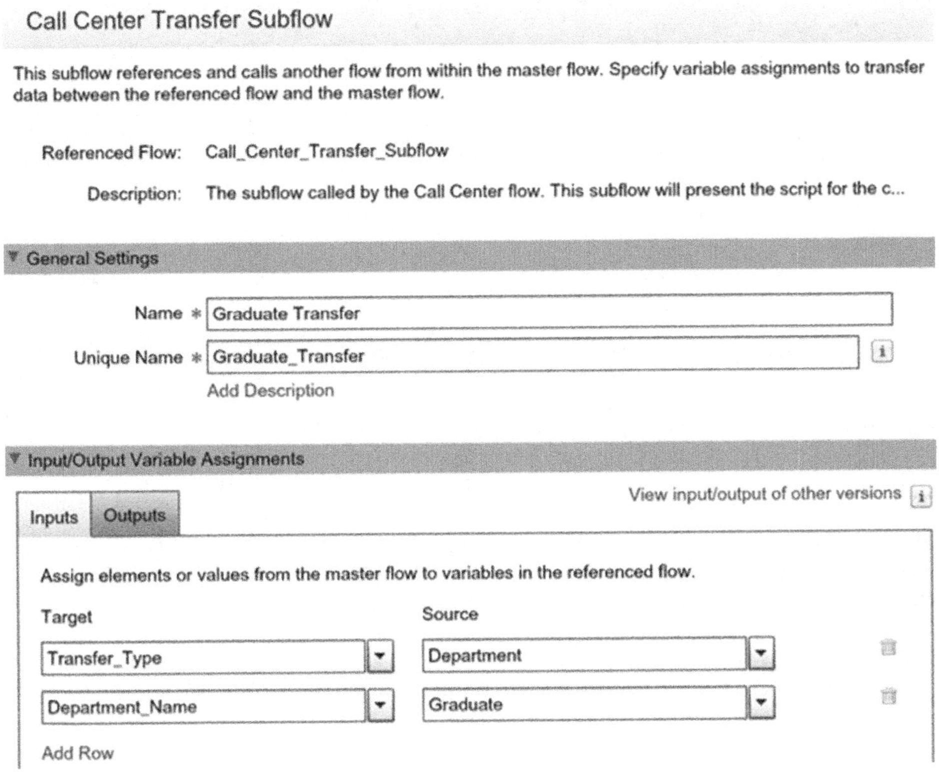

Call Center Transfer Subflow

This subflow references and calls another flow from within the master flow. Specify variable assignments to transfer data between the referenced flow and the master flow.

Referenced Flow: Call_Center_Transfer_Subflow

Description: The subflow called by the Call Center flow. This subflow will present the script for the c...

▼ General Settings

Name ∗ [Graduate Transfer]

Unique Name ∗ [Graduate_Transfer]   [i]

Add Description

▼ Input/Output Variable Assignments

View input/output of other versions [i]

| Inputs | **Outputs** |

Assign elements or values from the master flow to variables in the referenced flow.

Target   Source

[Transfer_Type] [▾]   [Department] [▾]   🗑

[Department_Name] [▾]   [Graduate] [▾]   🗑

Add Row

Figure 6-27. *The configuration for the Graduate_Transfer element*

For the Outputs tab we actually do not need any outputs. If you try to click the OK button to save these settings without touching the Outputs tab then you will see an error stating to "Correct the invalid field entries" and Cloud Flow Designer will highlight the fields in Figure 6-28. You do not need to configure them though. Instead, click the trashcan icon to remove the row for the Source/Target fields. Now you can safely click the OK button and continue to create more elements on the canvas.

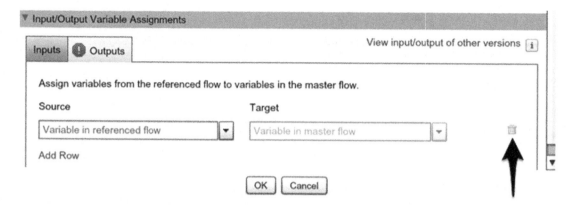

Figure 6-28. *The Outputs tab when the Source/Target fields are not configured*

The Main Flow

In order to speed things along and not get into every single aspect of every single screen, we are going to skip the setting up of each element from here on. The reason is that we have already covered how to set up Screen elements, Decision elements, and Flow elements. Instead, try to finish the remaining elements as per the design. When finished, connect them as they are connected in this complete flow in Figure 6-29. Once completed, save as "Call Center" if you have not already done so. Finally, activate this flow to make it available for the next step, which is very interesting: passing input variables into a flow from the Account detail page.

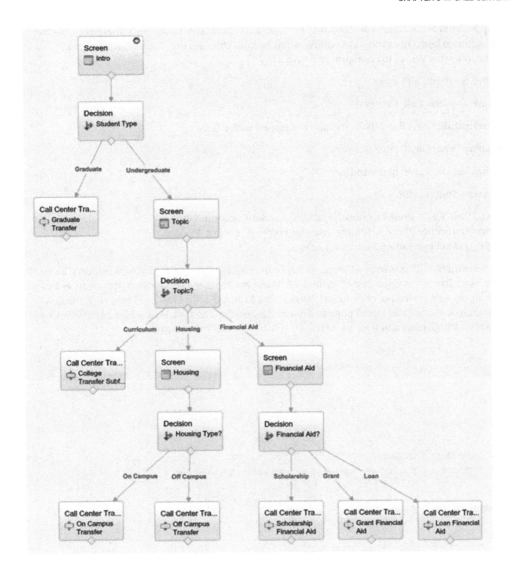

Figure 6-29. *The final flow layed out on the Canvas in Cloud Flow Designer*

Up to this point we have created the flows and tested them via the Run button in Cloud Flow Designer, but the flows have not be added to existing Salesforce functionality. In other words, they have not been easily accessible by Salesforce users. Our design calls for the ability to start the call center script from an Account record detail page. Doing this is quite simple. Let us begin.

Go to Setup ➤ Build ➤ Customize ➤ Accounts ➤ Buttons, Links, and Actions. Once there click the New Button or Link button to begin the process of adding a new button. Once on the "New Button or Link" edit page, use the following values to configure and save it:

- **Label**: Student Call Center

- **Name**: Student_Call_Center

- **Description**: Starts the Call Center app developed with a flow

- **Display Type**: Detail Page Button

- **Behavior**: Display in new window

- **Content Source**: URL

- **Text**: /flow/Call_Center?accountNumber={!Account.AccountNumber }&accountName={!Account.Name}&studentType={!Account.Student_ Type__c}&collegeName={!Account.College__c}

Notice the text entered? This is where the magic happens. First of all the URL (uniform resource locator) is the URL to the flow. To get this value just go to Setup ➤ Build ➤ Create ➤ Workflows & Approvals ➤ Flows as usual. This time, though, instead of clicking the "Open" link to go to Cloud Flow Designer click the flow name. This will take you to the Flow Detail page as seen in Figure 6-30. The URL is listed for each flow. Copy that URL on the Flow Detail page and then paste it as the URL to go to for the button.

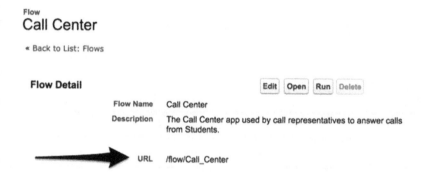

Figure 6-30. *Find the URL to the flow on the Flow Detail page*

Since this is a URL, though, we are allowed to enter in a query string just like the one you normally see in your browser's address bar. The trick is to use the name of each input variable we created in our main flow and put them in the query string. Then, for the value to pass, we can use standard merge fields. Pretty cool stuff!

■ **Note** The first query string parameter in a URL must start with "?" while all subsequent parameters start with "&".

While being able to pass variables in the URL query is convenient, there are some limitations.

- Flow SObject variables and sObject collection variables cannot be set.

- Only flow variables of Input/Output Type set to allow input access can be set.

- Variable names are case sensitive, so accountNumber and AccountNumber are considered two different variables

- Flow currency variables cannot be set by a currency merge field because currency merge fields include the currency symbol such as $. Flow currency variables must instead be set with a number field in order not to include the currency symbol.

You can set collection variables (not to be confused with sObject collection variables) with the following format:

```
http://instance.salesforce.com/flow/flowName?collectionName=value1&collectionName=value2
```

Table 6-1 shows a table of acceptable values that can be passed in the URL for each flow variable type.

Table 6-1. Table of allowed merge field types of values for each flow variable type

Flow Variable Type	Allowed Merge Field Types	Allowed Values
Text	Merge field of any type	Any string
Number	Merge field of type Number	Any numeric value
Currency	Merge field of type Number	Any numeric value
Boolean	Merge field of type Check box	For a TRUE value: "true" or "1" For a FALSE value: "false" or "0"
Date	Merge field of type Date	String of format "YYYY-MM-DD"
DateTime	Merge field of type Date/Time	String of format "YYY-MM-DDThh:mm:ssZ"

Finish Behavior

If you have ever reached the end of a flow and clicked the Finish button you may have noticed that the flow will start back at the very first screen of the flow. This normally isn't the desired behavior. Instead of relying on this default behavior you can set the retURL parameter on the URL to define what Salesforce page to redirect to once you've clicked the Finish button.

In the example that follows:

```
https://instance.salesforce.com/flow/flowName?retURL=pageName
```

would redirect to

```
https://instance.salesforce.com/pageName
```

Even the retURL has limitations though. These include the following:

- Flow users cannot be redirected to a URL external to your Salesforce organization

- Flow variables cannot be used as the value of the retURL parameter.

- Depending on the scenario, the retURL can cause nested top navigation and side navigation bars to render on the destination page. So be careful how it's used! To avoid this try making sure that the flow is on its own page and doesn't already have a top or side navigation. Having a retURL set to the calling record with a value such as "&retURL=/{!Account.Id}" helps too.

Update Account Page Layout

Now that the custom button is created we need to add it to the page layout for the Account. Do this by going to Setup ➤ Build ➤ Customize ➤ Accounts ➤ Page Layouts and once there find the appropriate Account page layout that the button belongs to. Click the edit link for that page layout and add the custom button to that page layout. Figure 6-31 illustrates the process of adding the custom Student Call Center button to the page layout.

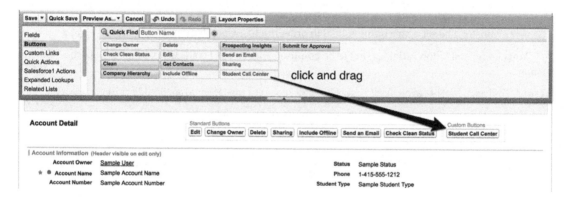

Figure 6-31. *Illustration of how to add the Student Call Center custom button to the Account page layout*

Click the Save button to keep the changes made to the page layout. Amazingly this is all that is needed to start the flow. Using a custom button is a very common practice to call a flow. By linking the flow to the button and then the button to a page layout, you can now define alternate business processes to your organization. Fun stuff!

Done, Done, and Wait There's More

If you made it this far then congratulations! We had to put a lot of work into this flow. Not only did the flow need to do a lot of different things, but we needed to do some work on the custom objects, fields, and button to get it to work seamlessly. Now if you go to an Account record, you can click the custom Student Call Center button and begin the call center script that was just implemented.

Hold on a minute, though! We thought we were done, but after your manager saw the demo for the call center script you got some feedback. Your manager does not like the out-of-the-box styles for the screens in the call center flow. Your manager thinks they look too plain and need to be jazzed up a bit. What are we going to do now? Do we disappoint your manager and say it cannot be done? Let's hope not, because while it isn't obvious, there actually is a way to style the implemented flow. Are you not entertained? Is that not why you are here?

The answer lies in Visualforce! You are thinking this was supposed to be a way to develop without code. Well, we might need a little help here but I assure you that the Visualforce code is very much a copy-and-paste activity. The styling might need some help from a user interface designer or possibly some sort of WYSIWYG tool where you can style web pages with point and click. That depends on what is available in your organization, but we will go through how we can style the flow and add some corporate branding to it.

Adding a flow to a Visualforce Page

To begin, you first need to create a Visualforce Page or edit an existing one. To create a new Visualforce Page go to Setup ➤ Build ➤ Develop ➤ Visualforce Pages and click the New button. Now we are going into an area that is usually more accustomed to developers. On the Visualforce Page edit screen you will see the normal fields you are used to, including:

- Label

- Name

- Description

While these look pretty standard, there are a couple of check boxes and this really large field labeled "Visualforce Markup" on a tab. Here we can enter Visualforce code that includes HTML (Hypertext Markup Language), CSS (Cascading Style Sheets), and JavaScript. This can be daunting for the uninitiated. To keep it simple, though, here are two boilerplate code samples you can use. Both of these examples will use the Call Center flow name (which is "Call_Center") as the flow. Both examples embed the flow using a special Visualforce tag, <flow:interview>, that embeds the flow onto a Visualforce page. The first example in Figure 6-32 simply embeds the Call Center flow on the page without any special options.

```
<apex:page>
    <flow:interview name="Call_Center" />
</apex:page>
```

Figure 6-32. *Visualforce markup for embedding a flow within a Visualforce Page*

The second example in Figure 6-33 also embeds the Call Center flow on the page but has several options. Notice that there are three attributes, sidebar, showHeader, and standardStylesheets, set to false. Setting these to false will remove the Salesforce sidebar, remove the Salesforce header, and remove the Salesforce user interface elements such as colors and font sizes to name a few. Any of these values could be changed from false to true in order to make that attribute's respective elements appear.

```
<apex:page sidebar="false" showHeader="false" standardStylesheets="false">
    <flow:interview name="Call_Center" />
</apex:page>
```

Figure 6-33. *Visualforce markup for embedding a flow within a Visualforce Page without standard Salesforce user interface elements*

Of course the Call Center flow expects some initial values at startup so the past few examples will not allow the flow to run correctly. If you need to set some variables at startup you cannot pass them in the URL. Instead, you can pass them in with Visualforce markup code. For example parameter we need to pass we need to have a <apex:param> tag include between the <flow:interview> start/end tags such as in Figure 6-34.

```
<apex:page standardController="Account">
    <flow:interview name="Call_Center">
        <apex:param name="accountNumber" value="{!Account.AccountNumber}" />
        <apex:param name="accountName" value="{!Account.Name}" />
        <apex:param name="studentType" value="{!Account.Student_Type__c}" />
        <apex:param name="collegeName" value="{!Account.College__r.Name}" />
    </flow:interview>
</apex:page>
```

Figure 6-34. *Visualforce markup for a flow with parameters*

There is much more you can do too that goes more into the developer aspect of Visualforce and Apex, such as using a custom controller instead of a standard controller as in the previous example. Another example would be to set the standardStylesheets attribute in the <apex:page> tag to false and then use custom CSS to make the background, fonts, and buttons appear a very specific way.

Find more information in the *Visualforce Developer Guide* at

https://developer.salesforce.com/docs/atlas.en-us.pages.meta/pages/pages_flows_intro.htm

Recap

In this chapter we covered how to develop a call center application that guides call center representatives with a script when they receive phone calls from students at the university. We showed how to plan and design a complicated flow that has many aspects to it, including several branches during the process plus retrieving specific data from Salesforce on the fly while walking through the flow screens. Some new material included showing you how to add the flow as an alternate business process by using a custom button added to a page layout. It is easy to tie a custom button to a flow via the flow's unique URL. Then that custom button can be added to a page layout, providing an easy way for a Salesforce user to execute the flow. Finally, we took it a step further and explained how a flow can be added to a Visualforce page with the <flow:interview> tag. Once the flow is called within the Visualforce page there are more options available on how to pass parameters and use custom HTML, CSS, and JavaScript to change the look and feel of the flows.

CHAPTER 7

■ ■ ■

Lightning Process Builder Basics

This book has spent a considerable amount of time diving into the details of Visual Workflow and how to develop with it while adhering to tried-and-true software development principles. Visual Workflow gives an extreme amount of power to the Salesforce administrator or developer to create software graphically. It is very flexible as well. Every twist and turn with the flows we have created so far is greeted with a configuration window that ensures that the element placed on the Canvas behaves exactly how we want it to behave. Not only that, but the connectors between all those elements can be wired, removed, and rewired to our heart's content. With that power and flexibility comes more complication though. On one hand we have standard Salesforce Workflows, which are very simple to create but also very simple in what they are able to do. Then, on the other hand, we have this sweet new technology from Visual Workflow that puts a development environment in our hands to achieve what we could only achieve before from Visualforce and Apex programming.

Visual Workflow is very flexible but also very complicated. On the other hand, standard Workflows are a lot simpler but lack the graphical interface. Lightning Process Builder takes the idea of Salesforce Workflowx to the next level by giving it a visual environment to create "processes." It takes the success of Visual Workflow but simplifies it to a point that it's just as uncomplicated as standard Salesforce Workflow.

Salesforce Workflow has that tried-and-true user interface that Salesforce has used successfully for years. With Salesforce Workflow you click the "New" button to create a Workflow then walk through a wizard that guides you through all the steps to put together a single workflow. It's the familiar interface filled with links and buttons. No graphical interface, no drag and drop, no special tool like the Flow Designer that Visual Workflow has. It was great for its time because it worked in all the major browsers and simplicity was king. These days though, modern web sites and apps provide a more robust experience for users. It seems like everyone has a smart phone to touch and move elements around. If not then they have access to a computer with a modern web browser to do the same.

Lightning Process Builder is actually built on top of Visual Workflow. It puts a layer on top of Visual Workflow to create workflows or processes that are not as complicated as a flow but actually do have more functionality than a standard Salesforce Workflow. Lightning Process Builder also is its own development environment that is separate from Visual Workflow. It does not use Flow Designer. Instead, Lightning Process Builder uses an approach similar to the Canvas in Flow Designer but has placeholders that guide you with the process on its version of a Canvas.

What Exactly Is a Process?

A process in Lightning Process Builder is basically a series of steps to take when an event occurs. Doing a quick web search gives the following definition of the word "process."

a series of actions or steps taken in order to achieve a particular end

© Jonathan Keel 2016

J. Keel, *Salesforce.com Lightning Process Builder and Visual Workflow*, DOI 10.1007/978-1-4842-1691-0_7

So, a process is a pretty general idea! The term can be applied to any sort of series of steps but it's important to not underestimate the power of a process. When you train someone to use Salesforce, you are training that person in a business process. When you define a Salesforce Workflow, then you are creating a process to be followed. When you configure approval steps in Salesforce, you are creating a process. If you make a peanut butter and jelly sandwich you likely follow a process! Processes are all around us. It's a part of everything we do daily.

With Lightning Process Builder a process is a series of steps as well. It's the combination of a workflow, approvals, and other new capabilities that were not available before. That's right! Instead of having to create a workflow in one tool and then a set of approval steps in another, you can do both with Lightning Process Builder. On top of that, some other actions are available as well. The full list includes the ability to

- Create a record for an object

- Update any related record (also includes any record besides itself or its parent)

- Submit a record for approval

- Send an e-mail

- Post to Chatter

- Use quick actions that can create or update records or even log a call

- Kick off a Flow created in Cloud Flow Designer

- Call invocable methods in Apex

The Anatomy of a Process

A process is composed of its properties, the records it applies to, its criteria, and its actions. Basically, to have a process one needs to specify the object it applies to, its criteria if the object's records should be evaluated for the process, and then the set of actions to take if the record falls within the set of defined criteria.

To get a better understanding, let's go to Lightning Process Builder in Salesforce. To do so, log into your Salesforce org and go to the Administration Setup just as we did with Visual Workflow. This time go to Create > Workflow & Approvals > Process Builder as seen in Figure 7-1.

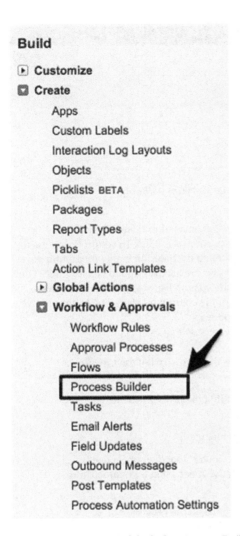

Figure 7-1. Location of the link to Process Builder in the Setup navigation menu

Once you click the "Process Builder" link you are presented with the new Lightning user interface. Salesforce has branded its newer user experiences as "Lightning" and they look very different from the previous Salesforce user experience (known as Salesforce Classic). Instead of the familiar screens, there are rich interfaces to interact with. Figure 7-2 shows what the first screen looks like for Lightning Process Builder.

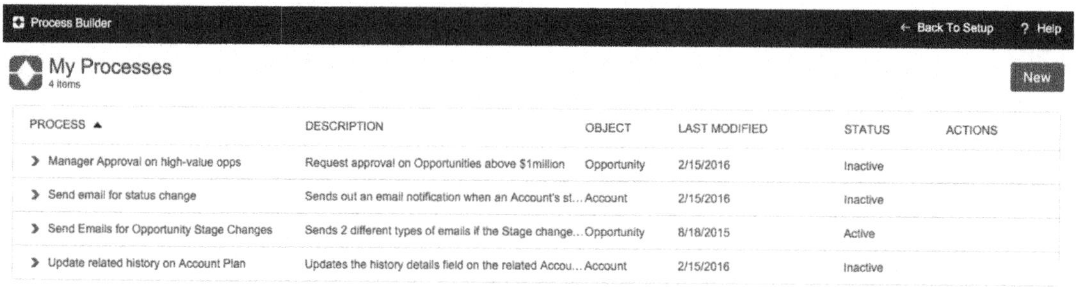

Figure 7-2. *The My Processes screen in Process Builder shows all the processes in the org*

The first thing to notice is that the colors are different and the left navigation menu is gone. It's as though you have left the administration setup altogether. No fear, as there is a "Back To Setup" link at the top right side of the screen. Also, next to that is a link for help to be taken to the Salesforce documentation pages.

Below all that is what takes the place of the standard list views we are accustomed to in Salesforce. The New button has been shifted to the far right and the ability to create custom list views has been removed. The view that remains can be sorted by clicking the name of one of the column headers. The columns have different information about each of the processes, described as follows:

- **PROCESS**: The name of the process created.

- **DESCRIPTION**: The details of the process. This helps distinguish what the process does since the process name length is limited.

- **OBJECT**: The name of the standard or custom object that the process will be triggered off of.

- **LAST MODIFIED**: The date that the process was last changed.

- **STATUS**: The current state of the process. The status can be "Inactive" or "Active." Inactive means that it is disabled and will not run. Active means that it's enabled and will run for the object listed.

- **ACTIONS**: A list of action links to perform certain actions on the processes themselves. An example of an action is "Delete." The Delete action allows the deletion of a specific version of a process.

This screen itself isn't the core of process builder's user interface though. To see that, first click the New button to open up the New Process window as seen in Figure 7-3.

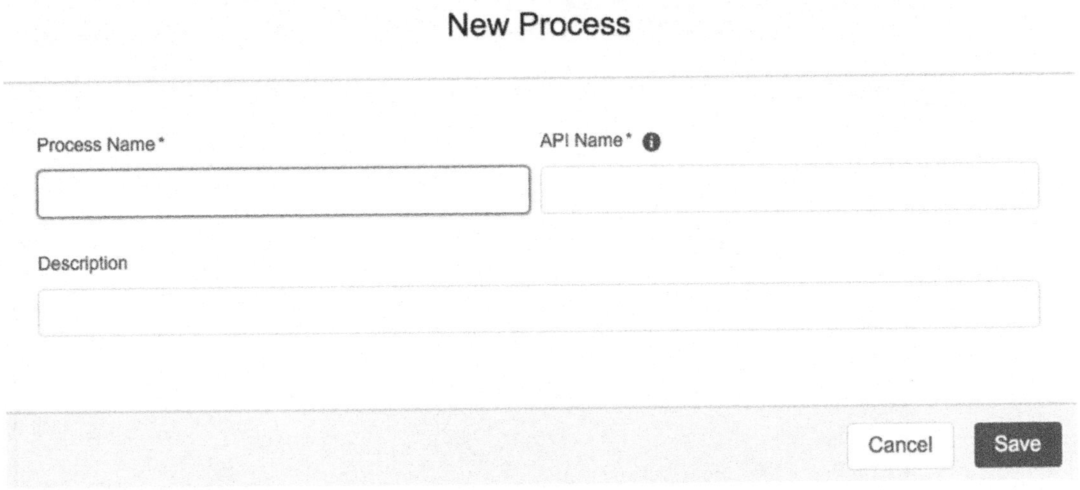

New Process

Process Name*

API Name* ⓘ

Description

Cancel   Save

Figure 7-3. *The New Process window seen before entering into the editor*

There are three fields on the New Process window.

- **Process Name**: The user-friendly name or label.

- **API Name**: The named used to reference the process elsewhere in the system, including managed packages. The API (application programming interface) name follows the standard naming rules regarding API names such as:

  - must begin with a letter

  - must use only alphanumeric characters and underscores

  - cannot include spaces

  - cannot end with an underscore, or

  - cannot have two consecutive underscores

- **Description**: The details to process to help explain further what it does.

■ **Note**   Once the API Name is set, it cannot be changed like other API Names in Salesforce. The reason for that is because inside the process, any component added in it is internally given an API Name that is based on the API Name of the process.

Once the proper entries are made in the New Process screen and the Save button is clicked, then the main Process Builder edit will finally come up as in Figure 7-4. This is the user interface that is used to build all processes for Lightning Process Builder.

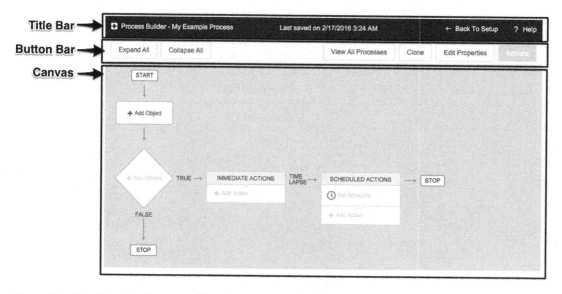

Figure 7-4. *The Lightning Process Builder editor with an empty process*

Lightning Process Builder User Interface

The first thing we notice when looking at how the user interface of the Lightning Process Builder is set up is that not only is it nothing like the Salesforce tools seen before, but it's also very different from how the Visual Workflow looks. While Process Builder is actually built on top of Visual Workflow, Salesforce has simplified the interface on how processes are built. Let's dive into some of the elements of Lightning Process Builder.

Title Bar

The dark blue bar at the top is the Title Bar. Its main purpose is really the same you might find in some full-fledged applications on your personal computer.

- Provide the name of the process being built

- Provide the last timestamp of when the process was saved

- Provide a way back to the Setup home screen

- Provide help for Lighting Process Builder

Button Bar

Under the Title Bar is the Button Bar. This closely resembles a Menu Bar in other applications. It has the following buttons:

- **Expand All:** expands all the actions on the canvas

- **Collapse All:** collapses all the actions on the canvas

- **View All Processes:** opens the My Processes page

- **Clone:** makes a copy of the current process to begin new development under a different process name

- **Edit Properties:** opens the Properties screen to view or edit the current properties of the process. Properties Screen contains:

  - Process Name

  - API Name

  - Description

  - Version History

- **Activate/Deactivate:** allows the process to be toggled from active to inactive. Active processes are allowed to execute while inactive processes are not.

Canvas

The Canvas is where you build the meat of the process. Please refer to Figure 7-4 and each number listed on it to match up the following descriptions:

- **Add Object:** Just like a standard Workflow, a process needs to start with a specific object to evaluate its records for a process.

- **Add Criteria:** Criteria to match which records of the object are to be a part of the process

- **Immediate Actions:** Actions to take on the records as soon as they meet the specified criteria

- **Scheduled Actions:** Actions to take on the records at a later scheduled time from when they met the specified criteria

Essentially, with those three parts of the process being built in the Canvas you can build simple to complex processes. That's because many more criteria/immediate actions/scheduled actions combinations can be added. You are not limited to just one. Every time there is a not a match in the criteria and the logic goes down the "FALSE" path, you get another chance to add another criteria before the process stops.

Figure 7-5 shows an example of a process with multiple criteria elements. As of the Salesforce Spring 2016 release, the limit of criteria nodes that can be evaluated and actions that are executed at runtime is 2000!

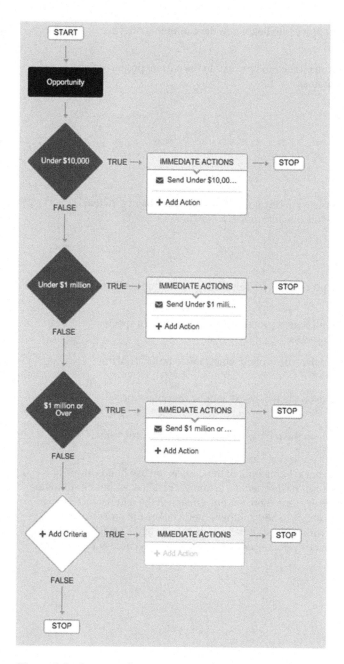

Figure 7-5. *An example process with many criteria nodes and its actions*

When to Use Lightning Process Builder vs. Salesforce Workflow

As you can see, things have changed a lot! The new Lightning Process Builder looks completely different from the standard Salesforce Workflow Rules and Workflow Actions. The way one goes about building processes is graphical, similar to Visual Workflow. Unlike Visual Workflow, the elements on the Canvas and how they are arranged are limited. That doesn't mean Lightning Process Builder is not powerful though. It just keeps the spirit of what Workflow Rules and Workflow Actions were meant for and improves upon that mission. It provides a more intuitive interface to build out the process for Salesforce to execute while not overcomplicating the process.

Beyond the new interface there are distinct functional differences between what Lightning Process Builder and Salesforce Workflow are capable of. To further illustrate these differences refer to Table 7-1.

Table 7-1. Lightning Process Builder vs. Workflow Capability Matrix

	Lightning Process Builder	Workflow
Conditional Statements (If/Then Logic)	Multiple if/then statements	A single if/then statement
Graphical Development	X	
Time-Based Actions	Multiple schedules per criteria	A single schedule per criteria
Call Apex Code	X	
Create Records	Standard and Custom	Tasks only
Delete Records		
Update Records	The record or any related record	The record or its parent
Launch Flows	X	(Pilot)[1]
Post to Chatter	X	
Send E-mail Alerts	X	X
Send Outbound Messages (without code)		X
Submit for Approval	X	

■ **Note**   While it says "PILOT," The Process Builder has superseded flow trigger workflow actions, formerly available in a pilot program. Organizations that are using flow trigger workflow actions can continue to create and edit them, but flow trigger workflow actions aren't available for new organizations.

Now that we have a nice reference table for the differences between Lightning Process Builder and Workflow Rules/Actions let's dive a little deeper into what these mean for us when developing on Salesforce.

Conditional Statements (If-Then Logic)

With both Lightning Process Builder and Workflow Rules you need to set up criteria to look at one specific object. Think of the criteria as a "listener." That "listener" can only listen to one object (standard or custom) at time. If that object is created or updated, then the listener will be aware of the change. Then, the criteria can be more specific regarding the details of what to look for. The criteria can say that not only is the object modified but only pay further attention to it if one or more fields are updated with specific values. This is the same for Lightning Process Builder and Workflow Rules. The big difference is that in Lightning Process Builder, multiple criteria can be defined (for a specific object). For each one of those criteria, then an appropriate action can be made. This gives you the capability of multiple "If/Then" logic statements. This means that a process criterion can be configured to say "if <criteria met> then <do action(s)." In Lightning Process Builder if that criterion is not met, then another criterion can be configured to ask another "if/then" statement. This gives an administrator a lot of power and flexibility with what actions are performed for specific scenarios. To make a simpler point, multiple Workflow Rules could be reduced to a single process in Lightning Process Builder.

■ **Note**   While Lightning Process Builder can do most of what Workflow Rules do, the one thing it cannot do as of yet is send outbound messages—unless Apex code is written to do so.

Graphical Development

As seen so far, Lightning Process Builder looks similar to Visual Workflow. There is a Canvas with multiple shapes and each has a specific purpose. Each shape can be clicked to display its properties in order to configure it to behave accordingly. While the shapes cannot be moved around on the Canvas there can be more added in order to accommodate more complicated process requirements. Meanwhile, Workflow Rules are completely textual. This means that every screen that is used just has text to display what it is to be configured. Workflow Rules are configured just like most other Salesforce configurations. A new button is clicked and the user is presented with a wizard that is a series of data entry screens. With complicated Workflow requirements, it can be difficult to get a holistic view of what the system is doing and what the requirements are since no single diagram to represent all the rules.

Time-Based actions

A time-based action is an action that can be scheduled later in time. Usually when criteria are met in a process or a workflow immediate action can be taken. However, with a time-based action the action can be delayed for a later period in time. This is useful for scheduling the action similar to scheduling an event on a calendar. For example, a time-based action could be created for Opportunities that have an amount over $1 million. That time-based action could send an e-mail to the owner of an Opportunity seven days from the close date as a reminder. This type of action is achievable in both Lightning Process Builder and Workflow. The big difference though is that in a Workflow Rule you can create only one time-based action per criteria, but in Lightning Process Builder you can create multiple time-based actions. Lightning Process Builder calls these "scheduled actions." With this ability to have multiple scheduled actions in Lightning Process Builder a process could be set up to send out e-mail reminders seven days before Opportunity close date, and then again two days before close date, and finally one day before. This can be done all in one single process. Figure 7-6 shows this Lightning Process Builder example.

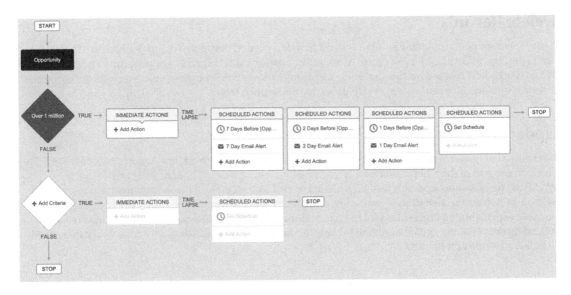

Figure 7-6. *An example process with multiple scheduled actions*

Call Apex Code

Workflow Rules have never been able to call Apex code. The closest feature to calling code is being able to send an Outbound Message that can, in turn, call a web service. With Lightning Process Builder, calling Apex is now possible. A process cannot call any Apex code though. It can only call an "invocable method" on an Apex class. What is an invocable method you ask? It's a static Apex method but with an extra line of code prepended to it. Salesforce calls this prepended line of code an "annotation." Adding the @InvocableMethod annotation above a static method allows the method to be called from a Process. The following code is an example of an invocable method that generates a random number from 0 to 999. Please keep in mind, that only one @InvocableMethod annotated method is allowed per Apex class.

```
@InvocableMethod
public static Integer getRandomNumber() {
    return Math.round(Math.random() * 1000);
}
```

Calling Apex code should be the exception and not the rule. Lightning Process Builder provides a lot of freedom and flexibility to create many different types of processes without code. That said, there are limitations to its capability, and sometimes having code perform complex logic is either the only way to meet a requirement or possibly a more efficient way to meet the requirement.

Create Records

Lightning Process Builder has the capability of creating records for both standard and custom Salesforce objects. This is a huge benefit! Workflow Rules and Actions can be used only to create Tasks. If the requirement were to create a custom object record or even a Standard object record (e.g., an Account), then a Trigger would need to be developed to do the necessary work. Such a needed task was limited to the realm of developers. Now with Lightning Process Builder this can be done with clicks, not code.

Delete Records

It may seem strange to note this in Table 7-1 and have this section devoted to it, but neither Workflow Rules nor Lightning Process Builder can delete records. This action is still limited to Triggers, Apex code, and Visual Workflow. The good news is that while Lightning Process Builder cannot delete records out of the box, there are options since processes can call Apex code and launch Flows.

Update Records

Workflow Actions can update records. It is a commonly used feature of Workflow Actions to update the object that is part of the criteria matched. It is done with Field Updates. A limitation though is that a Workflow Action cannot update a field on a related record. For example, if the requirement was to update a field on an Account related to an Opportunity, then that would not be possible with a Workflow Action. It is possible with Lightning Process Builder though. Lightning Process Builder has the ability to traverse down related records to do an update similar to the way the Advanced Formula tab in a formula field can be used to build cross-object formulas.

Launch Flows

This book has covered Visual Workflows extensively in the previous chapters. The flows that are built can be very sophisticated. Lightning Process Builder is a simpler way of building business processes, but sometimes what Lightning Process Builder can do is just not enough. That's where the capability to launch a flow can come in handy. Similar to how processes can call Apex code for more sophisticated requirements, a flow can also be called as long as it is an autolaunched flow. If the goal is to write as limited amount of code as possible (and it usually is), then having a process call a flow to pick up the heavy lifting could prove useful so Apex code does not have to be implemented. In the Salesforce Spring 2014 release, the capability to call a Flow from Workflow began its pilot program. Salesforce called these types of flows "Flow Triggers." They did not have a user interface aspect of standard flows. They were considered "headless," meaning that they had no pages that anyone would interact with. Instead, they just ran behind the scenes similar to an Apex Trigger. In October 2014, when Salesforce introduced Lightning Process Builder, the idea would be that it would supersede flow triggers. Organizations that are using flow trigger workflow actions can continue to create and edit them, but flow trigger workflow actions aren't available for new organizations.

Post to Chatter

This one is pretty straightforward. Lightning Process Builder can post to Chatter while Workflow cannot. The only type of notification that Workflow can do is an e-mail notification. Posting to Chatter is out of the question. With Lightning Process Builder, this is an option. When posting to Chatter there are several options. The Chatter post can be posted to the following areas:

- User (a specific user or a user related to the record)
- Chatter group
- This record (the record being evaluated in the process)

In addition, where the post is made, Lightning Process Builder allows for the configuration of the message to be posted. Any post message can be configured including the addition of merge fields from the record or related child record fields. Finally, topics can be added to the message as well.

Send E-mail Alerts

Lightning Process Builder and Workflow can both send out e-mail alerts. Both tools work fundamentally the same way. First you must create an E-mail Template and then an E-mail Alert that is associated with that template. Finally, in either Lightning Process Builder or a Workflow Rule, choose the E-mail Alert as an action that can be performed.

Send Outbound Messages (Without Code)

One of the greatest tools Salesforce has for integration with outside systems is outbound messages. Outbound messages essentially send out updated field values to external servers in a format known as SOAP (Simple Object Access Protocol). SOAP is an enterprise standard for sending information and it's used widely for sending data between different technologies. While sending outbound messages is possible with Workflow, it is not possible with Lightning Process Builder unless you make a call to Apex code.

Submit for Approval

Before Lightning Process Builder, if there was an approval process set up there were two ways to initiate it. The standard way was with an Approval button on the record's Detail page. Someone had to manually click the button to submit the record for approval and start the process. If there was a requirement to submit a record for approval based on a business rule like the change in an Opportunity change, for example, then a trigger needed to be implemented. That, of course, meant Apex code would have to be written. Now, with Lightning Process Builder a trigger does not have to be written. Instead, the process can be configured to submit a record for approval. The configuration for this is so flexible that not only can it submit the default approval process but also it can be configured to select a specific approval process.

Strengths and Weaknesses of Lightning Process Builder

After reviewing the list of differences between standard Salesforce Workflow and the new Lightning Process Builder one could come away with the impression that Workflows should be abandoned and all new development should be in Lightning Process Builder. For the most part this is a correct assumption. Almost everything you can do in a Workflow Rule/Action can be implemented in Lightning Process Builder—and then some. As you can see, though, Lightning Process Builder has some limitations. There are ways to overcome them though. Let's focus a little more the strengths and weaknesses of Lightning Process Builder.

Strengths of Lightning Process Builder

The strengths of Lightning Process Builder are very apparent when looking at the differences between it and Workflow. There were a lot of capabilities that were out of reach for a Salesforce administrator before if he or she didn't know how to develop Apex code. Any time the capabilities of Workflow were reached, an Apex Trigger could be developed. That would mean that a developer or consultant would need to get involved. Lightning Process Builder has less reliance on Apex code development. Some of the strengths that make Lightning Process Builder so great are

- **Visual Development:** Developing a process in Lightning Process Builder is more intuitive due to the visual development environment that is available. This makes it easy to see what is being built out.

- **Better Maintenance:** After a process is built, someone who is not the original author of the process can come in and at a glance see what the process is doing and what it is meant for. You could say that it is "self-documenting." That's due to the visual nature of Lightning Process Builder. Unlike Workflow, you do not have to go hunting around to find any other related Workflow Rules to get an understanding of what the process is doing.

- **Ease of Use:** An administrator can come in and start using Lightning Process Builder fairly quickly without a lot of training. The shapes on the canvas help to guide in the development of the process.

- **Many Capabilities:** Most requirements for an automated business process can be achieved using Lightning Process Builder. With all the capabilities of creating records, updating records, sending messages or notifications via e-mail and chatter, etc., there isn't much it cannot do. Anything that is out of its range can be achieved in a callout to Visual Workflow. Anything that cannot be achieved in a callout to Visual Workflow can be achieved with a callout to Apex code.

- **Versioning:** Processes created are versioned. This means that once a process is created and then activated it is set with a version number—the first version being version 1. Once activated, changes cannot be made to that version. Instead, the version has to be cloned to a new version, such as version 2. Then changes can be made to that version. Each of these versions can be enabled and disabled. This provides the ability not only to keep track of changes in the process but also to go back in time to a previous version of a process. This is useful when something does not work out as intended and a rollback needs to occur.

Weaknesses of Lightning Process Builder

Now that we have touched on some of the strengths of Lightning Process Builder, let's touch on its weaknesses. No system is perfect. Lightning Process Builder is being enhanced with every Salesforce release. At this time, here are some limitations to Lightning Process Builder.

- **Each process is associated with a single object:** Just like Workflow Rules, each process has to be associated with a single object. The criteria that can be configured for a process have to look at one object and the values of the fields on it. If the criteria logic needed to look at two or more objects to start a process, that would not be possible. That is something that would have to be developed in Visual Workflow or an Apex Trigger.

- **Possible infinite loops:** Workflow Rules has safeguards from kicking off and then kicking itself off again and essentially causing an infinite loop. That means that it just keeps going indefinitely. Apex Triggers may also kick themselves off, but you can put in safeguards. With processes, you need to be careful not to have an infinite loop. This unfortunate scenario could occur if, let's say, you have Process A make an update to a field and that update kicks off Process B. Then Process B makes an update to a field that kicks off Process A, and so on and so forth.

- **If any of the actions fail, the entire transaction fails and an error message displays:** If there are multiple actions in a process and one of them fails then none of the actions take place. It's all or nothing. Now some might see this as strength. It depends on your requirements and your frame of reference. Ultimately, it's good to be aware of this when developing and debugging processes built in Lightning Process Builder.

- **External Objects aren't supported in Process Builder:** Salesforce now supports having references to data outside Salesforce. These are known as External Objects. Processes cannot act on External Objects. They only support standard and custom objects.

- **Deployment:** With a workflow, you need to only deploy it to another organization with a change set and it's done. With a process, you can still use a change set but you have to find the processes under Flows. This is because behind-the-scenes processes are actually just flows. Then once in production or a sandbox, the process is not active. The version you would like needs to be activated to make it functional.

Recap

This chapter has served as a basic introduction to Lightning Process Builder. While it did not dive into any development, it did cover the key aspects of Lightning Process Builder. It covered the user interface that makes of the development environment so you can be acquainted with its usage. Also covered were the key differences between Lightning Process Builder and standard Salesforce Workflow. Lightning Process Builder has more capabilities and is developed in a graphical development environment. While Salesforce Workflow has fewer capabilities in total, it is still a key part of Salesforce for the time being. Workflow also can send outbound messages while processes cannot without code. Finally, we covered some strengths and weaknesses of Lightning Process Builder. While the strengths outweigh the weaknesses, it is important to understand its weaknesses while developing processes.

CHAPTER 8

■ ■ ■

Cross-Object Updates with Lightning Process Builder

While Lightning Process Builder is visually a lot different from Salesforce Workflow, it has a lot more functionality available. We have compared the differences between Lightning Process Builder and Salesforce Workflow and the list of additional functionality is very apparent. Besides the fact that Salesforce Workflow can send outbound messages, Lightning Process Builder excels in just about every other aspect.

One of the most useful features that sets Lightning Process Builder apart is its ability to update fields on objects related to the main object being worked with. So while Salesforce Workflow can be configured to work with a Case object and then have an update performed on a field on that Case, it cannot be configured to update the related Account if the requirements arose to do so. This is because Case has a Lookup field for relating to an Account. Salesforce Workflow field udpates can update a parent record but only from the child record in a Master-Detail relationship. Even then it has limitations. For Lookup fields, though, this is not possible. Lightning Process Builder on the other hand can be configured to do that.

In this chapter we will walk through an example process that will work off an object and do some field updates on it. It will also make field updates on an entirely different object that is related to it. We will be working with Salesforce in a new way that wasn't possible before without the aid of custom development such as an Apex Trigger.

The Business Case

In our example, we are going to look at a business case where a company's call center deals with incoming calls for customers. The company is Cable Runner, Inc., a cable provider that provides other services such as Internet and phone. For its Internet service plans Cable Runner offers home and business class versions. With both of these types of plans the company loses a lot of money if a customer decides to cancel and switch to another Internet service provider. This is so especially with the business class plans as they cost more due to their increased services around uptime and available service agents. Cable Runner management has found that in most cases when a customer cancels her Internet service plan, at one time or another she placed a call into the call center that foreshadowed her intent to cancel the service plan.

While researching, management found that past Cases in Salesforce had references to the customer being dissatisfied with Cable Runner's service and making mention of thinking of canceling even though he did not cancel at that time. Time after time, when looking through Case comments within one to three months before a customer canceled, management found statements such as "I'm not sure why I still use this service," or "I really think I should just cancel soon." While getting great feedback during the course of the service call due to the phone representative, the customer was still left with a bad taste in her mouth from her overall experience leading up to the event.

© Jonathan Keel 2016
J. Keel, *Salesforce.com Lightning Process Builder and Visual Workflow*, DOI 10.1007/978-1-4842-1691-0_8

After several meetings, it was decided that the Sales team was unaware of the issues occurring until it was too late and there needed to be some way of notifying them so they could take action for their Accounts. The company is very serious about its customer service and would like to be proactive in dealing with any customers who would potentially consider canceling their service. The call center gets many calls and hears from the customers first hand. They are the first line of defense in dealing with loss revenue due to unhappy customers.

To combat this problem, management decided that a new picklist value needed to be added to the Account Status field. This would designate the Account as being "At Risk." This "At Risk" status would be set when a phone service agent received a call that fit into the parameters of being "At Risk." One parameter of being "At Risk" is that, during the course of the call, the customer seemed especially upset or mentioned thinking of canceling his service. Even if the customer doesn't cancel during the call, his intention of doing so would mean that the service agent would check off an "Account At Risk" flag on his Case record. The checking of this flag would then bubble up and flip the status on the Account to "At Risk" without the phone representative having to touch the Account page. In addition, there was already an existing flag on the Case called "SLA Violation" that was used to indicate that Cable Runner had violated the service-level agreement. While the "SLA Violation" field didn't fit into the scenario of the customer claiming he had an intention of canceling, it certainly should throw off the same sort of alarm for the Account to be at risk.

Furthermore, if the "Account At Risk" flag is set on the Case, then there needs to be another field named "Account At Risk Reason" on the Case. The phone representative should be required to type a reason into this field as to why he or she decided to set the "Account At Risk" flag to true/checked. In the event that the Account is at risk because the "SLA Violation" flag is set, then the "Account At Risk Reason" doesn't need to be entered. Instead, it should be automatically filled out with the reason that "SLA Violation Occurred."

This presents a simple yet multifaceted example of a process to build. In this example we have the following properties:

- Updating check box field (Account At Risk) on Case record based on a Case field value

- Updating a text field (Account At Risk Reason) on a Case record to a specific text based on a Case field value

- Updating a picklist field (Status) on a related Account record based on a Case field value

- Updating a text field (At Risk Reason) on a related Account record by copying the Case record's text value. It's worth noting that this At Risk Reason field would only have the latest reason for being at risk. Any field value there previously would be overwritten if multiple at-risk scenarios were to occur.

In Figure 8-1 we see a flow chart of the design of this process just discussed. Again, before event beginning development of a process, taking the time to flesh out the design will make its implementation that much easier. Everything can be figured out and approved by management beforehand.

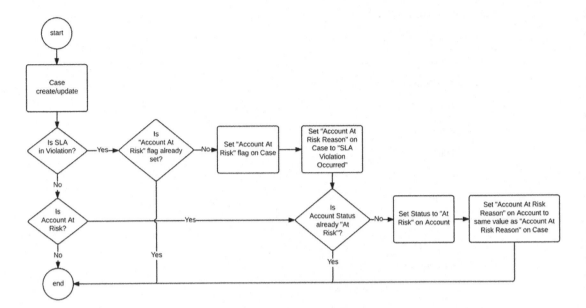

Figure 8-1. *Flow chart design of the new Account At Risk process*

Set Account At Risk from Case Process

With the requirements and the design set out before us we can now begin development of the process in Lightning Process Builder. The steps involved with building a process should feel a little more straightforward than building a Flow. In Visual Workflow you have complete control of the arrangement of the elements on the Canvas. A Flow can progress across the Canvas from left to right, right to left, up or down. Implementing Flows is almost an exercise in art. With Lightning Process Builder the direction and arrangement of the elements are laid out for us. We just need to fill in the blanks. Using the design previously discussed let's start building our first process.

Before touching Lightning Process Builder we need to make sure we have the necessary custom fields in place that the process will be using. This book assumes the reader has adequate knowledge of adding custom fields. So we will not be covering that aspect in detail. For now, use the information that follows to create the custom fields needed for this process and make sure each custom field has the appropriate permissions set up for the users:

- **Standard Object**: Account
  - **Custom Field**: Status
    - **Data Type**: Picklist
    - **API Name**: Status__c
    - **Picklist Values**: "New (< 1 Year)," "In Good Standing," "At Risk," "Closed"
  - **Custom Field**: Account At Risk Reason
    - **Data Type**: Text Area (255)
    - **API Name**: Account_At_Risk_Reason__c
- **Standard Object**: Case
  - **Custom Field**: SLA Violation
    - **Data Type**: Picklist
    - **API Name**: SLAViolation__c
    - **Picklist Values**: "Yes", "No"
  - **Custom Field**: Account At Risk
    - **Data Type**: Check box
    - **API Name**: Account_At_Risk__c
  - **Custom Field**: Account At Risk Reason
    - **Data Type**: Text Area (255)
    - **API Name**: Account_At_Risk_Reason__c

With all that setup out of the way, open up Lightning Process Builder in the setup screen. In Salesforce Classic go to Setup ➤ Build ➤ Create ➤ Workflow & Approvals ➤ Process Builder. Lightning Process Builder will open up to the My Processes screen first or a welcome screen if there are no existing processes. In the top right-hand corner of the screen is the New button. Click the New button to create a new process. The New Process screen will appear. Go ahead and enter the following information for each of the three fields:

- **Process Name**: Set Account At Risk from Case
- **API Name**: Set_Account_At_Risk_from_Case
- **Description**: Sets the Account to be "At Risk" from a Case when an issue has a potential to cause the Account to be closed.
- **The process starts when**: A record changes

The New Process Screen should look like Figure 8-2. At this point you can click the Save button to continue.

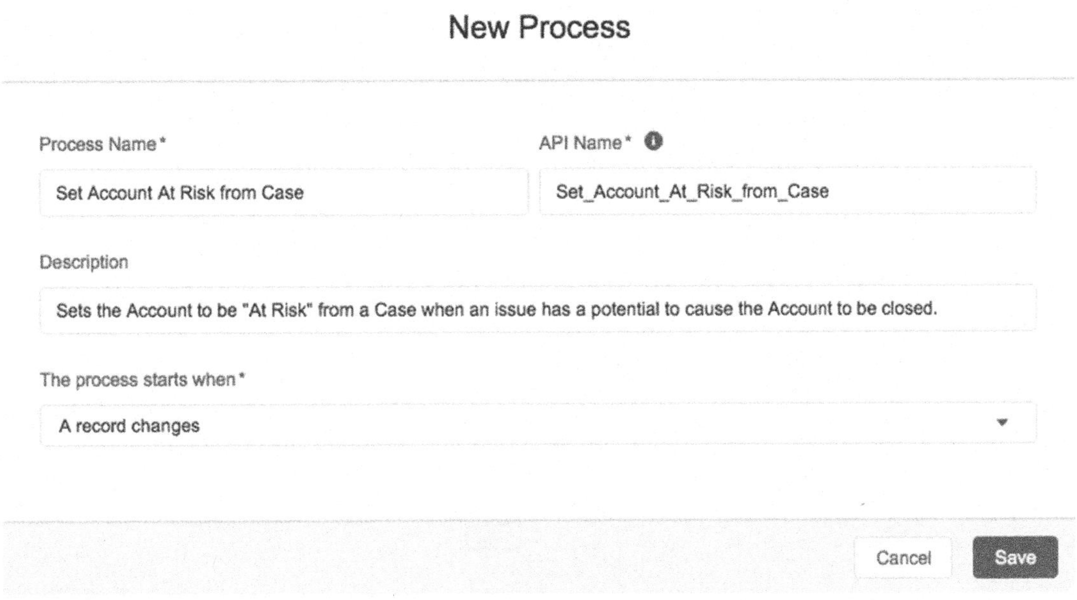

New Process

Process Name *

Set Account At Risk from Case

API Name * ⓘ

Set_Account_At_Risk_from_Case

Description

Sets the Account to be "At Risk" from a Case when an issue has a potential to cause the Account to be closed.

The process starts when *

A record changes ▾

Cancel   Save

Figure 8-2. *The New Process window to give the process a Name, API Name, and Description*

The next thing you will see is the Canvas in Lightning Process Builder as seen in Figure 8-3. As discussed previously, it contains several elements that you basically have to "fill in." The first element to configure is the object in which this process will act upon. To begin, the first thing you need to do is click the box with the label "+ Add Object." Doing so will open up a panel on the right side. You will find that whenever you click an element in the Canvas all the properties you can configure for that element will appear in this right panel. This is consistent with the entire configuration in process builder. The configuration settings are always in the right panel that appears after clicking an element in the canvas.

In the configuration panel, enter the following settings:

- **Object**: Case
- **Start the process**: when a record is created or edited

Under "Start the process" there is another radio button with the label "only when a record is created." This option can be chosen if you only want the process to occur during the "create new record" phase. In our case, we want the process to evaluate the criteria if a new record is created or an existing record is edited.

There is another option on this page under "Advanced" named "Recursion." We are not checking "Yes" for this option because in our case it would be unnecessary. Checking this option would allow for any updates that occur in this process to possibly rerun the process to see if more processing is needed. Usually this option will not be checked "Yes."

After entering in these values, click the Save button to save these settings for the "+ Add Object" element. Doing so will return you to the Canvas without the properties panel on the right side.

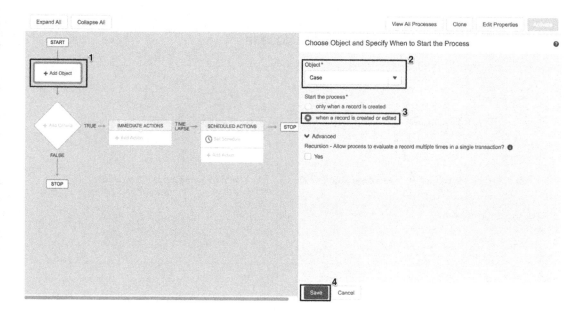

Figure 8-3. *Clicking "+ Add Object" opens up the configuration options in the right panel*

First Criterion–Is SLA in Violation?

The next step is configuring the criteria for the process to make sure they meet our qualification to continue with any actions. To do so, click the "+ Add Criteria" decision node. This will open up a configuration panel on the right side again. In it there are several sections. The first two are "Criteria Name" and "Criteria for Executing Actions." Criteria Name is the label to place on the criteria node in the Canvas. Interestingly enough, it does not have to be unique and you can have multiple criteria nodes with the same name. The second section, titled "Criteria for Executing Actions," is used for determining how criteria are passed and a TRUE or FALSE value is determined in the process execution. The three options and their descriptions are

- **Conditions are met**: Displays two extra sections named "Set Conditions" and "Conditions." They are determining how fields from the object should relate to a specific set of values such as "Type Equals Other" or "Closed Date Is Null." The Conditions section is for determining how the fields' comparisons are logically calculated either by AND, OR, or custom logic.

- **Formula evaluates to true**: Displays a "Build Formula" section for developing complex formula logic similar to how other formulas are developed in Salesforce, such as formula fields.

- **No criteria—just execute the actions!**: Performs no criteria checks. It skips the checking entirely and just runs the actions as it says.

In the configuration panel enter in the following options:

- **Criteria Name**: Is SLA in Violation?

- **Criteria for Executing Actions**: Conditions are met

Next under "Set Conditions" click "Find a field . . ." to display the "Select a Field" window as seen in Figure 8-4.

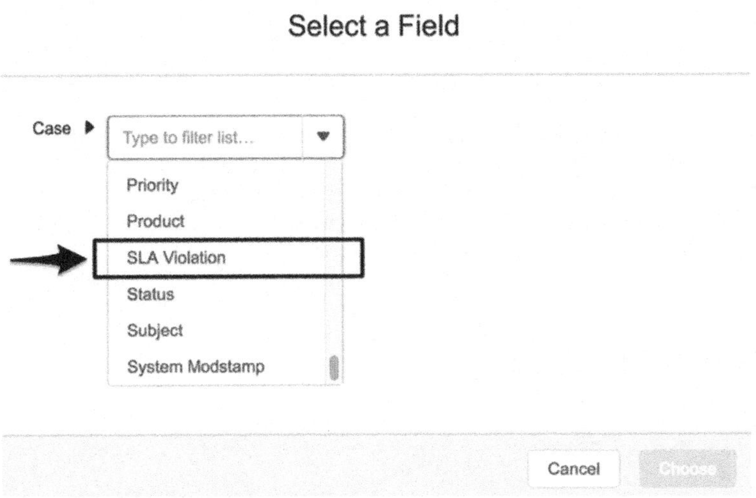

Figure 8-4. *The windows used to select the field on an object for the condition*

In this window you have the option of selecting the field to be used to set the condition on an object. In this scenario we are looking for the "SLA Violation" field. We want to test to see if this field that is a check box has been checked (set to a value of true). Scroll through the list and click "SLA Violation". The window should then change to look like Figure 8-5. Now click the "Choose" button to confirm the selection.

Select a Field

Case ▶ SLA Violation

You have selected the following field:

SLA Violation
Type: Picklist
API Name: SLAViolation__c

Cancel   Choose

Figure 8-5. *The Select a Field window after a "SLA Violation" has been selected*

After clicking the "Choose" button the criteria configuration panel will be visible again. The Field option under Set Conditions should read "[Case]. SLAViolation__c." There are still three more options to configure for this one condition. Configure them as follows:

- **Operator**: Equals
- **Type**: Picklist
- **Value**: Yes

Next we need to add a second condition because our design states that we need to make sure that the "Account At Risk" flag is not already set. We can do this here with a second condition to check it. Click "+ Add Row" to add another condition. When the new row appears, click "Find a field . . ." to bring up the Select a Field window. Select "Account At Risk" and the window should look like Figure 8-6. Now click the "Choose" button to confirm the selection.

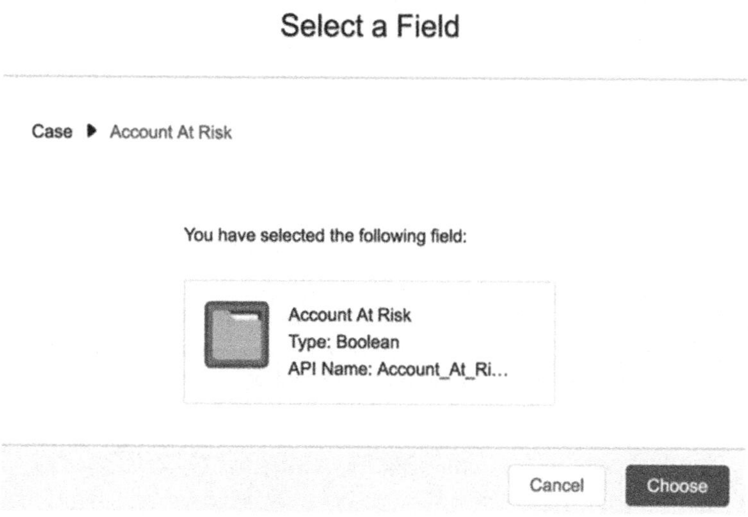

Select a Field

Case ▶ Account At Risk

You have selected the following field:

Account At Risk
Type: Boolean
API Name: Account_At_Ri...

Cancel   Choose

Figure 8-6. The Select a Field window after a "Account At Risk" has been selected

After clicking the "Choose" button the criteria configuration panel will be visible again. This second Field option under Set Conditions should read "[Case]. Acount_At_Risk__c". There are still three more options to configure for this one condition. Configure them as so:

- **Operator**: Equals
- **Type**: Boolean
- **Value**: False

That's all we need for the "Set Conditions" section of the configuration panel. The final options to configure are Conditions and the last option under the "Advanced" section. For those, use the following settings:

- **Conditions**: All of the conditions are met (AND)
- **Do you want to execute the actions only when specified changes are made to the record?**: Yes/checked

■ **Note** If the check box in the "Advanced" section is checked (Yes) then this guarantees that the criteria are only met when they were not met previously. The values involved in calculating the criteria must have been updated.

When all these configuration changes have been made the screen should look like Figure 8-7. Review these six changes made and if all of them look correct, the seventh and final step is to click the Save button.

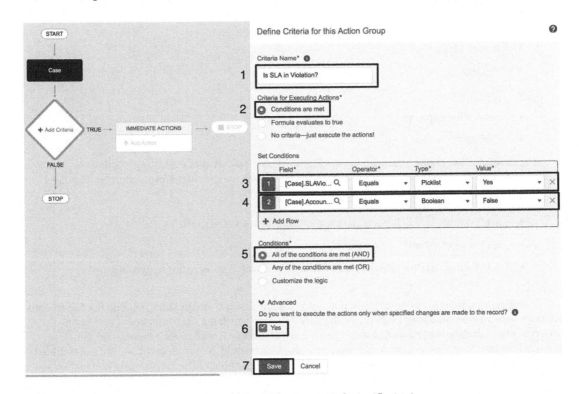

Figure 8-7. *The final configuration settings for the "Is SLA in Violation?" criterion*

Once the criteria are added for our Cases coming through this process we need to decide what to do with them if they qualify for taking an immediate action. There are two branches from the criteria node. One branch is labeled "FALSE." This is the branch the process takes if the Cases coming through this process do not meet the criteria we just configured. Before the criteria were added it simply pointed to "STOP." This meant that at this point, for the one Case record going through this process, the execution would halt. If there were more Cases to be evaluated, such as in a bulk update, then the next record would come through. If there were no more Case records to be evaluated, then the entire process would be complete.

Now that the first criteria node was added, the FALSE branch no longer points to stop. Instead it points to another "+ Add Criteria" node. At this point Lightning Process Builder is giving the option of adding another criterion if the requirements call for it. This "+ Add Criteria" node is just a placeholder at this point. It does not affect execution. If another criteria node is not added, then it simple runs straight to the STOP node as before.

For the time being we will focus on the first criterion, "Is SLA in Violation?" and its actions. To begin setting up an immediate action click "+ Add Action" under the "Immediate Actions" node. The configuration panel on the right should appear again with the heading "Select and Define Action." The configuration panel as before acts like a wizard and only shows you each step at a time as you begin configuring the action. The first setting to configure is "Action Type." This has a picklist of several types of actions we can take in a process. These were discussed before in more detail in Chapter 7, but to review, the options available are

- Apex
- Create a Record
- E-mail Alerts
- Flows
- Post to Chatter
- Processes
- Quick Actions
- Submit for Approval
- Update Records

The design for our example, as seen back in Figure 8-1, stated that after evaluating whether the Case is indeed an SLA Violation and the Account At Risk flag was not set, we should perform four record updates.

- Set "Account At Risk" flag on Case.
- Set "Account At Risk Reason" on Case to "SLA Violation Occurred."
- Set Status to "At Risk" on Account.
- Set "Account At Risk Reason" on Account to same value as "Account At Risk Reason" on Case.

These are all actions to update records, but notice that the first two are updating fields on the Case record while the other two are updating fields on the Account record to which the Case is related. These last two are cross-object updates and cannot be implemented in a Salesforce Workflow Rule because Account is a Lookup field on a Case. This is why we are all here! At this point though it may seem that we are still confined to working with a single type of object. In this scenario, it's the Case object. The first thing we had to do when setting up this process was define what type of object we are dealing with. We aren't allowed to configure it for multiple objects at once. However, notice that the last option in the "Action Type" picklist states "Update Records." It does not say "Update this Record." Maybe there is some flexibility here? Let's continue configuring. Since all four of our design requirements are record updates, select the following option:

- **Action Type**: Update Records

Once you have selected that option in the picklist, two new fields appear below it, "Action Name" and "Record Type." Use the following value for the first field:

- **Action Name**: Update Case as "Account At Risk"

Next click the Record Type field. A configuration window will appear titled "Select a Record to Update." Finally, this is where we get to determine if we want to update a field on the record that came through this process (Case) or a related record (Account). The first two steps in the design deal with updating the Case fields first and, as you can tell by the Action Name entered in, we are just going to update the Case fields at this point. Choose the following setting so that the window should then look like Figure 8-8 and click the Choose button to finish and return to the previous screen:

- Select the Case record that started your process

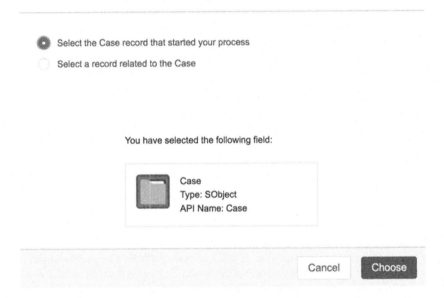

Figure 8-8. *The Select a Record to Update window after Case has been selected*

After returning to the configuration panel you will notice that the Record Type field has the value "[Case]" and that the following two additional sections have appeared:

- Criteria for Updating Records

- Set new field values for the records you update

Under "Criteria for Updating Records" there are two options. These two options give you the ability to filter which fields will receive the updates we are configuring to be applied or to simply apply the updates without any criteria whatsoever. If you select "Updated records meet all conditions," then an additional section appears to configure the filtering. It looks identical to the criteria configuration for when we added the first criteria node in this process. For our requirements we do not need any further criteria for updating the records, so select the following option:

- No criteria—just update the records!

The last section of this configuration panel to set up is "Set new field values for the records you update." This section allows you to put one or more fields to be updated along with their new values. It starts off with one field to update but notice the "+ Add Row" link at the bottom. Clicking that will add another row that allows you to configure another field update.

We need to update two fields on the Case record according to the design. Let's start off with the first field, "Account At Risk." It is a check box that needs to be checked (set to True). Click the input box under "Field" to see the options in the picklist. The picklist will have all the fields from the Case object to choose from. Select "Account At Risk" and notice the next field, "Type," with the following three options:

- Boolean

- Reference

- Formula

The first option, Boolean, is essentially the type that the field is. It is a check box field and this means that it takes two values of checked or unchecked. These equate to True and False in the context of a process. The second option, Reference, is used when you do not want to explicitly provide a value but instead reference another value in another field on the Case record or a related record. The third option, Formula, is used when you want to derive a value based on a calculation. It works similarly to formula fields except you do not need to create an extra field. The formula will just live within the process so you do not have to create yet another formula field on an object for a specific scenario. Pretty cool! In our case, we want to set the "Account At Risk" field to True, so select Boolean for the Type. Then in the Value field, the picklist shows True and False. Select True to ensure that this field gets set to a checked check box.

We now need to add another row because we need to set the "Account At Risk Reason" as well. Click "+ Add Row" and another set of Field, Type, Value will appear below the current row. For the Field select "Account At Risk Reason" from the picklist. Now the Type picklist should show the following options:

- String

- Reference

- Global Constant

- Formula

All these options are the same as the check box field we just configured except that because this field is a String (a text field), the additional option of "Global Constant" is also available. A Global Constant is a fixed, system-provided value. It is a value that the Salesforce platform provides depending on the type of field. For this instance that is a String, the following Global Constants will be available:

- **$GlobalConstant.Null**: a field with no set value

- **$GlobalConstant.EmptyString**: a field with a text value that has no characters entered.

■ **Note** $GlobalConstant.Null and $GlobalConstant.EmptyString seem the same, but when a process is running they are treated as two separate, distinct entities. It's essentially the difference in a field never being touched (Null) vs. a field being updated but with no characters, not even spaces (EmptyString).

For this design we want to literally enter some text to a specific value, so choose String for the Type field. When you click on the Value field now, notice there are no options. It is a blank field where you can type the text you want to set the field to. Enter in the text "SLA Violation Occurred." At this point you should have the following settings for these two fields:

- **Field**: Account At Risk

  - **Type**: Boolean

  - **Value**: True

- **Field**: Account At Risk Reason

  - **Type**: String

  - **Value**: SLA Violation Occurred

Perform a quick review over the settings in the configuration panel. It should look like Figure 8-9. After setting up those six items, then the last step is to click the Save button to keep these settings and return to the Canvas.

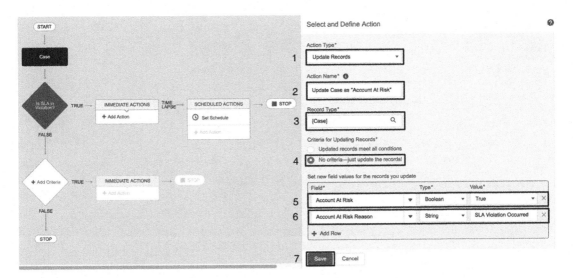

Figure 8-9. *The final configuration settings for the "Update Case as 'Account At Risk'" action*

After returning to the Canvas the screen should look Figure 8-10. The new immediate action has been added to update the two fields on the Case record. We still need to update the related Account record though. Individual actions that have the Action Type of "Update Records" have to update the record being processed or a related record but not both at the same time. To update the related Account record we need another action to be added to the list of immediate actions. To do so, click the "+ Add Action" link again to begin the process of setting up another action as seen highlighted in Figure 8-10.

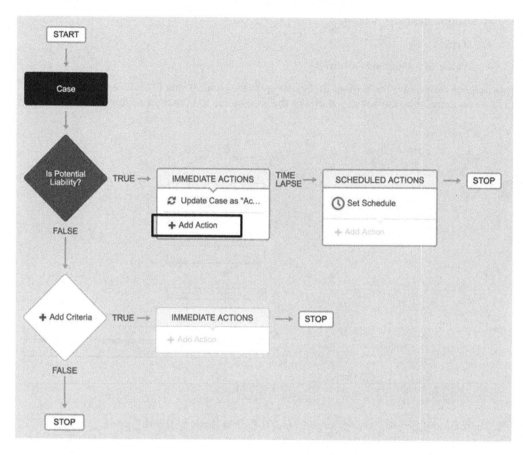

Figure 8-10. *The Lightning Process Builder Canvas after adding the first action*

Clicking the "+ Add Action" link starts the process again to set up another action. The configuration panel on the right appears just like last time. It starts off with just one field, "Action Type." Under "Action Type" choose "Update Records" again. Again, this causes the same two fields to appear, "Action Name" and "Record Type." Set the "Action Name" field to the following value:

- **Action Name**: Update Account as "Account At Risk"

Next click the "Record Type" field. A configuration window will appear titled "Select a Record to Update." Again, this is where we get to determine if we want to update a field on the record that came through this process (Case) or a related record (Account). The last steps for the "Is SLA in Violation?" criterion deals with updating the related Account. So we need to make the appropriate choice here by choosing the following setting:

- Select a record related to the Case

When this option is selected, a picklist appears with the list of lookup and master-detail fields on the Case object. Here we can navigate to find any related object we want to update. Since we want to update the Account object, we do this by selecting "Account ID" in the picklist as seen in Figure 8-11.

Figure 8-11. The "Select a Record to Update" window showing the selection of the related Account

■ **Note** When looking through the related record picklist it is a common mistake to select the values that end in ">" such as "Account ID >." This is only used if you would like to traverse to another record on that selected value.

After choosing the "Account ID" option in the picklist the window will be updated to look like Figure 8-12. If you find yourself accidentally choosing the wrong value, notice that there is an "Account ID" link in blue. Clicking that link will take you back to the picklist to choose another option. In our case we want the "Account ID," so finalize the choice by clicking the Choose button.

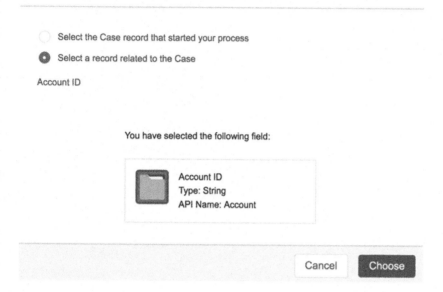

Figure 8-12. *The Select a Record to Update window after related Account ID has been selected*

After returning back to the configuration panel you will notice that the Record Type field has the value "[Case].Account ID" and that the following two additional sections have appeared:

- Criteria for Updating Records

- Set new field values for the records you update

Under "Criteria for Updating Records" there are two options again for whether to add additional criteria to filter which records get updated or to just update them without any criteria. This time we will be choosing the following option:

- Updated records meet all conditions

Since these next updates on the Account will set the Status of the Account, we are going to add criteria here to not apply to Accounts that already have a Status of "At Risk." That way we don't make any unnecessary updates, nor do we want to override the previous "Account At Risk Reason" field on the Account. Additionally, this gives us a good reason to see how this whole record filtering works here.

Notice now that the section titled "Filter the records you update based on these conditions" has appeared. It has the number 1 followed by the following inputs:

- Field

- Operator

- Type

- Value

These should look very familiar by this point. We want to filter records to any that do not have the Account Status set to "At Risk." To configure this correctly, choose the following settings:

- **Field**: Status
- **Operator**: Does not equal
- **Type**: Picklist
- **Value**: At Risk

This is the only criteria we will need, so we do not need to add another row.

■ **Note** When looking through a list of fields for a large object such as Account, you can save time by typing in the field name into the input box above the picklist. This will narrow down the options available in the picklist for you.

We need to configure the fields to update to their new values. According to our design we need to update the Account's "Status" field to "At Risk" and the Account's "Account At Risk Reason" field to the same value of the "Account At Risk Reason" on the Case. The first update is simple because we have set up a field update like this before. Set the Field, Type, and Value to the following settings:

- **Field**: Status
- **Type**: Picklist
- **Value**: At Risk

Next, click the "+ Add Row" link to add another field update. Now for the Field and Type settings choose the following values:

- **Field**: Account At Risk Reason
- **Type**: Reference

Notice we have something new here that we have not used before. A Type of "Reference" means that we are not going to put an explicit value in here. We could have chosen a Type of "String" and then copied the same text into the Value input as we did for the Case. The problem with that though is that now you have that text in multiple places. What if in the future the text needs to change in some way due to new requirements? Then there is a risk of updating one area and forgetting about the other. A better way to implement this and reduce this risk is to have the Value of this Field be a Reference to another field on Case. That would be the Case's "Account At Risk Reason" field, of course.

To set this up, click the input box under Value that has the words "Find a field . . ." to open up the "Select a Field" window as seen in Figure 8-13. The window will have a picklist with the fields on the Case record to choose from. Look for the "Account At Risk Reason" field and select it.

Figure 8-13. *The Select a Field window to allow a Reference in a field update*

After selecting "Account At Risk Reason" the window will update to confirm the selection. It should look like Figure 8-14. Just as in other windows in Lightning Process Builder where you have to select from a list of Object or Fields once you made a choice, you still have an option to change it before you click the Choose button. Notice in Figure 8-14 the "Account At Risk Reason" link in blue text at the top left. If you happen to ever choose the wrong value by accident you do not need to cancel out of this window and start over. Instead, you simple click that link and you will be back at the point where you can choose the correct field from the picklist of possible fields on the Case object. At this point we have done all we need so click the Choose button to finalize the selection and return to the previous screen with the configuration panel.

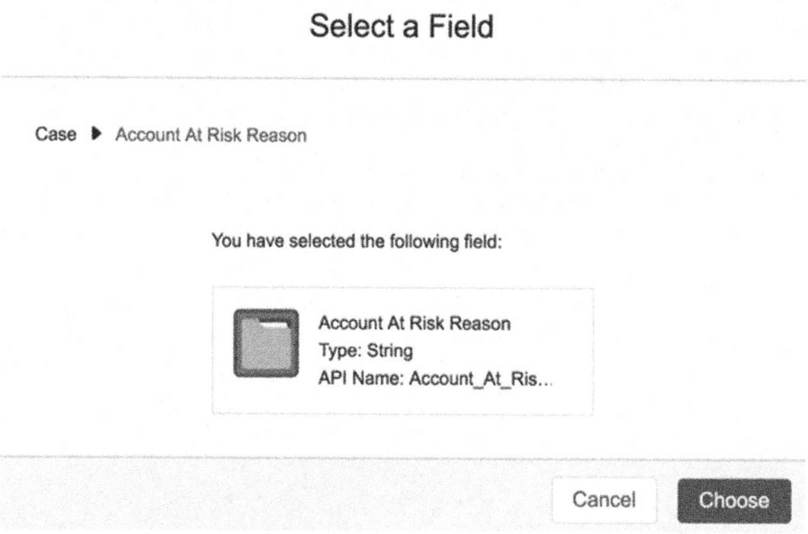

Select a Field

Case ▶ Account At Risk Reason

You have selected the following field:

Account At Risk Reason
Type: String
API Name: Account_At_Ris...

Cancel   Choose

Figure 8-14. *The Select a Field window after the "Account At Risk Reason" field is selected*

Perform a quick review of the settings in the configuration panel. It should look like Figure 8-15. After setting up those seven items, the last step is to click the Save button to keep these settings and return to the Canvas.

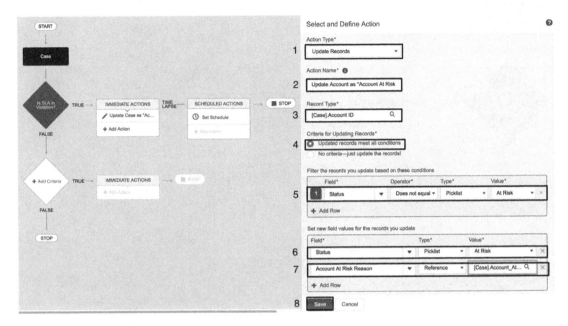

Figure 8-15. *The final configuration settings for the "Update Account as 'Account At Risk'" action*

After returning to the Canvas the screen should look Figure 8-16. The new immediate action has been added to update the last two fields on the Account record, "Status" and "Account At Risk Reason." According to the design we went over previously, this takes care of the list of actions for this first criterion, "Is SLA in Violation?" You will notice to the right there is a section for scheduled actions. In this chapter we will not be covering scheduled actions so this section will be left untouched for the process we are setting up.

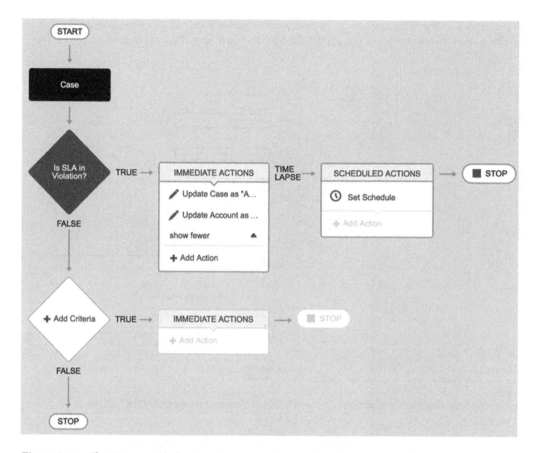

Figure 8-16. *The Canvas with the first criterion and its associated actions complete*

Second Criterion–Is Account At Risk?

The design we came up with earlier in the chapter has a second set of criteria to look at if the Case does not have an SLA violation flag set. That set of criteria is whether or not the Account is at risk due to something noted on the call that the phone representative noticed. This could be something the caller stated, such as thinking of canceling, or the caller seeming very upset. At this point the business process is for the phone representative to check the "Account At Risk" check box on the Case. Then he or she would enter the reason for doing so in the "Account At Risk Reason" on the Case.

To start configuring this criterion click the "+ Add Criteria" placeholder that is on the canvas. This will present the configuration panel on the right again with the heading "Define Criteria for this Action Group." Since we have gone through this setup procedure before, we can go a little faster this time. Use the following settings to set up this set of criteria:

- **Criteria Name:** Is Account At Risk?

- **Criteria for Executing Actions:** Conditions are met

- **Set Conditions:**

    - **Condition 1:**

        - **Field:** Account At Risk

- • **Operator**: Equals
- • **Type**: Boolean
- • **Value**: True
- • **Conditions**: All of the conditions are met (AND)
- • **Advanced**:
  - • **Do you want to execute the actions only when specified changes are made to the record?**: Yes/checked

Going through these five settings should yield a configuration panel as seen in Figure 8-17. Take a moment to review your settings to see if they match. Essentially we have set it up to go into the next group of actions if the "Account At Risk" flag is checked on the Case record. If all looks good, then click the Save button to save the changes and return to the canvas.

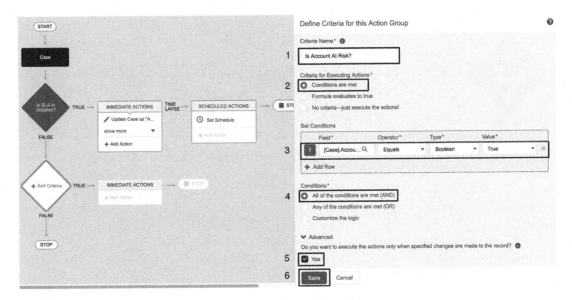

Figure 8-17. *The "Define Criteria for this Action Group" configuration panel for "Is Account At Risk?" criterion*

The canvas should now look like Figure 8-18. It currently contains the first criterion and its group of actions and also the second criterion without any actions added as of yet. The process as seen will flow from the start with a Case record down to the first criterion. If that set of criteria is found to be TRUE then it will execute its related action group. If it is found to be FALSE then it will flow to the second criterion to see if it is TRUE or FALSE. Right now, since we have no actions associated if it is TRUE or FALSE, it will stop. We need to add some actions if it is found to be TRUE though.

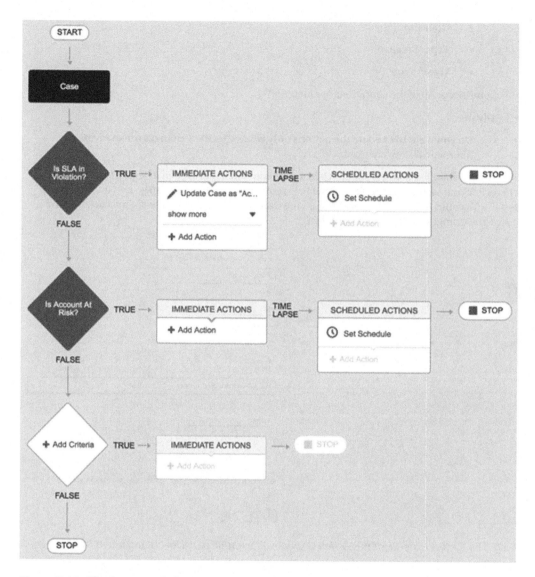

Figure 8-18. *The Canvas with the "Is Account At Risk?" criterion added*

The design states that the two actions needed are to set the "Status" field on the Account to "At Risk" and also to set the "Account At Risk Reason" field on the Account to the same value of the "Account At Risk Reason" field on the Case. These two actions are identical to the last two actions we added to the previous criterion's action group. Click the "+ Add Action" link under "IMMEDIATE ACTIONS" to the right of the "Is Account At Risk?" criterion to start configuring the first action.

As before, the configuration panel appears to the right of the screen with the heading "Select and Define Action" along with one picklist field labeled "Action Type." From the picklist choose the following option:

- Update Records

This will cause two fields to appear, "Action Name" and "Record Type." For the "Action Name" field enter the following value:

- Update Account as "Account At Risk"

Then click the "Record Type" field to open the "Select a Record to Update" window as seen in Figure 8-19. Since we want to update fields on the Account record only with this action we need to choose the following option:

- Select a record related to the Case

Once you have chosen that option the picklist with the lookup and master-detail fields will appear. Here you will select "Account ID" just as we did in the previous action we created. This will allow us to update the related Account record for the Case record being processed.

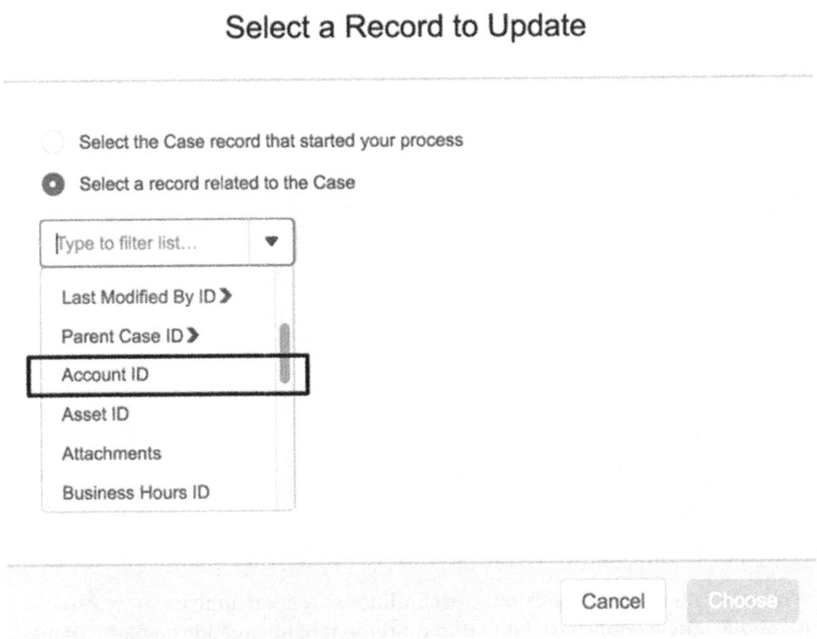

Select a Record to Update

Select the Case record that started your process

● Select a record related to the Case

Type to filter list... ▼

Last Modified By ID ❯
Parent Case ID ❯
Account ID
Asset ID
Attachments
Business Hours ID

Cancel   Choose

Figure 8-19. The "Select a Record to Update" window to choose the Account ID

Once you have chosen the Account ID field the window will update to show you a confirmation of what you selected, as seen in Figure 8-20. If all looks well, click the Choose button to finalize your selection.

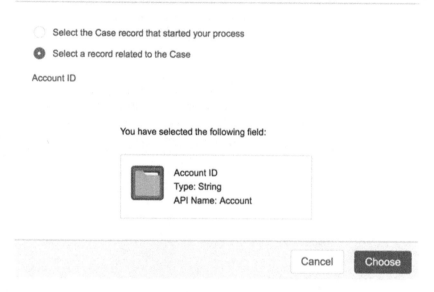

Select a Record to Update

○ Select the Case record that started your process

● Select a record related to the Case

Account ID

You have selected the following field:

Account ID
Type: String
API Name: Account

Cancel | Choose

Figure 8-20. The "Select a Record to Update" with the Account ID field chosen

The configuration panel will now show the following two sections to set up:

- Criteria for Updating Records

- Set new field values for the records you update

For the "Criteria for Updating Records" section select the following option to make sure we don't update Account objects that already have a Status of "At Risk":

- Updated records meet all conditions

As before, the "Filter the records you update based on these conditions" section appears so we can configure the field updates to modify only records based on our requirement of not already having a Status of "At Risk." Set the Field, Operator, Type, and Value settings to the following values:

- **Field**: Status

- **Operator**: Does not equal

- **Type**: Picklist

- **Value**: At Risk

Scroll down a bit to the "Set new field values for the records you update" section and configure first field update with the following settings:

- **Field:** Status

- **Type:** Picklist

- **Value:** At Risk

Next click the "+ Add Row" to add another field update for the "Account At Risk Reason" using the following settings:

- **Field**: Account At Risk Reason

- **Type**: Reference

- **Value**: [Case].Account_At_Risk_Reason__c

At this point you can review your changes and compare them to Figure 8-21 where we see the seven main places to update plus the Save button. Let's go ahead and Save to finalize the changes.

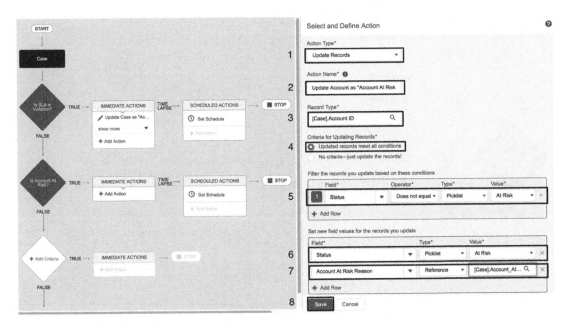

Figure 8-21. *The final configuration settings for the "Update Account as 'Account At Risk'" action*

Upon saving and returning to the Canvas you will see all of our hard work laid out before us, as shown in Figure 8-22. The Canvas should have everything the design had in it. It has the two different sets of criteria plus their related actions to update the Case record and its related Account record. While it may have seemed tedious to walk through each of these screens and set up the process this time, rest assured that the more processes you build in Lightning Process Builder the faster you will get. Even in this one example we were repeating the same steps over again several times. All processes follow a nice layout of configuring the object for the process, the criteria, its actions, and repeating for any more sets of criteria and actions.

Where the same requirements could have been met with an Apex Trigger, this method of implanting it with Lightning Process Builder allowed for faster development—plus there was no need to create unit tests (something developers need to do when writing Apex Triggers). Of course, this also gives a lot of power to Salesforce administrators to implement processes without needing to get a developer involved.

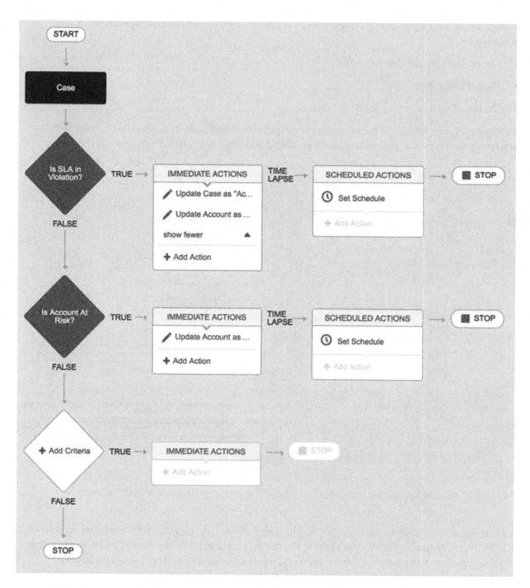

Figure 8-22. *The Canvas with both sets of criteria and their related action groups*

The final step is activating this process. As of now we have everything built, but if someone updates a Case, then that Case record will not go through this new process. To make it available we simply just click the blue Activate button at the top right side of the screen. This will bring up a window to allow for confirmation that this is what you indeed are ready to do, as shown in Figure 8-23. Notice that the text states that achieving this process will deactivate any other versions. Since this is the first time you are activating this process, this does not apply because there are no other versions to deactivate. If there were a previous version that was active, of course, that version would be deactivated and this one activated. That is because once a process is active, it cannot be changed. Instead, a new version (with the same name if you like) needs to be created that starts off as inactive.

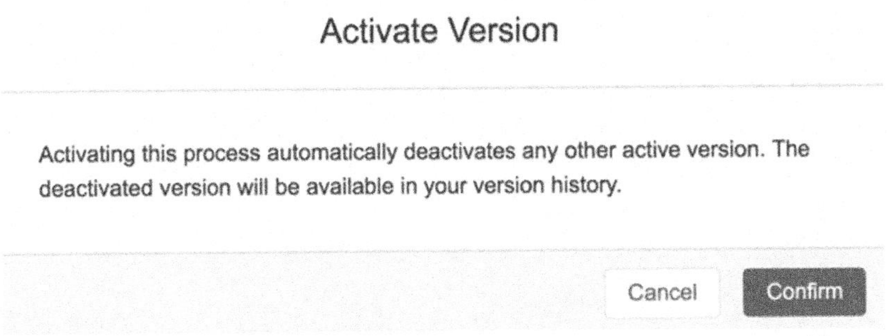

Activate Version

Activating this process automatically deactivates any other active version. The deactivated version will be available in your version history.

Cancel   Confirm

Figure 8-23. *The Activate Version window for confirmation*

There can only be one active version at a time and all the versions show in the process's version history so that you can essentially roll back to a previous version if needed by deactivating a newer process and activating and older process. Now that is something that not even an Apex Trigger can do!

Click the Confirm button to be returned to the Lightning Process Builder Canvas. Notice that there is no Deactivate button where there used to be an Activate button. Also, next to that button is a status of "Read Only." This is letting us know that we can no longer make changes to this process. We are done here! If you look at Figure 8-24 you will notice there is a Back To Setup button at the very top right side. Click that button to go all the way back to the standard Salesforce Setup screen. If you would like instead to go back to the listing of processes at the beginning of Lightning Process Builder, then click the View All Processes button.

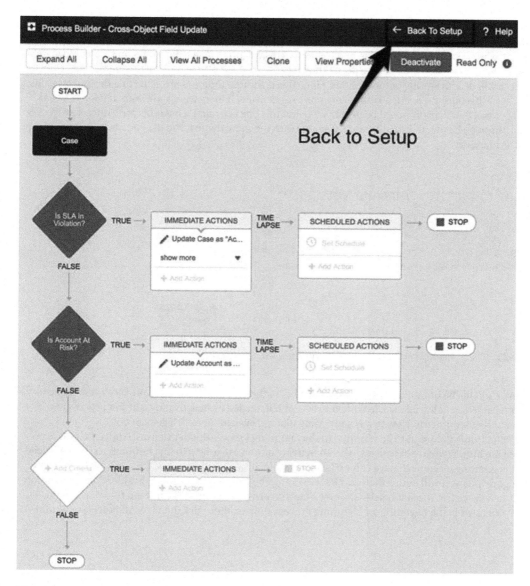

Figure 8-24. *The active process in the Canvas*

To test our active process, create an Account that does not have an "At Risk" status. Then create a Case record and save the Case record. Figure 8-25 provides an example of a Case that does not have the Account At Risk flag set to true, and it also does not have the Account At Risk Reason field populated.

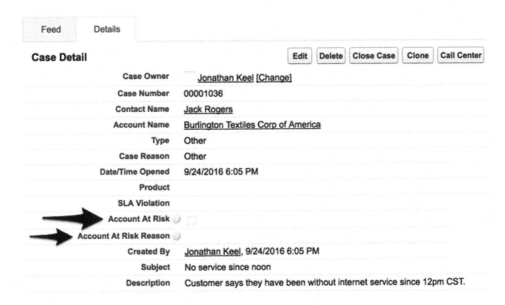

Figure 8-25. *A Case record before Account At Risk was set to true/checked*

Figure 8-26 shows the related Account record. Notice it has a status of "In Good Standing" and its Account At Risk Reason field is empty.

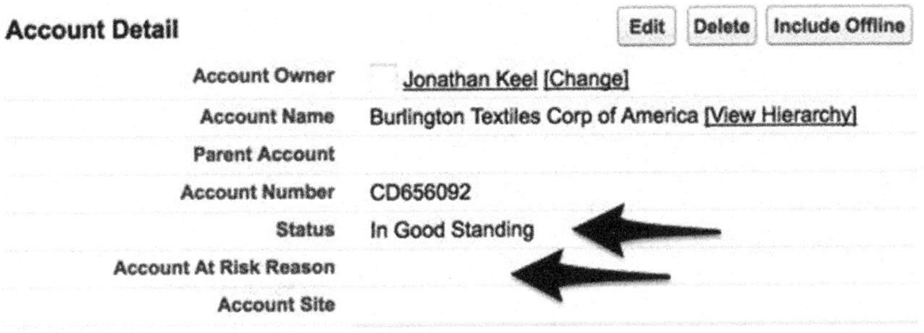

Figure 8-26. *The Case's related Account record with a status of "In Good Standing"*

If we then set the Account At Risk flag to true/checked on the Case and its Account At Risk Reason as seen in Figure 8-27, then the Account will be automatically updated.

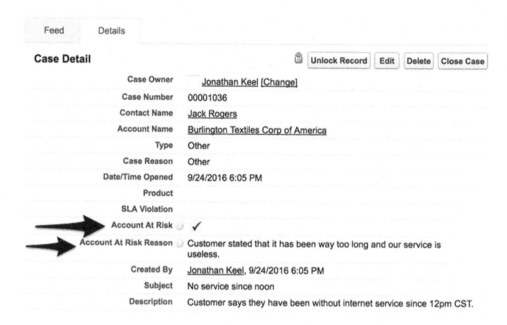

Figure 8-27. A Case record after Account At Risk was set to true/checked with Account At Risk Reason

Here in Figure 8-28 we see now that the Account has been updated to have a status of "At Risk" and the Account At Risk Reason is copied from the Case record.

Figure 8-28. The Case's related Account record with a status of "At Risk" and an Account At Risk Reason

Recap

In this chapter we introduced our first process in Lighting Process Builder. With it we implemented a feature that went beyond the capability of Salesforce Workflow. Not only did the process update specific fields on the object the process was working off of, the Case, but it also updated fields on a related record, the Account. Before Lightning Process Builder such a requirement might have been met by developing an Apex Trigger. This would have resulted in pulling in a developer skill set. It would have also meant more custom code along with unit tests to make sure the custom code worked correctly. With the process implemented in this chapter the requirements were met 100% without any coding. It was strictly through configuration, keeping with the Salesforce principle of clicks, not code.

■ ■ ■

CHAPTER 9

Approval Process with Lightning Process Builder

Lightning Process Builder can do many things. We have now looked at how it can be used to go beyond what Salesforce Workflow can do. Lightning Process Builder can be used to update objects and fields related to the object that initiated the process. It offers features that were only available to Apex coding, specifically Apex Triggers. There are more areas that Lightning Process Builder can be used to augment though. What about approval processes? Does Lightning Process Builder offer any features around approval processes? What are the capabilities and limitations? These are questions we will answer. In the past, when a Salesforce administrator set up an approval process he or she had to go through a lot of steps to define how it functioned. Once complete, the Salesforce administrator then depends on an individual to click an Approve button to start the approval process he or she had defined. With all the work the put into setting it up, the administrator still depends on an individual to start the approval process. Even if the administrator wants to start the approval process systematically, he or she they would need to offload the work to a developer to develop custom Apex code to do so. Now with Lightning Process Builder the game has changed!

In this chapter we will cover approvals and how Lightning Process Builder works to augment the features already existing in Salesforce Approval Processes. This chapter will dive into the capabilities and limitations that exist currently in Lightning Process Builder when it comes to implementing an approval process. Finally, we will build an example process where we implement an approval process that in the past would require custom Apex development to achieve. Now with Lightning Process Builder the work can be handled in a simpler fashion without any custom Apex code.

Approval Processes

An approval process in the context of Salesforce is an automated process used to approve or reject records in Salesforce. When an approval process is set up in Salesforce it defines the necessary steps for a record to be approved and who is allowed to approve it during each step in that process. It also gives the approver the ability to reject rather than approve the record. In the event that the approver cannot approve or reject then there are facilities in place to have another person approve or reject the record.

To state it simply, an approval process is a great way to set up checkpoints in a business process to make sure everything is in order before moving on to the next step. It is a place where human intervention is required to look over the integrity of the data in a record or to ensure that the purpose of the record is in line with business goals. Computers do a great job of being fast! They are excellent tools at validating the rules we specify to make sure all the fields required are inputted and formatted correctly. When it comes to the details, though, computers just do not have the same level of complexity as a human. While we can configure Salesforce with validation rules, workflow rules, and processes, we cannot configure Salesforce to understand the complexity of written language, or to know about any events that happen outside Salesforce, such as in-person meetings, conference calls, and so on. It is much too complicated and is subject to the human intervention mentioned earlier.

© Jonathan Keel 2016

J. Keel, *Salesforce.com Lightning Process Builder and Visual Workflow*, DOI 10.1007/978-1-4842-1691-0_9

Usually these approvals must come from someone with authority in the area impacted by the record. One example would be the manager of the person creating the record. The person creating the record might need to have it reviewed by her supervisor for quality assurance before the record can proceed to the next step in the business process. Another example would be having a record approved by an owner of an Account. There could be a scenario where a child record, related to the Account, needed some sort of action taken upon it. The record could have an impact on the Account so in this scenario the owner of the Account might need to review and approve the record. Approval processes can have multiple levels of approvers too. In the two scenarios just described, it could be a requirement that first the manager of the creator of the record has to approve. Then, once it receives the manager's approval, it moves on to get the approval of the Account owner. This would be very helpful as to not overwhelm the Account owner with too many approvals. The manager could "weed out" the records he or she deemed unfit by rejecting the records. Doing this would not only limit the amount of work needed by the Account owner but would also give the Account owner peace of mind that someone else had already reviewed the record. The chance of the record not being in a good position to be approved would then be lower.

In Salesforce we have two options of initiating a record to go through a defined approval process. There are manual approval initiations and automatic approval initiations. A manual approval initiation is the default behavior in Salesforce that includes an Approve button on the record detail page. The user would be viewing the record and then at his or her discretion click the Approve button to start the record on its way through a define approval process. An automatic approval initiation involves the system, in this case Salesforce, starting the approval process when some sort of criteria are met when an action is taken on a record. It can be an action such as an update to the record with a field or set of fields that the system waits for an update and once it occurs starts the process. Let's go into some more details about how these two types of processes can happen in Salesforce.

Manually Submitted Approvals

As stated previously, the out-of-the-box solution for approvals in Salesforce is manually submitted approvals. By "manually submitted" I mean in the sense that the approval is kicked off manually by an individual using Salesforce. A record for an option has to be created and saved. It could be a standard object such as an Account, an Opportunity, or a Contract. Then, once saved, the detail page can be viewed. Depending on whether an approval process is set up for the object in question, a Submit for Approval button will be available on the detail page in a related list named "Approval History." This can be seen in Figure 9-1. "Submit for Approval" can be clicked by an individual and, depending on how the approval process is set up, either the record will be sent to the approver for approval or the individual who clicked the button will get an opportunity to select an approver. Again, this all depends on how it's configured, and approval processes have a lot of options.

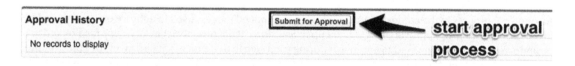

Figure 9-1. *The default location of the Submit for Approval button in the Approval History*

All these options make it extremely flexible to meet any business need that may arrive, but it also means there are a lot of steps that a Salesforce administrator has to go through to get the approval process going. Speaking of options, "Submit for Approval" can be applied to the top of the page layout by going to the "Edit Layout" link at the top of the page. Just look at Figure 9-2, for another example of the many ways that you can configure Salesforce approval processes. In this figure the Submit for Approval button was added to the top of the page layout to make it easier for individuals to find and click the Submit for Approval button.

Figure 9-2. *An example record detail screen on the Contract that allows for submitting for approval*

It is not the goal of this book to go through every aspect of how to set up an approval process along with all available options. We will show you how to set up the particular one, for the example, in this chapter, but only to get the data and process ready for the aspect of proving that Lightning Process Builder provides a lot of value to the approval process when the requirements are right.

Automatically Submitted Approvals

In the context of this book an automatically submitted approval is one where an individual does not have to click the Submit for Approval button in order to start a configured approval process in Salesforce. However, if a user does not click the out-of-the-box Submit for Approval button to start an approval process, then how does an approval process get initiated? One would need a mechanism for kicking off the approval process based on some sort of specified criteria—basically, the mechanism that would start the approval after you create or update a record. This sounds like a perfect job for a Workflow Rule except for one issue. Workflow Rules cannot start an approval process.

So, let's say there was a requirement to allow Opportunities to go through their defined stages as usual, except that an Opportunity over $1 million needs to be approved before moving to a specific stage. The requirement would be that the user could not decide when to submit for approval. That would happen when the Opportunity meets the specified criteria. How could this be implemented? Previously, it was done with the development of an Apex Trigger. Since the Apex language gives the most amount of freedom for implementing functionality in Salesforce, this became the way to solve this particular problem. In this case an Apex Trigger would be developed on the Opportunity object. It would get called every time there was an insert (create) or update (edit). Then Salesforce allowed Apex to call and start approval processes that were associated with Opportunity. Of course, this pattern of solving the problem could be for standard and custom objects.

Thus an administrator who was developing declaratively on Salesforce would have to go from one extreme (clicks) to the next (code) in order to solve the problem. A halfway point was needed— a tool had to be created that could bridge this gap and be an advanced method for a Salesforce administrator to start an approval process without the aid of Apex coding. This is another great example of Lightning Process Builder stepping up to the plate! There are some pros and cons to going from an Apex Trigger to Lightning Process Builder including:

- **Pros**

    - **No unit tests**: Without Apex code there is no need to write unit test, which is, in turn, more code to develop. This usually means less development time. However, if you do make a call to Apex code from Lightning Process Builder you will still need to have unit test coverage.

    - **Versioning**: A process built in Lightning Process Builder will have versions. That means that if you have a newer version and want to go back to an old version you can. You can also go back to a new version from an old version.

- **Cons**

    - **Simple logic may have a lot of configuration**: For simple logic, sometimes just a few lines of Apex code can do the trick. With a process in Lightning Process Builder, a lot of steps and screens need to be clicked through in order to get everything built.

    - **Less flexibility**: Lightning Process Builder is very flexible, but Apex code is extremely flexible. Sometimes you can write a process with a set of requirements without issue, but then if the requirements change and get very complicated you may find yourself needing an Apex Trigger again.

Approval Process Using Lightning Process Builder

Let's get some things clear about what Lightning Process Builder does for approval processes. It cannot be used to create an approval process. While its graphical nature that is reminiscent of a flow chart could seem like it could lend itself to being able to build an approval process, it just isn't meant for that. Lightning Process Builder excels at performing functionality that was once the realm of Apex Triggers. It's a more advanced Workflow. But while approval processes seem just like any other process, they are completely different concepts.

Lightning Process Builder has one function when it comes to approval processes and it's starting them. While a Salesforce user can manually submit a record for approval, Lightning Process Builder can submit a record for approval too. So let's think of Lightning Process Builder another way. Let's say you had instructions for Salesforce users to always submit a record for approval when it meets certain criteria. Even today you can think of examples of records that may not have all the information they need to be submitted for approval. They are not in a ready state. So you need those instructions to let users be aware of when it is appropriate to submit the record for approval. However, when you depend on human intervention typically there will be errors. Nobody is perfect 100% of the time. Everyone has good days and bad days. So some records might not get submitted for approval at the correct time.

Lightning Process Builder can replace that human intervention if it is a requirement. It runs with the simple idea of having a set of criteria to evaluate against every time you create or update a record and then execute a set of actions. It can be used to "watch" for records that need to be sent through an approval process. One of the choices available for an action in a process is "Submit for Approval." Let's continue by walking through the options available for us when we use the type of action for a process.

The Parts Used for Approvals

When you click the "+ Add Action" link on the Canvas the configuration panel appears on the right side of the screen. This configuration panel is titled "Select and Define Action." At first there is a single field labeled "Action Type." It is a picklist field with several options, as discussed previously. Upon selecting the "Submit for Approval" option, the "Select and Define Action" configuration panel will update to show more fields as seen in Figure 9-3. That list of fields includes

- **Action Type**: the specific action to take; in this case "Submit for Approval"

- **Action Name**: the label to give the action; it appears on the Canvas and helps to tell one action from another

- **Object**: the object the approval process is for; this is read-only and comes from the object that this process starts from in Lighting Process Builder

- **Approval Process**: a picklist to choose which approval process to submit; the options include

  - Default approval process

  - Specific approval process

- **Submitter**: the user that should be used to submit the approval process on behalf of; the options include

  - Current User

  - User field from a Record

  - Other User

- **Submission Comments**: free-form text that can be added to appear in the history of the approval. It can also be employed in e-mail templates using the {!ApprovalRequest.Comments} merge field

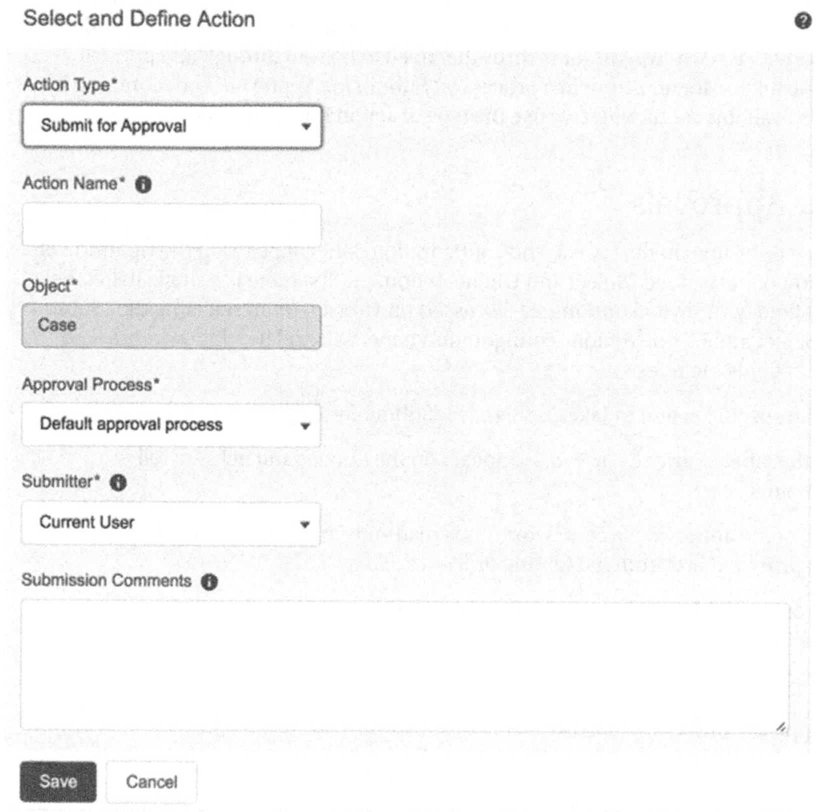

Select and Define Action

Action Type*

Submit for Approval

Action Name* ●

Object*

Case

Approval Process*

Default approval process

Submitter* ●

Current User

Submission Comments ●

Save   Cancel

Figure 9-3. *The initial "Select and Define Action" window for the "Submit for Approval" Action Type*

For the "Approval Process" section the default option is "Default approval process." This option launches the same approval process that would be launched if the Submit for Approval button existed on the record detail page and a user clicked it. Selecting this option automates what a user would normally perform (a click of a button). It is very useful and probably sufficient for many scenarios.

If you have requirements to have different approval processes for different scenarios for an object, then using the second option of "Specific approval process" will give you just what you need. When the "Specific approval process" option is selected a second input field appears to the right with the text "Find an approval process..." as seen in Figure 9-4. When an approval process is configured outside Lightning Process Builder it is required to have a name for it. That name can be typed into the "Find an approval process..." field and a picklist will appear to find matches. It is essentially a search box limited to the names of approval processes. Just start typing in that field and the picklist will become more and more limited with its search results as you type the name in.

In addition to the above-mentioned fields we find the check box titled "Skip the entry criteria for this process?" which gives an extra level of flexibility. If you select this check box, then something interesting happens. Normally, an approval process is configured to have some entry criteria to filter out any records that should not go through the approval process. When you are configuring a process in Lightning Process Builder you can decide the criteria that should be used before calling submitting for approval. So there could be a business requirement to bypass the entry criteria for an approval process and just run it. This is what the "Yes" check box signifies. It tells the process to submit the approval and run it no matter what because the process is handling the criteria. It gives you more control when designing the process.

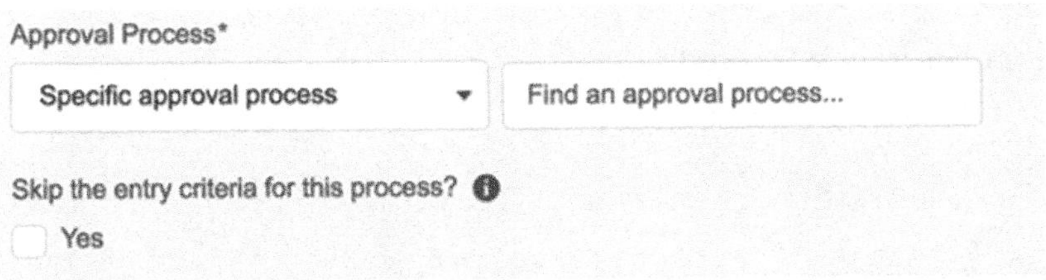

Approval Process*

| Specific approval process ▼ | Find an approval process... |

Skip the entry criteria for this process? ⓘ

☐ Yes

Figure 9-4. *The Approval Process section with the fields related to selecting a specific approval process*

The next section is the Submitter section. Here is where the process can be configured to choose who should be used to submit the approval. This is necessary because there is not a person physically pushing a Submit for Approval button on a record detail page. When a user pushes that button then he is the one submitting the record for approval. When nobody is pushing a button anymore then who is submitting?

One idea is that since a process is triggered by a create or an update on a record the person who created or updated the record should be the submitter. This is the default option for the Submitter section. It's labeled "Current User" and it causes the approval to be submitted by whomever this process is running as. So, for example, let's say there is a process on the Opportunity object that will submit a record for approval. In this example, the process is configured to only do an update when it is $1 million or more and it's placed into the "Qualification" stage. Now if the "Current User" setting was chosen for the submitter on this process, then whoever saved that record automatically becomes the submitter, even if he is not aware of it. For a lot of scenarios this may be the requirement. It certainly follows a similar pattern as a record manually submitted for approval.

What happens if you need more control over which submitter it is? There could be a requirement that the original creator of the record should be the one who should be listed as the submitter even in the event that someone else with access happens to be updating the Opportunity in our example. For this type of requirement we have this second option for the Submitter section, "User Field from a Record" as seen in Figure 9-5. The "User Field from a Record" allows the process to be configured to look at a related user on the record and submit the approval as that user.

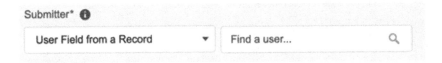

Submitter* ⓘ

| User Field from a Record ▼ | Find a user... 🔍 |

Figure 9-5. *The Submitter section with the fields related to finding a User lookup field for the record*

Next to the "User Field from a Record" input box is the "Find a user . . ." search box. Click here and start typing the name of a field on the record. There will be picklist with possible results to choose from. Figure 9-6 shows an example of this picklist on a Case. Select the field that meets the requirement and then click the Choose button and you are good to go!

Figure 9-6. *The results as a picklist for selecting a field on a Case*

After a field is chosen for the Submitter, the lookup will show the names of the object and fields similar to those in Figure 9-7. The field you chose is replaced with this text. It has the form of "[Object].Field. RelatedField." Depending on how deep you traverse through the relationships, there can be more and more related fields. From the object there can be up to ten fields deep if needed. When clicking on this text, you are not allowed to manually change the text. Instead, the "Select a user from a Record" window appears again to allow you to make the updates required. Here only fields of type User show up to be selected.

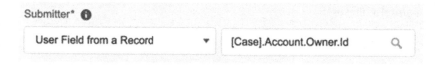

Figure 9-7. *A field selected off the Case object as the submitter*

The third option for the Submitter section is "Other User." The "Other User" option also enables a Find a User . . . field as well, as seen in Figure 9-8. It works a little differently, though, compared to the previously discussed "User Field for a Record." Upon clicking the "Find a User . . . field, instead of a window appearing a picklist appears for matching user records as you type the user's name in the field. Once the appropriate user is found, simply click his or her name to select it. While this does give the ability to select specific users, it is not always the best approach. That is because people change positions and having them specified directly here will mean having to change the process any time the user needs to be replaced. Sometimes requirements dictate that you do not have a choice, but if possible try to have the user run off a field so that way the data can be updated without having to modify the process any time a person changes. It makes the process less brittle and more hardened.

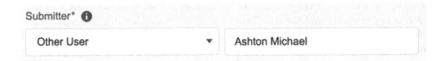

Figure 9-8. The "Other User" option for the "Submitter" section with a user chosen

When all the settings are configured and saved in the "Select and Define Action" configuration panel, the action is added to the list of immediate actions in the Canvas for its related criteria. In Figure 9-9 you can see that the action has a stamp icon to represent that the action is a "Submit for Approval" action. Having different icons allows you to distinguish the different action types at a glance without needing to click the action and look at the settings in the configuration panel.

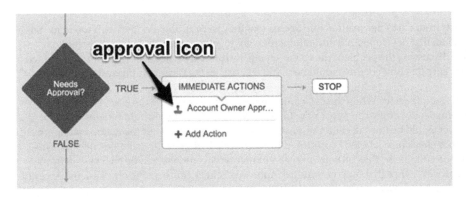

Figure 9-9. A "Submit for Approval" action with its stamp icon

The Business Case

For actions in Lightning Process Builder all the settings are limited to the single configuration panel that appears on the right of the Canvas. This keeps the implementation of a process nice and tidy. By having everything self-contained on that configuration panel it keeps an administrator from context switching or having to move about the Canvas doing different tasks for different items. This consistency makes working with Lightning Process Builder easier to use; once you have configured one type of action, the rest follow a similar pattern.

We have walked through what that configuration panel looks like for a "Submit for Approval" action. Luckily there are not too many fields required to set it up. In fact, most of the work comes from just two sections, the "Approval Process" section and the "Submitter" section. The other sections are important too, of course, but these two sections drive the core of the behavior for the process to submit an approval.

Now that we understand what each of the sections of the "Submit for Approval" action do, let's put this into action. To do so, let us return to the scenario we just handled in the last chapter. As a recap, that scenario was that customers were calling into a call center for any issues they had. During research it was found that while the call center was handling the issue from the customer, many times the customer would mention about how unhappy he or she was—so much so that sometimes the caller would cancel service. Even if it didn't happen during the call to the call center, it would happen eventually. It was then decided that in order to be proactive about the customer cancellations, modifications would be made to Salesforce to allow a phone representative to flag an account as "at risk," meaning the account was at risk of being canceled. Customer relationship agents could then call the customer back and discuss options to make the service more attractive in order to keep the customer.

In the previous chapter we set up a process in Lightning Process Builder to handle the scenario we just recapped. Now, with the new process, visibility into the volatility of the account was possible. Whenever someone called in and seemed upset or even irate, the customer service agent could then flag the Case, which in turn would flag the Account. Someone could contact the customer later in hopes of keeping the customer happy and keeping him as a customer.

Of course, there is always room for improvement. The best-kept intentions rarely work out the way you would expect. In actuality, when the process was put in place a new problem cropped up. Call center representatives were afraid of not flagging an Account as at risk when it should be, so they ended up flagging Accounts that really were not at risk at all. This ended up causing more work down the line for customer relationship agents, who were trying to call so many people to understand and rectify any issues, many of which were nonexistent. So that's a problem!

The Design

After some complaints from customer relationship agents that they were getting flooded with too many false positives the initial team that developed the implementation got together again. As before, everyone sat down around a table discussing the problem they were seeing. By the end of the meeting it was determined that in order to make sure that an Account should be marked at risk by the Case, an approval needed to be set up.

The solution was simple really. When the call center representative marked a Case as "Account At Risk," instead of automatically setting the Account's status to "At Risk," the action would be submitted for approval. The approver would be the call center representative's manager, and after the action was approved there would be another check box, labeled "Account At Risk Approved," that would become checked. This check box would not be editable by the call center representative and would instead be checked off by the Salesforce approval process. Once that "Account At Risk Approved" check box became checked, the Account be updated to an "At Risk" status along with the "At Risk Reason" comments.

The beauty of Lightning Process Builder is that you can take an existing process and clone it into a new version. This means a copy is made that will be in an inactive state so you cannot alter the existing process. This is very useful for backing out changes in case something does not work out correctly in production. So let's take the design from the last chapter and update it with the new steps just discussed. Putting it all together should look like Figure 9-10.

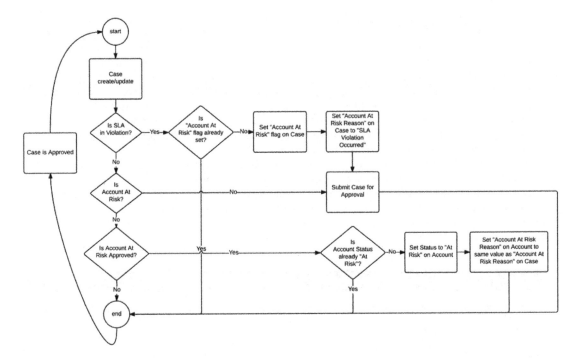

Figure 9-10. *Flow chart design of the Account At Risk process updated to include Approval*

The newly updated design now has a third set of criteria checking if the "Account At Risk Approved" flag is true. If so, it finishes off the process as it did before. Before that, though, we can see that the first two sets of criteria now all end up as an action to submit the Case for approval. When this happens, the process in Lightning Process Builder ends. Then we just wait until a manager approves. At that point the Case is updated and it will go through our same process again as designated in by the loop from the end to the start of the process in the design. Lightning Process Builder allows this all to be in the same process so it can be clearly seen and managed in one place. There is no need to create separate processes in Lightning Process Builder for different scenarios.

First Set up the Approval Process

There is one aspect that cannot be implemented when working within Lightning Process Builder. That's the actual approval process. As stated earlier, Lightning Process Builder can be used to submit an approval but it cannot be used to create an approval process. That feature is still where it has always been, in the Approval Process functionality of Salesforce. Let's begin setting up the Approval Process so that we can see how this all ties together with Lightning Process Builder. Since the focus of this chapter is learning and building a process in Lightning Process Builder, we will not dive into the details of building an Approval Process and all of its features. There are plenty of other great books on that topic such as *Practical Salesforce.com Development Without Code* (Apress, 2015) by my good friend Philip Weinmeister.

Let's quickly walk through setting up the approval process so we can use it later within Lightning Process Builder. Create an approval process as usual by going to Setup ➤ Build ➤ Create ➤ Workflow & Approvals ➤ Approval Processes. The first screen you will see will look like Figure 9-11. At the top of the page in the drop-down list select "Case" to manage approval processes for the Case object. Then, in the next drop-down menu that reads "Create New Approval Process" select the "User Standard Setup Wizard" to begin setting up our approval process.

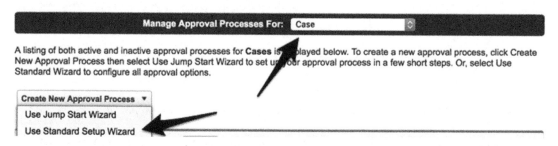

Figure 9-11. *The start page for creating a new Approval Process*

In the next screen we will want to define the basics such as the Process Name, Unique Name, and Description. It's very important to add a description for approval processes as they are complex and the title alone makes it difficult sometimes to understand its intention. Use the values as seen in Figure 9-12 to set up step 1 of the approval process configuration. Then click "Next" to move on to step 2.

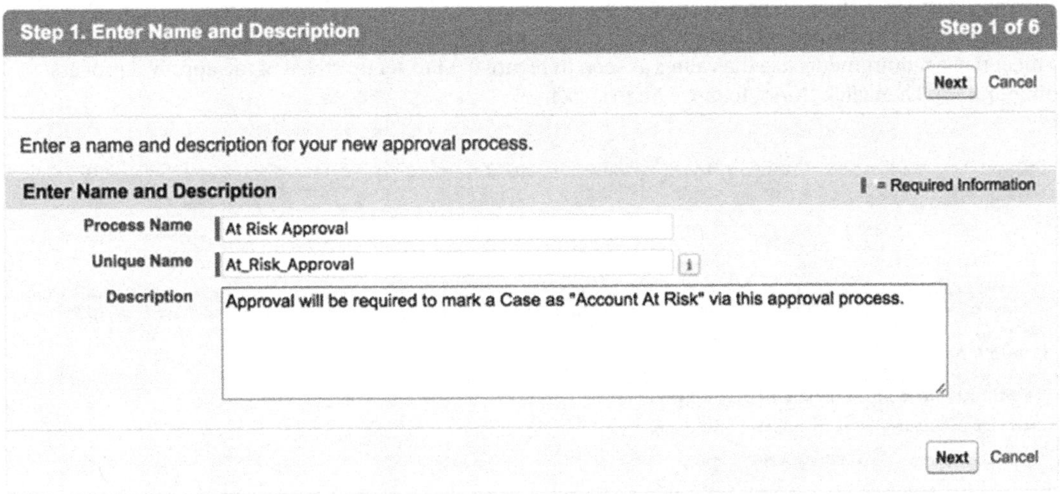

Figure 9-12. *Step 1 of the approval process configuration with the Process Name, Unique Name, and Description*

The requirements are that approvals for this approval process should only happen with Case records that were checked off with the "at risk" flag. Step 2 of the configuration of the approval process defines the entry criteria of the approval, so it needs to be set up to apply only to records where the "Account At Risk" field on the Case record is equal to "True" (checked). Use the values as seen in Figure 9-13 to set up step 2 of the approval process configuration. Then click "Next" to move on to step 3.

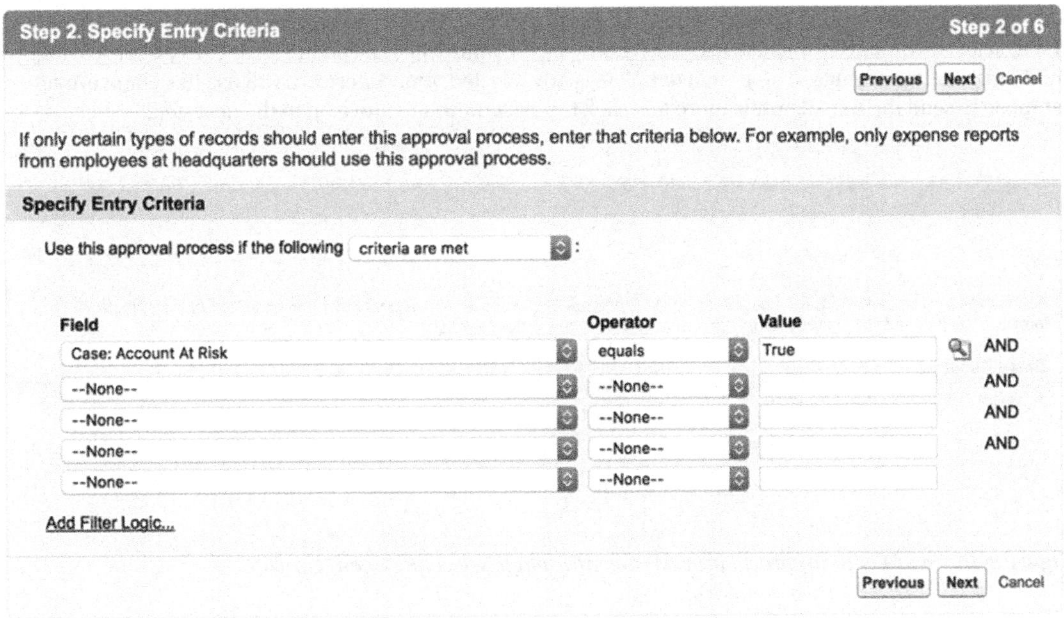

Figure 9-13. *Step 2 of the approval process configuration with the entry criteria*

Next, we need to define who can approve the Case and edit its values. The requirements state that we need the manager of the person working the Case to approve the Case. To configure the approval process to meet these requirements use the values as seen in Figure 9-14 to set up step 3 of the approval process configuration. Then click "Next" to move on to step 4.

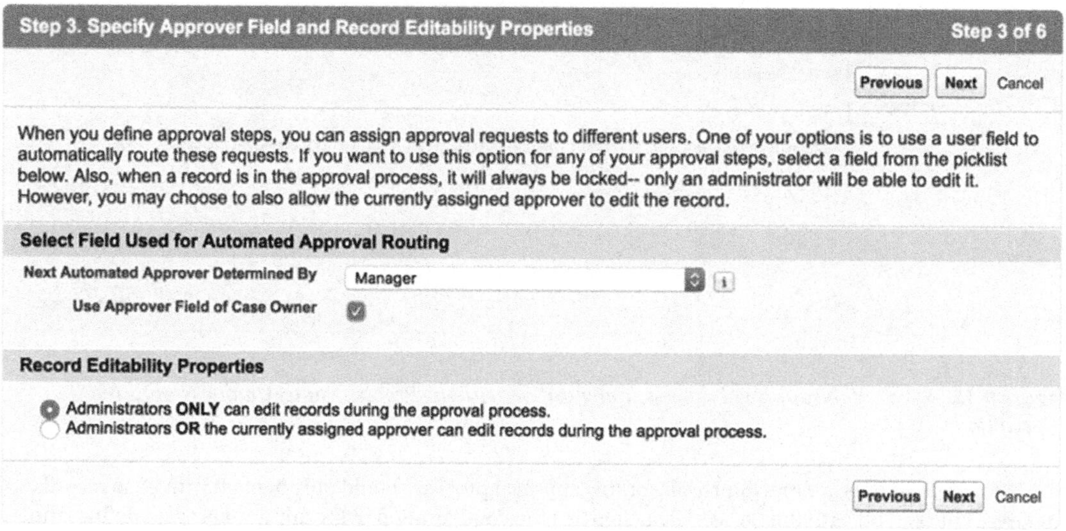

Figure 9-14. *Step 3 of the approval process configuration to define who can approve the record and who can edit it*

Approval processes need a way to notify the approver that there is a record to approve. Step 4 allows you to select an e-mail template to use when notifying the approver. As seen in Figure 9-15 we are leaving this blank for this example. If an e-mail template is not selected, then Salesforce will use its default e-mail template to send the e-mail notification. Just click the Next button to move on to the next step.

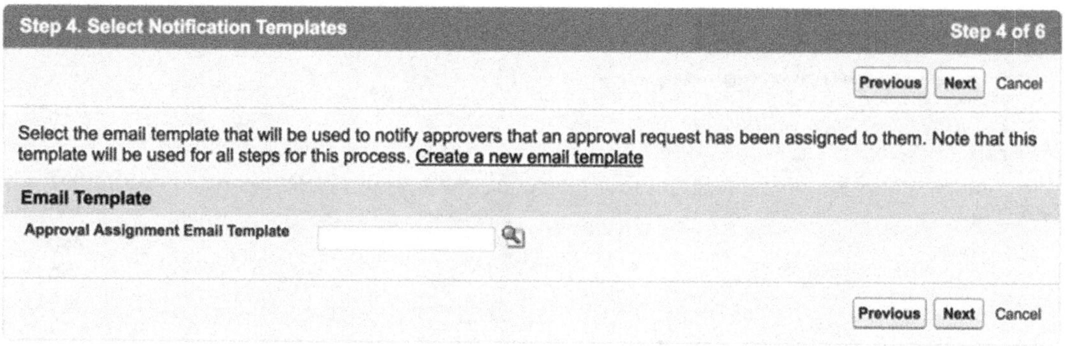

Figure 9-15. *Step 4 of the approval process configuration to select an e-mail template*

We also need to define what will be on the approval page layout. Step 5 is for configuring these settings. Use the values as seen in Figure 9-16 to set up step 5 of the approval process configuration. Then click "Next" to move on to step 6.

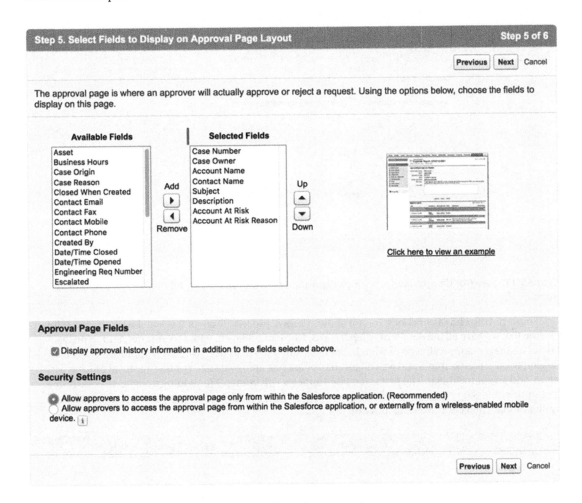

Figure 9-16. Step 5 of the approval process to configure the approval page

In step 6 we finally need to specify who can initially submit a Case for the approval process. With the requirements the process defined in Lightning Process Builder will submit the Case. However, we still need to define who will be allowed to submit it. Logically it will be the Case Owner who is editing and saving the Case. Then, the Case is saved, it will be evaluated by the criteria we set up in Lightning Process Builder to see if it needs to be submitted for approval. Once we configure that part of course here in this chapter. For this step, configure the screen as seen in Figure 9-17 to select the Case Owner as the user who can submit the Case for approval. Finally, click the Save button to save this approval process.

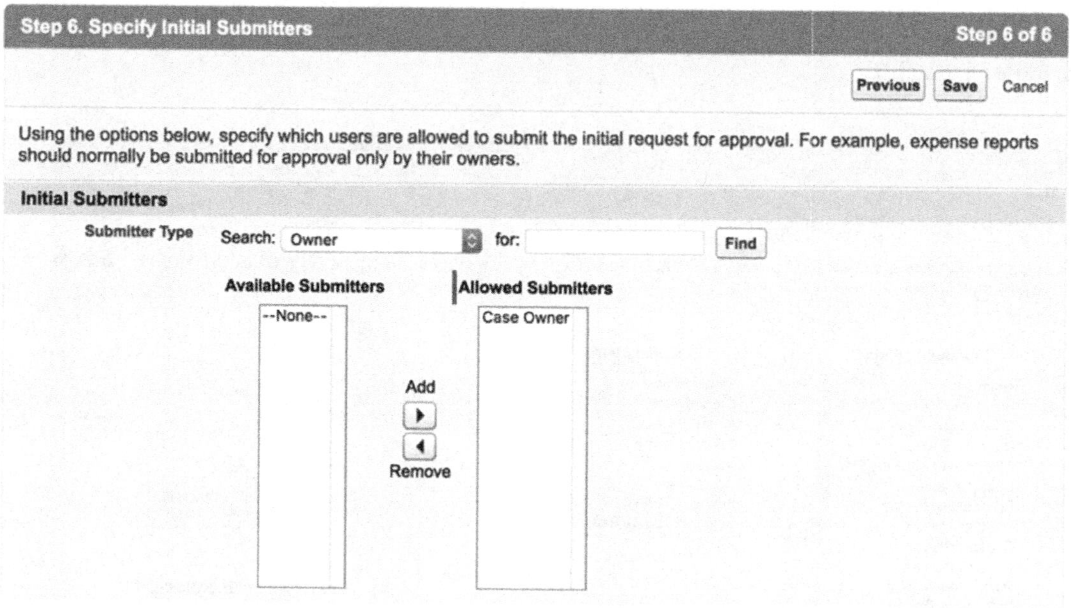

Figure 9-17. *Step 6 of the approval process configuration to specify the initial submitters to the approval process*

This is not the end of our configuration of the approval process, though. It is just the beginning. While it is true that we have all the details of when it starts, who can initiate it, who can approve, and so on, we did not define our approval steps or what happens at different states (e.g., when it is approved or rejected). This approval is pretty simple and we will just be adding one approval step. For this approval process we just set up, add an approval step. The first screen that appears will be step 1 for adding a Name, Unique Name, Description, and Step Number. Use the values as seen in Figure 9-18 to set up step 1 of the approval step configuration. Then click "Next" to move on to step 2.

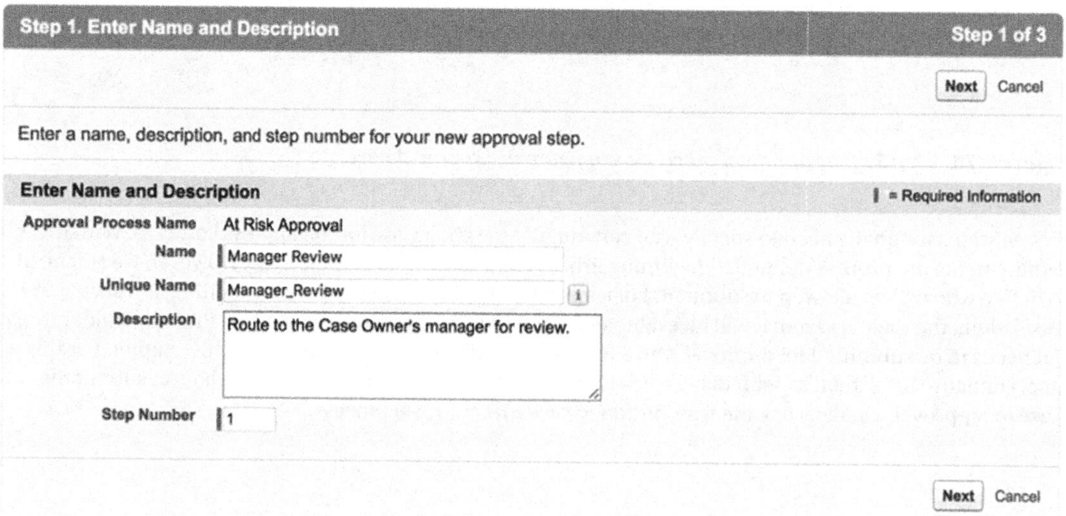

Figure 9-18. *Step 1 of the approval step configuration for the approval process*

The second step is to define any criteria needed in the record to move on to this particular step in the approval process. We have no use for criteria for this step, so leave everything as seen in Figure 9-19. Then click "Next" to move on to step 3.

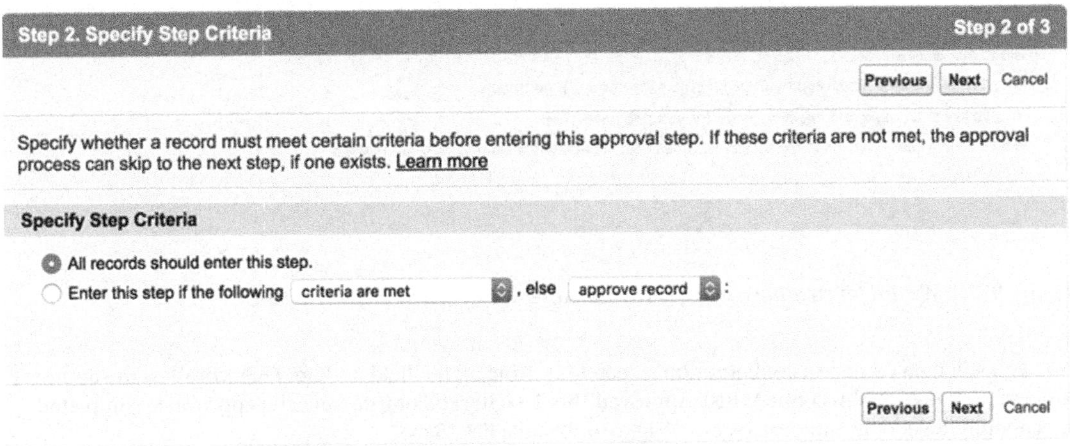
Step 2. Specify Step Criteria
Step 2 of 3
Previous
Next
Cancel
Specify whether a record must meet certain criteria before entering this approval step. If these criteria are not met, the approval process can skip to the next step, if one exists. Learn more
Specify Step Criteria
All records should enter this step.
Enter this step if the following
criteria are met
, else
approve record
Previous
Next
Cancel

Figure 9-19. *Step 2 of the approval step configuration for the approval process*

The final step is to configure who is assigned as the approver for this step in the approval process. Our requirements are to have the manager of owner of the Case be the approver. So select the option as shown in Figure 9-20 and click "Save."

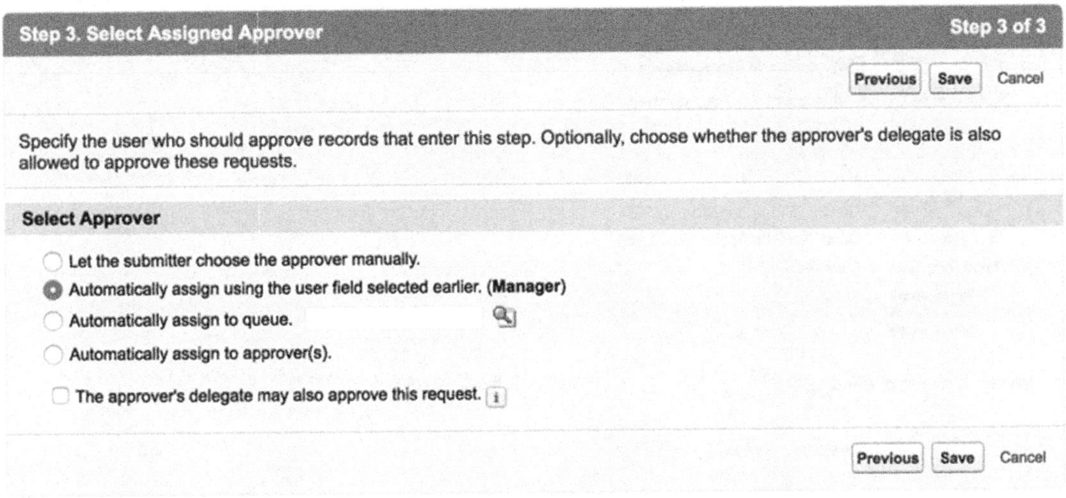
Step 3. Select Assigned Approver
Step 3 of 3
Previous
Save
Cancel
Specify the user who should approve records that enter this step. Optionally, choose whether the approver's delegate is also allowed to approve these requests.
Select Approver
Let the submitter choose the approver manually.
Automatically assign using the user field selected earlier. (Manager)
Automatically assign to queue.
Automatically assign to approver(s).
The approver's delegate may also approve this request.
Previous
Save
Cancel

Figure 9-20. *Step 3 of the approval step configuration for the approval process*

After creating the approval step for the first time you will see a screen with some options as in Figure 9-21. We now want to do a field update because we have a check box we want to set to checked or true when the action is approved. To begin setting up this aspect, select options as shown in Figure 9-21 and click "Go!"

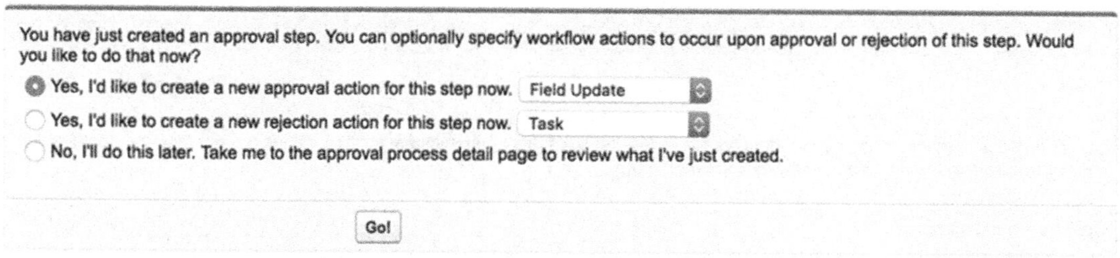

You have just created an approval step. You can optionally specify workflow actions to occur upon approval or rejection of this step. Would you like to do that now?

- Yes, I'd like to create a new approval action for this step now. Field Update
- Yes, I'd like to create a new rejection action for this step now. Task
- No, I'll do this later. Take me to the approval process detail page to review what I've just created.

Go!

Figure 9-21. *Wizard for creating a workflow action after the approval step is created*

You will then come to a configuration screen for setting up the field update. This will allow the approval process to change the "Account At Risk Approved" field to checked or true once the approval is completed successfully. Select the options as seen in Figure 9-22 and click "Save."

■ **Note** It's important to check off the "Re-evaluate Workflow Rules after Field Change" as that will cause the record to run through our process in Lightning Process Builder again once we create it.

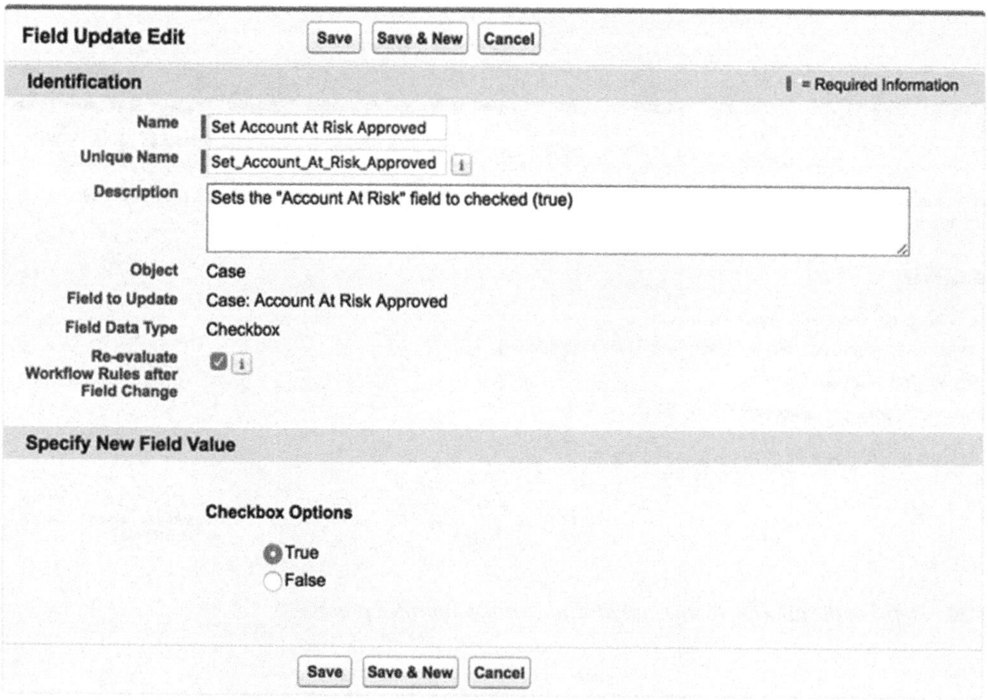

Field Update Edit Save Save & New Cancel

Identification ▌ = Required Information

Name	▌ Set Account At Risk Approved
Unique Name	▌ Set_Account_At_Risk_Approved [i]
Description	Sets the "Account At Risk" field to checked (true)
Object	Case
Field to Update	Case: Account At Risk Approved
Field Data Type	Checkbox
Re-evaluate Workflow Rules after Field Change	☑ [i]

Specify New Field Value

Checkbox Options
- True
- False

Save Save & New Cancel

Figure 9-22. *The "Set Account At Risk Approved" field update action*

Finishing with Lightning Process Builder

We just finished setting up a quick approval process so we can show how to use it in Lightning Process Builder. The steps we went through previously were done in an expedited manner just so we could have the approval process ready. There is a lot to configure with approval processes, so even though it seemed lengthy, it is still a simple approval process compared to what a lot of organizations set up in their production Salesforce orgs.

To begin we will open up the process we built in the last chapter. It was named "Set Account At Risk from Case" and once it's opened you will notice a few things at the top of screen. First, it is set to "Read Only" because it has been made active from our previous work. Also noticeable is the Deactivate button that will set it to not active. There is no button that says "Edit" on it. Lightning Process Builder will not allow a process to be edited once it has been activated. In fact, at this point even if the Deactivate button were clicked, the ability to edit the process would still not be there. In order to edit this process from the last chapter it will have to be cloned (copied) into either a new version of the process with the same name or an entirely new process with a different name. Go ahead and click the Clone button, as seen in Figure 9-23, so we can make a new version of this process.

Figure 9-23. *The Clone button located at the top of Lightning Process Builder*

New Version or New Process

Upon clicking the Clone button, the window in Figure 9-24 will appear to give the ability to clone as a "Version of current process" or "A new process." This window presents a fork in the road. On one hand you could go with the default selection of "Version of current process" that will essentially allow you to edit this process by creating a new version. On the other hand, you could select "A new process" and it will present you with a different screen that looks just like the screen you have when you create a new process in Lightning Process Builder from scratch.

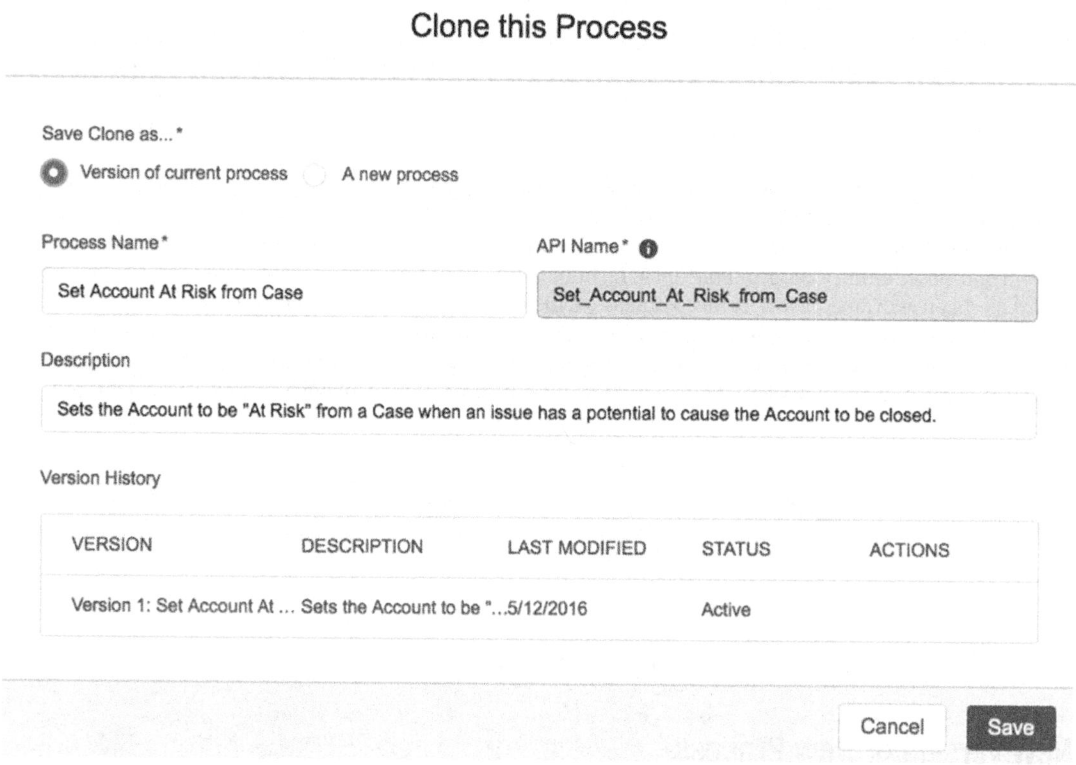

Clone this Process

Save Clone as...*

◉ Version of current process   ○ A new process

Process Name*

| Set Account At Risk from Case |

API Name* ⓘ

| Set_Account_At_Risk_from_Case |

Description

| Sets the Account to be "At Risk" from a Case when an issue has a potential to cause the Account to be closed. |

Version History

VERSION	DESCRIPTION	LAST MODIFIED	STATUS	ACTIONS
Version 1: Set Account At ...	Sets the Account to be "...	5/12/2016	Active	

Cancel   **Save**

Figure 9-24. *Clone this Process window*

So which do we choose? Well, that depends on intent. If the intent is really just to edit the current process, then choose to create a new version. Having a new version of the same process means that you can never have the two versions run at the same time since only one version can be active at any one moment in time. If you plan on needing to use the process as a starting point to build another process that can run side by side with the original, then you would want to choose to create a new process. Just be sure though that the new process does not do anything to "step on" the original process since you can have the new process active alongside the process that it was cloned from.

For our example we are truly just editing the current process and will go with the default choice to create a new version of the same process. From a business process modeling perspective this makes sense since we are basically doing the same thing except that we need to add approvals to an already existing process. To continue, click the Save button to save the new version.

■ **Note**   With the "Version of current process" option the Process Name and Description can be modified but the API Name cannot. If you change the Process Name or Description, it changes not only for this version but also for all versions of the process.

Once the new version has been created it should look exactly like the original except that it's not in read-only mode and there is an Activate button now. We will not be activating anything quite yet though. Instead, let's change up this new version to meet the design.

Adding a New Criteria

The design calls for a third criterion to be added, labeled "Is Account At Risk Approved?" and it will essentially have a group of actions identical to the actions that were originally associated with the "Is Account At Risk?" criterion. Unfortunately, we cannot create a new criterion and drag over its actions to it to save us time. We could just recreate all the actions on the new criterion and remove the old action from the "Is Account At Risk?" criteria, but let's be creative and try to save some time.

Let's add an additional set of criteria but also name it "Is Account At Risk?" so that we can build this one to be the replacement for the existing criteria set with the same name. This is also a good exercise to show that Lightning Process Builder allows duplicate names with the criteria. It can be confusing to have multiple names, but after we are complete this will not be the case.

Add the new criteria using the following settings:

- **Criteria Name**: Is Account At Risk?

- **Criteria for Exciting Actions**: Conditions are met

- Set Condition 1

  - **Field**: [Case].Account_At_Risk__c

  - **Operator**: Equals

  - **Type**: Boolean

  - **Value**: True

- **Conditions**: All of the conditions are met (AND)

- **Advanced**: checked

When complete, the configuration panel for the criteria should look like Figure 9-25. Click "Save" to continue.

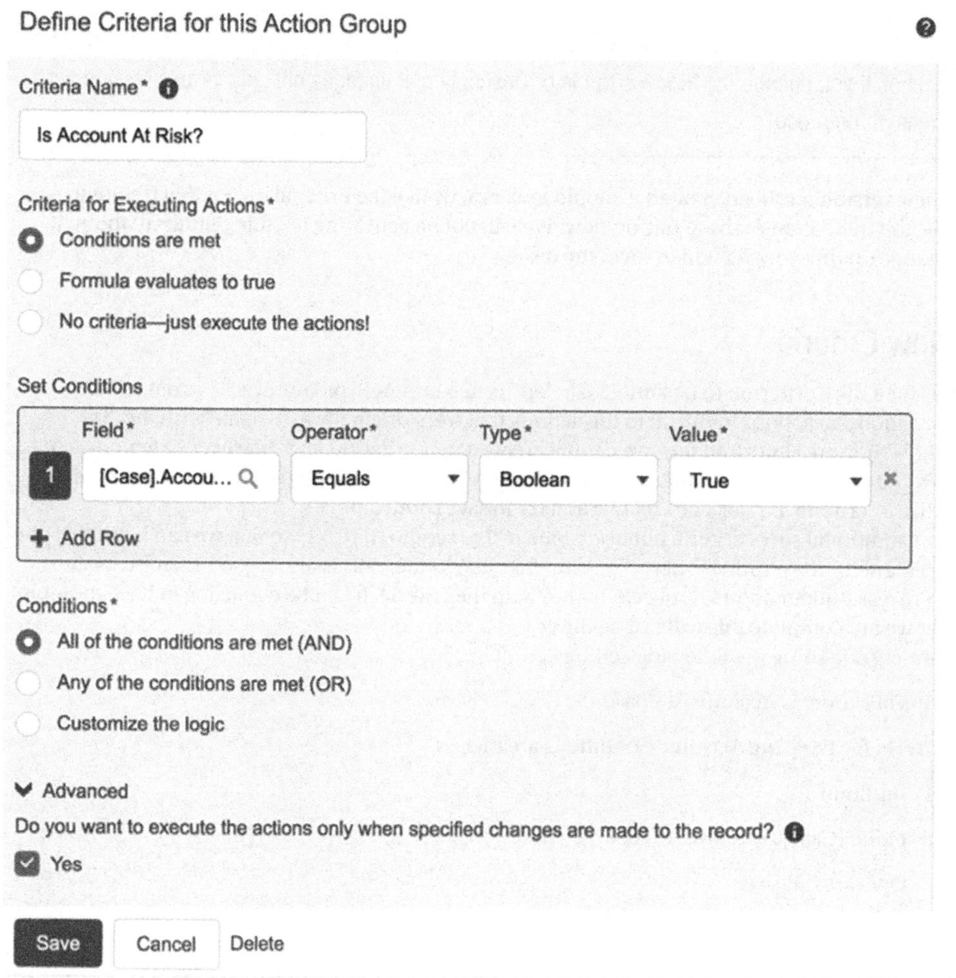

Define Criteria for this Action Group ❓

Criteria Name* ⓘ

[Is Account At Risk?]

Criteria for Executing Actions*

🔘 Conditions are met

⚪ Formula evaluates to true

⚪ No criteria—just execute the actions!

Set Conditions

	Field*	Operator*	Type*	Value*	
1	[Case].Accou... 🔍	Equals ▾	Boolean ▾	True ▾	✕

➕ Add Row

Conditions*

🔘 All of the conditions are met (AND)

⚪ Any of the conditions are met (OR)

⚪ Customize the logic

∨ Advanced

Do you want to execute the actions only when specified changes are made to the record? ⓘ

☑ Yes

[Save] Cancel Delete

Figure 9-25. *Configuration panel for additional "Is Account At Risk?" criteria*

Having two sets of criteria can be confusing, so now click the original "Is Account At Risk?" criteria so its configuration panel opens up. The design states that there should be a criteria set named "Is Account At Risk Approved?" and if true, it performs the actions of updating the Account record.

To meet the design, update the current settings for this criteria with the following settings:

- **Criteria Name**: Is Account At Risk Approved?

- **Criteria for Executing Actions**: Conditions are met

- Set Condition 1

    - **Field**: [Case].Account_At_Risk_Approved__c

    - **Operator**: Equals

    - **Type**: Boolean

    - **Value**: True

- **Conditions**: All of the conditions are met (AND)

- **Advanced**: checked

Almost everything should be the same as in the original except the Criteria Name and the Field in the Set Condition. The Field is now looking at [Case].Account_At_Risk_Approved__c. This is the field that the approval process updates to true (checked) at the end when it is approved. Click the Save button to continue and go back to the Canvas. At this point our process in Lightning Process Builder looks flipped compared to our design. The "Is Account At Risk Approved?" criteria should be at the bottom and the "Is Account At Risk?" criteria should be in the middle. No worries though! We can fix this. You might have noticed while moving the mouse around over the Canvas that a blue box would appear around a criterion and its related actions. You might also have noticed that in the top right corner of that box is an icon showing two arrows with one pointing up and the other down. This box represents the ability to move or reorder the criteria and their related actions.

We need to move the "Is Account At Risk Approved?" criteria to the bottom so hover the mouse over any of the area around that criterion or its actions until the blue move box appears. Then, while the move box is visible, click and hold anywhere inside the move box and drag the box down below the "Is Account At Risk?" criteria until a green line appears showing where the new placement will be. When the green line appears let go of the mouse button to finalize its placement. To illustrate this movement please refer to Figure 9-26, which shows the Canvas before and after the criteria were reordered.

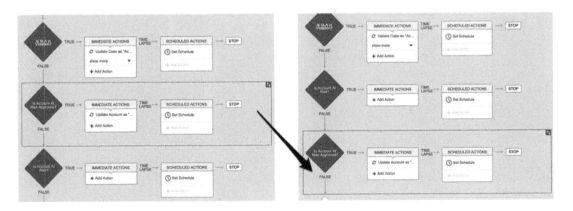

Figure 9-26. *The reordering of the criteria in action*

We are getting closer! It's starting to look a lot more like the design conceived back at the start of the chapter. We still haven't added the action to submit the approval though. Have no fear because this is next!

Submit for Approval Action

All this anticipation is killing me. We have gone through all these steps to set up the fields, field updates, and approval process and to edit the new version of the process we created in the last chapter to finally add this next step to submit a record for approval. To do so, click the "+ Add Action" link under "Immediate Actions" for the "Is Account At Risk?" criteria. As expected, the configuration panel opens up. We previously went through all these settings to understand what they do so there is no need to walk through them again. Instead, use the settings that follow to set up the "Submit for Approval" action:

- **Action Type**: Submit for Approval

- **Action Name**: Account Owner Approval

- **Object**: Case

- **Approval Process**: Specific approval process ➤ At Risk Approval – At_Risk_Approval

- **Submitter**: Current User

- **Submission Comments**: Case is marked "Account At Risk." Please approve to change Account status to "At Risk."

When complete the configuration panel should look like Figure 9-27. It's worth noting that in our example we only have one approval process for our Case. So we could use the "Default approval process" option under the "Approval Process" setting. In production systems it might not be so straightforward. I've seen such complex Salesforce implementations that there have been scenarios with multiple approval processes. So it is more explicit to call upon a specific approval process in case the default approval were to ever change; then at least you know are still calling the approval process you need. This also has the positive side effect of self-documenting the process in Lightning Process Builder. We can literally see what approval process will be called for submission. If we instead chose the "Default approval process" option, we would not necessarily know what approval process we were using to submit for approval for.

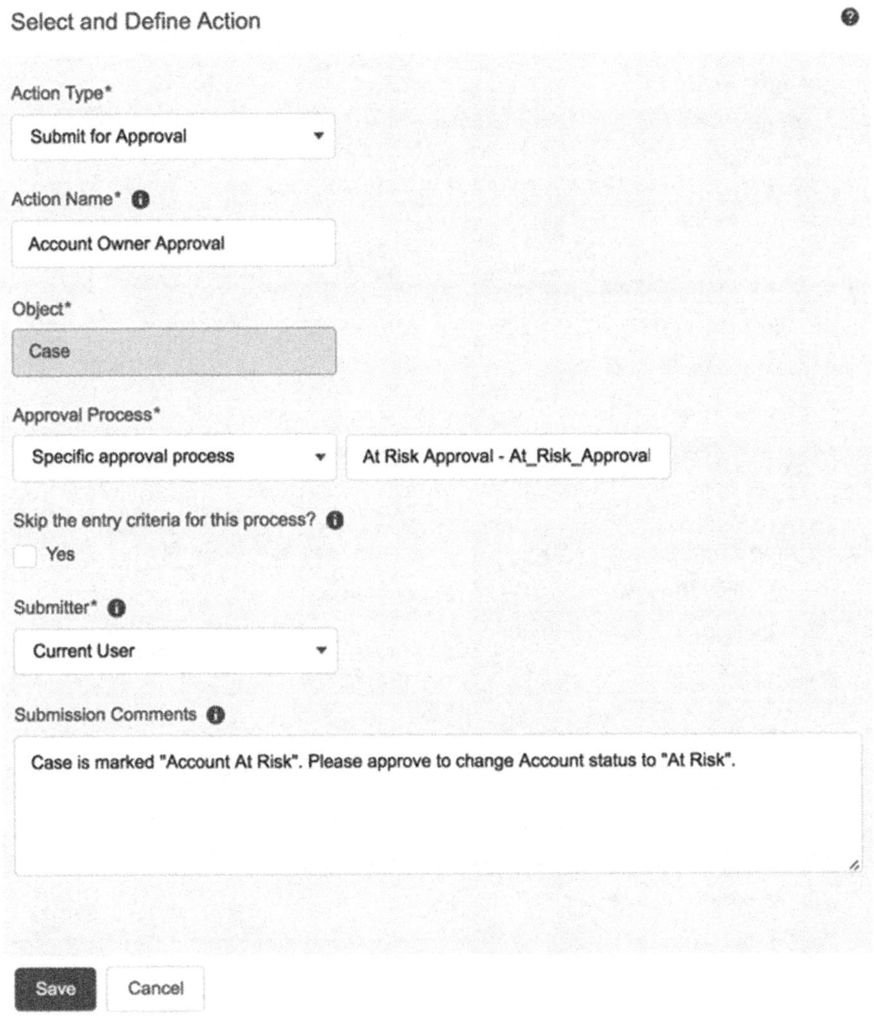

Select and Define Action

Action Type*

Submit for Approval ▼

Action Name* ⓘ

Account Owner Approval

Object*

Case

Approval Process*

Specific approval process ▼   At Risk Approval - At_Risk_Approval

Skip the entry criteria for this process? ⓘ

☐ Yes

Submitter* ⓘ

Current User ▼

Submission Comments ⓘ

Case is marked "Account At Risk". Please approve to change Account status to "At Risk".

[Save] [Cancel]

Figure 9-27. *Submit for Approval configuration*

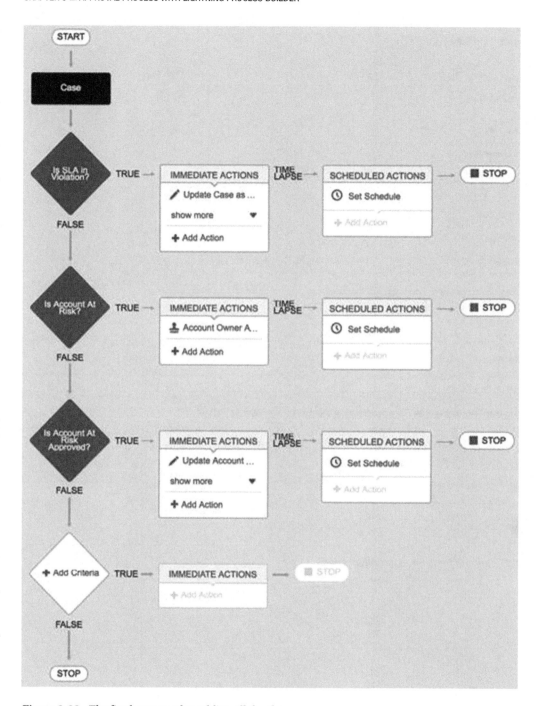

Figure 9-28. *The final process after adding all the changes*

Click the Save button to continue and be taken to the Canvas again. At this point we are done with the changes to the process. It should look like Figure 9-28. Even though all the changes are made and saved, it still is not active. The previous version we cloned this from is still active. This means that Salesforce is using the original version of the process, not this new version we just finished updating. In order to make Salesforce use this version, just click the Activate button on the top right. A confirmation screen will appear stating that the previously active version will be automatically deactivated when this newer version is made active. Again, we can only have one active version of a process at any one time. Just activating our newer process here saves time from having to deactivate the older version. Salesforce does this for us automatically.

To see how this process works, Figure 9-29 presents a Case without the Account At Risk flag or the Account At Risk Reason set. Next to it is an image of the related Account that is still in good standing.

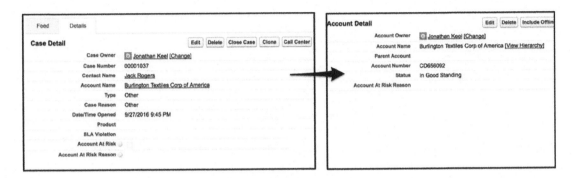

Figure 9-29. *A case and its related Account, which is in Good Standing*

Once the Case is updated to have the Account At Risk flag checked and the Account At Risk Reason set, the approval process will be initiated, as shown in Figure 9-30. The Account status will remain In Good Standing until the approval is complete.

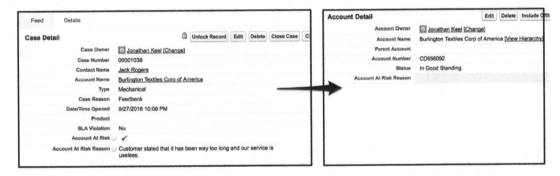

Figure 9-30. *The case that has the Account At Risk flag (and reason) set and the Account status still In Good Standing*

An e-mail will be sent to the approver and the approver will see the Approve/Reject Approval Request screen, as in Figure 9-31.

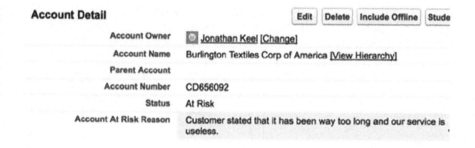

Figure 9-31. The Approve/Reject Approval Request screen used to approve (or reject) the request

The approver can then approve, and once he or she does, the Account will be updated to At Risk and the Account At Risk Reason will be set as well, as shown in Figure 9-32.

Account Detail

Account Owner	Jonathan Keel [Change]
Account Name	Burlington Textiles Corp of America [View Hierarchy]
Parent Account	
Account Number	CD656092
Status	At Risk
Account At Risk Reason	Customer stated that it has been way too long and our service is useless.

Figure 9-32. The Account now in an At Risk status along with its Account At Risk Reason set

Recap

In this chapter we covered the difference between manually submitted approvals and automatically submitted approvals. Manually submitted approvals require a user to literally click a Submit for Approval button, while automatically submitted approvals have the system submit a record for approval based on some rule that is defined. With this understanding, we walked through how Lightning Process Builder helps to define the rule to automatically submit a record for approval. Lightning Process Builder is not used for building the actual approval processes, so we still have to configure them just as we did in the past. What Lightning Process Builder does is allow us to create a process to submit a record for approval that in the past would have required an Apex Trigger to do so. We also walked through an example where we took the process from the previous chapter and modified it to use an approval process. In doing so we learned about other aspects of Lightning Process Builder such as cloning, versions, and reordering of criteria/actions.

CHAPTER 10

■ ■ ■

Calling Autolaunched Flows

Ideally, by now you are getting more and more excited about the possibilities that you have to get tasks completed faster than ever. It really seems that with Lightning Process Builder, you can now complete many different scenarios where you had to use an Apex Trigger, or maybe some sort of overly complicated configured workaround. The fact that a process can contain several criteria and actions also makes that process more maintainable. That is because everything can be kept together in the process. Well, almost everything! We just saw in the last chapter that approval processes are not implemented in process builder. We instead have to call out to an approval process. This is good though. It's good because it keeps processes in Lightning Process Builder streamlined to do what they are good at. And that approval process we called? Well, it was implemented in the tried-and-true method that Salesforce has used for years to build approval processes.

So as we saw with the approval process, when we implement a process, in some aspects it needs to be implemented outside Lightning Process Builder. Sometimes requirements become complicated and we reach the limit of what can be done in a process. At that point, though, Lightning Process Builder allows for other options to call out to different features of Salesforce. One of those features we can call out to is a Flow. We've converted flows built in Visual Workflow in earlier chapters. They can be quite complicated. In fact, using Lightning Process Builder feels much simpler than using Visual Workflow. However, their capabilities and their interfaces are so different.

Lighting Process Builder keeps you confined to a simple yet powerful pattern of criteria and actions linked to other criteria and actions. The chaining of these is what makes the processes in Lightning Process Builder simple yet powerful. Yet you aren't really confined. While Lightning Process Builder is simpler than Visual Workflow, it does not give you as much control. Visual Workflow, as stated earlier in this book, is a way to develop graphically. It gives a lot of control. It has a lot of the same capabilities as a programming language such as Apex. It has decision elements to provide if-then logic. It has a loop element to iterate through multiple records of information. All these things add up to a great tool to fill in any gaps in functionality by augmenting processes via a call out to a flow.

Although as we saw in the chapters covering Visual Workflow, the flows had elements that required a user to interact with screens or choices. How can a flow be called in a process when flows are run without user interaction? Salesforce allows flows to be created without elements that need user interaction so that they can be called from a process built in Lightning Process Builder. These types of flows are called autolaunched flows. They are yet another example of a type of flow that Salesforce allows to run on the platform. It may make sense at this point to dive into these different flow types and what separates them from each other. Once we do so, we can focus on the autolaunched flow types and how we will set up a process to take advantage of its special qualities.

Introducing Even More Flow Types

We've seen in previous chapters how to create a Flow in Visual Workflow. We've grown quite familiar with the way they are structured. Many elements are placed on the Canvas and connected to determine the processing path that will take place when a Flow is executed. We have also discussed that when we use

Lightning Process Builder, it is actually creating a Flow behind the scenes. These two types of flows give us some hint that not only are Flows a powerful tool for Salesforce users to utilize but they are also powerful enough for Salesforce to utilize as well.

It might not be apparent when Salesforce is using Flows behind the scenes, so let's go over some of the different types of Flows. A Flow or Flow versions type determines a lot about what it is capable of doing and what elements are supported to run within them. We can break down a Flow into two categories, standard flows and other flows. Let's walk through what those two categories mean.

Standard Flow Types

The standard flow types will be anything that you can create in Cloud Flow Designer. Those three types are Flow, Autolaunched Flow, and User Provisioning Flow. Again, you can create all these via Cloud Flow Designer. You specify the type during creation. The type determines the elements that are allowed within the flow and the way the flow can be utilized. In Table 10-1 we see a table showing the flow types and their characteristics.

Table 10-1. *Table of flow types and their characteristics*

Type	Description	Elements Not Supported
Flow	The standard flow developed in Cloud Flow Designer with required interaction by a user via screens, steps, choices, or dynamic choices. This type of flow can be implemented and launched with a custom button, custom link, URL (pointing directly to the flow), Visualforce page, or a Salesforce1 action.	Wait
Autolaunched Flow	A flow that does not require user interaction. It does not have any of the user interaction elements such as screens, steps, choices, or dynamic choices. This type of flow can be implemented and launched just like a standard flow, as well as via a Lightning Process Builder action or Apex code.	Screen Step Choice Dynamic Choice Picklist Choice
User Provisioning Flow	A flow for provisioning users for third-party services. Implemented by associating it with a connected app when running the User Provisioning wizard. This type of flow can be started from Apex.	

Other Flow Types

As mentioned before, the standard flow types are any flow that can be created in Cloud Flow Designer. It may not come as a surprise but Salesforce actually uses flows in other parts of the system. Why not take advantage of a good thing? These flows cannot be created or edited in Cloud Flow Designer. If you go to the list of flows to edit they will not show up in that list. They are excluded, although there are other places to go to see them in action. On the "Paused and Waiting Interviews" list on the flow management page you can see these types of flows. Figure 10-1 shows where this section is located.

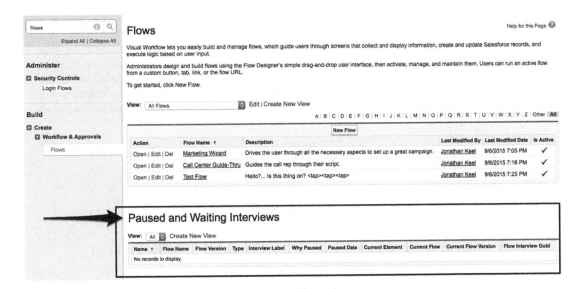

Figure 10-1. *The "Paused and Waiting Interviews" section on the flow management page*

Table 10-2 lists the one example of this type of flow. It's the flow that is created behind the scenes for processes created in Lightning Process Builder. As stated previously, Lightning Process Builder is a simpler interface than Cloud Flow Designer, but behind the scenes it still creates a flow. In this case it is not considered a standard flow type since it is not created in Cloud Flow Designer.

Table 10-2. *Table of flow types and their characteristics*

Type	Description	Elements Not Supported
Workflow	A running flow that was created in Lightning Process Builder.	

Autolaunched Flow from Lightning Process Builder

Now that we've gone over the different types of flows and what makes them so special let's get to the point of this whole chapter, calling autolaunched flows from a process. Autolaunched flows are created in Cloud Flow Designer and do not need to be created with any special properties, which means that when a flow is created it is not necessary to designate its type during creation. What makes a flow type different is the elements that are included in it and what it is used for. So, when creating a flow, as long as it is created without any user interface elements it can be used an autolaunched flow. Thus, stay away from the following elements:

- Screen
- Step
- Choice
- Dynamic Choice
- Picklist Choice

The Flows Action Type

Lightning Process Builder provides an option to add an action that is a "Flows" Action Type. As in the prior processes created, when you click the "+ Add Action" link on the Canvas the "Select and Define Action" configuration panel appears on the right side of the screen. At first there is a single field labeled "Action Type." It is a picklist field where we will select "Flows" to continue to see the configuration of calling a Flow. There are multiple fields that will appear, as shown in Figure 10-2. That list of fields includes the following:

- **Action Type**: the specific action to take—in this case "Flows"

- **Action Name**: the label to give the action; it appears on the Canvas and helps to tell one action from another

- **Flow**: a search/picklist to find and choose an Active Autolaunched flow

- **Set Flow Variables**: used to pick values as input into the selected active autolaunched flow:

  - **Flow Variable:** the input variable that is a part of the select flow that can be set from the process in Lightning Process Builder

  - **Type:** the type of variable to use as the value for the Flow Variable field including:

    - **String:** allows the Value field to be a hardcoded value

    - **Reference:** allows the Value field to be a reference to a field from the controlling Object in the Process

    - **Global Constant:** a value available from Salesforce that cannot be changed

    - **Formula:** allows the Value field to be set by a formula; choosing this option will display a formula builder to use

  - **Value:** the value used to set the Flow Variable field; this value depends on the Type selected

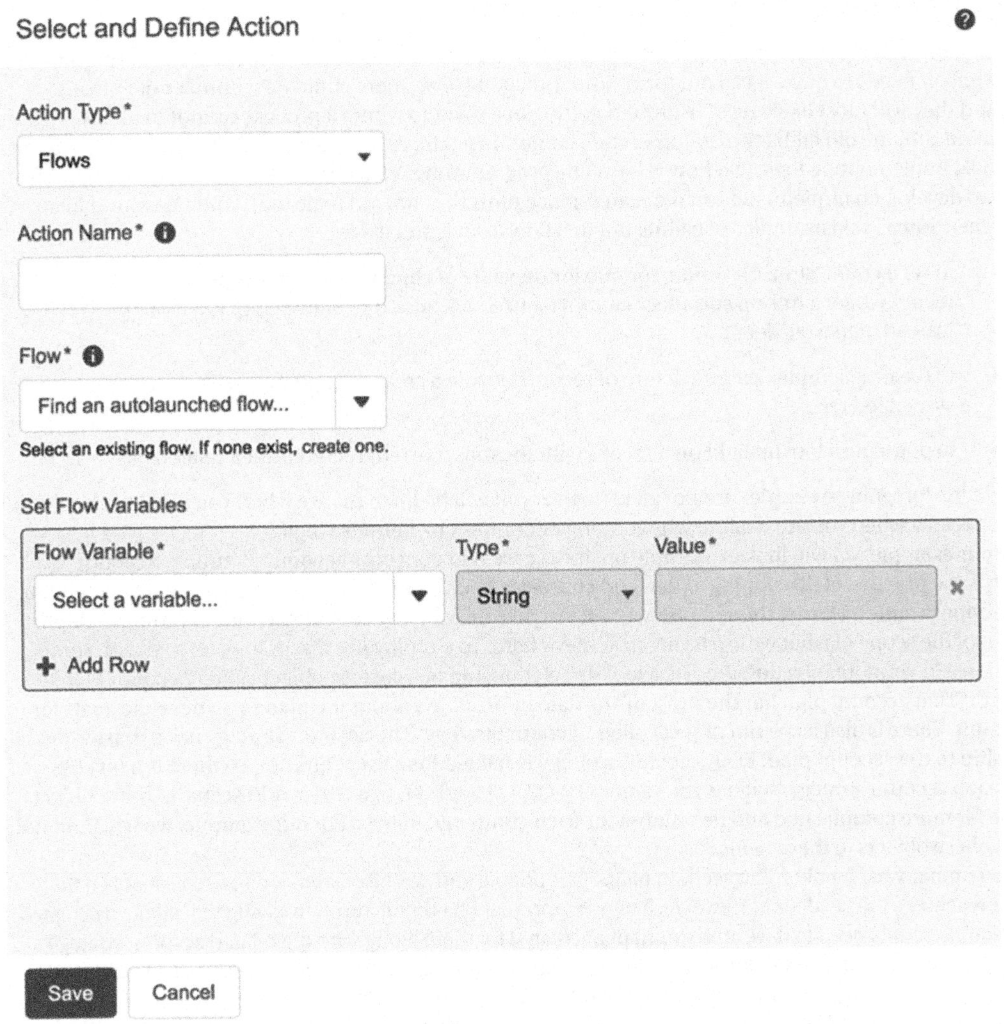

Select and Define Action

Action Type*

Flows ▼

Action Name* ⓘ

Flow* ⓘ

Find an autolaunched flow... ▼

Select an existing flow. If none exist, create one.

Set Flow Variables

Flow Variable*		Type*	Value*	
Select a variable... ▼		String ▼		✖

➕ Add Row

[Save]   [Cancel]

Figure 10-2. *The "Select and Define Action" window for the "Flows" Action Type*

There are not a lot of options when calling a Flow. Since the process will basically pass control over the Flow for additional processes until the Flow is completed, we can expect that the Flow will contain all the necessary implementation and logic. The process will merely wait for the Flow processing to be complete before it continues.

Figuring Out Requirements and Design

There are many tasks that can be completed with Lightning Process Builder, so it can be difficult to get to a point where it needs to make a call out to an Autolaunched Flow. There could be a number of reasons though and they will most likely revolve around getting to a point to where a process cannot meet the requirements and the old fallback of going to code comes up again. As we have seen in the first few chapters of this book, implementing logic in a flow is basically programming. Visual Workflow has all the constructs we need to develop an implementation that can replace most (but not all) logic that would be found in an Apex Trigger. Some good examples of calling out to a flow from a process are

- to set a count, sum, minimum, or maximum value of child records on a parent record where a roll-up summary cannot be used because the relationship is a lookup instead of master-detail

- to create a complex data structure of records during a create or update event on an associated record

- to populate a lookup field on a record with the most current record from a related list

While the foregoing examples are not all inclusive, you will begin to realize when you need to call out to a flow, especially when you are dealing with looping or complex if-then-else logic.

For our example, we will look at a simple business case that concerns account planning. Account planning is the practice of developing a plan and strategies to unlock the most potential from an account in winning opportunities. During this chapter we will not dive into the concept of Account Planning in depth as it is out of the scope of what we are trying to achieve here. To simplify the discussion, let's go with some assumptions. In your organization there is a lookup relationship of a custom object called Account Plan to an account. That account plan has the most up-to-date information about the plan to achieve the goals for that account. There is also a custom object called Account Strategy. The account strategy has a master-detail relationship to the account plan. Each account strategy is related for a fiscal quarter. So there is a picklist field on each account strategy that has the values Q1, Q2, Q3, and Q4. In a real-world scenario these objects would be far more complicated and be tailored for each company's needs. For our example, we will limit the design of these objects to these fields.

Your company has a policy that account plans are optional and can be created for an account only if the account owner sees the need for it. However, a new requirement has come through saying that all newly created "high-value" accounts need to have an account plan created for them along with the related account strategies for each quarter. Your company defines high-value accounts as any account with a revenue over $1 billion.

You decide to implement this requirement with Lightning Process Builder. You realize that when you create an Account, you can create a new account plan. However, you cannot create four new account strategies and relate them to the newly created account plan because you do not have access to the record ID of the account plan after it's created. You are left with two options. Option A is to create another process that then says when you create an account plan, in turn you should create four account strategies (one for each fiscal quarter) and relate them to the account plan. Option B is to do everything in one implementation of a flow where the flow creates the account plan and all four account strategies and links them up.

Options A and B have their pros and cons, but you hear from management that the whole account planning process is going to continue to get more and more complicated. So you decide to go with option B so any additional logic can be encapsulated into the single flow, making this more maintainable for the future.

From this we can formulate our design of how it would look for the logic of dealing with the Account object in a process and calling out to a flow and then having the flow do the work we just described. The design should look something like Figure 10-3.

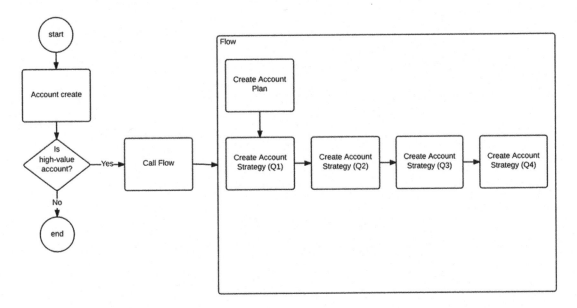

Figure 10-3. *The design for the creation of Account Plans and Account Strategies for high-value Accounts*

Building the Flow

The first thing to do is build the flow. We have spent several chapters building flows, so we will go through this process as quickly as possible. As stated in the requirements and design, the flow will create an Account Plan object. At this point we are assuming this custom object is already created with at least a lookup field named "Account" and "Account__c" for the API (application programming interface) name. Go ahead and create a new flow just as you did in other chapters. Add a Record Create element to the canvas and use the configuration settings as shown in Figure 10-4.

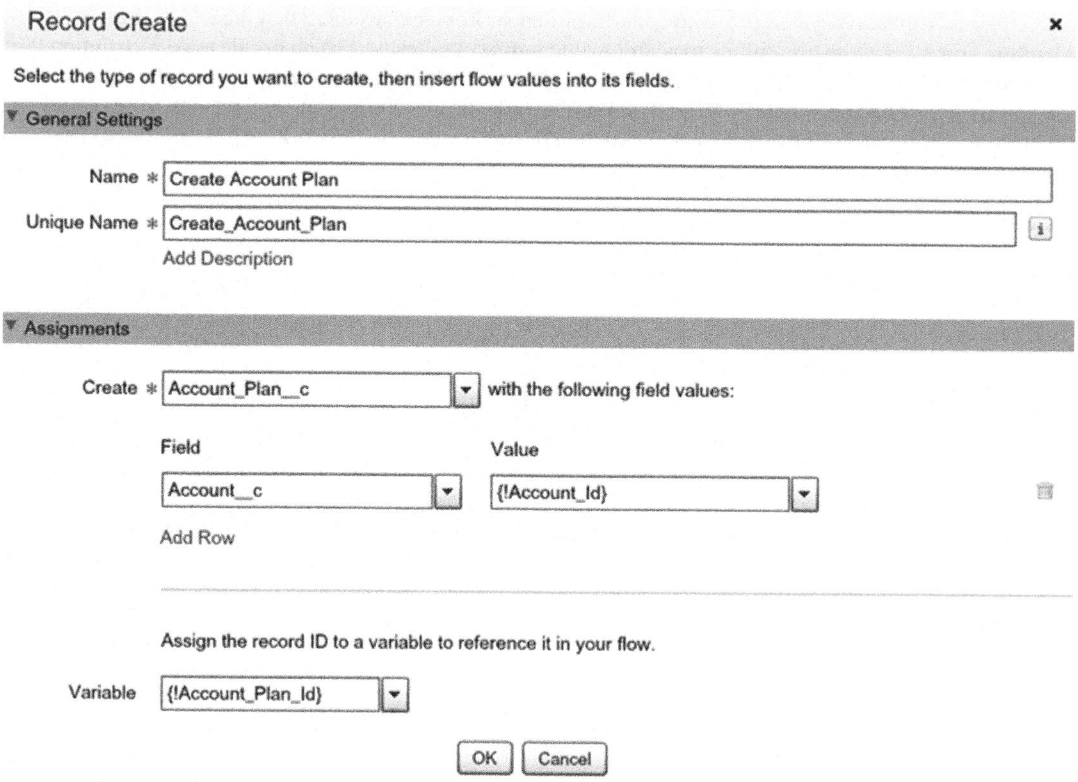

Record Create   ✕

Select the type of record you want to create, then insert flow values into its fields.

▼ General Settings

Name * [Create Account Plan]

Unique Name * [Create_Account_Plan] [i]

Add Description

▼ Assignments

Create * [Account_Plan__c] [▼] with the following field values:

Field	Value	
[Account__c] [▼]	[{!Account_Id}] [▼]	🗑

Add Row

Assign the record ID to a variable to reference it in your flow.

Variable [{!Account_Plan_Id}] [▼]

[OK] [Cancel]

Figure 10-4. *The configuration settings for the Record Create element to create a new Account Plan record*

While configuring this element, you will have to create two new variables as well. Use the following setting for these two variables:

- **Account_IdUnique Name**: Account_Id

  - **Description**: The Account Id that the newly created Account Plan will be associated to.

  - **Data Type**: Text

  - **Input/Output Type**: Input Only

  - **Default Value**: <leave blank>

- **Account_Plan_Id**

  - **Unique Name**: Account_Plan_Id

  - **Description**: The Id of the Account Plan of the newly created Account.

  - **Data Type**: Text

  - **Input/Output Type**: Private

  - **Default Value**: <leave blank>

Once you are complete with setting up the configuration window for the Create Record element, click the OK button to continue.

The next step is to create the four Account Strategy records that will be related to the newly created Account Plan record. Before continuing, make sure you have a custom object named "Account Strategy" with at least two fields. One field is a master-detail field with the name "Account Plan" and then "Account_Plan__c" for the API name. The other field will be a picklist field with the name "Fiscal Quarter" and then "Fiscal_Quarter__c" for the API name. The picklist values for it should be Q1, Q2, Q3, and Q4.

On the flow, drag another create Record Create element to the Canvas and use the following configuration settings shown in Figure 10-5 to set it up. No new variables need to be created need to finish this step.

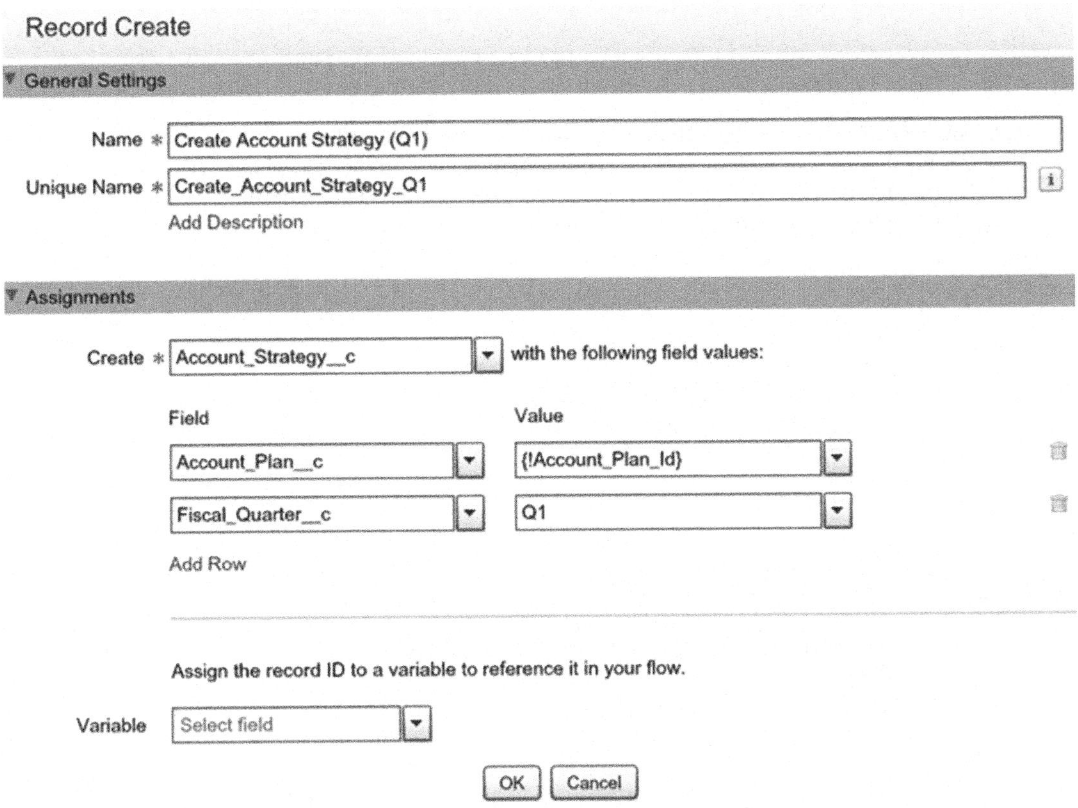

Figure 10-5. The configuration settings for the Record Create element to create a new Account Strategy record

Once complete with the configuration, go ahead and click the OK button to continue. We need to create three more records for Q2, Q3, and Q4. Go ahead and repeat the process we just went through to configure the other Record Create elements, but everywhere that you used Q1 (such as the Name, Unique Name, and Value for the Fiscal_Quarter__c field), use the last three quarters that we need to set up. Once all that is complete, connect the elements so that they look like Figure 10-6.

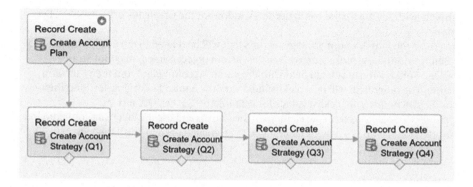

Figure 10-6. *The finished flow with all the elements connected on the Canvas*

If all looks well, let's save the flow. Upon clicking the Save button the Flow Properties window will appear to give the flow its Name, Unique Name, Description, Type, and Interview Label. Use the values as seen in Figure 10-7. Please make sure that you choose "Autolaunched Flow" for the Type. The two requirements for calling a flow from a process is that it is an Autolaunched Flow and that it is active.

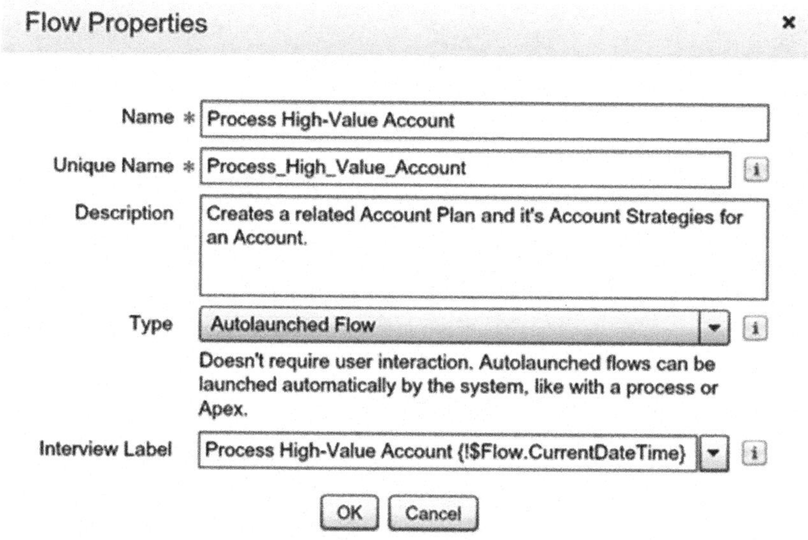

Flow Properties ✖

Name *	Process High-Value Account
Unique Name *	Process_High_Value_Account ⓘ
Description	Creates a related Account Plan and it's Account Strategies for an Account.
Type	Autolaunched Flow ▼ ⓘ
	Doesn't require user interaction. Autolaunched flows can be launched automatically by the system, like with a process or Apex.
Interview Label	Process High-Value Account {!$Flow.CurrentDateTime} ▼ ⓘ

OK   Cancel

Figure 10-7. *The Flow Properties window for the "Process High-Value Account" flow*

Click the OK button to save. After saving you should see your flow on the Flow detail page. Click the "Activate" link to activate it or else we will not be able to use in the process we create in the next step.

Calling the Flow

Wow! We just flew through all those steps. Remember back in the beginning of this book when we went through ever step in detail. Well, you are getting the hang of it now and creating flows is second nature to you. The new skill to learn here is calling this flow from a process. As per the design, go to Lightning Process Builder and create a new process. Use the settings seen in Figure 10-8 for the New Process window that appears and click the Save button.

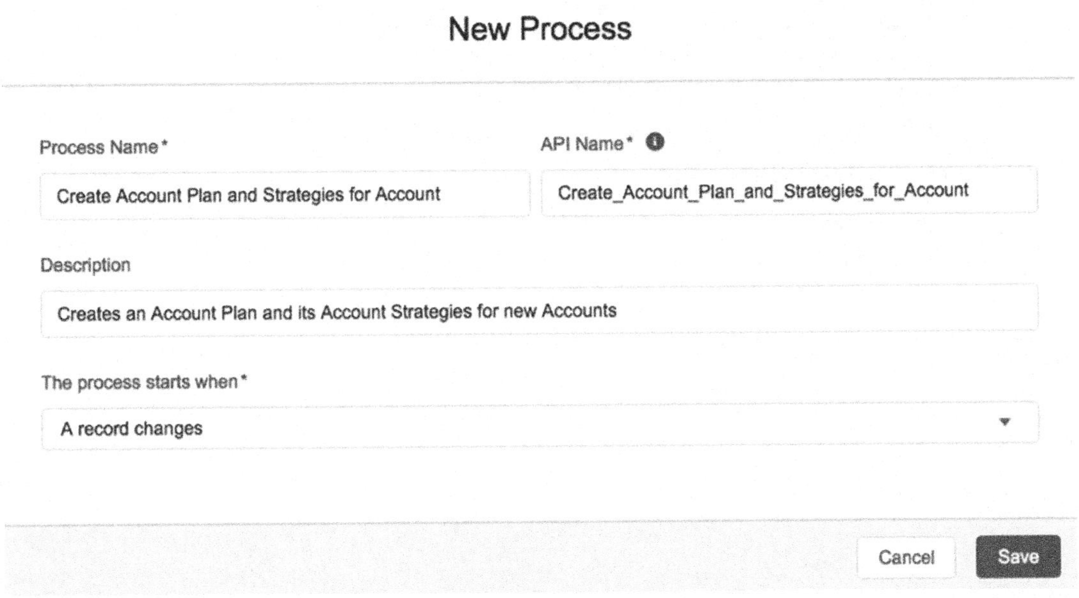

New Process

Process Name*

Create Account Plan and Strategies for Account

API Name* ⓘ

Create_Account_Plan_and_Strategies_for_Account

Description

Creates an Account Plan and its Account Strategies for new Accounts

The process starts when*

A record changes ▾

Cancel   **Save**

Figure 10-8. *Configuration settings for the New Process window*

Next we will be taken to the Canvas in Lightning Process Builder. Click "+ Add Object" and enter the following settings in the configuration panel as seen in Figure 10-9. These settings will configure the process to run only when you create an Account record but not when you edit/update the Account record. After you are complete, click the Save button to return to the Canvas.

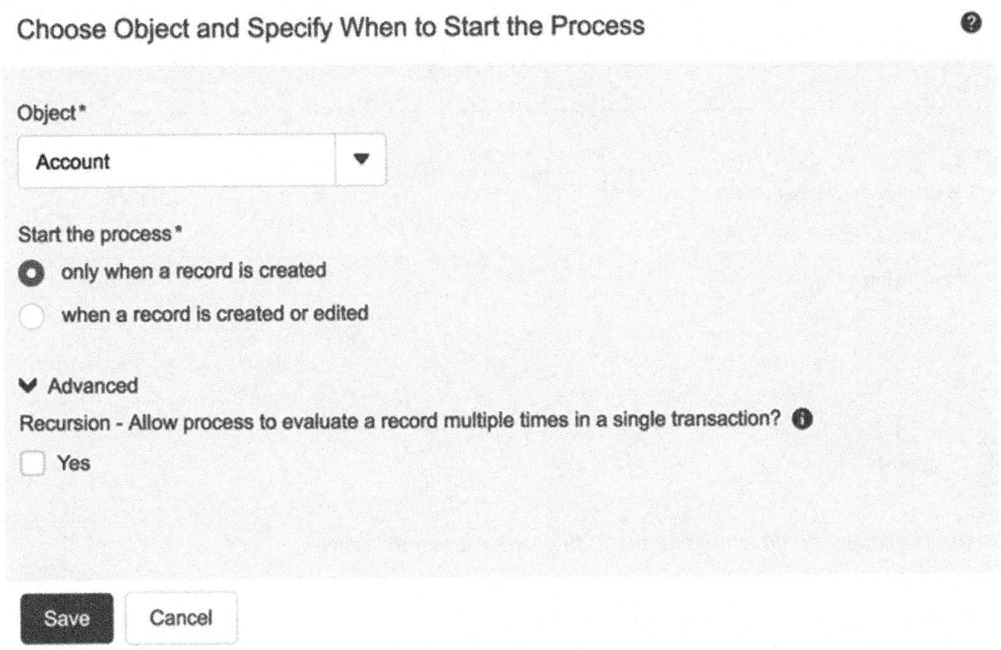

Choose Object and Specify When to Start the Process ❓

Object*

Account ▼

Start the process*

● only when a record is created

○ when a record is created or edited

❤ Advanced

Recursion - Allow process to evaluate a record multiple times in a single transaction? ⓘ

☐ Yes

Save   Cancel

Figure 10-9. *The configuration panel for setting up the object to act on*

Next click "+ Add Criteria" to see the configuration panel for defining the criteria for the actions needed to run. Use the settings as seen in Figure 10-10 to configure the criteria and click the Save button once complete. Note that the Set Condition should be the following settings:

- **Field:** [Account].AnnualRevenue
- **Operator:** Greater than or equal
- **Type:** Currency
- **Value:** 1000000000

Define Criteria for this Action Group

Criteria Name* ⓘ

Is high-value account?

Criteria for Executing Actions*

🔘 Conditions are met

⚪ Formula evaluates to true

⚪ No criteria—just execute the actions!

Set Conditions

	Field*	Operator*	Type*	Value*	
1	[Account].Ann... 🔍	Greater than or ▾	Currency ▾	1000000000	✕

+ Add Row

Conditions*

🔘 All of the conditions are met (AND)

⚪ Any of the conditions are met (OR)

⚪ Customize the logic

Save   Cancel

Figure 10-10. The configuration settings for the "Is high-value account?" criteria

Having laid down the groundwork for what we came here to do, we simply need to call a flow from a process. Yet we needed to do so much just to get to this point. So, without further hesitation, click "+ Add Action" under the immediate actions section to begin the final steps to configure this process. In doing so, you will see only the Action Type field in the configuration panel. Select "Flows" from the picklist and the panel will update to have two more fields, Action Name and Flow. Use the following values for the two fields. While doing so the panel should look like Figure 10-11.

- **Action Name:** Process High-Value Account
- **Flow:** Process_High_Value_Account

Select and Define Action

Action Type *

| Flows | ▼ |

Action Name * ❶

| Process High-Value Account |

Flow * ❶

| Find an autolaunched flow... | ▼ |

| Process_High_Value_Account |

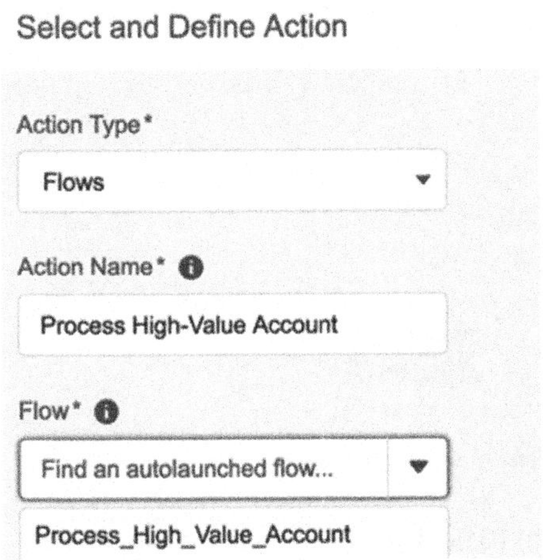

Figure 10-11. *Action Type, Action Name, and Flow picklist in the configuration panel*

The Process_High_Value_Account is the API name of the flow we created earlier. If other active autolaunched flows are in the organization they will appear in the picklist of available flows to choose as well. So make sure to choose the correct flow. After choosing the flow, the "Set Flow Variables" section will appear as seen in Figure 10-12.

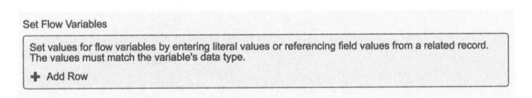

Set Flow Variables

Set values for flow variables by entering literal values or referencing field values from a related record. The values must match the variable's data type.

✚ Add Row

Figure 10-12. *The Set Flow Variables section before adding a row*

The flow we created earlier creates the account plan and related account strategy records based on an Account ID field that is passed into the flow. That is why we chose the type of the Account_Id field in the flow to be an "Input Only" type. We want to take the Account Id of the account that this process is working on and pass it to the flow. To do that click "+ Add Row" to see the three fields appear ("Flow Variable," "Type," and "Value") that we need to configure. Click the "Flow Variable" input field to bring up the "Select a Field" window. We have seen this type of window before. We want to pass the value into the flow and store it in the Account ID field that is in that flow. To do so select the Account ID field from the Account. Upon selection, this window should update to look like Figure 10-13. If it looks correct, then click the Choose button to continue.

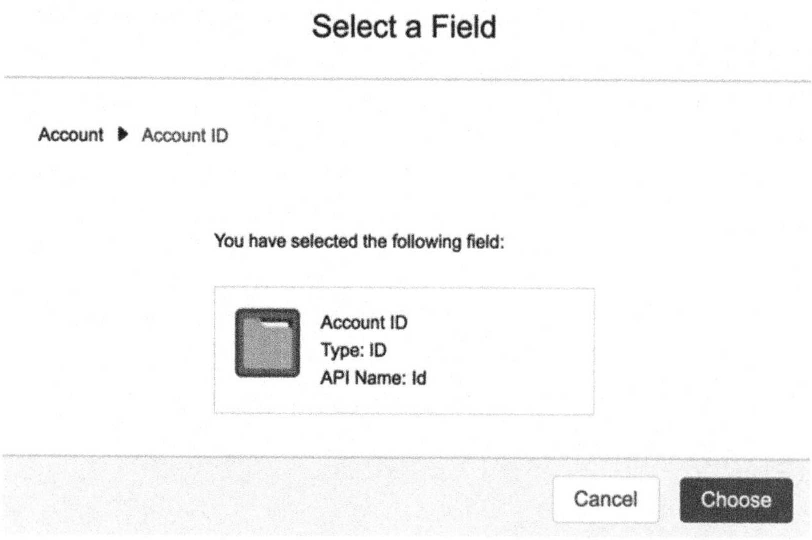

Select a Field

Account ▶ Account ID

You have selected the following field:

> Account ID
> Type: ID
> API Name: Id

Cancel   Choose

Figure 10-13. *The Select a Field window to pick the Account ID field to send to the flow*

We do not want to hard-code the value to send to the Account ID field in the flow. Instead, we want to send the value that comes from the Account that this process is acting on. To do this, choose the "Reference" option from the Type picklist. In the Value field you should now be allowed to traverse through the fields on the Account object and choose "Account ID" from the picklist. Once complete, the configuration panel will look like Figure 10-14.

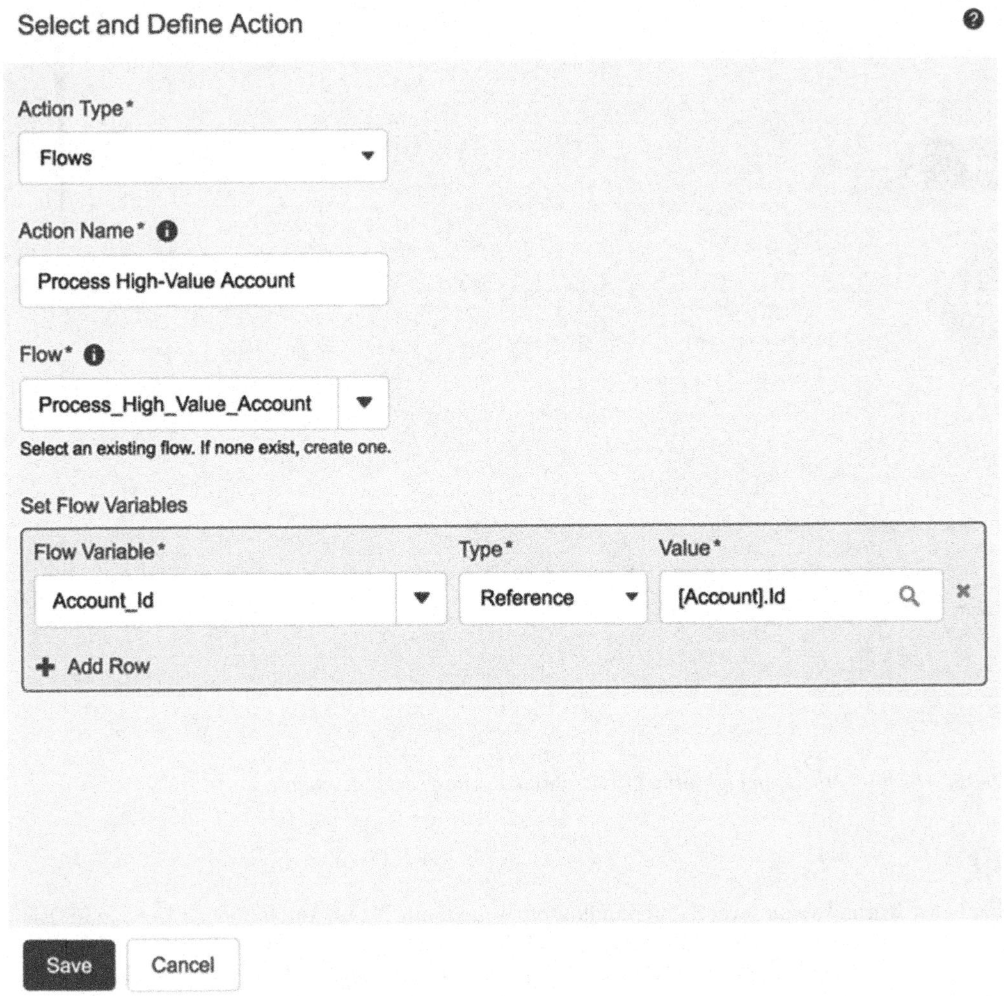

Select and Define Action

Action Type*

Flows ▼

Action Name* ⓘ

Process High-Value Account

Flow* ⓘ

Process_High_Value_Account ▼

Select an existing flow. If none exist, create one.

Set Flow Variables

Flow Variable*		Type*		Value*		
Account_Id	▼	Reference	▼	[Account].Id	🔍	✖

➕ Add Row

[Save] Cancel

Figure 10-14. *The configuration panel for setting up the Flows action*

Click the Save button to continue and be returned to the Canvas in Lightning Process Builder. The process should look like Figure 10-15. Notice that there is a special Flow icon next to the newly added action. The final thing to do is to activate this process. To do so, click the Activate button.

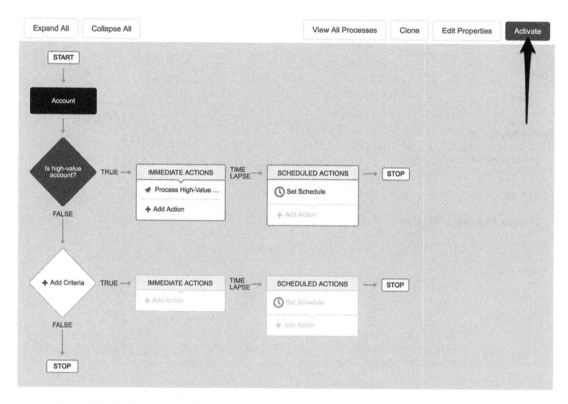

Figure 10-15. *The final process in Lightning Process Builder before clicking Activate*

Recap

In this chapter we learned about several different flow types including Flows, Autolaunched Flows, and User Provisioning Flows. They are all standard flows that can be developed in Cloud Flow Designer. There are other flow types, specifically the Workflow flow, which is what a process runs as that was created in Lightning Process Builder. We learned that the only flow type that can be called from a process is an autolaunched flow and it needs to be active as well. Autolaunched flows are any flows that do not contain user interface elements such as Screen, Step, Choice, Dynamic Choice, and Picklist Choice. Finally, we put everything we learned into practice by building a process that makes a call out to a flow in order to provide some complex functionality that a flow could handle quite easily.

CHAPTER 11

■ ■ ■

Notifications with Lightning Process Builder

As stated before, Lightning Process Builder gives administrators the power to do so much that previously had to be implemented with Apex Triggers. In the past, if there were a requirement to create a new record (other than a task), perform a cross-object field update via a lookup field, or autosubmit an approval process then a developer would need to create an Apex Trigger. In the last few chapters we've covered how Lightning Process Builder can be used to meet these needs with clicks, not code. We have also seen how Flows can be used, as long as they are Autolaunched Flows and not the standard Flows created by Visual Workflow with user interface elements associated with screens. However, the nice thing about Flows with user interface elements is that the user is interacting with the system and is aware of what is happening.

How do users know about the actions that are going on behind the scenes in a process created in Lightning Process Builder? Much of the time there may not be a requirement to let them know all the gory details of the internals of a process, although sometimes there are requirements to notify users of certain actions taken. What if we had a need to create a new record and then notify the user that the new record was created and he or she is the owner? What if we need to notify a group of users and not necessarily just one? Maybe there could be an instance in which they are not even notified when the process completes. There could be a requirement to postpone the notification to a later date, such as a couple of days or weeks in the future. Can that be handled with Lightning Process Builder? The answer is yes.

Types of Notifications

Salesforce has many ways of notifying people when something occurs. There are on-screen notifications, E-mail Alerts, Chatter Posts, in-app notifications in Salesforce1, and so on. Notifications are useful because they let users know when something happens or will happen. They function to give reassurance that the system is working as intended or maybe not working as intended. Notifications are also useful when something goes wrong and someone needs to be alerted.

Lightning Process Builder can be used to send out notifications. Specifically, it can be set up to send two types of notifications: E-mail Alerts and Chatter Posts. Additionally, these two types of notifications can also be sent out either as immediate actions or as scheduled actions in a process. A notification sent out as an immediate action is perfect for letting someone know of what the process just finished performing. With a scheduled action the notification can be sent out at a later time (e.g., sending out a notification 30 days before a contract's end date).

© Jonathan Keel 2016
J. Keel, *Salesforce.com Lightning Process Builder and Visual Workflow*, DOI 10.1007/978-1-4842-1691-0_11

E-mail Alerts

E-mail Alerts are useful because they deliver an e-mail to someone's inbox that can be read anywhere that e-mail is accessible. These days, with mobile phones in such great use, e-mail has become one of the most widely used forms of keeping in contact with an individual. Due to this fact, E-mail Alerts will most likely be the most used form of notifications from a process unless your organization is heavily invested in Chatter and would prefer that form of notification. E-mail provides a lot of traceability and is an important part of Salesforce.

In fact, the actual E-mail Alerts are not configured in Lightning Process Builder. Instead, it uses the existing functionality of Salesforce E-mail Alerts and E-mail Templates. Essentially it's very similar to the way standard Salesforce Workflow rules work. First you create an E-mail template, then an E-mail Alert uses the E-mail Template, and finally a process calls the E-mail Alert. If you are comfortable with using E-mail Alerts in standard Salesforce Workflow rules and actions then you will be right at home using them in Lightning Process Builder.

It's also worth noting that processes share the E-mail Alert limits with workflow rules, flows, approval processes (but not approval notification emails), and the REST API. The daily limit is 1,000 per standard Salesforce license per organization. The daily limit means a 24-hour period that starts at and ends at midnight Greenwich Mean Time (GMT), the time zone that Salesforce stores dates and times internally. The overall organization limit is 2 million and if you send an E-mail Alert to a group, every person in that group counts against the daily limit. If the organization is a free Developer Edition or trial organization, then the daily workflow E-mail Alert limit is 15 per standard Salesforce license. Table 11-1 shows the E-mail Alert limits at a glance for the different Salesforce editions.

Table 11-1. *Workflow e-mail limits*

	Personal Edition	Contact Manager	Group Edition	Professional Edition	Enterprise Edition	Developer Edition	Unlimited and Performance Edition
Workflow E-mails Per Day	N/A	N/A	N/A	N/A	1,000 per standard Salesforce license 2million per organization	15 per standard Salesforce license 2 million per organization	1,000 per standard Salesforce license 2 million per organization

Chatter Posts

Sending a notification from a process as a Chatter Post is an interesting concept. Salesforce has been pushing for the adoption of Chatter since its inception. While not every organization makes use of Chatter, it is getting harder to ignore its impact on the way business is conducted. More than ever people are using social media to communicate and stay informed. With the adoption of social media everyday people are used to seeing features such as feeds, likes, and @mentions. Chatter has brought those concepts to the workplace and found unexpected ways to use them to increase efficiency, awareness, and communication.

Within Lightning Process Builder you can configure a Chatter Post to be made when a process runs. Just like an E-mail Alert the Chatter Post can notify a user or a group of users. Unlike an E-mail Alert, though, a Chatter Post can be made to a specific record in Salesforce. Objects in Salesforce can have feed tracking turned on so that each record for that object can have its own Chatter feed that users can follow. With the ability to Post to Chatter from a process, any object with feed tracking turned on can have a post made to its feed. Then anyone who follows that feed can be updated to any activity that shows in the records Chatter feed.

Just like E-mail Alerts, Chatter has limits as well. While there are a lot of limits regarding Chatter in general, Table 11-2 shows limits that relate to posting to Chatter.

Table 11-2. *List of Chatter limits*

Feature	Limit
Characters in single post	10,000
Mentions in a single post	25
Topics on a single post	10
Topics on a single record	100
Characters in a topic name	99

Notification Deep Dive

With so much that Lightning Process Builder can implement, it is important to have a way to keep individuals aware of any important actions taken. In the event that a status change was made to an Account, a Case, or any other type of standard or custom object then people will want to be notified. It's important when gathering requirements for a project to figure out if any notifications need to be sent out from a process. It's not always the case that notifications are necessary, but it is a question that should be asked. If it is decided that notifications are needed, then the next two questions are what type of notification and when are they sent out?

We have covered the two types of notifications in Lightning Process Builder: E-mail Alerts and Chatter Posts. While we have covered them at a high level to understand why they are useful and when one type of alert would be used vs. another, we have not stepped through the details of how they can be configured in Lightning Process Builder. Let's dive into those details now.

E-mail Alerts Configuration Details

Adding an E-mail Alert to a process is the same as adding any other type of action. The Canvas has an option to add an action to the Immediate Actions group or the Scheduled Actions group. While a lot of actions tend to be most useful as immediate actions, E-mail Alerts do well as both types. When adding an action, the "Select and Define Action" configuration panel appears. In it you need to choose the "E-mail Alerts" Action Type. When you choose that action type, the configuration panel should look like Figure 11-1. It will consist of the following two extra fields besides the Action Type field:

- **Action Name:** A user-friendly name that will show on the canvas to distinguish this action from others.

- **Email Alert:** This search field can be used to look up an existing E-mail Alert already defined in Salesforce. If a new E-mail Alert needs to be created then below this field is a link to create one. To create it, click the blue "create one" link.

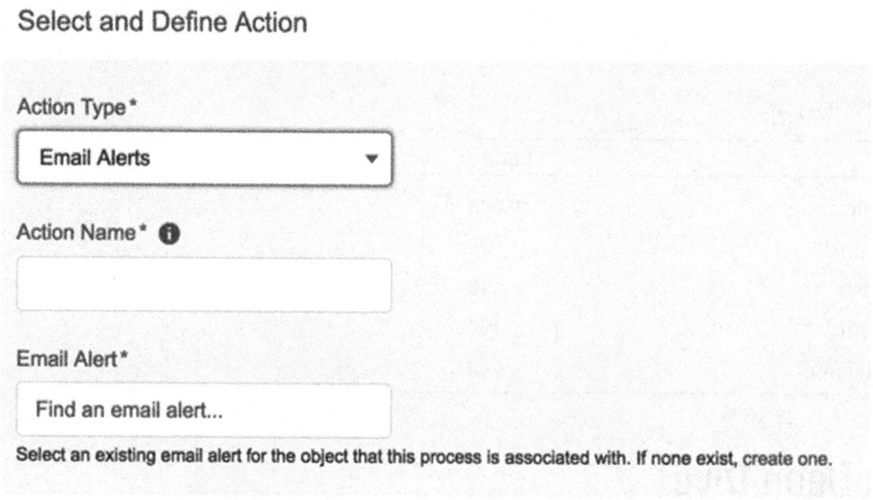

Select and Define Action

Action Type*

Email Alerts ▼

Action Name* ⓘ

Email Alert*

Find an email alert...

Select an existing email alert for the object that this process is associated with. If none exist, create one.

Figure 11-1. *The initial "Select and Define Action" screen for the E-mail Alerts Action Type*

The E-mail Alerts action type actually does not have a lot of options in it. This is because it depends on the existing E-mail Alerts and E-mail Templates that Salesforce administrators have been accustomed to for years.

While there is a link named "create one" that can be used to create a new E-mail Alert, it is recommended to do all this beforehand to make the configuration process more efficient. Instead of stepping out of Lightning Process Builder while in the midst of creating a process, be sure to create an E-mail Alert and its E-mail Template (if a new E-mail Template is needed) to have it ready before including it in the process. Once you create an E-mail Alert and E-mail Template beforehand, adding an E-mail Alerts action to a process takes a matter of seconds to complete. Once you select an E-mail Alert, it appears in the E-mail Alert text field with just the name as seen in Figure 11-2. Also, if the exact name is known, you can copy and paste it in this field without having to do the lookup and clicking its name. Once the Action Name and E-mail Alert are entered, you can click the Save button and then the configuration is complete.

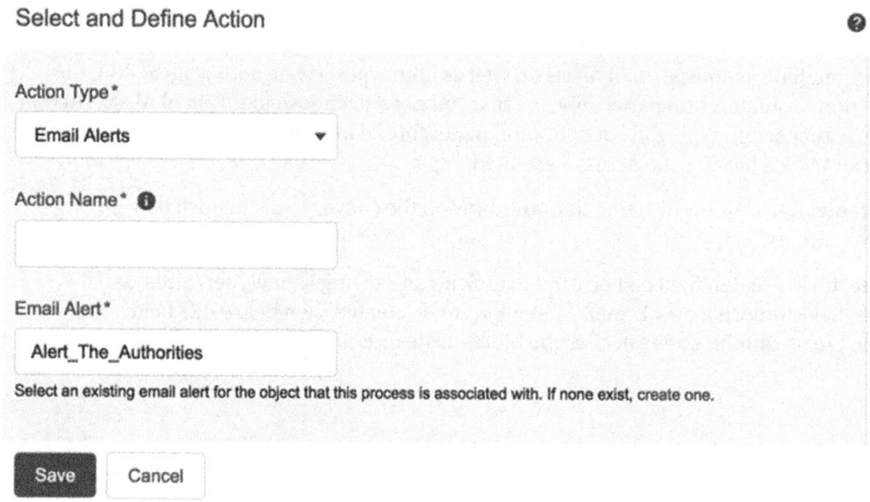

Select and Define Action   ❷

Action Type*

Email Alerts ▼

Action Name* ⓘ

Email Alert*

Alert_The_Authorities

Select an existing email alert for the object that this process is associated with. If none exist, create one.

Save   Cancel

Figure 11-2. *An example of a selected E-mail Alert*

The details that go into creating the Salesforce E-mail Alert and the E-mail Template are not covered here as it they are beyond the scope of this book. However, later we will see an example of setting this up. Otherwise, there are plenty of great resources that cover this topic (see *Practical Salesforce.com Development Without Code* by Philip Weinmeister [Apress, 2015], mentioned in Chapter 9).

Post to Chatter Configuration Details

Implementing a Post to Chatter action takes a little bit more work. The E-mail Alerts Action Type takes advantage of the pre-existing E-mail Alert and E-mail Template feature in Salesforce. Implementing a notification via e-mail can make use of this feature and shortens the amount of configuration needed. With a Post to Chatter Action Type, there is not a pre-existing Chatter Alert or Chatter Template idea like e-mail notifications have. This actually gives a lot of flexibility in Lightning Process Builder when a Chatter notification is required. Let's walk through the configuration option to see what is available to set up. In Figure 11-3 we see that similar to the E-mail Alerts Action Type, once you have selected the Post to Chatter Action Type two additional fields appear. Those two fields are

- **Action Name**: A user-friendly name that will show on the Canvas to distinguish this action from others.

- **Post to**: The field that is used to configure where the Chatter message is posted. There are three options which include

    - **User**: Post to a single user, which can be directly entered here by name. While typing the name, it performs a search and shows possible matches via a picklist. The user can also be selected via a reference from the object being acted upon in the process. These two options are in a picklist as:

        - Search for a user

        - Select a user from a record

    - **Chatter Group**: Post to a Chatter group that can be entered directly by name. While typing the name, it performs a search and shows possible matches via a picklist.

    - **This Record**: This option simply posts to the feed of the object being acted upon in the process. This option will only appear if Feed Tracking is enabled for the object. To enable Feed Tracking go to Setup ➤ Build ➤ Customize ➤ Chatter ➤ Feed Tracking. Then select the object and check the "Enable Feed Tracking" option.

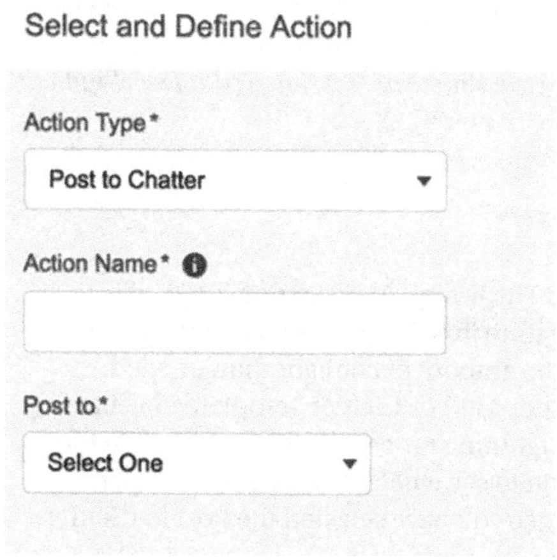

Select and Define Action

Action Type*

Post to Chatter ▼

Action Name* ⓘ

Post to*

Select One ▼

Figure 11-3. *The initial "Select and Define Action" screen for the Post to Chatter Action Type*

Depending on where the message needs to be posted, you will have a different set of fields to configure. If you need to post a Chatter message to a User, then selecting "User" from the Post to field will display the User field as seen in Figure 11-4. The User field has the two options discussed previously, "Search for a user" and "Select a user from a record." These two options allow the post to go directly to one person. By selecting "Search for a user" a third field will appear in which you are able to type in the name of the user directly in the field. While typing a drop-down menu will appear to help autocomplete the selection if it can find the user's name that is being typed in. Then the name can be selected from the drop-down menu. If "Select a user from a record" is selected then a third field also appears, but instead of typing a name you just click the field in order to get the familiar window that allows you to search across the object or related objects for a Lookup field for a User record.

Post to*   User*

User ▼   ✓ Select One
              Search for a user
              Select a user from a record

Figure 11-4. *The additional field to configure a post to a User*

The next option is Chatter Group. A lot of times the requirements dictate to let several people know about a notification via Chatter. Instead of several single posts to different users it is for more useful and efficient to post a message to a Chatter group. This way, many people can be aware. When you select "Chatter Group" for the "Post to" field, the "Group" field will appear as seen in Figure 11-5. This Group field works the same way as when searching for a user record. Just start typing the name of the group in the field and a drop-down menu will appear showing the matching results. When the group you are looking for appears, click its name to select it. That's all it takes to select many individuals to send a message to.

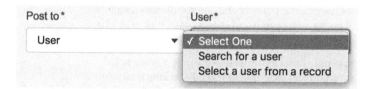

Post to*   Group*

Chatter Group ▼   Find a group...

Figure 11-5. *The additional field to configure a post to a Group*

Figure 11-6 shows the final option, "This Record." It is also the simplest to configure in Lightning Process Builder. While the other two options allow the message to be posted to a user or a group of users, this option posts the message to the record directly. This is useful when you are not sure who is an interested party. As long as you select the "Enable Feed Tracking" option for the object, you can see a feed on the record's detail page.

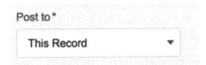

Figure 11-6. *The post to "This Record" option has no additonal fields to configure*

Finally, the last section to configure is the actual message to be posted to Chatter. This is where you can be most creative. As seen in Figure 11-7, there is are two search fields at the top to help add merge fields and existing topics to the message box located at the bottom. The Merge Field search opens up a window to traverse the fields on the object being acted upon in the process. It can also be used to traverse fields of related objects as well. The "Add an existing topic . . ." field is a search field as well, but instead of opening a window it allows text input. Typing in a topic name will cause an autocomplete drop-down list to appear when the first two characters are typed in. Then you can select a value from the list to add topics to the message.

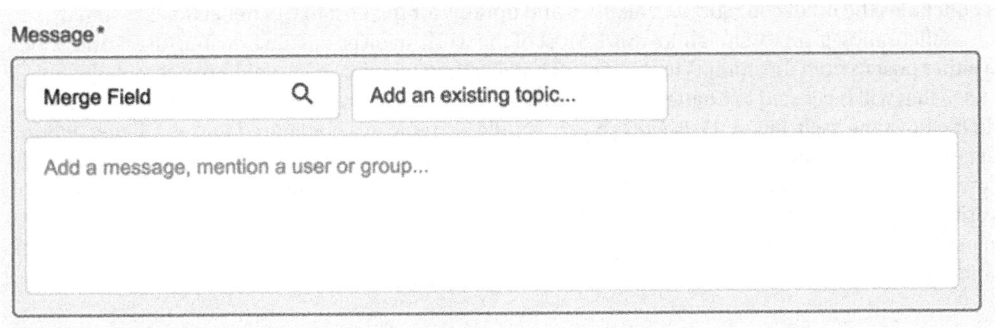

Message*

| Merge Field 🔍 | Add an existing topic... |

Add a message, mention a user or group...

Figure 11-7. *The fields used to configure the message to Post to Chatter*

Let's go into a little more detail of what you can do with the message. For example, while you can certainly search for a merge field and select it to be added to the message, you can also type it in manually. When adding a merge field it will look something like "{! [Case].OwnerId}" if the OwnerId field of the case was inserted into the message. As you see, it uses the same convention for Salesforce merge fields (the curly braces with an exclamation mark preceding the field's API name). What is a little different, though, is that the object is also specified here. The object's API name is included in square brackets before the field's API name with a period separating the two. While the merge fields can be typed in this way, it is always safer to use the built-in merge field search tool to ensure that there are no misspellings.

Next up are topics! In Salesforce a Topic is a word or phrase that can be associated with Salesforce records to organize them around common themes. In Chatter, a topic can be added by merely including the "#" sign before the topic name. If a topic was never used before, Chatter will automatically add it to the list of topics. It's a very dynamic way of creating them, but as stated in the topic search widget you need to have an existing topic to search for so you can't create a new topic via the search widget. However, that does not stop you from including a new topic in the message. To do so use the convention that the search widget uses.

This convention is to surround the topic name in the message with square brackets and precede the whole thing with the "#" sign. An example topic of "Winning" would be "#[Winning]" to correctly include it in the message. Spaces are also allowed in topic names since they are within the square brackets.

Finally, we have @mentions. Those are the way to mention users so the Chatter message shows up on their feed and they are notified that they are mentioned. The mentioned user will have the mention show up on his or her feed in Chatter. If enabled, the user will also receive an e-mail notification that he or she was mentioned. These @mentions work a little different from the merge fields and the topics in that there is not a search field to use like the other two. Instead, after typing in the "@" sign in the message box a pop-up menu will appear below it that states the following: "Notify a person or group about this update." This is letting us know that the @mention search feature is now activated. As you begin typing even after the first character is typed in the pop-up menu will refresh to show potential matches for users or groups. After selecting a name from the pop-up menu some text will be inserted into the message that will include the user or group that was selected. The text is similar to that of the topic format. It has the name of the user or group surrounded by square brackets, but instead of being preceded by a "#" sign, it is preceded by an "@" sign. This is the reason these are called @mentions. Just like merge fields and topics they can be manually typed in as well if you don't have time waiting for autocomplete menus to appear. An example @mention for a user named "Abigail Marie" would be "@[Abigail Marie]."

■ **Note**   If you would like to do an @mention dynamically off a merge field, just surround the merge field text with the "@" sign and square brackets like so, "@[{![Case].Owner ID}]".

That concludes the list of configuration features and options for the Post to Chatter action. As stated earlier, the configuration is pretty straightforward. Most of the work involves utilizing existing users and groups to either post to from the options in the "Select and Define Action" configuration panel or in the message itself that will be posted to Chatter. Since Chatter messages are text-based and so dynamic, a lot can be done in the message itself. Figure 11-8 shows a very simple example of a configured Post to Chatter action. Again, get creative with the message part of the configuration. In this example, a message is simply posted to the Case's feed stating that an automated process closed the case. Much more information could be added to the message. A great example might be to include some important values from the Case at the time of closing to use as a type of snapshot of what state the Case was in at the time. Now that we have covered all the configuration options at length, let's dive into a real-world example of using notifications in a process.

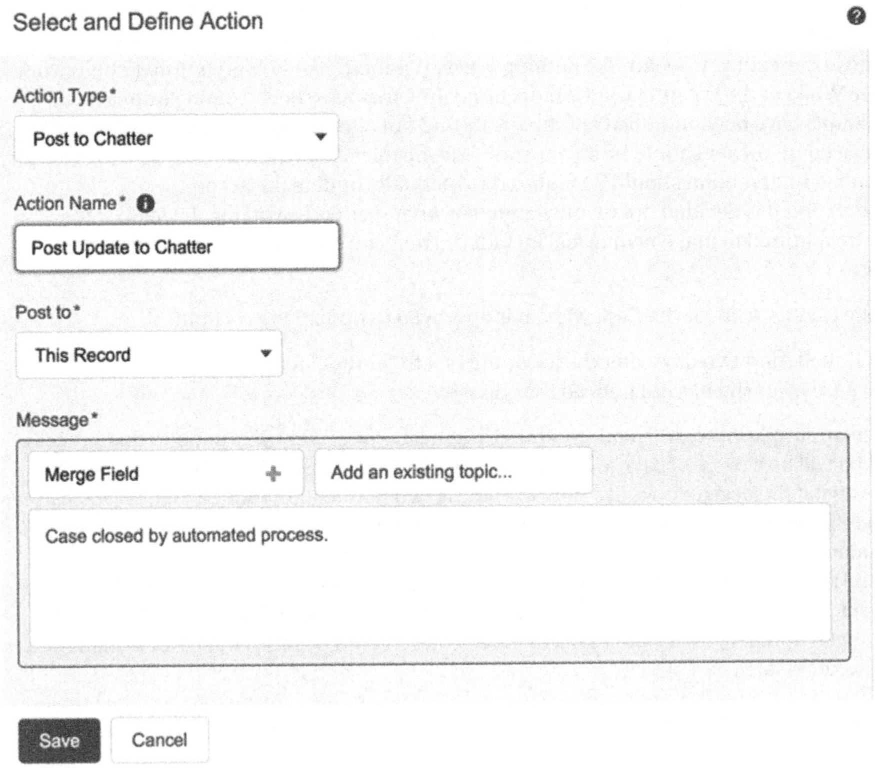

Select and Define Action

Action Type*

Post to Chatter ▼

Action Name* ⓘ

Post Update to Chatter

Post to*

This Record ▼

Message*

| Merge Field | ＋ | Add an existing topic... |

Case closed by automated process.

Save   Cancel

Figure 11-8. *An example Post to Chatter configuration*

Add Notifications to an Existing Process

Many processes could benefit from notifications being sent out. Sometimes it is appropriate for the notifications to be sent out immediately when the process runs and sometimes it is appropriate for the notifications to be scheduled to be sent out later. Lightning Process Builder can be used to fulfill both of these requirements. In Chapter 8, we created a process to set the status of an account to "At Risk" but to be driven by a Case record. This was an interesting scenario, but Lightning Process Builder proved itself to be a great tool to get the job done. In our implementation though there is a slight problem. That problem is that accounts were being modified and no notification was being sent out.

Let's return to the scene of our office. We are sitting there working away on Salesforce administrative work. A report here, a dashboard there, a little dash of data scrubbing is all in a day's work. Suddenly, you are pulled into another ad hoc meeting. It seems like nothing is ever planned. If only everyone else could work as calculatedly as you! While in the meeting you hear of complaints that have been coming from account owners that their accounts have been modified and they only find out after the fact. Many solutions are proposed. Maybe the account owner should be an approver. Maybe the account should not be automatically updated at all and human intervention should be required to manually update the account.

After much deliberation it is decided not to touch much of what is already working. Instead, some simple notifications are required to make people feel included. There are only two requirements that are agreed upon. They are

- Post to the Chatter feed for the Case when it is approved to update the account

- Send an E-mail Alert two days after the account is set to "At Risk" to the account owner in case he or she has not noticed the change.

These changes seem simple enough. Thank goodness, because a lot of work was put into that process. Adding these two alerts will be a piece of cake for you, especially since the design really has not been impacted. Let's review what the design looks like now with these two notifications added to it. As you can see in Figure 11-9 the highlighted elements are the only two elements added to the previous design. So now, as before, if a Case is updated as Account At Risk then the Case will be submitted for approval. Once the Case record is approved, the related Account will be set to the At Risk status. The Account At Risk Reason on the Account will also be set. That was the process built out in earlier chapters, which this design shows. Now, after the account has been updated, the Chatter Post to the Account record occurs. Finally, an E-mail Alert is scheduled to go out two days later.

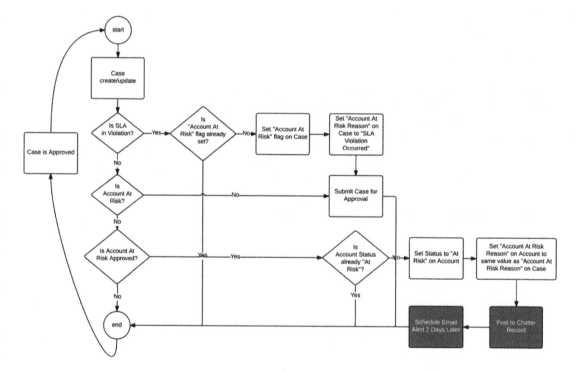

Figure 11-9. *Updated design diagram with the two newly added notifications highlighted*

In Lightning Process Builder, making updates to a process is easy because we just need to clone the already existing process version and make the updates. Then the new process version will not go into effect until it is activated. Activating a process version deactivates all other process versions since only one process version can be active at a time.

Adding the Post to Chatter

Let's begin implementing the solution by opening the processed titled "Set Account At Risk from Case" and then clicking the Clone button to make a copy. This will open up the "Clone this Process" window as seen in Figure 11-10. From here we want a new version of the current process and not a new process. So select the appropriate radio button at the top. Everything else can stay the same. We are only making a minor modification to the process to send these two notifications. We are not altering any of the business logic within the process or changing how it handles records. Go ahead and click the Save button to continue.

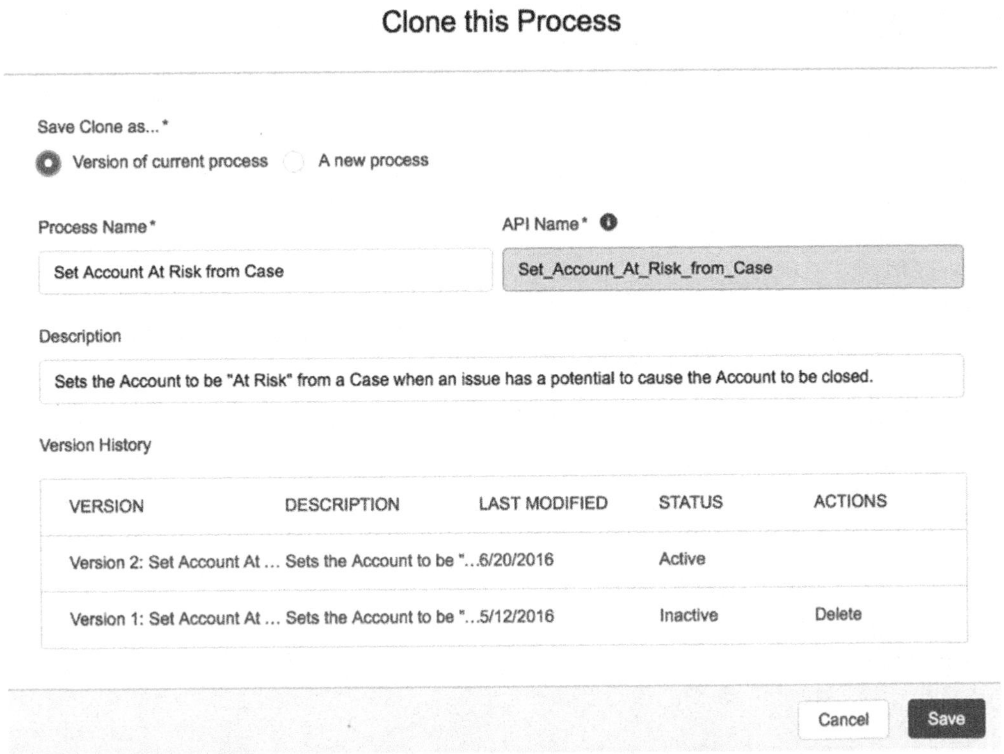

Clone this Process

Save Clone as...*

⦿ Version of current process   ○ A new process

Process Name*

Set Account At Risk from Case

API Name* ❶

Set_Account_At_Risk_from_Case

Description

Sets the Account to be "At Risk" from a Case when an issue has a potential to cause the Account to be closed.

Version History

VERSION	DESCRIPTION	LAST MODIFIED	STATUS	ACTIONS
Version 2: Set Account At ...	Sets the Account to be "...	6/20/2016	Active	
Version 1: Set Account At ...	Sets the Account to be "...	5/12/2016	Inactive	Delete

Cancel   Save

Figure 11-10. The "Clone this Process" screen to make a copy of the process version to edit

The first notification we are going to add is the Post to Chatter action. According to our requirements, this post should come right after the approval "Account At Risk" flag on the Case. After a successful approval, there is another flag named "Account At Risk Approved" that gets set to true. Looking at the process in the Canvas the last criterion, named "Is Account At Risk Approved?," is the area of interest. This is where the check is done to see if the "Account At Risk Approved" flag is set to true. Currently only the "Update Account as 'Account At Risk'" action is in the immediate actions group. This action does the actual work of updating the account status to "At Risk," as mentioned in Chapter 8. Since we want the Chatter notification to come immediately after the approval we will add the new Post to Chatter action here.

Also, we want the post to be made to the owner of the account that was moved to an "At Risk" status. So we will need to configure the Post to Chatter action accordingly. Click the + Add Action button to open up the "Select and Define Action" configuration panel and enter the following configuration values:

- **Action Type**: Post to Chatter
- **Action Name**: Chatter Account Approved At Risk
- **Post to**: User
- **User**: Select a user from a record
- **Find a user**: [Case].Account.Owner.Id
- (this is found by traversing Case ➤ Account ID ➤ Owner ID ➤ User ID)
- **Message**: Case Number {![Case].CaseNumber} has been approved to set Account {![Case].Account.Name} to At Risk #AccountAtRisk

After entering in all the values, the "Select and Define Action" configuration panel should look like Figure 11-11. Click the Save button to continue.

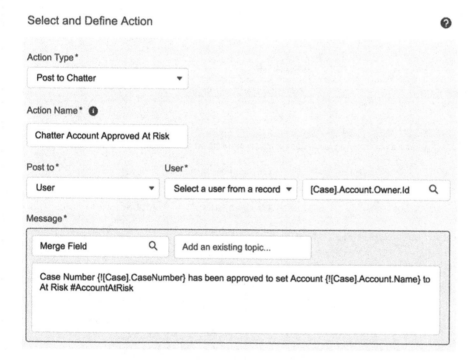

Figure 11-11. *The configured Post to Chatter action when a Case is approved to set the Account to "At Risk"*

The message entered for the post will show up on the account owner's Chatter feed. It will include the case number, the account name, and the AccountAtRisk topic similar to Figure 11-12.

Jacob Obst to Patricia Gail:

Case Number 00001034 has been approved to set Account North Alamo Farm
Supply to At Risk #AccountAtRisk

Topics: AccountAtRisk

Figure 11-12. An example of what the Chatter Post may look like on a user's feed

Adding an E-mail Alert

The next requirement is to set up an e-mail reminder that goes out two days later to remind the account
owner to take action in order to move the account out of "At Risk" status. While this could also be Post to
Chatter action technically, for this example we are using an E-mail Alert to show how one is properly set up.
Also, in case the account owner did not pay attention to the Chatter Post, sending an e-mail is another way
to reach the account owner in case he or she has Chatter settings configured to not get timely e-mail updates
about Chatter Posts.

To get all of this to work done we need to perform two steps beforehand.

- Create a new E-mail Template to be used by the E-mail Alert.

- Create a new E-mail Alert to be called the process.

Create a new E-mail Template by going to Setup ➤ Administer ➤ Communication Templates ➤ Email
Templates. Then click the New button to start setting up a new E-mail Template. In the first screen select
"Text" to create a text-based E-mail Template and click the Next button. The final screen has all the inputs for
creating the E-mail Template. Use the following configuration settings to set it up and click Save afterward:

- **Folder:** Unfiled Public Email Templates

- **Available For Use**: <checked>

- **Email Template Name**: At Risk Email Reminder Template

- **Template Unique Name**: At_Risk_Email_Reminder_Template

- **Encoding**: General US & Western Europe (ISO-8858-1, ISO-LATIN-1)

- **Description:** Email template for the reminder e-mail when an Account has been put
  into "At Risk" status.

- **Subject**: Account At Risk 2-Day Reminder

- **E-mail Body**: The account {!Account.Name} was set to a status of "At Risk" 2 days
  ago. If you have not already checked, please follow up to resolve and move the
  account into another status.

Once you have saved the E-mail Template, it should look like Figure 11-13.

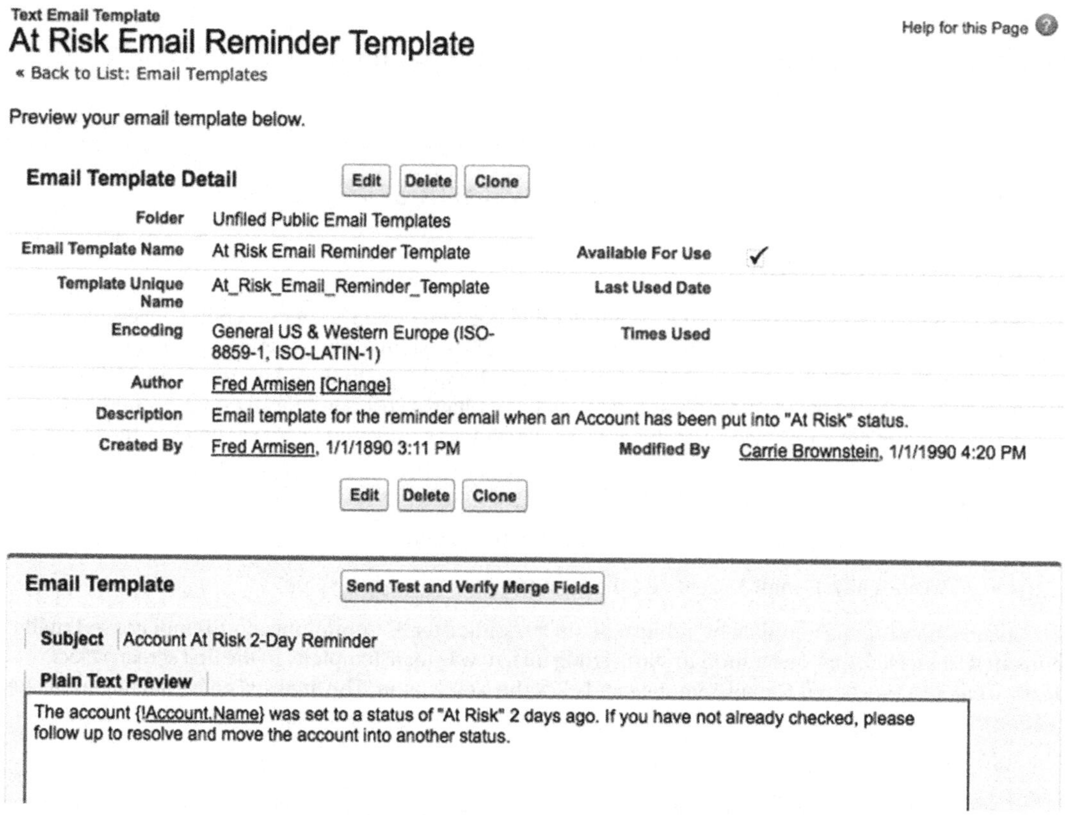

Text Email Template
At Risk Email Reminder Template

« Back to List: Email Templates

Help for this Page ❓

Preview your email template below.

Email Template Detail   [Edit] [Delete] [Clone]

Folder	Unfiled Public Email Templates		
Email Template Name	At Risk Email Reminder Template	Available For Use	✓
Template Unique Name	At_Risk_Email_Reminder_Template	Last Used Date	
Encoding	General US & Western Europe (ISO-8859-1, ISO-LATIN-1)	Times Used	
Author	Fred Armisen [Change]		
Description	Email template for the reminder email when an Account has been put into "At Risk" status.		
Created By	Fred Armisen, 1/1/1890 3:11 PM	Modified By	Carrie Brownstein, 1/1/1990 4:20 PM

[Edit] [Delete] [Clone]

Email Template   [Send Test and Verify Merge Fields]

Subject	Account At Risk 2-Day Reminder

Plain Text Preview

The account {!Account.Name} was set to a status of "At Risk" 2 days ago. If you have not already checked, please follow up to resolve and move the account into another status.

Figure 11-13. *The completed E-mail Template for the "At Risk" reminder*

The second step is to create the E-mail Alert that will be called from our process. To create the E-mail Alert, go to Setup ➤ Build ➤ Create ➤ Workflow & Approvals ➤ Email Alerts. Once there click the New Email Alert button. Once on the New Email Alert page, enter the following values:

- **Description**: At Risk Email Reminder
- **Unique Name**: At_Risk_Email_Reminder
- **Object**: Case
- **Email Template**: At Risk Email Reminder Template
- **Recipient Type**: User
- **Selected Recipients**: Case Owner
- **From Email Address**: Current User's email address

Once all these fields have been entered in click the Save button. Once saved the page should look like Figure 11-14.

Figure 11-14. *The completed E-mail Alert for the "At Risk" reminder*

Phew! Now that all that preparation is complete let's go back to our process in Process Builder. Remember that it is the "Set Account At Risk from Case" process. Once the process is open for editing, the next step that needs to be completed before adding the E-mail Alert is setting the schedule in the Scheduled Actions in the action group related to the "Is Account At Risk Approved?" criteria. To do so, click "Set Schedule" as shown in Figure 11-15.

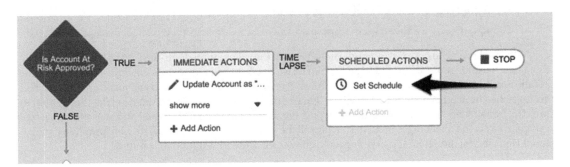

Figure 11-15. *The Set Schedule link under Scheduled Actions*

After clicking "Set Schedule," the "Set Time for Actions to Execute" configuration panel will open to the right. In it click the bottom radio button and enter "2" in the first field and "Days" in the second so that it should look like Figure 11-16 when complete. Finally, click the Save button to continue. This will set the schedule for any actions in this list of schedule actions to run two days after the Case was approved to update the account to "At Risk" status. Now we need to add some actions to this list.

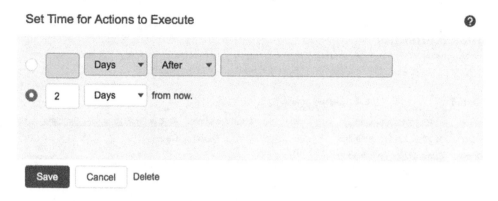

Set Time for Actions to Execute

Figure 11-16. *The configured Scheduled Action set to kick off two days from when the process runs*

Notice how that the schedule has been set that the "+ Add Action" link is enabled. Click it to open the "Select and Define Action" configuration panel. Now we can finally reap the rewards of our hard work. We have our E-mail Template in place that is used by the E-mail Alert we created. So now in the configuration panel enter the following values:

- **Action Type**: Email Alerts

- **Action Name**: At Risk Email Reminder

- **Email Alert**: At_Risk_Email_Reminder

What we have done here is very simple now. With all the preparation done, the E-mail Template and the E-mail Alert handle most of the work. At this point all we need our process to do is fire the E-mail Alert. So the Action Type just says we want to fire an E-mail Alert. The Action Name is just the usual name entered, so it is distinguished from other actions in the Canvas. Finally, the E-mail Alert is just the name of the E-mail Alert to run. The E-mail Alert field allows you to start typing the name of the E-mail Alert and an autocomplete list will appear to select the matching E-mail Alert. When all the values have been entered, the configuration panel should look like Figure 11-17. If everything looks correct, click the Save button to continue.

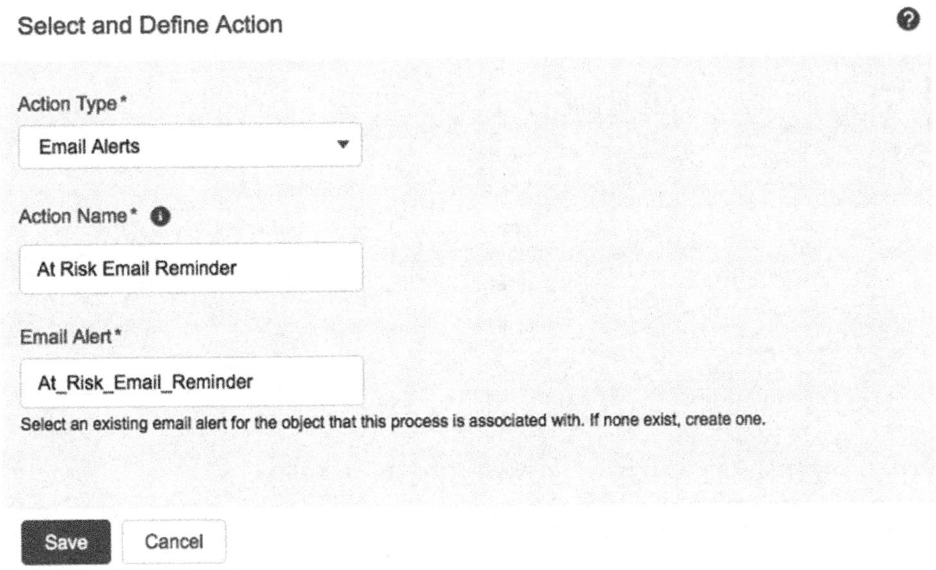

Select and Define Action

Action Type *

Email Alerts ▼

Action Name * ①

At Risk Email Reminder

Email Alert *

At_Risk_Email_Reminder

Select an existing email alert for the object that this process is associated with. If none exist, create one.

Save   Cancel

Figure 11-17. *The configured action to call the "At_Risk_Email_Reminder" E-mail Alert*

At this point we have met our new requirements. A Chatter Post is made immediately after the Case is approved to set the account to an "At Risk" status and two days later a reminder e-mail is sent out to have the account owner follow up on resolving the issue. The process should look like Figure 11-18.

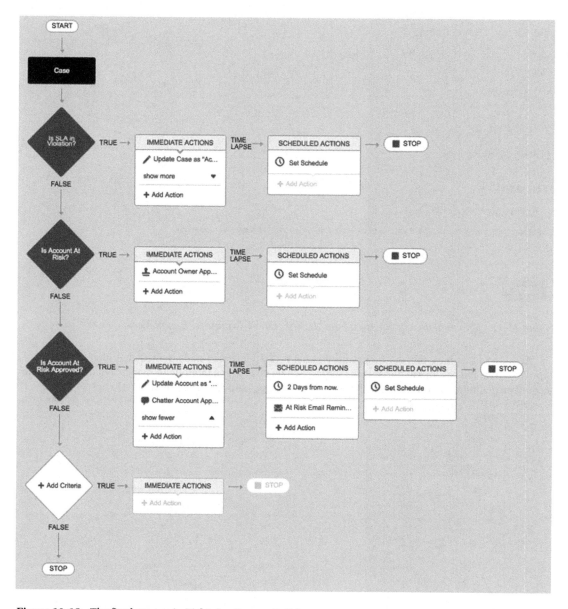

Figure 11-18. *The final process in Lightning Process Builder*

Now this new process will not run until the other process created earlier is deactivated and this new version is activated. Fortunately, Lightning Process Builder allows for the immediate deactivation of previous versions of a process when another version is activated. So the last step needed here is to click the Activate button and you are all set.

Recap

In this chapter we covered the two types of notifications that can be sent from a process: E-mail Alerts and Chatter Posts. Each type of notification has its use. E-mail Alerts are great because so much communication is performed with e-mails and they can be accessed almost anywhere. A Post to Chatter is also a great way to notify to a user or a group or to post to record. Chatter Posts are recorded in Salesforce while sometimes e-mails can get lost in an inbox. Which notification is appropriate depends on the requirement and also the organization's adoption of Chatter. We also covered the details of configuring e-mails of these types of notifications for use in Lightning Process Builder. E-mail Alerts have to be primarily configured outside Lightning Process Builder and are just called from a process without many configuration options. On the other hand, a Post to Chatter is entirely configured within Lightning Process Builder. In the configuration, the post can be made to a user, to a Chatter group, or to the record being handled in the process. The message of the post is configured within Lightning Process Builder too, and it can include text, merge fields, @mentions, and topics (new or existing). Finally, we went through an existing process and altered it by created a new version to add the notifications required. One notification was an Immediate Action, Post to Chatter, and the other was an E-mail Alert, which was a Scheduled Action sent two days after the Chatter Post was made.

■ ■ ■

CHAPTER 12

Extend Visual Workflow and Lightning Process Builder with Apex

Until now, this book has been focusing on not using code by taking advantage of the expressiveness that is available in Visual Workflow and Lightning Process Builder. There is a lot that can be achieved with the features that these two tools have. A lot of what could have been implemented before with Apex Triggers can now be achieved with Lightning Process Builder. Its simple interface makes it easy to use. Its abundance of actions, both immediate and scheduled, make it robust in what it can achieve. When requirements get more complicated and they cannot be implemented in Lightning Process Builder alone, they can also be handled by calling an autolaunched flow created in Visual Workflow. Also, Visual Workflow is great at creating not only autolaunched flows but standard flows that have a user interface elements such as screens. With Visual Workflow you can create pages that you would normally create with Visualforce and Apex.

Although these two tools have a huge breadth of features, they cannot account for every single requirement that Salesforce customers from across the globe may have. In those instances it may be necessary to use Apex in order to augment the current capabilities of flows and processes. This chapter will not dive into learning Apex. Salesforce provides Trailhead and there are plenty of awesome books on the subject. Instead, this chapter provides some simple but powerful examples of calling Apex to get the job done!

What Is Apex?

Apex is a programming language developed specifically for the Force.com platform. It contains many of the same attributes found in other programming languages used by other systems. It contains conditional statements such as if, then, and else to help with the flow of logic. It contains assignment operators to allow for saving and retrieving information in memory. It has the ability to interact with the database using DML (Data Manipulation Language), SOQL (Salesforce Object Query Language), and SOSL (Salesforce Object Search Language). It can work with data formats such as JSON (JavaScript Object Notation) and XML (Extensible Markup Language). It can do a lot more, but I think you get the picture. As you can see, once you dive into Apex it is a whole other world filled with abbreviations and mixing of other technologies. Apex is the ultimate tool for customizing Salesforce. It is a very expressive language that can take advantage of other languages, previously noted, to fully customize the user and customer experience on Salesforce's platform.

As stated earlier we are not going to learn Apex in this chapter, but let's cover some basics to get started. First of all, Apex code is just plain text. That plain text is stored in a file stored within Salesforce. There are different file types that Salesforce uses depending on the purpose of the file. Some of the files that Salesforce has are Visualforce Pages, Visualforce Components, Apex Classes, and Apex Triggers.

This is not an exhaustive list, but when working with flows and processes the only files you need to work with are Apex Classes. They have a `.cls` extension and can be created and located in Salesforce in a few ways. One way is with the Force.com Developer Console located at the top right side of the window when you log into Salesforce. Another way is just simply going to Setup ➤ Build ➤ Develop ➤ Apex Classes and there you can create, edit, and delete classes. In addition to these two ways, there are a lot of different tools for accessing and editing Apex code. One example is the Force.com IDE (Integrated Development Environment). It is a tool used by developers to manage their code within Salesforce. Developers use other tools as well to edit code (e.g., MavensMate, which is used with text editors such as Sublime and Atom).

That said, if you don't plan on diving into developing Apex on a full-time basis, then stick with the Force.com Developer Console. The Force.com Developer Console, as seen in Figure 12-1, is always up to date with the latest edition of Salesforce, plus it works in a browser and does not require any software to be installed on your computer.

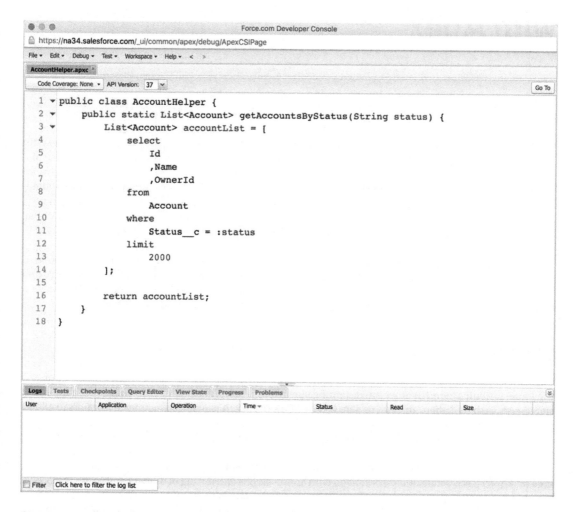

Figure 12-1. *The Force.com Developer Console*

Deciding on the best tool for you often comes down to personal preference, but in general you will want a tool that allows you to create, read, edit, save, and delete Apex, Visualforce, and Lightning Components. Some things to keep in mind when comparing the Force.com Developer Console vs. other external developer tools are the following:

- Force.com Developer Console
  - Pros
    - 100% browser-based
    - Works directly with the organization's code (no local copies on your computer)
  - Cons
    - No ability to compare a changed version with the organization's version (since no local copy is made)
    - No ability to deploy code to another organization
- Other Tools
  - Pros
    - Does not depend on being connected 100% of the time to develop (except saving)
    - Compare local version to organization's version
    - Most allow the ability to deploy code to other organizations
  - Cons
    - Must work with a local copy of code that needs to be kept in sync with the organization's version
    - Can be a little slower to save local copy to the organization

Salesforce Developers are accustomed to working with development environments such as the Force.com Developer Console to write code that can be run by the Force.com platform. If you are looking to branch out from Salesforce administrator to Salesforce developer you can use this tool to get started in learning Apex. If that is not the case, then the Force.com Developer Console is still useful. Let's say you are a full-time Salesforce administrator who has not touched Apex code before and you need a solution that requires a flow or a process to call some Apex code. There are many web sites where you can find code solutions to copy and paste into an Apex class to be used. Another scenario could be where a Salesforce developer could write some custom Apex code to meet the requirement you need. Then you can do the rest of the work with a flow or a process. So, even though you might require some Apex code, there are still a lot of benefits to using Visual Workflow or Lightning Process Builder to build something that does the bulk of the work and only calling out to a small amount of logic in Apex code. It's a great way to augment these two tools that Salesforce provides.

Calling Apex from a Flow

Let's look at the first tool Salesforce provides, Visual Workflow, and its output, the flow. This book has spent a considerable amount of time going over Visual Workflow and flows. We have converged all that is clicks, not code, but today it's all about the code. Flows actually have two ways of calling Apex code. One is through the use of custom plug-ins that can be built and actually show up in the toolbox for Visual Workflow. The other is a simple call out to some code that is available to "invoked" by Visual Workflow but does not show up as a custom plug-in in the Visual Workflow toolbox.

This may not be clear unless it's seen. So look at Figure 12-2 to see an example of a custom plug-in build for Visual Workflow. Do your eyes betray you? In the list of elements that can be dragged to the Canvas in Visual Workflow is a new element. That's a custom plug-in and, yes, code can be written to create more elements to be used in Visual Workflow.

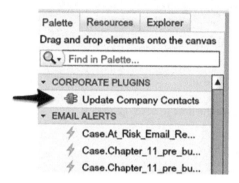

Figure 12-2. *Example of a custom plug-in in Visual Workflow*

We will get to an example later on how this is done, but it sure is convenient. It's like taking a pile of Apex code and putting it into a box that you can use any time. Having the added feature of seeing something tangible that you can click and drag onto the Canvas is a bonus. To do this an Apex class has to be written that implements Salesforce's "Process.Plugin" interface. What this means is that Salesforce has a set of Apex code named Process.Plugin that does some work in letting Cloud Flow Designer know where the necessary data is for showing some information about the custom plug-in. This frees up the developer to only write code that makes this plug-in different or special from other plug-ins. As long as a custom plug-in uses this Process.Plugin interface then Cloud Flow Designer knows how to work with it.

The other way of using Apex is a just a call out to an Apex method directly within Cloud Flow Designer. This is done by marking a section of Apex code known as a "method" with a special keyword of "@ InvocableMethod," which tells Cloud Flow Designer that it is usable in a Flow. The @InvocableMethod keyword is what is called an annotation and is a newer feature than Process.Plugin. It can be applied as a standard Apex method as long as the method follows some rules.

InvocableMethod rules include the following:

- An Apex class can only have one InvocableMethod.

- The invocable method can only have one parameter and it is required to be one of the following:

- A list of primitive data type (cannot be the generic type Object but must be a child of that type)

- A list of lists of primitive data type (cannot be the generic type Object but must be a child of that type)

- A list of an sObject type (cannot be the generic type sObject but must be a child of that type)

- A list of lists of an sObject type (cannot be the generic type sObject but must be a child of that type)

- A list of user-defined type, containing variables of the above supported types and must have the "InvocableVariable" annotation as well

- The invocable method must be defined as static and either public or global.

- The invocable method must either return a List (but not of type Object or sObject) or be of return type null.

- Other annotations cannot be combined with the InvocableMethod annotation.

- Invocable methods can be used in packages, but once you add an invocable method you can't remove it from later versions of the package.

- Public invocable methods in a managed package will not appear in Cloud Flow Designer's list of actions when editing a flow, although they can still be referenced by flows within the same managed package.

- Global invocable methods in a managed package will appear in Cloud Flow Designer's list of available actions even outside the managed package.

- Invocable methods cannot be used in Apex Triggers.

While it does appear that there are a lot of rules surrounding invocable methods, they tend to require less Apex code than their Process.Plugin counterparts. Later on, when we get to some examples, this will become very apparent, as the Process.Plugin interface requires a lot of code to interface with Cloud Flow Designer. This is because creating plug-ins gives a lot of flexibility in how the individual building flows can configure the plug-in element at the time of usage compared to using an invocable method. However, invocable methods can be used in many places besides flows and they also support bulk operations. This means that they are "bulkified" and when, loading large amounts of data in Data Loader, more efficient and can run all the records through a method at a time, while plug-ins have to be one at a time. This can cause issues in Salesforce organizations with large amounts of data.

■ **Note**　Salesforce recommends using the @InvocableMethod annotation instead of the Process.Plugin interface.

To see more about the differences of the Process.Plugin interface compared to the @InvocableMethod annotation please refer to Table 12-1.

Table 12-1. *Process.Plugin interface vs. @InvocableMethod annotation*

	Process.Plugin Interface	@InvocableMethod Annotation
Apex data types not supported	Blob Collection sObject Time	Generic Object Generic sObject Sets Maps Enums Note: The Cloud Flow Designer doesn't support mapping an Apex method's input or output parameters to an sObject collection variable.
Bulk operations	Not supported	Supported
Element name in the Cloud Flow Designer	Class name or the value of the name property	Class name
Reusability	Classes with this interface implemented are available in flows	Classes with this annotation implemented are available in: Flows Processes Rest API
Section in the Cloud Flow Designer	Apex Plug-in or the value of the tag property	Apex

Example: Generate Random Number

Now that we have described the two ways to augment Flows with code, let's look at an example of each. The amount of code that can be used can be very simple or very complex. Since the book is mainly aimed at staying with the principle of "clicks, not code" as much as possible we will keep the example code as short as possible to illustrate the idea of how utilizing Apex in a flow works. We will look at an example of using code and how it would be implemented with Process.Plugin and then with the @InvocableMethod annotation. That way the contrasts and similarities can be realized even for a small bit of Apex code.

A nice, concise example is a random number generator that can pick a number between a configurable minimum and maximum range. While the use of a random number generator may not seem apparent, it can be useful for, let's say, wanting to randomly send out one of several e-mail templates when communicating with a lead or contact to keep the conversation a bit more natural. For that example, five e-mail templates could be configured and when sending out an e-mail from a flow, the e-mail alerts could be named NewLeadEmailAlert1 NewLeadEmailAlert2, and so forth. The flow could call upon some Apex code to generate a number from 1 to 5 and append the number to the name of the alert to call. This is one example. If you want to have a bit more fun, you could use the same concept to create a Magic 8 Ball-style game: a game where you enter a question and it randomly chooses between a set of canned responses such as yes, no, maybe, ask again later, or outlook unlikely.

We won't go into creating these two examples in their entirety. It's a great exercise for you to try on your own. Instead, we will lay down groundwork of generating the random number using the Apex System. Math class. It's an Apex class that contains several methods for mathematical operations. In the System.Math class there is a random() method, but this method takes no parameters and produces a decimal greater than or equal to 0.0 and less than 1.0. This method does not give us many options does it? In fact, there are no parameters so how is this going to meet our needs of creating a configurable plug-in or method that takes a minimum and maximum value? Luckily searching on the Internet will bring all sorts of interesting ways to achieve this. Listing 12-1 shows a simple way using one line of Apex code to give us what we need.

Listing 12-1. Apex code to generate a random number using the Math.random() method

```
Long randomNumber = min + (Long)(Math.random() * ((max - min) + 1));
```

In the single line of code the "min" variable represents the configurable minimum threshold we want and the "max" variable represents the configurable maximum threshold we want. There are other mathematical formulas that can be found on the Internet as well, but this is one that will meet our needs. Essentially, it uses the configurable min value as the floor of that we want. It uses `Math.random()` to generate a number from 0.0 to 1.0 but then uses the difference of the max and min (plus 1) to give a multiplier effect to add to the min value. So on one end of the spectrum you could get a min of 1 multiplied by 1, which would be itself (1). Then, on the other end, you can have the maximum value you configured. It works out well for most needs. So now that we have the basic mathematical formula and Apex code ready, let's apply this to our two options for including Apex in flows.

Generate Random Number with Process.Plugin

First, to use Process.Plugin, we need to create an Apex class. This can be done several ways depending on whether or not you use a third-party development tool. The two easiest ways are by going either to the Salesforce Admin Console or through the Force.com Developer Console. In the Admin Console go to Setup ➤ Build ➤ Develop ➤ Apex Classes and click the New button. There you can enter Apex code and save the class with a name such as RandomNumberPlugin. If you prefer to use the Developer Console, then under your name in the header go to Developer Console to open it up. Once there go to File ➤ New ➤ Apex Class and then give it a name such as RandomNumberPlugin, as stated before. Then Apex code can be entered and it can be saved by going to File ➤ Save.

For the RandomNumberPlugin class enter the code seen in Listing 12-2. There are 40 lines here in this class. It could be a little shorter by not using lines 2-8 and instead typing these values straight into the code below, but these final variables are included at the top to make the code more readable and more maintainable.

Listing 12-2. Apex code for the RandomNumberPlugin that implements the Process.Plugin interface

```
global class RandomNumberPlugin implements Process.Plugin  {
    private final static String FLOW_NAME = 'Random Number';
    private final static String FLOW_DESC = 'The Random Number flow plugin takes a low
    number, a high number, and returns a random number in between those values.';
    private final static String TAG = 'Math';
    private final static String INPUT1  = 'Min';
    private final static String INPUT2  = 'Max';
    private final static String OUTPUT1 = 'Random Number';
    private final static Boolean FLOW_REQUIRED = true;

    global Process.PluginResult invoke(Process.PluginRequest request) {
        // Get low and high numbers
        Decimal min = (Decimal)request.inputParameters.get(INPUT1);
        Decimal max = (Decimal)request.inputParameters.get(INPUT2);

        // Input validation
        if (min == null || max == null) return null;
```

```
        return new Process.PluginResult(new Map<String, Object> {
            OUTPUT1 => min + (Long)(Math.random() * ((max - min) + 1))
        });
    }

    global Process.PluginDescribeResult describe() {
        Process.PluginDescribeResult result = new Process.PluginDescribeResult();
        result.name = FLOW_NAME;
        result.description = FLOW_DESC;
        result.tag = TAG;

        result.inputParameters = new List<Process.PluginDescribeResult.InputParameter> {
            new Process.PluginDescribeResult.InputParameter(INPUT1, Process.
            PluginDescribeResult.ParameterType.LONG, FLOW_REQUIRED),
            new Process.PluginDescribeResult.InputParameter(INPUT2, Process.
            PluginDescribeResult.ParameterType.LONG, FLOW_REQUIRED)
        };

        result.outputParameters = new List<Process.PluginDescribeResult.OutputParameter> {
            new Process.PluginDescribeResult.OutputParameter(OUTPUT1, Process.
            PluginDescribeResult.ParameterType.LONG)
        };

        return result;
    }
}
```

The values that we defined in lines 2-8 are described in more detail next.

- **FLOW_NAME:** The name to show as the element name in palette of Cloud Flow Designer.

- **FLOW_DESC:** The description to show for the element in the palette of Cloud Flow Designer.

- **TAG:** The tag name used to group the element into. Several plug-ins can be categorized into the same tag. For example, there could be multiple math-related plug-ins created in a "Math" tag and then multiple other plug-ins created under a tag named "Acme Corp." to distinguish them separately.

- **INPUT1:** The name of the first input field to be shown in Cloud Flow Designer when configuring the plug-in instance.

- **INPUT2:** The name of the second input field to be shown in Cloud Flow Designer when configuring the plug-in instance.

- **OUTPUT1:** The name of the first (and only) output field to be shown in Cloud Flow Designer when configuring the plug-in instance.

- **FLOW_REQUIRED:** This is a value of true to let Cloud Flow Designer know that there must be a value entered here when the instance of the element is configured. So it is not optional.

Again, these lines are here to help the code be more readable and maintainable. These values could have been entered without the use of these variables in Apex, but using this format makes it easy to change. Let's say you want to change the name, description, or tag. Then you would just need to change the text within the single quotes to anything you want. Nice and easy!

OK, so once the code is entered and saved the plug-in will be usable. Open up Cloud Flow Designer with a new or existing flow and you should see the Math tag in the palette along with the custom "Random Number" element as seen in Figure 12-3.

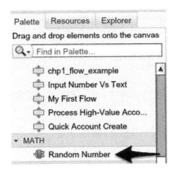

Figure 12-3. *The finished Random Number plug-in seen in the Visual Workflow palette*

Pretty cool, right? Now you can drag this new element to the Canvas to open up its configuration screen. It should look like Figure 12-4.

Random Number   ✕

Class name: RandomNumberPlugin

Description: The Random Number flow plugin takes a low number, a high number, and returns a random number...

▼ **General Settings**

Name ∗ [   ]

Unique Name ∗ [   ] ⓘ

   Add Description

▼ **Inputs/Outputs**

Inputs	**Outputs**

Assign elements or values from your flow to the Apex keys.

              Target   Source

          Max   [Enter value or select resource   ▼]

          Min   [Enter value or select resource   ▼]

[OK] [Cancel]

Figure 12-4. *Configuration screen in Visual Workflow for the Random Number plug-in*

In this configuration screen we can enter in the values we need. Go ahead and enter in the name, unique name, and description in the "General Settings" section as seen in Figure 12-5.

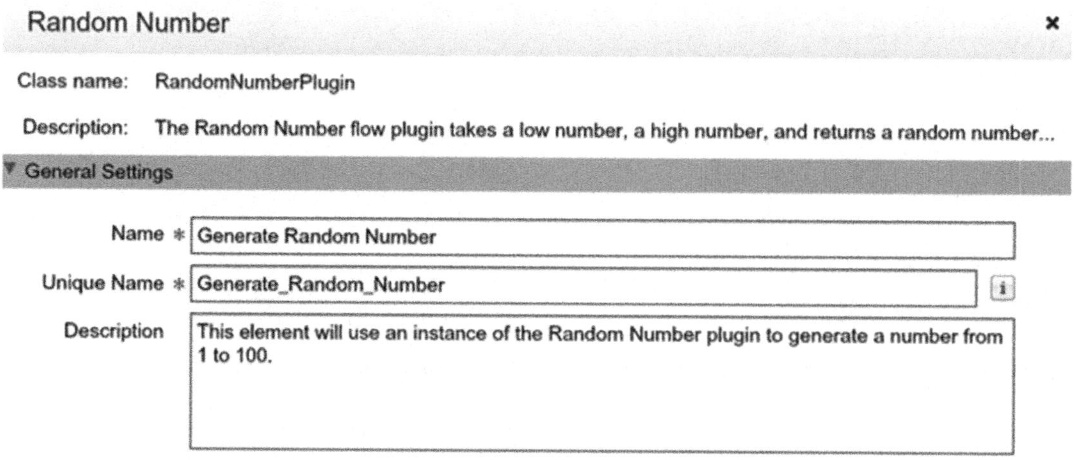

Figure 12-5. *Configured "General Settings" section of the Random Number plug-in*

After configuring the General Settings, enter the following values for the Inputs tab in the "Inputs/Outputs" section as seen in Figure 12-6. Here is where the Max and Min values are entered. For now we are using a minimum of 1 and a maximum of 100 just as an example, but any positive or negative values can be used.

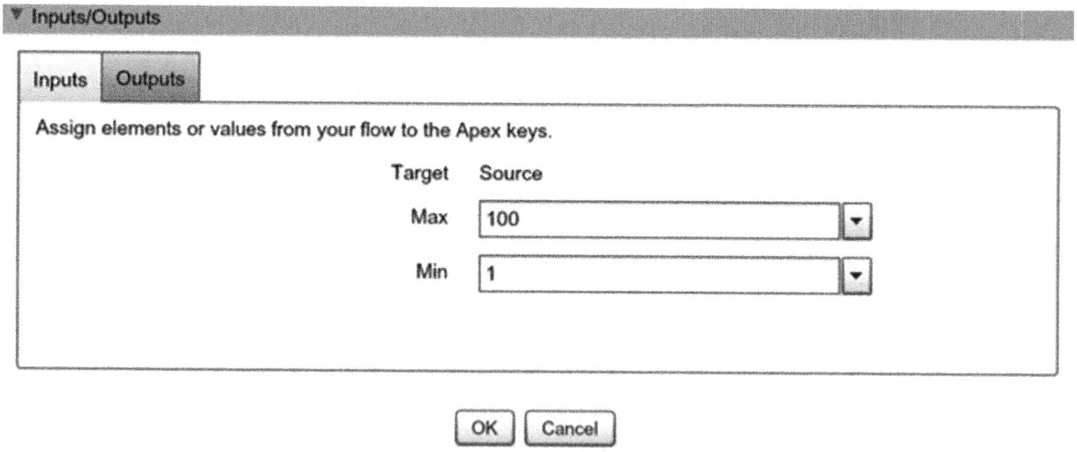

Figure 12-6. *Configured Inputs tab of the "Inputs/Outputs" section for the Random Number plug-in*

Next click the Outputs tab and select "Random Number" under the Source field. Under the Target field select CREATE NEW ➤ Variable. Enter the configuration settings as shown in Figure 12-7.

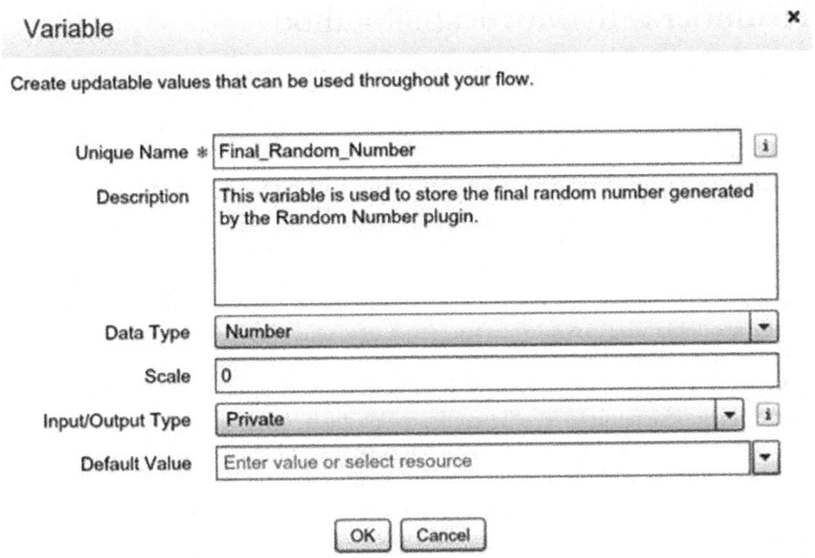

Variable

Create updatable values that can be used throughout your flow.

Unique Name ✳	Final_Random_Number
Description	This variable is used to store the final random number generated by the Random Number plugin.
Data Type	Number
Scale	0
Input/Output Type	Private
Default Value	Enter value or select resource

OK   Cancel

Figure 12-7. *Configuration for the Final_Random_Number variable for use in the flow*

After clicking the OK button the Target field on the Outputs tab will be updated to look like Figure 12-8.

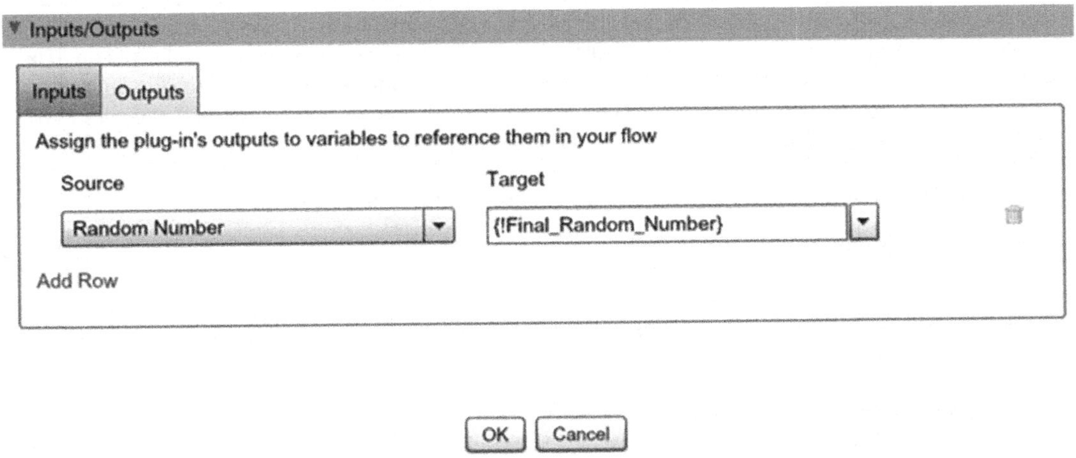

▼ Inputs/Outputs

Inputs	Outputs

Assign the plug-in's outputs to variables to reference them in your flow

Source	Target
Random Number	{!Final_Random_Number}

Add Row

OK   Cancel

Figure 12-8. *Configured Outputs tab of the "Inputs/Outputs" section for the Random Number plug-in*

At this point after configuring the Random Number element you can set it as the start element of a flow and add a Display element afterward to show the Final_Random_Number variable. Then, when running this flow, a new number will show each time that will be between the minimum and maximum value that was configured.

Generate Random Number with @InvocableMethod

Let's say you don't want or need a plug-in like we just described. Maybe the requirement is simply to call a small piece of Apex code without a lot of the fuss of adding extra code that does not have anything to do with the main goal. Salesforce recommends the @InvocableMethod annotation over the Process.Plugin approach. There are a few reasons for this.

One reason is that the additional code required to make some Apex code usable in a flow is literally the single @InvocableMethod annotation on an Apex method. Salesforce takes the work off our hands with this annotation. Instead of having to create a lot of the same code over and over again to get our Apex logic to be usable in a flow like we do with Process.Plugin, Salesforce looks at the @InvocableMethod annotation and does the heavy lifting for us. That's basically what an annotation is in Apex. It's a single keyword that tells Salesforce how some Apex code should be used without the developer having to write the same amount of tedious code over and over again. Apex has other annotations for numerous reasons such as creating web services or unit tests.

Another reason that Salesforce recommends @InvocableMethod is that it is designed with "bulkification" in mind. You may be wondering what bulkification is. It is the ability to handle large amounts of records, as in a bulk data import from Data Loader, without having to handle each record individually. Salesforce has many governor limits in place since it is a multitenant platform. Since many organizations share the same systems it is important that one customer is not affected by another customer's actions. One way Salesforce handles this is by putting governor limits in place. There are limits on how much code can run and how many operations can be performed to the database in a length of time. These limits help to promote efficiency and to prevent excessive processing. So if a method was not bulkified, it would have the potential to slow things down by having to perform logic on one record in the database at a time. Bulkification works by performing logic on all the records before accessing the database and then finally at the end updating all the records in the database at one time. It's much more efficient than the Process.Plugin approach.

We've seen some examples of why using the @InvocableMethod annotation is a great idea, but let's look at an example of how to use it in a flow. To make an adequate comparison we will use the random number generator example again here. First we need an Apex class, so create a new Apex class in the Force.com IDE or by going to Setup ➤ Build ➤ Develop ➤ Apex Classes and clicking the New button. Name the Apex class RandomNumberGenerator when prompted for a name. Next, use the code seen in Listing 12-3 and click Save. If you are in the Developer Console you would go to File ➤ Save.

Listing 12-3. Apex code to generate a Random Number using the @InvocableMethod annotation

```
public class RandomNumberGenerator
{
    @InvocableMethod
    public static List<Long> randomNumber(List<RandomNumberRange> ranges) {
        List<Long> randomNumberList = new List<Long>();

        for(RandomNumberRange range : ranges) {
            Long randomNumber = (range.min + (Long)(Math.random() * ((range.max - range.min)
            + 1)));
            randomNumberList.add(randomNumber);
        }

        return randomNumberList;
    }

    public class RandomNumberRange {
        @InvocableVariable(required=true)
        public Integer min;

        @InvocableVariable(required=true)
```

```
        public Integer max;
    }
}
```

On line 7 of the code you can see the formula we use to generate the random number. That part stays the same even though this is an implementation using @InvocableMethod instead of Process.Plugin. The rest of the code is mainly to deal with making the method configurable from Cloud Flow Designer and also to handle bulk data. The invocable method is named randomNumber and it takes a List (a type of collection). The List is needed by an invocable method as an input to handle the bulkification aspect. In order to not handle one record at a time, such as the case with a plug-in, we have to be able to handle a number of items at a time. If we just get one value to deal with then Salesforce will simply use a List of one value. Likewise, the output of this invocable method is also a List. This is again due to its being bulkified. If we get several values coming in, then after being processed it would make sense that we would get multiple outputs.

Notice also that the type of List does not have to match for the inputs to the invocable method and the outputs. The input is a List of type RandomNumberRange while the output is a List of type Long. The Long data type is what is known as a primitive data type in Apex. It is essentially a very large or very small number without a decimal point. Longs have a minimum value of -2^{63} and a maximum value of $2^{63}-1$. On the other hand, the RandomNumberRange type is not a primitive data type at all. It's a custom data type we created starting on line 14. It is what is called an inner class, an Apex class inside an Apex class. The reason we need this is because to create a random number, we need two values: a minimum number and a maximum number. They come in pairs and if we can get a List then we would be getting a List of pairs. Well, there really isn't a perfect fit for a Salesforce data type that represents a pair of numbers, but Apex allows the creation of our own data type.

Looking at the code that makes up this inner Apex class we can see the min and max variables to hold our pair of numbers. However, do you notice that there is another annotation above them? It's the @InvocableVariable annotation! This is something similar to the @InvocableMethod annotation. It works off the same principle. While the @InvocableMethod annotation allows a method to be seen in Cloud Flow Designer and called in a flow, the @InvocableVariable allows for a variable used as an input or output parameter for an invocable method's invocable action. That is to say, an invocable variable can be seen and used in Cloud Flow Designer and in a flow. This will be much clearer once we look at this example in Cloud Flow Designer.

Go ahead and create a new flow in Cloud Flow Designer. In the palette there will now be an APEX tag with the RandomNumberGenerator action as seen in Figure 12-9. This is from our invocable method.

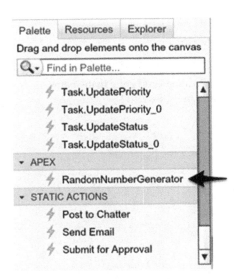

Figure 12-9. *The RandomNumberGenerator action seen in the Visual Workflow palette*

Click and drag the RandomNumberGenerator action onto the canvas. This will open up its configuration screen. It should look like Figure 12-10.

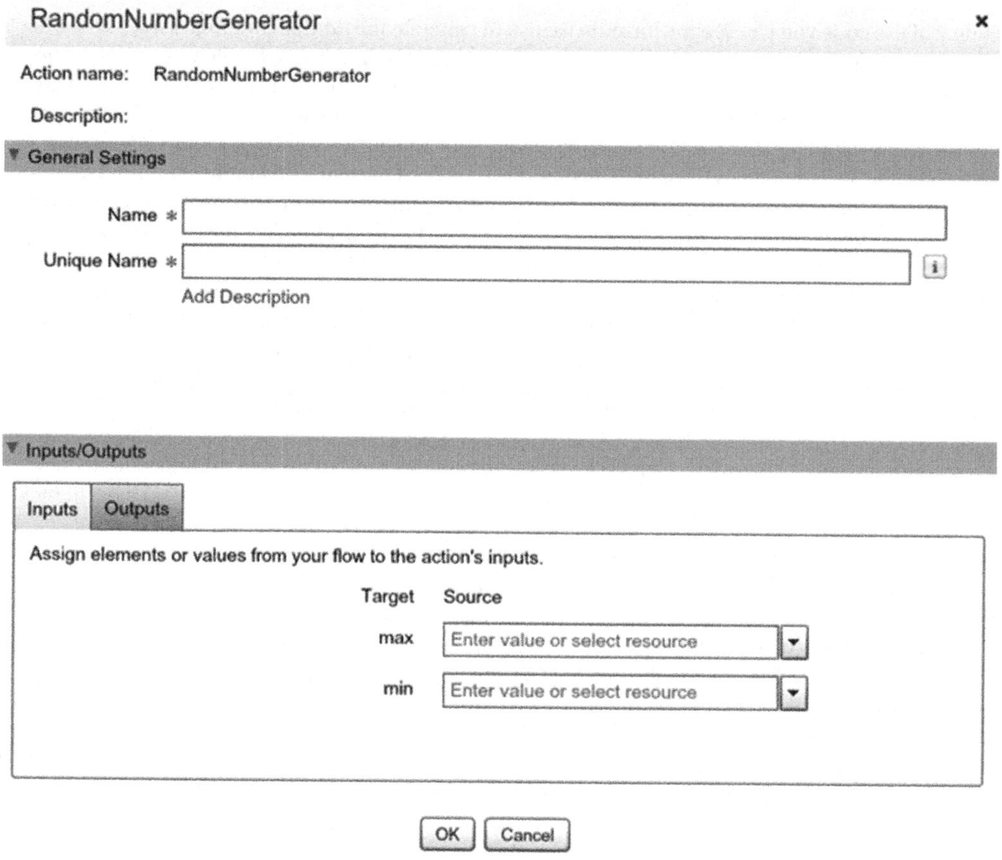

Figure 12-10. Configuration screen for the RandomNumberGenerator action

In this configuration screen we can enter in the values we need. Go ahead and enter in the name, unique name, and description in the "General Settings" section as seen in Figure 12-11.

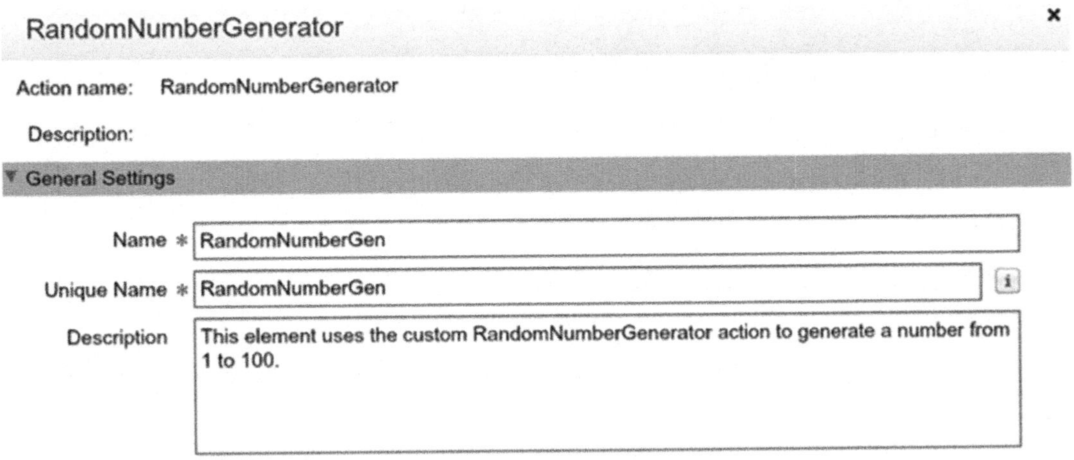

RandomNumberGenerator ✕

Action name: RandomNumberGenerator

Description:

▼ General Settings

Name * RandomNumberGen

Unique Name * RandomNumberGen [i]

Description This element uses the custom RandomNumberGenerator action to generate a number from 1 to 100.

Figure 12-11. Configuration of the "General Settings" section of the RandomNumberGenerator action

After configuring the General Settings, enter in the following values for the Inputs tab in the "Inputs/ Outputs" section as seen in Figure 12-12. Here is where we enter the max and min values. For now we are using a minimum of 0 and a maximum of 100 just as an example, but we can use any positive or negative values.

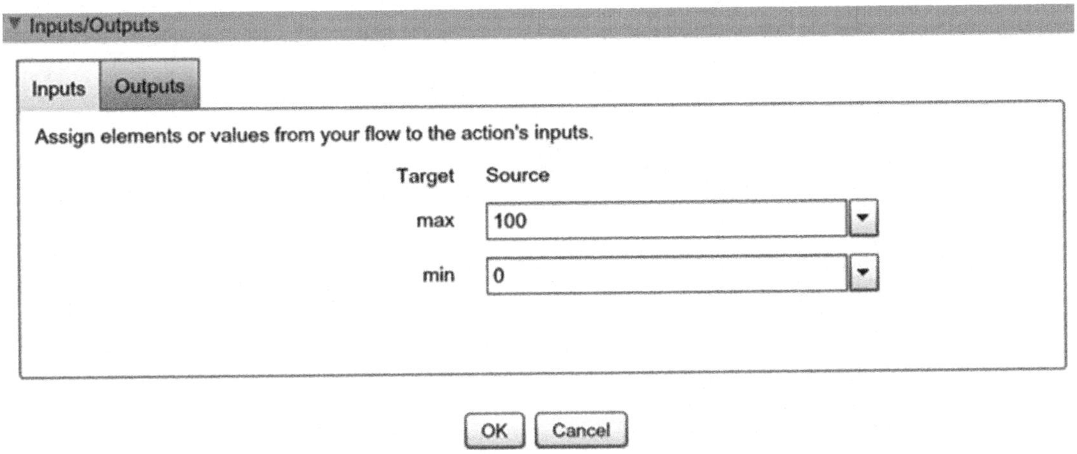

▼ Inputs/Outputs

| Inputs | **Outputs** |

Assign elements or values from your flow to the action's inputs.

	Target	Source
	max	100 ▼
	min	0 ▼

[OK] [Cancel]

Figure 12-12. Configuration of the Inputs tab in the "Inputs/Outputs" section of the RandomNumberGenerator action

Next click the Outputs tab and enter the values as seen in Figure 12-13. You will need to create a new variable named Final_Random_Number. For the values to configure that variable, refer to Figure 12-14.

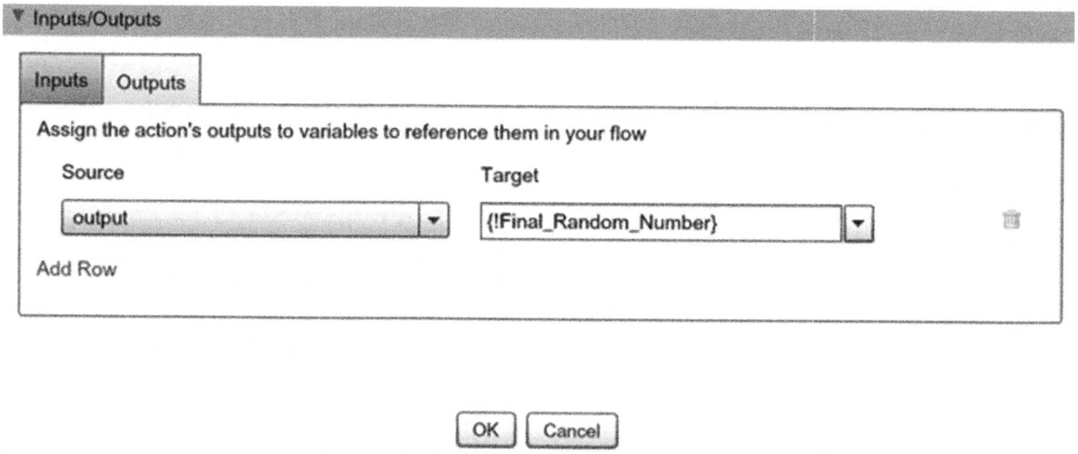

Figure 12-13. Configuration of the Outputs tab in the "Inputs/Outputs" section of the RandomNumberGenerator action

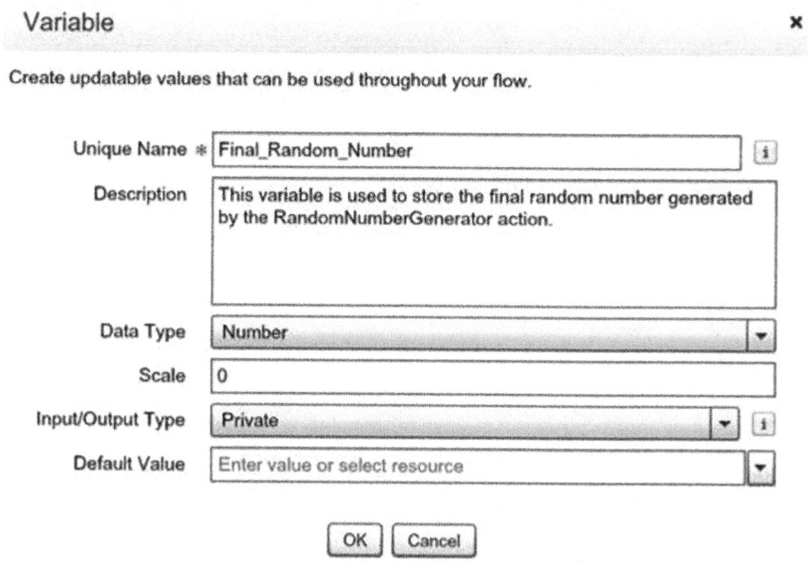

Figure 12-14. Configuration of the Final_Random_Number variable for use with the RandomNumberGenerator action in the flow

At this point, after configuring the RandomNumberGen element you can set it as the start element of a flow and add a Display element afterward to show the Final_Random_Number variable. Then, when running this flow, a new number will show each time that will be between the minimum and maximum value that was configured. It gives the same functionality in the running flow as the Process.Plugin implementation we discussed previously.

Calling Apex from Lightning Process Builder

Lightning Process Builder, while it is powerful in its simplicity, does not have the amount of flexibility as building a flow in Cloud Flow Designer. Thus, it is more likely that you would be calling Apex from a process built in Lightning Process Builder than from a flow built in Cloud Flow Designer. Fortunately configuring Lightning Process Builder to call Apex in a process is an easy task. Let's run through the main configuration settings in Lightning Process Builder before we look at an example. To use Apex in Lightning Process Builder, while in the Canvas add an action, such as an immediate action, and in the configuration panel for the action choose the Apex Action Type as seen in Figure 12-15.

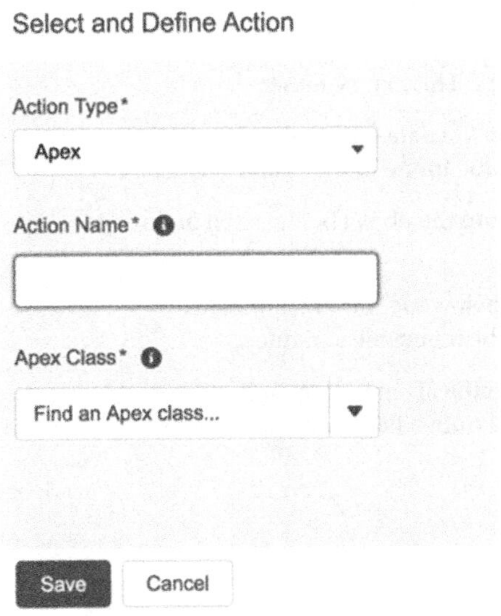

Select and Define Action

Action Type*

Apex ▼

Action Name* ❶

Apex Class* ❶

Find an Apex class... ▼

Save   Cancel

Figure 12-15. *The Select and Define Action configuration screen for the Apex Action Type*

Once you have selected Apex, two fields appear to configure. The first is the Action Name, which we all know by now is the name to give the action to distinguish it from other actions on the Lightning Process Builder Canvas. The other is "Apex Class" and it is specific to the Apex action. This field allows you to select the Apex class to call in this action. Keep in mind that not all Apex classes can be called. Only those that have an @InvocableMethod annotation will show up on this list. Furthermore, an Apex class can have multiple methods but only one invocable method. So the configuration does not require a method from the class to be selected. It automatically uses the annotated invocable method.

After selecting the Apex class, several events could take place. If the one invocable method does not have any variables it takes as parameters then no additional steps will be needed to configure the Apex action in Lightning Process Builder. Simply clicking the Save button will finish the configuration of the action. If the invocable method does have input variables to take, meaning there are variables that have been annotated with the @InvocableVariable annotation, then the "Set Apex Variables" section will appear as seen in Figure 12-16. This section will only look like this, though, if all the invocable variables are not required. This is because they are essentially optional and you can decide if you need to pass a value to them by clicking "+ Add Row" to start adding a row to the screen that can be used to configure the variable.

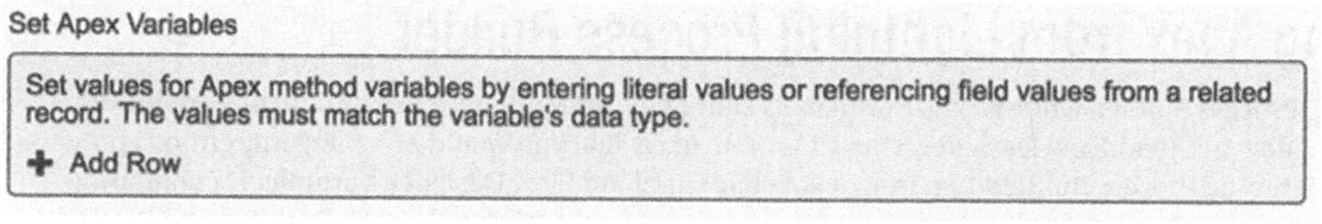

Set Apex Variables

Set values for Apex method variables by entering literal values or referencing field values from a related record. The values must match the variable's data type.

＋ Add Row

Figure 12-16. *The "Set Apex Variables" section when all input variables are optional*

Once the row is added the "Set Apex Variables" section will update to look like Figure 12-17 with the following three fields to configure:

- **Field:** The invocable variable for this class that a value can be stored in.

- **Type:** The type of value that is going to be used to store. This can be either

  - **Defined data type:** Such as ID, String, etc. This is the data type defined in the code and this would be selected to type in the value inline in the "Value" field.

  - **Reference:** This is a reference to another field from the object being acted on in the process or a field from a related object.

  - **Formula:** Allows the formula builder to appear below the row and configure a formula to produce a dynamic value to store in the invocable variable.

- **Value:** This is the value to store into the invocable variable. Depending on the Type selected, the value can be typed directly inline, pulled from a field or related object's field, or from a formula.

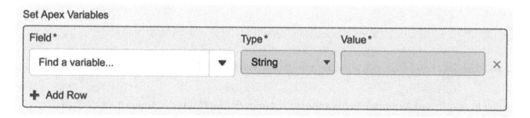

Figure 12-17. *Adding a variable in the "Set Apex Variables" section when all input variables are optional*

At this point more rows can be added or removed depending on how many optional fields there are.

If there is a mix of required variables and optional variables then the required variables would show up in the "Set Apex Variables" section. There would also be the ability to add a row so that the optional variables could be added as well as seen in Figure 12-18.

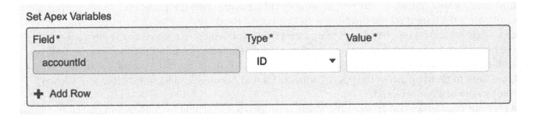

Figure 12-18. *Example of the "Set Apex Variables" section when some input variables are optional and one is required*

Finally, if all the fields are required then they would show up in the "Set Apex Variables" section to configure and there would be no option to add a row, as there are no optional variables to set as seen in Figure 12-19.

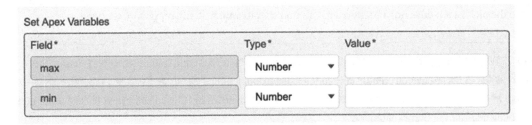

Figure 12-19. *Example of the "Set Apex Variables" section when all input variables are required*

■ **Note**   There is not a section to configure the output of the invocable method because Lightning Process Builder does not have the ability to store the values to be used by another action.

Example: Using Apex in a Process

In this last example we will be calling some Apex code from a process built in Lightning Process Builder. The example is pretty straightforward. In Lightning Process Builder a process can be built to update a record as we have seen but it's only one related record. There are times where records need to be updated but are not related so conveniently. One example can be where maybe a Salesforce ID of an object is stored in a record's field, but it actually is not a lookup or a master-detail record. While that seems like something you don't want to do, it is actually something seen quite often in the wild. There are all sorts of implementations and workarounds that cause this.

Another example of needing to update the most current child record is when its parent record is updated. For example, let's say you have a Student object with multiple related Semester objects. If logic was required to change the most recent Semester record for a Student when the student's status changes when the Student withdraws, then getting that most recent Semester would require some workaround. Maybe adding a related field to the Student object that points to the most current Semester would help. Then it would be easier to update using Lightning Process Builder.

A third example and one we will look at in more detail is having special logic to update all appropriate child records when the parent record is updated. In Lightning Process Builder we can configure the process to update a single related record. If we want to update a whole related list of records or maybe a subset of the related list of a parent record then we can get a little bit of help from Apex. In the following example we will have an Account with its related Contracts. The requirement is that when an Account's status is set to "Closed," we want to clean up any of the open Contracts for that Account by also setting them to "Closed" status if they were not already closed.

In a previous chapter we had an example where we added a Status field to the Account object, but if that field is not created yet then go ahead and create a picklist field on Account with the following values:

- New (< Year)

- In Good Standing

- At Risk

- Closed

Now under the Contract object there should already be a Status field that is a picklist. Add the "Closed" status to the picklist if it does not already exist. OK, that's pretty much all the prep work we need.

■ **Note** When adding a new Contract Status value it needs to be assigned to a Status category. Assign the "Closed" status to the "Activated" Status category for this example under Setup ➤ Build ➤ Customize ➤ Contracts ➤ Fields ➤ Contract Standard Fields ➤ Status. Once there, add "Closed" as a new picklist value and select "Activated" for the Status category.

Next we need some Apex code. Remember that in order for it to be visible in Lightning Process Builder it needs to have the @InvocableMethod annotation. In Listing 12-4 we have the Apex code to do this work for us. To break it down, it consists of taking in a List of Account IDs because invocable methods are required to take a List for bulkification. Next we have some SOQL that pulls the records we need, which is the list of Contracts that are related to the Account IDs in question. Also, the SOQL only looks for Contracts that are not in a "Closed" status. We even have criteria to make sure the Account is actually in a "Closed" status as well just in case someone tries to call this method without checking on the Account status beforehand. Next the Apex code simply iterates over every Contract in our result list and sets the Status to "Closed" before finally updating all the Contracts.

Listing 12-4. Apex code for the RelatedContractHandler that sets Contracts to the "Closed" status

```
public class RelatedContractHandler {
    @InvocableMethod
    public static void closeContractsForAccounts(List<ID> accountIdList) {
        List<Contract> contractList = [
            SELECT Id, Status
            FROM Contract
            WHERE Status != 'Closed'
            AND Account.Status__c = 'Closed'
            AND AccountId in :accountIdList
        ];
```

```
        for(Contract c : contractList) {
            c.Status = 'Closed';
        }

        update contractList;
    }
}
```

Now we can start building the process in Lightning Process Builder. Go ahead and create a new process and use the following values as seen in Figure 12-20:

- **Process Name**: Update Closed Contracts for Closed Account

- **API Name**: Update_Closed_Contracts_for_Closed_Account

- **Description**: Updates all Closed Contracts for a Closed Account

New Process

Process Name *

| Update Closed Contracts for Closed Account |

API Name * ⓘ

| Update_Closed_Contracts_for_Closed_Account |

Description

| Updates all Closed Contracts for a Closed Account |

The process starts when *

| A record changes   ▼ |

Cancel   Save

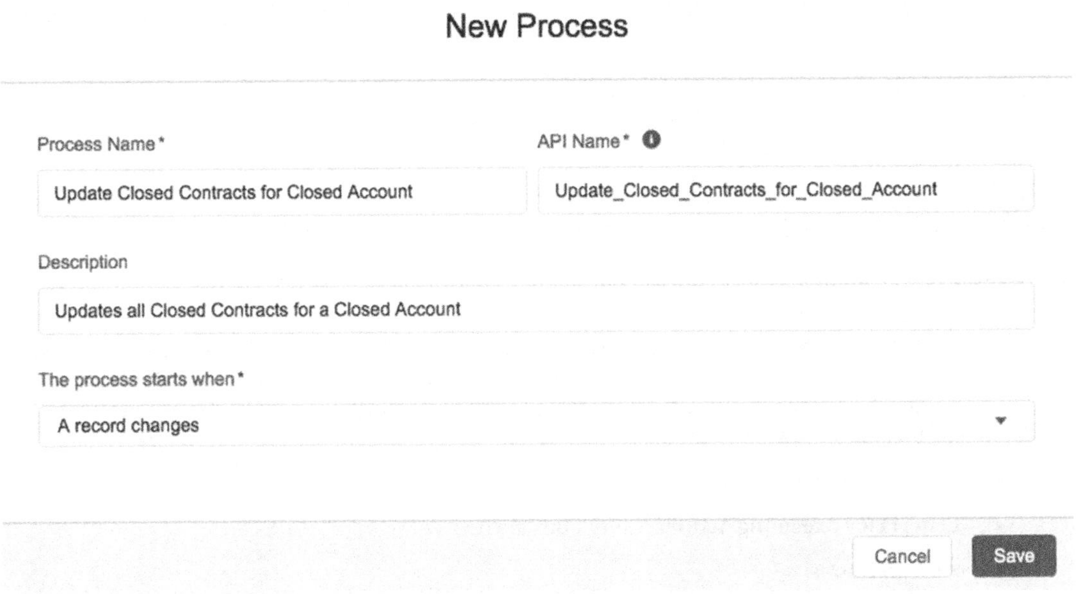

Figure 12-20. New Process screen for the "Update Closed Contracts for Closed Account" process

Once the canvas appears for the process we first need to add the object that this process is acting on. Our requirements are to take action if the Account is updated to a "Closed" status, so it's the Account object we need to act on. Click "+ Add Object" and in the configuration panel use the following settings:

- **Object**: Account

- **Start the process**: when a record is created or edited

The configuration panel should look like Figure 12-21. Once all the settings are entered correctly, click the Save button.

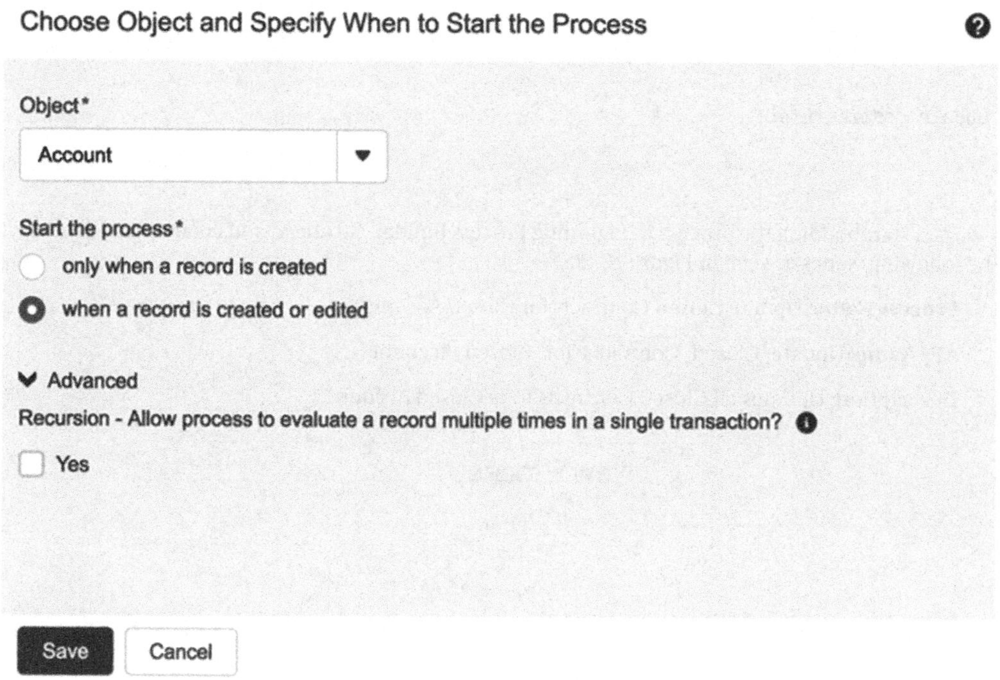

Choose Object and Specify When to Start the Process ❷

Object*

| Account | ▼ |

Start the process*

○ only when a record is created

◉ when a record is created or edited

❤ Advanced

Recursion - Allow process to evaluate a record multiple times in a single transaction? ❶

☐ Yes

Save   Cancel

Figure 12-21. *Configuration settings for using the Account object in the process*

Even though the Apex code only looks at Accounts with a status of "Closed" we do not want to do any unnecessary processing by calling the Apex code when it is not needed. So we will limit the criteria to only call an action when the Account is in the "Closed" status. Click "+ Add Criteria" to start configuring. In the configuration panel that appears, use the following settings:

- **Criteria Name**: Is Account Closed?

- **Criteria for Executing Actions**: Conditions are met

- **Set Conditions**:

    - **Field**: [Account.Status__c]

    - **Operator**: Equals

    - **Type**: Picklist

    - **Value**: Closed

- **Conditions**: All the conditions are met (AND)

Once all the settings are entered, the configuration panel should look like Figure 12-22. Click the Save button to continue.

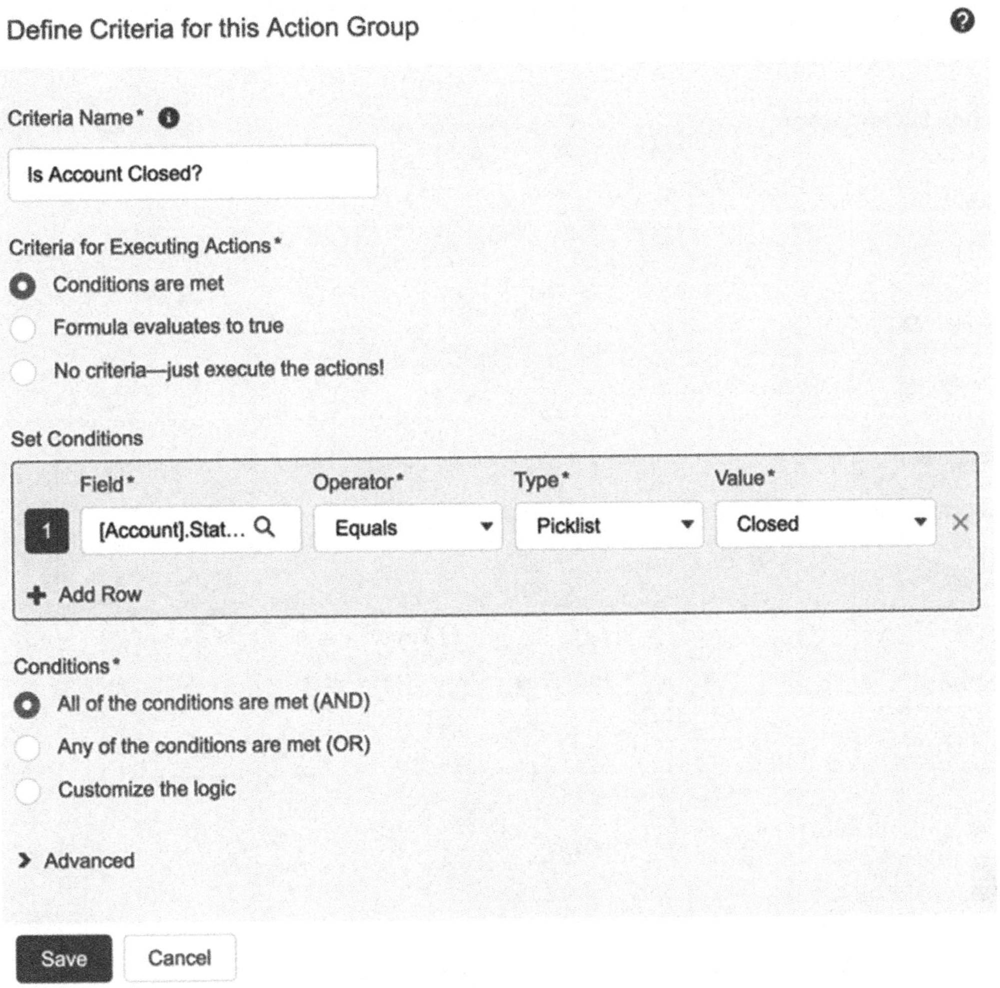

Define Criteria for this Action Group

Criteria Name* ⓘ

Is Account Closed?

Criteria for Executing Actions*
- ● Conditions are met
- ○ Formula evaluates to true
- ○ No criteria—just execute the actions!

Set Conditions

	Field*	Operator*	Type*	Value*
1	[Account].Stat... 🔍	Equals ▼	Picklist ▼	Closed ▼ ✕

➕ Add Row

Conditions*
- ● All of the conditions are met (AND)
- ○ Any of the conditions are met (OR)
- ○ Customize the logic

❯ Advanced

Save   Cancel

Figure 12-22. *Configuration settings for adding the "Is Account Closed?" criteria*

Now we need to call the Apex code to perform this magic for us. Click "+ Add Action" and in the configuration panel use the following settings:

- **Action Type**: Apex
- **Action Name**: Close Contracts
- **Apex Class**: RelatedContractHandler
- **Set Apex Variables**:
  - **Field**: accountIdList
  - **Type**: Reference
  - **Value**: [Account].Id

Once all these settings have been configured the configuration panel should look like Figure 12-23. Click the Save button to continue.

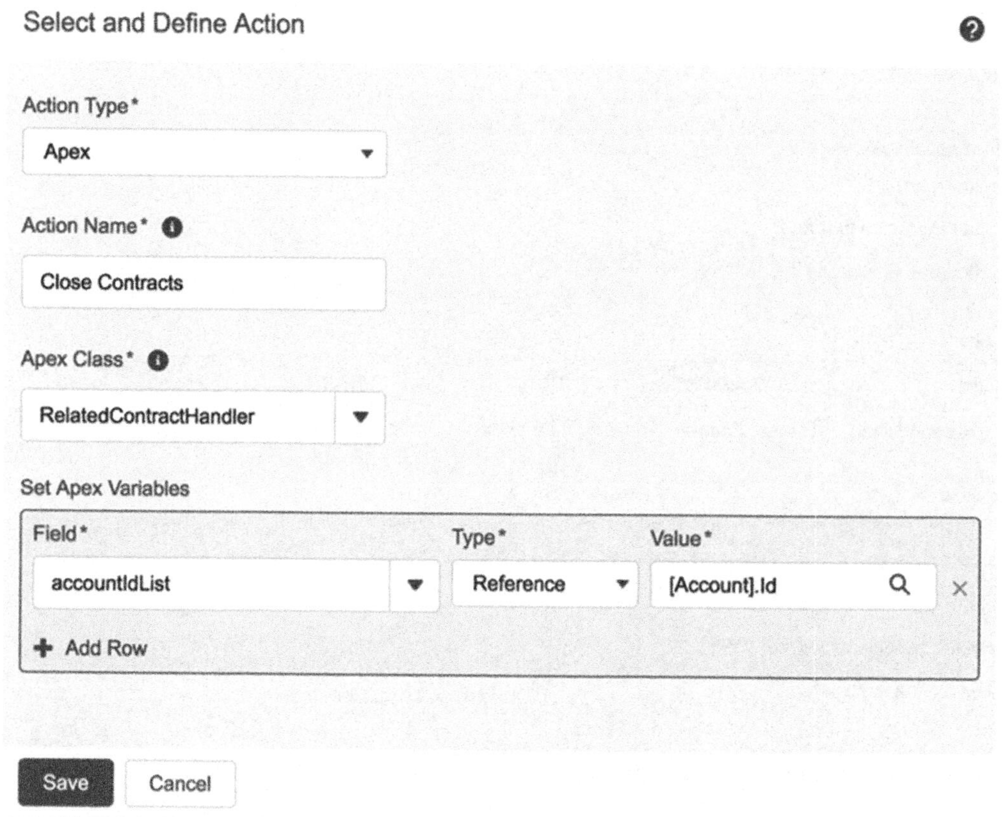

Figure 12-23. *Configuration settings for the Apex action to use the RelatedContractHandler class*

The Apex code does most of the work for us in this example, so it's nice and simple. By this point the Canvas in Lightning Process Builder should look like Figure 12-24. It is easy to see the flow of the process thanks to the graphical nature of Lightning Process Builder. Clearly the process flows from the start for an Account and then checks that the Account is closed. If the Account is closed, then call Apex code that closes the contracts. You can see the unique icon in the action that denotes this is an Apex action type. It looks like ">_" which represents a command prompt for entering or running code.

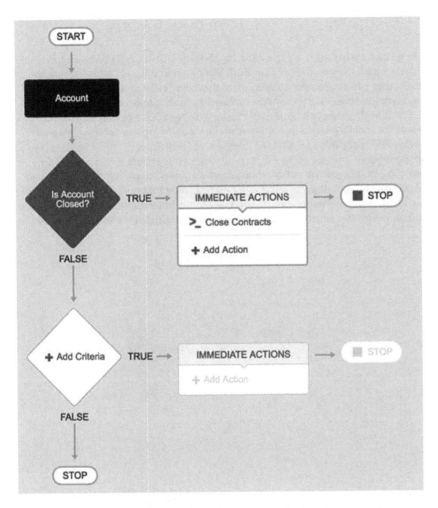

Figure 12-24. *The finished "Update Closed Contracts for Closed Account" process*

Finally, activate the process by clicking the Activate button. Now that it's active, go ahead and test this out by creating a few contracts for an account in different statuses. You can add the Contract related list to the Account page layout to make it easier to view. You will notice that once you change the Account status to "Closed," all the related Contracts for that Account will now be closed.

Recap

In this chapter we covered how Apex can be used to extend the capabilities of flows and processes in Visual Workflow and Lightning Process Builder, respectively. While both Visual Workflow and Lightning Process Builder are very powerful tools, they can't meet every requirement that every customer may have. Using Apex is a fantastic way to augment the abilities of these tools so that they are not limited to what is provided out of the box. With Visual Workflow there are two options to extend with Apex. One option is using the Process.Plugin interface to create a special plug-in that appears in the Visual Workflow palette. This allows for a highly configurable interface for users who are allowed to create and edit flows. A second option is to use the @InvocableMethod annotation. This is a quick way to make Apex code visible to Visual Workflow for use without creating a full plug-in. The @InvocableMethod annotation also happens to be the only way to make Apex code available for use in Lightning Process Builder. In Lightning Process Builder there is not an option to store the output of an invocable method as in Visual Workflow, but with the use of an invocable method you are able to build processes that normally would not be possible without the use of Apex code.

■ ■ ■

CHAPTER 13

Production Deployment—Giving the People What They Want!

We have come a long way in understanding how to develop using Visual Workflow and Lightning Process Builder. By this point you should have a good grasp of not only building flows and processes but doing so in a planned manner using time-tested software development principles. Those principles we covered include gathering and understanding requirements and then using them to design what is to be built. Finally, the design can be used to implement the flows and processes with Visual Workflow and Lightning Process Builder, respectively. All the hard work put into designing and developing should be shared with others! We need to let the world see these great ideas put into motion. To do that they need to be available for your Salesforce users to see, use, and interact with.

The great thing about the Salesforce platform is that many of the changes can be implemented directly in the production Salesforce org that users are interacting with on a daily basis via declarative or point-and-click. Changes can be made on the fly, and that is a testament to the power and configurability of Salesforce. However, in the spirit of proper software development practices this chapter is going to cover the concept of having a separate sandbox org to develop and test in and then migrating those changes to the production org that your users depend on daily. By having a separate org to develop in, you reduce the risk and impact that the changes might have on your business processes. Think of the chaos that could occur if during the day, a change was made in the production org without proper rigorous testing.

This chapter will only go into the basic details of creating a separate sandbox org as there is plenty of available material on the matter to do a deeper dive on that subject. This chapter will go into the details of taking the implemented flows and processes from a sandbox, putting them into a change set, and migrating to production. This chapter will then continue by covering how to deploy the migrating change set and ensuring that the correct versions are enabled. Finally, we will go over how to debug or problem-solve any issues that may come up with active running flows and processes.

Creating a Sandbox to Develop in

This section will go through the steps of setting up a sandbox quickly to develop in so that it can be used to deploy to production later. If you already have a sandbox that you have been developing in or know how to set one up then you can skip this section. Processes and flows can be implemented straight in a production org, but it is best practice to implement them in a sandbox first. This is because in a sandbox, you can experiment with the implementation of flows and processes without inadvertently affecting the users in the production Salesforce org. Testing can also be performed in the sandbox to ensure that the implemented flows and processes behave exactly as expected without bugs or side effects. It is even possible to have a combination of development orgs and to use an external tool such as the Force.com IDE (Integrated Development Environment) to develop on other orgs and move changes to production.

© Jonathan Keel 2016

J. Keel, *Salesforce.com Lightning Process Builder and Visual Workflow*, DOI 10.1007/978-1-4842-1691-0_13

Also remember that one of the goals of this book is to foster good habits that have been used in software development for years. One of those good habits is having a separate environment for developing and another for testing. The development environment can be used to make multiple changes that may never get pushed to production, while the test environment should stay as close to production as possible except with test data that is as close to production data as possible. After making changes in development that work as intended, those changes can be moved to the test environment for more real-world testing. Once everything is tested successfully in the test environment, it can be moved to production.

In the following example we will look at creating just one sandbox. The same process can be repeated to create a second sandbox. To create the sandbox, go to Setup in the production org. From there go to Administration Setup ➤ Data Management ➤ Sandboxes.

■ **Note**   If the option to create a sandbox is not available or if more licenses are needed, contact Salesforce to order sandboxes for your org.

Once there, you should see a list of sandboxes if there are any already created. Click the New Sandbox button to see the Create Sandbox screen in Figure 13-1. Depending on the Salesforce edition you have, there will be different available types of Salesforce licenses that you can create the sandbox with. For the purpose of this chapter we will just create a Developer sandbox. To do so enter the following values in the Name and Description fields:

- **Name**: Test

- **Description**: Test Sandbox to develop flows and processes.

Once complete, click the Next button on the bottom left under the Developer column.

Create Sandbox

Help for this Page ❓

Sandbox Information			❘ = Required Information
Name	Test		
Description	Test Sandbox to develop flows and processes.		

Sandbox License

Developer	Developer Pro	Partial Copy	Full
Refresh Interval: **1 Day**	Refresh Interval: **1 Day**	Refresh Interval: **5 Days**	Refresh Interval: **29 Days**
Capacity: **200 MB**	Capacity: **1 GB**	Capacity: **5 GB**	Capacity: **Same as Source**
Includes:	Includes:	Includes:	Includes:
• Configuration	• Configuration	• Configuration	• Configuration
• Apex & Metadata	• Apex & Metadata	• Apex & Metadata	• Apex & Metadata
• All Users	• All Users	• All Users	• All Users
		• Records (sample of selected objects)	• Records (all or selected objects)
		• Sandbox Template Support	• Sandbox Template Support
			• **History & Chatter Data (optional)**
Available: 25 (0 in use)	Available: 0 (0 in use)	Available: 1 (0 in use)	Available: 0 (0 in use)
Next	Next	No templates exist for this organization.	No licenses are available for your selected sandbox type. Contact your Salesforce representative to purchase additional licenses.

Figure 13-1. *The Create Sandbox screen with different types of sandbox options*

The next screen that will appear is for the Sandbox Options as seen in Figure 13-2. Our example has an option to enter the name of an Apex Class that we may want to run after the sandbox is activated. Just leave this field blank, as it is not required. Click the Create button to begin the process of creating the sandbox.

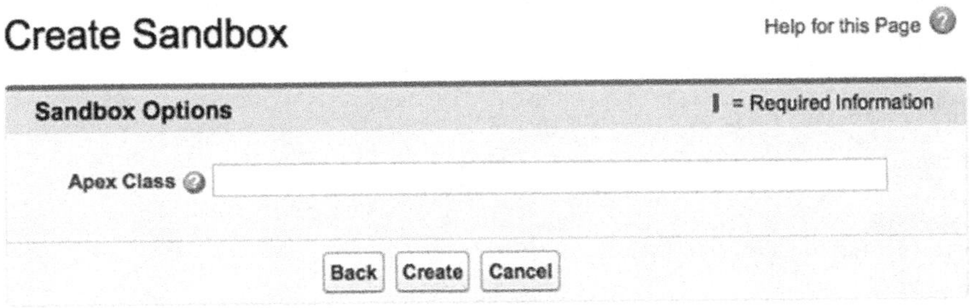

Create Sandbox

Help for this Page ❓

Sandbox Options	❙ = Required Information
Apex Class ❓	

Back   Create   Cancel

Figure 13-2. Run Apex Class on sandbox creation option

After clicking the Create button, the initial screen appears again with the list of sandboxes. This time, though, the sandbox just created will appear but with a status of "Pending" as seen in Figure 13-3.

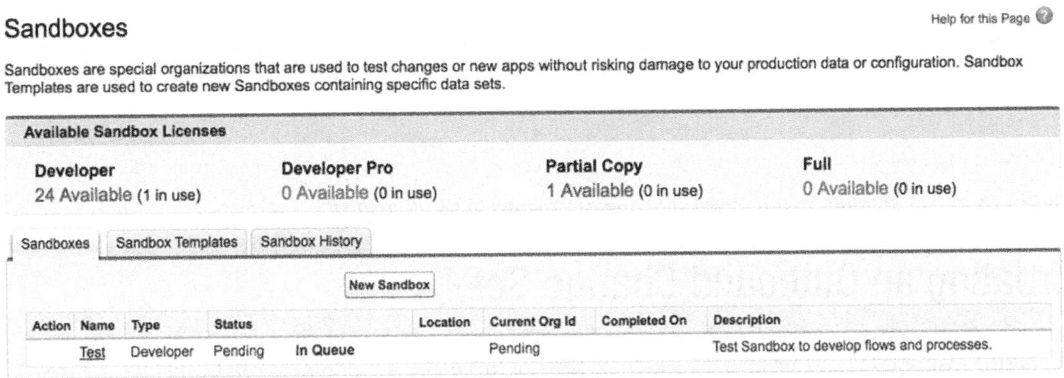

Sandboxes

Help for this Page ❓

Sandboxes are special organizations that are used to test changes or new apps without risking damage to your production data or configuration. Sandbox Templates are used to create new Sandboxes containing specific data sets.

Available Sandbox Licenses

Developer	Developer Pro	Partial Copy	Full
24 Available (1 in use)	0 Available (0 in use)	1 Available (0 in use)	0 Available (0 in use)

Sandboxes | Sandbox Templates | Sandbox History

New Sandbox

Action	Name	Type	Status		Location	Current Org Id	Completed On	Description
	Test	Developer	Pending	In Queue		Pending		Test Sandbox to develop flows and processes.

Figure 13-3. List of sandboxes showing sandbox pending for being created

At this point it is a waiting game. Creating a new sandbox is not immediate. It is usually best to wait until an e-mail is received stating that the sandbox is ready for use. In order to see more detail, though, clicking the name of the sandbox will take you to the sandbox detail screen as seen in Figure 13-4. This will show you the progress as it is being created.

Sandboxes > **Test Detail**

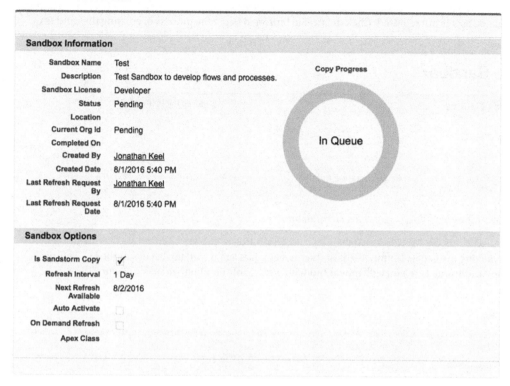

Figure 13-4. The sandbox detail screen showing its progress in being created

Creating an Outbound Change Set

Once the sandbox is created and ready, you should receive an e-mail with instructions on logging in. Follow the instructions and log in to the sandbox. Now, at this point, development can begin on any flows or processes. Once they are successfully completed and ready to move to production we will need to create a Change Set. A Change Set is a group of Salesforce items such as Objects, Fields, Visualforce Pages, Apex classes, and Flows to move across connected Salesforce orgs. As a Salesforce administrator you are probably familiar with what they are and how they work at this point. While not all items in a Salesforce org can be included in a Change Set, a flow/process can be included. A Change Set is how we will move any implemented flows and processes to the production org.

To create a new Change Set go to Setup and then go to App Setup ➤ Deploy ➤ Outbound Change Sets. If this is your first time going here then you will see an introduction screen. Just click the Continue button and you will see the Outbound Change Sets screen as in Figure 13-5. Here is where a new Change Set can be created so that it can be sent outbound to another connected org. In this example we will create a Change Set that has one flow created with Visual Workflow and one process created with Lightning Process Builder. To begin click the New button.

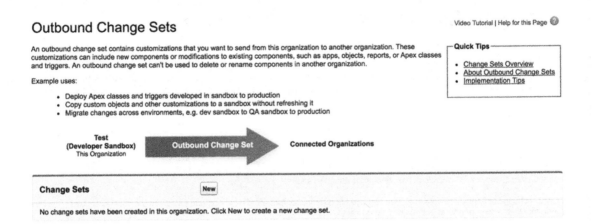

Figure 13-5. *The Outbound Change Sets screen to create a new Change Set*

The New Change Set screen will appear as seen in Figure 13-6. At this point we only need to configure one required field, the Name field. However, as best practice let's enter the Description field as well so we can have more detail about why this Change Set is created and its purpose. For this example enter the following values:

- **Name**: Call Rep Scripts

- **Description**: This change set contains flows used for the call scripts for call center.

Click the Save button to continue.

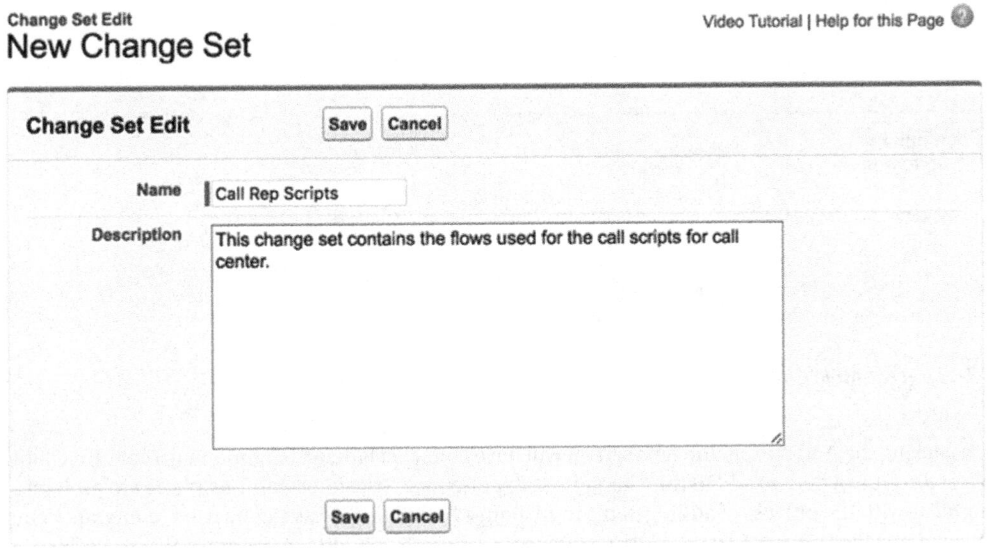

Change Set Edit
New Change Set

Video Tutorial | Help for this Page

Change Set Edit   Save Cancel

Name   Call Rep Scripts

Description   This change set contains the flows used for the call scripts for call center.

Save Cancel

Figure 13-6. *The New Change Set screen with example values*

Adding the Components to the Change Set

The detail screen will now appear for this Outbound Change Set. For this example we named the Change Set "Call Rep Scripts," so the screen will appear as seen in Figure 13-7. Depending on the name and description entered you will those values here on this screen. Here is where items need to be added to the Change Set. To add an item to the Change Set, just click the Add button in the "Change Set Components" section.

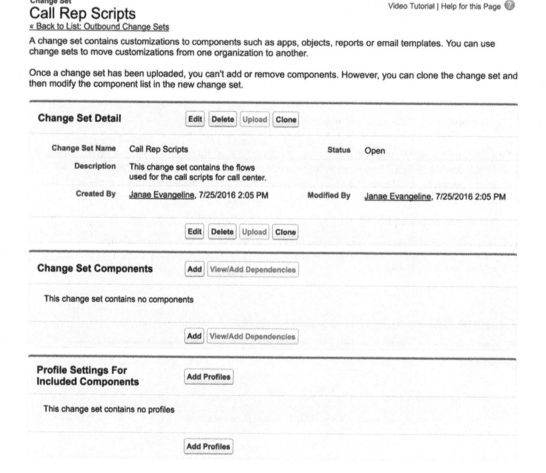

Figure 13-7. An example Change Set detail screen

Upon clicking the Add button, the next screen will have a picklist labeled "Component Type" that allows you to select the type of item to add to the Change Set. Experienced Salesforce administrators are probably already familiar with the process of adding items to a Change Set. Change Sets can be used to migrate items such as Visualforce Pages, Apex Classes, Custom Objects, Custom Fields, and many more. When working with flows and processes we have to remember something we discussed earlier in this book: the fact that processes built in Lightning Process Builder are actually flows behind the scenes. Since processes are just a different type of flow, Salesforce does not go through the trouble of distinguishing them in the Component Type picklist. Instead, if you want to select a flow or a process, then with both cases you need to select the

"Flow Definition" option in the Component Type picklist as seen in Figure 13-8. While you can't tell in this example the "Welcome Script" flow is a standard flow and the "Create New Account Plan For Approved Account" flow is actually a process built in Lightning Process Builder.

Figure 13-8. *An example Add To Change Set screen with a flow and a process listed under Flow Definition*

For our example, let's add "Welcome Script" to the Change Set. We do this by clicking the check box to the left of "Welcome Script" and then clicking the Add To Change Set button.

Once the "Welcome Script" flow is added to the Change Set you will be taken back to the Change Set detail screen. In the "Change Set Components" section the "Welcome Script" Flow Definition will be added to the list as seen in Figure 13-9.

Change Set Components	Add View/Add Dependencies			
Action	**Name**	**Parent Object**	**Type**	**API Name**
Remove	Welcome_Script		Flow Definition	Welcome_Script
				Previous (1 - 1 of 1) Next

Add View/Add Dependencies

Figure 13-9. *The example Change Set with the example "Welcome Script" Flow Definition added*

Now, if you would like to add the "Create New Account Plan For Approved Account" process/flow to the list, you would go through the same steps—first clicking the Add button, then selecting "Flow Definition" from the "Component Type" picklist, then clicking the check box next to the process/flow, and then clicking the Add To Change Set button.

Half the battle is realizing that you do not need to look for a separate "Process Definition" option in the picklist. It would seem as though you would, but again everything is just a flow behind the scene. Remember that and migrating Change Sets will be so much easier. Just look for flow and processes under the "Flow Definition" option.

Pushing the Change Set to Production

Once the Change Set has everything needed you will want to migrate it to the production org. Unfortunately, you will not be able to migrate it unless the sandbox is configured to be allowed to deploy to the production org. Let's go log in to the production org and check out how it is configured now. After logging in to production go to Setup ➤ App Setup ➤ Deploy ➤ Deployment Settings. Once there you will see the Deployment Connections in the Deployment Settings screen. In Figure 13-10 we have an example of an organization for Ashton Michael Automotive Inc. and it looks as though it is not configured to allow the Test org to migrate to production. We can tell because the red broken icon means that Change Sets are not allowed to pass between the environments. In order to get our Change Set in production we will need to make a little change.

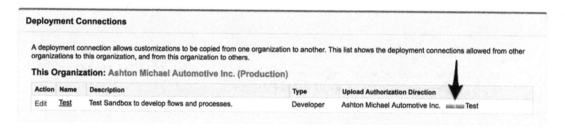

Figure 13-10. *Deployment Connections section showing that uploads are not allowed from the Test org to the production org*

Click the "Edit" link to be taken to the Deployment Connection Detail screen as seen in Figure 13-11. There is a check box labeled "Allow Inbound Changes" that we need to make sure is checked in order to allow Change Sets to be uploaded to this org. Click it to check it off and click the Save button to commit the changes.

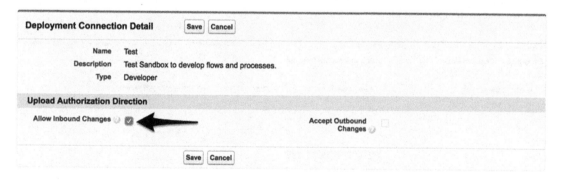

Figure 13-11. *The Allow Inbound Changes check box used to control whether Change Sets can be migrated to this org*

Now that inbound changes are allowed, the Deployment Settings screen will show the connection from the Test org to the production org as allowed in precisely that direction seen in Figure 13-12. The red broken icon has now been updated to a green arrow pointing from the Test org to our production org.

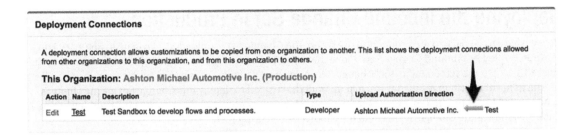

Deployment Connections

A deployment connection allows customizations to be copied from one organization to another. This list shows the deployment connections allowed from other organizations to this organization, and from this organization to others.

This Organization: Ashton Michael Automotive Inc. (Production)

Action	Name	Description	Type	Upload Authorization Direction
Edit	Test	Test Sandbox to develop flows and processes.	Developer	Ashton Michael Automotive Inc. ⟵ Test

Figure 13-12. *"Deployment Connections" section showing that uploads are allowed from the Test org to the production org*

With the sandbox now allowed to migrate our Change Set to the production org we can log back in to sandbox to do the next step. We need to get the Change Set we created earlier moved to the production org. Go ahead and log back in to the sandbox if you are not still logged in. Then go to Setup ➤ App Setup ➤ Deploy ➤ Outbound Change Sets. Here we will see our Change Set, named "Call Rep Scripts" in our example. The Change Set name will be a link that can clicked. Go ahead and click it to get to its detail screen. There you will see an Upload button. After clicking the Upload button you will see a screen like Figure 13-13. It will have a list of orgs that the Change Set is allowed to upload to. In this example we only have one org and that is the production org. Click the radio button to the left of the name, "Production" and then click the Upload button to start the upload process.

Upload Change Set   Video Tutorial | Help for this Page 🌐
Call Rep Scripts

Choose the organization that will receive the change set. Once the upload completes, the administrator responsible for authorizing deployments in the target organization will be notified.

⚠ Once you upload this change set, you won't be able to edit it or recall it from the target organization.

Upload Details   [Upload] [Cancel]

Target Organization   ❙ = Required Information

	Name	Description	Type	Platform Version
⦿	Production	Production organization	Production	37.0

[Upload] [Cancel]

Figure 13-13. *The Upload Change Set screen with the list of Target Organizations we are allowed to upload to*

After the Change Set is uploaded successfully to the production org you will see a message appear as in Figure 13-14. This confirmation message lets you know that it has been uploaded, but we are not done yet.

✓ **Your change set was uploaded successfully.**
  It will be available shortly, so that an administrator can deploy it.

Figure 13-14. *Confirmation message for the uploaded Change Set*

Deploying the Inbound Change Set in Production

Now we have to go back to the production org where the Change Set is uploaded. Navigate to Setup ➤ App Setup ➤ Deploy ➤ Inbound Change Sets. Once there you will see the Inbound Change Set screen such as in Figure 13-15. On the screen there is a "Change Sets Awaiting Deployment" section. In this section you will see the name of the Change Set that you just uploaded. We need to deploy this Change Set for the changes to be applied to the production org. It is merely copied here, but nothing is in use yet in the production org. Click the name of the Change Set to get to the Change Set Detail screen.

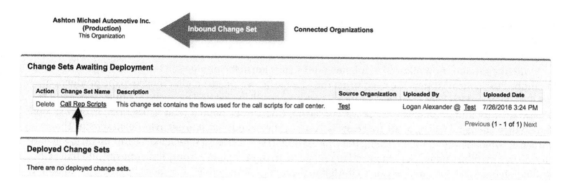

Figure 13-15. *"Change Sets Awaiting Deployment" on the Inbound Change Set screen*

■ **Note**   It takes a while for an uploaded Change Set to be ready to deploy. So if you go to the Change Set Detail screen and it says that it is not ready, just wait a few minutes and try again.

Now that we are at the Change Set Detail screen you will see a lot of detail such as the list of components in the Change Set. You will also see a set of buttons at the top of the screen including Validate, Deploy, and Delete as shown in Figure 13-16. The Validate button allows you to simulate the deployment without actually committing the deployment to the org. Using this action will give you an early warning regarding any possible issues before trying to deploy. This feature comes in handy if you need to deploy later in the day or evening and want to make sure there are not any unexpected errors when you actually deploy. Running a validation will give you early warning about any issues and give you time to correct them and possibly upload another Change Set that will not get those errors. The Deploy button actually will still do a validation before deployment, but it will automatically deploy and commit the changes if there are no errors. Use this feature when you know you are ready to have these changes applied to the org. Finally, the Delete button just removed the Change Set from the list so it can't be deployed.

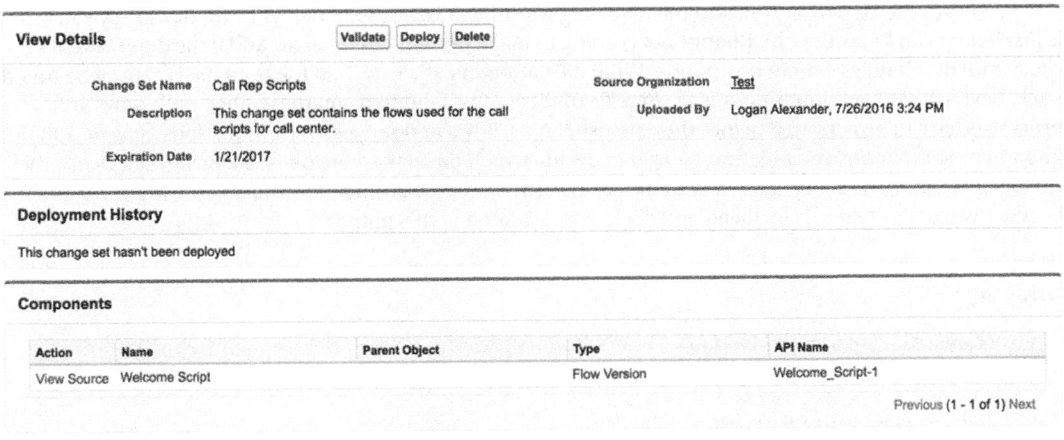

View Details Validate Deploy Delete

Change Set Name	Call Rep Scripts	Source Organization	Test
Description	This change set contains the flows used for the call scripts for call center.	Uploaded By	Logan Alexander, 7/26/2016 3:24 PM
Expiration Date	1/21/2017		

Deployment History

This change set hasn't been deployed

Components

Action	Name	Parent Object	Type	API Name
View Source	Welcome Script		Flow Version	Welcome_Script-1

Previous (1 - 1 of 1) Next

Figure 13-16. *Change Set Detail screen showing the components and buttons to Validate, Deploy, or Delete the Change Set*

Let's continue down this joy ride of moving our Flow Definition into production. Click the Deploy button to continue to the Deploy Change Set screen as seen in Figure 13-17. Here we see that we have to choose a Test Option when deploying. These options all have their pros and cons depending on what changes you are deploying. These options decide which unit tests from Apex to run, but in our example we do not have any Apex code. So if we choose Default, then no tests would be run because it states that if the Change Set does not contain any Apex components no tests are run. If you are just deploying Flow Definitions (flows and processes) by themselves, this is the best option to pick. However, what if the flows or processes make use of Apex as described earlier in this book? Well, remember that Salesforce requires 75% code coverage for deploying to production. In Chapter 12, where we discussed using Apex code, we did not cover writing unit tests since writing a good unit test might need a whole chapter unto itself. There are lots of other books and online resources for developing Apex and writing unit tests. The main thing to remember here is that if you have Apex code in the Change Set you will have to decide which of the four options best fit your scenario for deploying to the org. If in doubt, the Default option works because it will run the tests if they need to be run and otherwise try to run Apex tests if the Change Set has no Apex components.

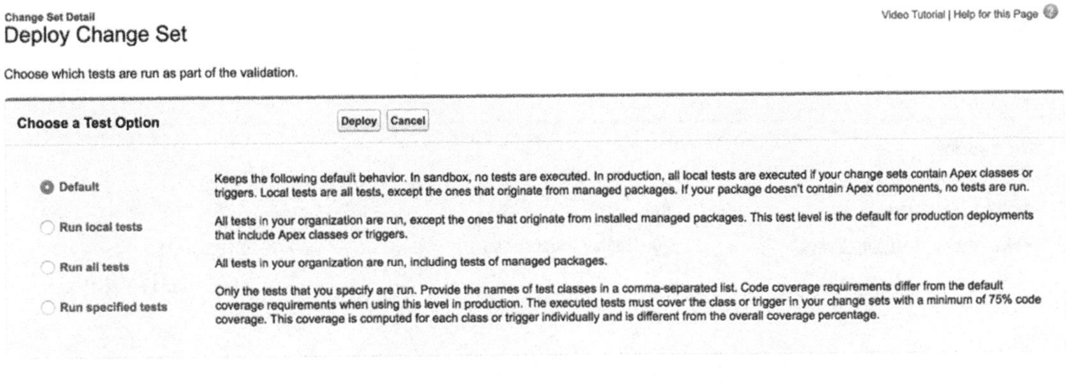

Change Set Detail Video Tutorial | Help for this Page
Deploy Change Set

Choose which tests are run as part of the validation.

Choose a Test Option Deploy Cancel

◉ Default	Keeps the following default behavior. In sandbox, no tests are executed. In production, all local tests are executed if your change sets contain Apex classes or triggers. Local tests are all tests, except the ones that originate from managed packages. If your package doesn't contain Apex components, no tests are run.
○ Run local tests	All tests in your organization are run, except the ones that originate from installed managed packages. This test level is the default for production deployments that include Apex classes or triggers.
○ Run all tests	All tests in your organization are run, including tests of managed packages.
○ Run specified tests	Only the tests that you specify are run. Provide the names of test classes in a comma-separated list. Code coverage requirements differ from the default coverage requirements when using this level in production. The executed tests must cover the class or trigger in your change sets with a minimum of 75% code coverage. This coverage is computed for each class or trigger individually and is different from the overall coverage percentage.

Figure 13-17. *Deploy Change Set screen with all the Test Options to pick from while deploying*

Next click the Deploy button and the following warning message seen in Figure 13-18 will appear. This is just letting you know that the Change Set is going to make permanent changes and if the deployment is successful the changes cannot be undone. While this is technically true, that these changes cannot be rolled back, having Flow Definitions does give some flexibility to this matter. If you remember, both flows and processes have to be activated before they are used. Also, flows and processes have versions. So a flow or a process can have many versions and you get to decide which the active version is. So, while technically the Change Set cannot be rolled back, any of the flows or processes can be deactivated and the older version can be reactivated. Pretty neat! Go ahead and click the OK button at this point.

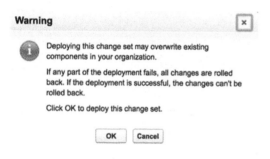

Figure 13-18. Deployment warning message

After clicking OK, the deployment will begin. There will be a message on the screen stating that the deployment has started. There is also a link to the "Deployment Status" page. Go ahead and click that link. Next, you will see the Deployment Status page that looks like Figure 13-19. If the Change Set is large, meaning it has a lot of components, then it could take a while to complete. Refreshing this page after a few minutes will give you the current status of this Change Set. As we see here, our example Change Set has been successfully deployed. In the event that deployment had not been successful, it would show in the "Failed" section of this page.

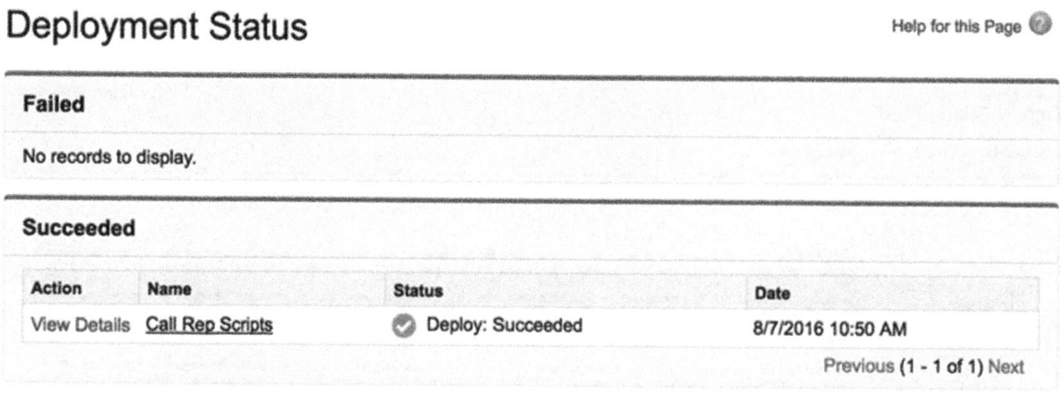

Deployment Status

Help for this Page

Failed

No records to display.

Succeeded

Action	Name	Status	Date
View Details	Call Rep Scripts	✅ Deploy: Succeeded	8/7/2016 10:50 AM

Previous (1 - 1 of 1) Next

Figure 13-19. Deployment Status page with a successfully deployed Change Set

Enabling Most Recent Versions of Flows/Processes

We are almost at the finish line! We deployed the Change Set successfully, but we are not done yet. While most components in Salesforce would be 100% functional for users after a successful deployment, flows and processes are not. Remember how flows and processes are versioned? Remember how we need to activate a version them for it to be usable? This is our next and final step. The Change Set deployment merely puts the flow/process version in place. It does not activate it automatically. You will need to manually complete this step.

To activate a flow built in Cloud Flow Designer, go to Setup ➤ App Setup ➤ Create ➤ Workflow & Approvals ➤ Flows. Once there is a list view that has several options. We want to see our flow is that not active, so two options we could select to see our newly deployed flow is either the "All Flows" or "Inactive Flows" option. As seen in Figure 13-20, the "All Flows" option is chosen so that our "Welcome Script" flow is now visible. To the far right is the "Is Active" column. Well look at that! As expected, the flow is not active. We need to get that check box checked off! So, to do so, click the link for the "Welcome Script" flow name (not the Edit link).

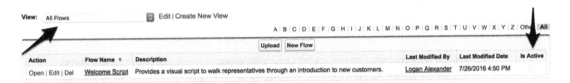

Figure 13-20. List of all flows with the example flow, Welcome Script, not active yet

That link will take you to the "Flow Detail" page. On that page there is a "Flow Versions" section as seen in Figure 13-21. Notice that there three links in the Action column. Those are

- **Open**: Opens the flow in Cloud Flow Designer for editing.

- **Run**: Runs the implemented flow (even if it is an autolaunched flow)

- **Activate**: Sets the current version as active and disables other versions

There is also a column named "Version," which has the version number for the flow. If there were multiple versions there would a row for every version each with a different number in this column. This is the first time we have had a flow deployed to production, so we only have version 1 in this example. Go ahead and click "Activate" to make version 1 the active version for this flow.

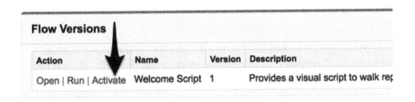

Figure 13-21. The Activate link for the example flow

Upon making version 1 the active version, the link will now change to "Deactivate" as seen in Figure 13-22, so that you can make it not active anymore. You can only have at most one active version at a time. You can also have none of the versions active as well. That is also an option.

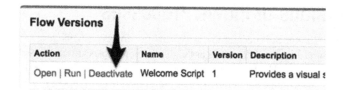

Figure 13-22. *The Deactivate link for the example flow*

If you move a process built in Lightning Process Builder, that latest version needs to be activated too. Let's look at those steps. Let's assume that we built another Change Set and moved over the process we saw earlier named "Create New Account Plan For Approved Account" to production. While it is added to the Change Set as a Flow Definition also, you do not activate the same way you activate flows built in Cloud Flow Designer. Instead, go to Setup ➤ App Setup ➤ Create ➤ Workflow & Approvals ➤ Process Builder and where you see the process name, click the icon to the left of the name. This will expand and show all the available versions of the process. In this example in Figure 13-23 we have only version 1 because we just deployed it. To activate it click the name of the process to the right of the "Version 1" label.

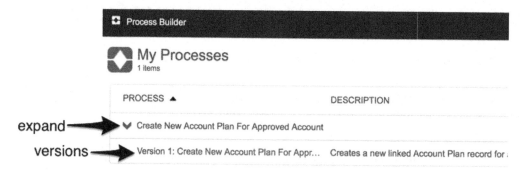

Figure 13-23. *My Processes page with the process expanded to see the list of versions available*

You should see a prompt that asks you to confirm the activation of the process. It warns you that it automatically deactivates all other versions. If you are ready to commit to this new phase of life then click the Confirm button.

Other Considerations

While this explains the steps of adding flows and processes to a Change Set, deploying them, and activating them, you still need to include other items that are typical Salesforce components that you may already be familiar with deploying. Make sure to include components that your flows and processes need, such as

- Custom Objects
- Custom Fields
- Custom Buttons
- Visualforce Pages
- Visualforce Components
- Approvals
- And Many More . . .

To ensure that all your dependent items are in the Change Set after adding the items you need to move, you can click the View/Add Tendencies button on the Change Set details screen. This functionality will look at your items, such as flows, and see what dependencies the item needs to run properly once moved to another org. If you know that the most recent changes already exist in the destination org, then they do not always need to be included. To ensure that nothing is missed, having Salesforce show you a list of what is needed is very helpful.

A rare consideration needs to be made with subflows (flows being called by other flows). There have been instances where Change Sets that contain parent flows (flows that call other flows) and subflows (flows called by parent flows) will not deploy because the parent flow will fail to see the related subflow it calls. This does not happen all the time, and it appears to happen mostly when there are many interconnected flows and subflows. If you run into a situation in which you have a Change Set with all your flows and the Change Set fails to deploy due to a dependent flow not being accessible but it is indeed in your Change Set, don't despair. Simply create two Change Sets where one has the subflows and deploy that Change Set first. Then create a second Change Set that has the parent flows and deploy it last. Again this issue does not always happen, but on the occasion that it does, these are the steps to migrate the Change Sets.

Debugging Active Flows/Processes

That concludes our overview of deploying flows and processes to your production org, but now what? Once they are running, what if there are issues? Well here is a bonus section on debugging these tricky little things. There may be instances where, out of the blue, you get an e-mail or a phone call that an error occurred. At that point it's best to ask the person using the system at the time how he or she came about the error. In addition to getting this information, Salesforce will send out an e-mail to the Salesforce administrator who created the associated flow. The e-mail message is extremely helpful as it not only contains the error message but details of every flow element that was executed during the flow. Figure 13-24 shows an example of what the e-mail can look like. Notice the third line that says Type: Flow. This means that this flow was built in Cloud Flow Designer. If this was a process built in Lightning Process Builder, the type would be Workflow.

Flow Details
Flow Name: Test_Error_Fault
Type: Flow
Version: 1
Status: Inactive

Flow Interview Details
Interview Label: Test Error Fault 8/20/2016 6:28 PM
Current User: Logan Alexander (005j000000BgBJh)
Start time: 8/20/2016 6:28 PM
Duration: 2 seconds

How the Interview Started
Logan Alexander (005j000000BgBJh) started the flow interview.
SCREEN: Intro
Display Text: Intro_Text
Value at run time: This is to test an error in a flow.

Selected Navigation Button: NEXT

RECORD CREATE: Create_Record_Error
Create one Account record where:
OwnerId = 123456789012345
Result
Failed to create record.|

Figure 13-24. Example e-mail when a flow encounters an error

Sometimes though these e-mails are not available. An example where this occurs is during deployments of Change Sets. If a Change Set has Apex Classes then it will need to have unit tests to run to verify that there is at least 75% code coverage as per Salesforce rules. When those unit tests run the code to do things such as inserts, updates, and so on, then they can trigger processes built in Lightning Process Builder. In this case the Change Set will show error messages if the errors are due to flows/processes not functioning. Those error messages look more like Figure 13-25.

```
CANNOT_EXECUTE_FLOW_TRIGGER, The record couldn't be saved because it failed to trigger a flow. A
flow trigger failed to execute the flow with version ID 301210000000ViE. Contact your
administrator for help.
```

Figure 13-25. *Example error message caused by a process during the deployment of a Change Set*

Notice that while the e-mail stated the name of the flow/process in question, this message does not. Administrators and developers in an effort to figure out which flow/process caused the problem have spent many hours trying to solve this problem. The natural reaction is to take the version ID (in this case 301210000000ViE) and paste it in the browser address bar so that the address would look like https://na16.salesforce.com/301210000000ViE. That does not work here. Instead, the "Insufficient Privileges" message appears as in Figure 13-26.

Insufficient Privileges

You do not have the level of access necessary to perform the operation you requested. Please contact the owner of the record or your administrator if access is necessary. For more information, see Insufficient Privileges Errors.

Figure 13-26. *The standard Salesforce "Insufficient Privileges" message*

The next step people fall into is to manually go through every process and try to see which one could be affected. There is a nice trick that works though. While Cloud Flow Designer is not used to build processes, it can be used to view them. Follow the next few steps to see the offending process:

- Go to Setup ➤ App Setup ➤ Create ➤ Workflow & Approvals > Flows

- Open an existing flow in Cloud Flow Designer

- Look at the address in the browser address bar and change the "ID" parameter to the version ID of the process in the error (In this example https://na16.salesforce.com/designer/designer.apexp#Id=301j0000000kJJY becomes https://na16.salesforce.com/designer/designer.apexp#Id=301210000000ViE)

- The process will load as an autolaunched flow and the name will be visible

In Figure 13-27 we see this example. Notice how the elements on the Canvas are compacted together. Since this was not developed in Cloud Flow Designer there is no information as to their exact placement.

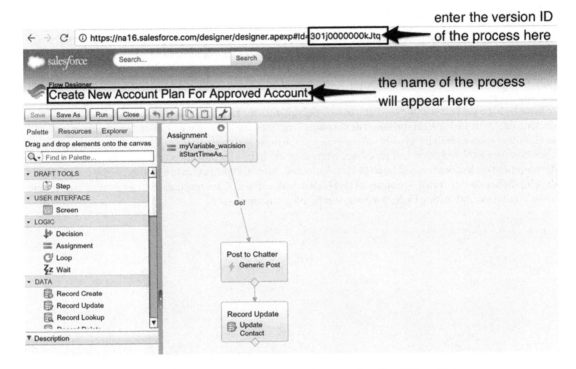

Figure 13-27. *A process created in Lightning Process Builder opened in Cloud Flow Designer*

Remember that we are just here to debug and find out which process is causing the issue seen in the error. Using Cloud Flow Designer to modify the process built in Lightning Process Builder is not recommended. In fact, you can't do it. If you try to save the flow backing this process you will only be given the three types of flows allowed in Cloud Flow Designer.

- Autolaunched Flow

- Flow

- User Provisioning Flow

We know the process's name now, so just click the Close button and get out of there. Then go back to Lightning Process Builder and look for the activated version of that particular process. Now you can take a more accurate look at the process and what it is doing. Once there you can figure out what steps are being taken and deduce what might be causing the error. Happy debugging!

Recap

In this chapter we covered how to migrate our beautifully crafted flows and processes into production. Moving them involves creating a Change Set and adding them as a Flow Definition. Since flows built in Cloud Flow Designer and processes built in Lightning Process Builder are both types of flows they are both moved as Flow Definitions. In case it was not completed before, we configured the production org to accept inbound Change Sets from the sandbox. After deploying the Change Sets for our flows and processes they will not be used yet because they are inactive by default. So they must be activated. Flows are activated by clicking the "Activate" link on the flow's detail page. Processes are activated by clicking the Activate button in Lightning Process Builder. Finally we went over some tools and tricks to debug any issues that might arise from the activated flows and processes while they are in production. This is important because the development cycle does not end once the implemented flows and processes are pushed to the users. Good development practices must continue, as this book has discussed, from requirements gathering to design to implementation and testing to deployment and finally to maintenance.

Index

Get the eBook for only $4.99!

Why limit yourself?

Now you can take the weightless companion with you wherever you go and access your content on your PC, phone, tablet, or reader.

Since you've purchased this print book, we are happy to offer you the eBook for just $4.99.

Convenient and fully searchable, the PDF version enables you to easily find and copy code—or perform examples by quickly toggling between instructions and applications.

To learn more, go to http://www.apress.com/us/shop/companion or contact support@apress.com.